Data Protection in a Profiled World

Serge Gutwirth • Yves Poullet • Paul De Hert
(Editors)

Data Protection in a Profiled World

Springer

Editors
Prof. Serge Gutwirth
Law, Science, Technology & Society
(LSTS)
Vrije Universiteit Brussel
Pleinlaan 2, 1050 Brussels
Belgium
serge.gutwirth@vub.ac.be

Prof. Paul De Hert
Law, Science, Technology and Society
Studies (LSTS)
Vrije Universiteit Brussel
Pleinlaan 2, 1050 Brussels
Belgium
paul.de.hert@vub.ac.be

Prof. Yves Poullet
Research Centre for Information
Technology & Law
University of Namur
Rempart de la Vierge 5
5000 Namur
Belgium
yves.poullet@fundp.ac.be

ISBN 978-90-481-8864-2 e-ISBN 978-90-481-8865-9
DOI 10.1007/978-90-481-8865-9
Springer Dordrecht Heidelberg London New York

Library of Congress Control Number: 2010930625

Cover design: eStudio Calamar S.L.

Printed on acid free paper

Springer is part of Springer Science+Business Media (www.springer.com)

Foreword

One of the most challenging issues facing our current information society is the accelerating accumulation of data trails in transactional and communication systems, which may be used not only to profile the behaviour of individuals for commercial, marketing and law enforcement purposes, but also to locate and follow things and actions. Data mining, convergence, interoperability, ever-increasing computer capacities and the extreme miniaturisation of hardware are all elements which contribute to a major contemporary challenge: the profiled world. This interdisciplinary volume offers twenty contributions that delve deeper into some of the complex but urgent questions that this profiled world poses to data protection and privacy.

The chapters of this volume are a peer-reviewed elaboration of presentations that were presented during one of the 12 panel sessions of the second *Conference on Privacy and Data Protection (CPDP2009)—Data protection in a profiled world* held in Brussels in January 2009 (www.cpdpconferences.org). In this sense, this book can be seen as a sequel of *Reinventing data protection?* (Springer 2009) which stemmed from the first CPDP conference of November 2007.

The yearly CPDP conferences aim to become Europe's most important meeting where academics, practitioners, policy-makers and activists come together to exchange ideas and discuss emerging issues in information technology, privacy, data protection and law. The second edition of the conference, of which this book is a reflection, was again very successful.[1] During the two conference days (16 & 17 January 2009) 61 speakers took the floor representing a worldwide palette of stakeholders and specialists of privacy and *data protection*, including members of academia, national, European and international administration, people from the private sector, representatives of the civil society, law firms, data protection authorities and so on. Around 200 motivated and highly qualified participants attended the conference, and at some point the *deBuren's* wide room seemed to come apart at

[1] The CPDP2009 conference was organised by LSTS from the Vrije Universiteit Brussel, the CRID from the University of Namur, TILT from the University of Tilburg, the INRIA in Grenoble, the Vlaams-Nederlands huis deBuren and last but not least, the VUB instituut voor PostAcademische vorming (iPAVUB). It was further supported by the Fonds voor Wetenschappelijk Onderzoek (FWO), the Brussels Capital Region, Microsof, Hunton & Williams and Stibbe.

the seams. The evening event, the *Pecha Kucha*, in the Belgian Rock&Roll temple *Ancienne Belgique* was also highly appreciated and three conference experts courageously went on stage, presenting ideas in the lively and challenging format of the event.

The present volume reflects the richness of the conference, containing chapters by leading lawyers, policy makers, computer, technology assessment and social scientists. It is structured in six parts, respectively dealing with generic, specific and third pillar issues, and with views from legal practitioners, technologists and technology assessment. The chapters cover a wide range of themes such as the evolution of a new generation of data protection laws, the constitutionalisation of data protection, profiling, the European human rights approach, security breaches, unsolicited adjustments, social networks, Eurojust, transatlantic data sharing, the Prüm agreement, surveillance, electronic voting, privacy by design, PETs, and more … In respect of the diversity of nationalities, disciplines, and perspectives represented in this book, the editors and the publisher have left the choices concerning the use of reference systems to the authors of the contributions.

This book not only offers a very close and timely look at the state of data protection and privacy in our profiled world, but it also explores and invents ways to make sure this world remains a world we want to live in.

We hope this book will find and interest many readers and we thank all authors, speakers, participants, discussants, supporters and organisers that helped contributing to its accomplishment.

Brussels, Belgium — Serge Gutwirth
Namur, Belgium — Yves Poullet
Brussels, Belgium — Paul De Hert

Contents

Contributors

Rosa Barcelo is legal advisor to the European Data Protection Supervisor (EDPS) since 2006. In her role at the EDPS, she serves on both the policy and supervision teams on all facets of privacy issues, particularly those related to challenges related to new technologies. She has worked extensively on the recent amendments to the ePrivacy Directive, including the security breach notification framework. Prior to joining the EDPS, she worked in the Data Protection Unit of the European Commission in Brussels where she was responsible for, among others, privacy issues related to new technologies, the U.S. Safe Harbor agreement, BCRs and contractual arrangements for transferring personal data from the EU. She has also worked as a private lawyer in the Brussels offices of Morrison and Foerster and DLA Piper where she advised clients on European privacy and data protection issues, as well electronic commerce and technology laws. Rosa is the author of books and articles on data protection and Internet related issues and often lectures on those topics.

Rocco Bellanova is currently researching data protection applied to security measures at both the Vrije Universiteit Brussel (VUB) and the Facultés universitaires Saint-Louis (FUSL). He is member of the interdisciplinary Research Group on Law Science Technology & Society or LSTS and of the Centre de Recherche en Science Politique, or CReSPo. At FUSL, he also works as assistant in international relations, political science and contemporary political issues. He takes part in the organisation of the Computers, Privacy and Data Protection conferences (2009–2010) and the Celebrating European Privacy Day activities. His research interests are: European and transatlantic security policies based on data processing, data protection and fundamental rights, the development of the European Area of Freedom, Security and Justice.

Ralf Bendrath is a policy advisor in the European Parliament. His work for MEP Jan Philipp Albrecht (Greens/EFA) mostly deals with privacy, civil liberties, and internet governance. As a former C-64 hacker, he studied political science in Bremen and Berlin, with a specialization in international affairs and security policy. After graduating, he did research at Free University Berlin, University of Bremen and Delft University of Technology, with visiting fellowships at George Washington

University and Columbia University. His research interests centered on the information revolution and its impact on security and privacy. He has widely published in German and English, and is also blogging at netzpolitik.org and bendrath.blogspot.com. In 2003 and 2005, Ralf Bendrath was a civil society member of the German government delegation to the World Summit on the Information Society. Since 2005, he has helped to build up the new German privacy movement, which developed around the protests against mandatory telecommunications data retention. He still is active in groups like the Working Group against Data Retention (AK Vorrat), European Digital Rights, and Open Network Coalition.

Bettina Berendt is a professor in the Hypermedia and Databases group at the department of computer science at Katholieke Universiteit Leuven, Belgium. She obtained her habilitation in information systems from Humboldt University Berlin, Germany, and her PhD in computer science/cognitive science from the University of Hamburg. She holds Masters degrees in artificial intelligence, economics and business studies from the universities of Edinburgh, Cambridge and Berlin (Free University). Her research interests include Web and Social-Web mining, digital libraries, personalization and privacy, and information visualization. Recent co-authored or co-edited publications include Intelligent scientific authoring tools: Interactive data mining for constructive uses of citation networks (Information Processing & Management 2009), a privacy-protecting business analytics service for online transactions (International Journal of Electronic Commerce 2008), and Knowledge Discovery Enhanced with Semantic and Social Information (Springer 2009). More information can be found at http://www.cs.kuleuven.be/~berendt.

Diana Alonso Blas LL.M. in European Law, is the Data Protection Officer of Eurojust, the European Union's Judicial Cooperation Unit, in The Hague, since November 2003. She studied Law at the universities of San Sebastián (Spain), Pau et les Pays de l'Adour (France) and Leuven (Belgium). Subsequently she followed a LL.M. European Law postgraduate programme at the University of Leuven where she graduated magna cum laude in 1993. From 1994 to 1998 she worked as research fellow for the Interdisciplinary Centre for Law and Information Technology (ICRI) of the Catholic University of Leuven (K.U.L.) where she carried out several data protection comparative research projects for the European Commission. In this same period she spent one year acting as privacy expert for the Belgian Data Protection Authority in Brussels. In April 1998 she joined the Dutch Data Protection Authority where she was a Senior International Officer working under the direct supervision of Peter Hustinx until the end of January 2002. During this period she dealt with the international cases and represented The Netherlands in several international working groups, such as the Article 29 Working Party, in Brussels and Strasbourg. From February 2002 to November 2003 she worked at the Data Protection Unit of Directorate General Internal Market of the European Commission, in Brussels. She was closely involved in the activities of the Article 29 Working Party as a member of the secretariat and was responsible within this unit for topics such as Internet, e-commerce, privacy-enhancing technologies, European codes of conduct, bilateral negotiation with several countries (including USA) and so forth. She is author of numerous articles and reports dealing with data protection at European level in the first and third pillar and is often invited as speaker at European and international data protection conferences. She has also performed as guest lecturer at the universities of Tilburg (Netherlands) and Edinburgh (UK). She is a Spanish national and speaks five languages.

Johann Čas holds a degree in Communications Engineering from a Higher Technical College and a degree in economics from the University of Graz. He is a researcher at the Institute of Technology Assessment of the Austrian Academy of Sciences since 1988. He has worked on several aspects of the Information Society and on societal impacts of Information and Communication Technologies. Past foci of research include technological development programmes, impact on employment and regional development, information systems for policy makers, regulatory issues of new telecommunication technologies and privacy. He has also been giving lectures on technology assessment at technical universities. His current research focus is on data protection and privacy in the information society, privacy enhancing technologies and their deployment within Ambient Intelligence, security technologies and health related applications. He was the coordinator of the PRISE EU-Project (http://prise.oeaw.ac.at/), which applied a participatory research approach to develop guidelines and criteria for privacy enhancing security technologies.

Guillaume Couneson is Associate in the Technology, Media & Telecommunications (TMT) practice of the international law firm Linklaters LLP in Belgium and is a member of the French-speaking Bar of Brussels. Guillaume is graduated from the University of Leuven (KUL). He has also obtained an LL.M. from the University of London with focus on IT, telecommunications and data protection matters. He has contributed in a number of data protection compliance projects from clients primarily in the pharmaceutical and financial sectors.

Franck Dumortier is senior researcher at the Information Technology and Law Research Centre (CRID) since 2005. His research particularly focuses on the impact of technologies such as RFIDs, biometrics, surveillance cameras and online social networks on the fundamental human right to privacy.

Gloria González Fuster is a researcher at the research group Law, Science, Technology & Society (LSTS) of the Faculty of Law and Criminology of the Vrije Universiteit Brussel (VUB). She joined the VUB to work on the EU-funded project *Reflexive governance in the Public Interest (REFGOV): A thematic application in the field of data protection* at the Institute for European Studies (IES), and currently participates in the *Converging and conflicting ethical values in the internal/external security in continuum in Europe* (INEX) research project. Additionally, she is preparing a PhD thesis on the relation between the right to respect for private life and the European fundamental right to personal data protection. She has studied Law, Journalism and Modern Languages and Literatures. Her professional experience includes working at the Citizenship Unit of the Education and Culture Directorate-General of the European Commission and at the Education, Audiovisual and Culture Executive Agency (EACEA), as well as different jobs in the field of EU Affairs and European Law information, and writing on music and new technologies.

Seda Gürses is a PhD candidate at the Department of Computer Science of the Katholieke Universiteit Leuven in Belgium. She has previously obtained her Master's in Computer Science from the Humboldt University in Berlin, Germany and Bachelor's in International Relations and Mathematics from the University of Redlands, USA. Her work focuses on multilateral privacy requirements engineering, social networks, security engineering and surveillance studies. She is also a researcher at COSIC/ESAT, K.U. Leuven working on TAS3, an integrated European Project with the objective of developing a trusted architecture for securely shared services. Her current focus lies in collaborative models for privacy design, feedback and awareness tools, and open source technologies.

Serge Gutwirth is a professor of human rights, legal theory, comparative law and legal research at the Faculty of Law and Criminology of the Vrije Universiteit Brussel (VUB), where he studied law, criminology and also obtained a postgraduate degree in technology and science studies. Since October 2003 Gutwirth is holder of a 10 year research fellowship in the framework of the VUB-Research contingent for his project 'Sciences and the democratic constitutional state: a mutual transformation process'. Gutwirth founded and still chairs the VUB-research group Law Science Technology & Society (http://www.vub.ac.be/LSTS). He publishes widely in Dutch French and English. Amongst his recent co-edited publications are *Safeguards in a world of ambient intelligence* (Springer, 2008), *Profiling the European Citizen* (Springer 2008) and *Reinventing data protection?* (Springer 2009). Currently, Serge Gutwirth is particularly interested both in technical legal issues raised by technology (particularly in the field of data protection and privacy) and in more generic issues related to the articulation of law, sciences, technologies and societies.

Paul De Hert is an international human rights expert. The bulk of his work is devoted, but not limited, to criminal law and technology & privacy law. At **Brussels**, Paul De Hert holds the chair of 'Criminal Law', 'International and European Criminal Law' and 'Historical introduction to eight major constitutional systems'. In the past he has held the chair of 'Human Rights', 'Legal theory' and 'Constitutional criminal law'. He is Director of the VUB-*Research group on Fundamental Rights and Constitutionalism* (FRC), Director of the Department of Interdisciplinary Studies of Law (Metajuridics) and core member of the internationally well-accepted VUB-*Research group Law Science Technology & Society* (LSTS) (see: www.vub.ac.be/LSTS). At **Tilburg** he holds a position as an associated-professor in the internationally renowned Institute of Law and Technology at the Tilburg University (http://www.tilburguniversity.nl/faculties/frw/departments/tilt/profile/). He is member of the editorial boards of several national and international scientific journals such as the *Inter-American and European Human Rights Journal* (Intersentia), *Criminal Law & Philosophy* (Springer). He is co-editor in chief of the

Supranational Criminal Law Series (Intersentia) and of the New Journal of European Criminal law (Intersentia).

Mireille Hildebrandt is Associate Professor of Jurisprudence at the Erasmus School of Law, Rotterdam and Senior Researcher at the centre for Law Science Technology and Society at Vrije Universiteit Brussel. She has been coordinator of research on profiling technologies in the EU funded project on the Future of Identity in the Information Society (FIDIS) and has published widely on the subject of profiling and the rule of law. Together with Serge Gutwirth she edited 'Profiling the European Citizen. Cross-Disciplinary Perspectives' (2008). She is Associate Editor of two peer reviewed international journals (Criminal Law and Philosophy and Identity in Information Society). Next to her research on law, technology and society she focuses on criminal law theory and legal philosophy, publishing on the role of expertise in court and the import and meaning of fair criminal proceedings in a constitutional democracy. She is presently dean of education of the Research School for Safety and Justice in the Netherlands.

Gerrit Hornung LL.M., studied law and philosophy at the University of Freiburg (1996–2001). After his first state exam, he attended an LL.M. course at the University of Edinburgh which focused on European law and European and international human rights and afterwards completed his legal clerkship in Hamburg in 2006. Since 2002, he has been a member of provet, the Projektgruppe verfassungsverträgliche Technikgestaltung (Project Group Constitutionally Compatible Technology Design, http://provet.uni-kassel.de/) at the University of Kassel, where he assumed the office of managing director in August 2006. His PhD thesis (2005) deals with legal problems of smartcards, particularly biometric identity cards and patient data cards. Additionally, he has worked in several projects in the field of electronic government, data protection, electronic signatures and multimedia law. Currently, he is focusing on the legal aspects of new surveillance technologies.

Bart Jacobs studied mathematics and philosophy at Nijmegen. He got his PhD in 1991, also at Nijmegen, in the area of theoretical computer science. He worked at universities of Cambridge (UK) and Utrecht, and at the Centre for Mathematics and Computer Science in Amsterdam. In 1996 Jacobs returned to Nijmegen on a research position of the Royal Netherlands Academy of Sciences (KNAW). Since 2002 he is full professor in the area of security and correctness of software. His work was supported by a prestigious Pioneer grant of the Netherlands science foundation NWO. With his research group he has worked over the last decade on a number of societally relevant topics such as chipcards (e.g. in passports and transport), electronic voting and privacy. Since 2005 Jacobs is also parttime professor at the Technical University Eindhoven. In 2007 he was a member of the "Korthals Altes" committee that advised on the future of the voting process in the Netherlands. In 2008 his research group attracted worldwide attention by showing severe security vulnerabilities in the Mifare Classic, the most widely used smart card. See also his personal webpage www.cs.ru.nl/B.Jacobs.

Sylvia Kierkegaard (LLB, LLM, PhDM, MSc, MA, BA) is Professor-PhD supervisor at the Communications University of China, Visiting Professor of Law at the University of Southampton, and Visiting Professor of Law at numerous universities. She is the President of the International Association of IT Lawyers (IAITL), Chairman of the the LSPI-ILTC-IBLT Conference series, and editorial board member of over 25 top-ranked international journals. She is the editor in-chief of the International Journal of Private Law, International Journal of Liability and Scientific Enquiry, Journal of International Commercial Law and Technology. Sylvia is the Principal Investigator of the co-Reach, a project funded by several European countries and China, which is conducting a somparative analysis of copyright law in the New Media. She is also an advisor to several governments and a legal expert for the EU and the Council of Europe. Sylvia has published over 2000 articles and books and writes on various legal aspects involving Information Technology.

Christopher Kuner is a partner in the Brussels office of the international law firm Hunton & Williams. Mr. Kuner is also Chairman of the International Chamber of Commerce (ICC) Task Force on Privacy and Data Protection and of the European Privacy Officers Forum (EPOF), and sits on the academic advisory board of the German Association for Data Protection and Data Security (GDD). He lectures at a number of universities around Europe, is author of the book "European Data Protection Law: Corporate Compliance and Regulation" (Oxford University Press 2007), which has also been published in Chinese, and has published several other books and over 30 articles on various legal topics having to do with data protection and electronic commerce. Mr. Kuner has also been a Visiting Fellow at the Oxford Internet Institute of Oxford University.

Daniel Le-Metayer Grenoble Rhône-Alpes Research Center, INRIA (Institut National de Recherche en Informatique et Automatique), 655 avenue de l'Europe, 38000 Montbonnot, France.

Gordon Nardell is a Barrister at 39 Essex Street Chambers in London, specialising in public law, human rights and environmental law. He previously practised at the former European Commission of Human Rights and the Legal Affairs Directorate of the Council of Europe, and was a member of the drafting team for the 1998 UK Human Rights Act. Gordon regularly appears in high-profile human rights cases involving privacy and surveillance. He acted for the UK NGO *Liberty* in its successful application to the European Court of Human Rights in the interception case *Liberty and others v. UK*. He is a visiting lecturer at the UK National School of Government, training public sector lawyers on ECHR Article 8.

Tanguy Van Overstraeten is the Global Head of Privacy and Data Protection of the international law firm Linklaters LLP. He is heading the Technology, Media & Telecommunications (TMT) practice in Belgium and has been a member of the French-speaking Bar of Brussels for 22 years. Tanguy has developed a thorough practice in the field of information governance. He has a long-standing experience in advising multinationals on large-scale data protection projects and audits. Listed among leading lawyers recommended in TMT (Chambers Europe 2009), his practice includes advisory and transactional work as well as the conduct of litigation. He is Vice-Chair of the ICT Committee of the British Chamber of Commerce and an active member of the Digital Economy Committee of the American Chamber of Commerce to the EU. Graduated from the University of Brussels (ULB) and the Law School of the University of Chicago (LL.M. 1991), he is also a fellow of the Belgian American Educational Foundation. He regularly contributes to conferences and publications (including "La Protection des données à caractère personnel: quelques réflections d'un practicien, in les 25 marchés émergents du droit", Bruylant, 2006) and is Lecturer of the Solvay Brussels School of Economics and Management (University of Brussels) teaching data protection laws.

Walter Peissl holds a PhD in social sciences. He is Deputy Director of the Institute of Technology Assessment, Austrian Academy of Sciences (ITA/AAS). He has also been lecturing at various Austrian universities since 1992. During 1986/87 he worked as consumer policy adviser at the Federal Ministry for Family, Youth and Consumer Protection, and for the Society for Consumer Information. His major research fields include social and economic effects of new ICT and methodological issues of Technology Assessment. His current focus is on privacy, ICT in health care and participatory methods in Technology Assessment.

Andreas Pfitzmann is a professor of computer science at Dresden University of Technology. His research interests include privacy and multilateral security, mainly in communication networks, mobile computing, identity management, and distributed applications. He has authored or coauthored about 120 papers in these fields. He received diploma and doctoral degrees in computer science from the University of Karlsruhe. He is a member of ACM, IEEE, and GI, where he served as chairman of the Special Interest Group on Dependable IT-Systems for ten years.

Wolter Pieters (1978) is a postdoc researcher in information security at the University of Twente. He studied computer science and philosophy of science, technology and society at the same university. His PhD research at the Radboud University Nijmegen resulted in the interdisciplinary thesis "La volonté machinale: understanding the electronic voting controversy". After finishing his PhD, he worked for the Dutch Ministry of the Interior for one year, on electronic voting and electronic travel documents. Since September 2008 he is employed as a postdoc researcher in the VISPER project at the University of Twente. The project concentrates on deperimeterisation, the disappearing of traditional boundaries in information security. Pieters is program chair of the 2010 workshop on Security and Privacy in Cloud Computing, to be held at the Computers, Privacy and Data Protection Conference. He is an editor of "Jaarboek Kennissamenleving", a Dutch annual on the knowledge society. He published on electronic voting, verification of security properties, access control, and philosophy and ethics of information security.

Yves Poullet PhD in Law and graduated in Philosophy, is full professor at the Faculty of Law at the University of Namur (FUNDP) and Liège (Ulg), Belgium. He teaches different topics like: "Sources and Principles of the Law", "Internet

Regulations", "International Commercial Law", "Human Rights in the Information Society". Yves Poullet heads the CRID, since its creation in 1979. He conducts various researches in the field of new technologies with a special emphasis on privacy issues, individual and public freedom in the Information Society and Internet Governance. He is legal experts near the European Commission, UNESCO and Council of Europe. He has been during 12 years (1992–2004) member of the Belgian Commission on Data Protection (Commission belge de protection de la vie privée). In addition, he was since its origin, member of Legal Advisory Board of European Commission. He has received the Franqui Chair in 2004. He also chaired the Belgian Computer Association ABDI (Association Belge de Droit de l'Informatique). Yves Poullet is an active member of the Editorial Board of various famous law reviews. He is a founder of the European Telecommunication Forum, ECLIP and FIRILITE. Recently (2009), he has been nominated as member of the Royal Belgian Academy.

Sylvie Rousseau is Managing Associate in the Technology, Media & Telecommunications (TMT) practice of the international law firm Linklaters LLP in Belgium and is a member of the French-speaking Bar of Brussels. Sylvie has over eight years experience of data protection, privacy and information governance. She has developed extensive expertise in compliance programs and audits, drafting of processing and transfer agreements, review of privacy policies as well as filing of notifications with the regulator. Sylvie has taken on a key role in managing the data protection aspects of some major international projects, where she coordinated the work of both Linklaters offices and corresponding firms in this legal area. She has also been heavily involved in dealings with the Belgian regulator, the EU authorities and the Article 29 Data Protection Working Party. Sylvie is an active member of the Digital Economy Committee of the American Chamber of Commerce to the EU regarding data protection matters. She has been involved in the drafting of a number of data protection and privacy position papers for that committee.

Peter Traung is a lawyer and administrator working in the secretariat of the European Parliament. He was the Parliament administrator responsible for the "Citizens' Rights" Directive, which includes the security breach notification provisions and other amendments to the 2002/58 Directive on privacy and electronic communications.

Melanie Volkamer studied Computer Science at the Saarland University (Germany). She received her Doctor degree in October 2008 from the Koblenz University. The topic of her thesis is "requirements and evaluation methods for electronic voting systems" (http://www.springerlink.com/content/g7r7v7/). Here she improves existing requirement documents by the application of the Common Criteria in order to be flexible with respect to underlying trust models and evaluations depths. Melanie Volkamer gave presentations on arbitrary eVoting events and conferences and was/is a member of different advisory boards in eVoting initiatives and projects—in particular she joints the OSCE mission to Estonia in 2007 and supported the Federal Constitutional Court in the voting machine case. She co-authors Protection Profile

(PP) for the Digital Election Pen and the PP for Online-Voting (http://www.bsi.bund.de/zertifiz/zert/reporte/pp0037b_engl.pdf). Since 2009, she is working as a senior researcher at CASED (www.cased.de)/Technical University Darmstadt.

Tal Zarsky is a Senior Lecturer at the University of Haifa—Faculty of Law. His research focuses on Information Privacy, Internet Policy, Telecommunications Law and Online Commerce. He has also taught Contract and Property law. He has written and presented his work on these issues in a variety of forums, both in Israel and worldwide. In addition, he has advised various Israeli regulators and legislators on related issues. Dr. Zarsky is also a Fellow at the Information Society Project, at Yale Law School.

Part I
Generic Issues

Chapter 1
About the E-Privacy Directive: Towards a Third Generation of Data Protection Legislation?

Yves Poullet

The main purpose of this contribution is not to analyse provision by provision the E-Privacy Directive[1] presently in course of revision,[2] but to describe the emergence of new principles which, in our view, might be considered as going far beyond the traditional principles enshrined in the Council of Europe Convention 108 and already translated in the EU Directive 95/46/EC. These new principles fully take into account the new Privacy threats incurred by individuals, due to the characteristics of modern and future information systems on a more and more global interactive and convergent Internet.

To summarize, since privacy has been enacted by the Council of Europe Human Rights Convention, we assist to a progressive extension of its legal protection. We notice that this extension has been realized by two successive generations of legislation, as described in the previous report which Antoinette Rouvroy and myself

Thanks to Karen Rosier, lawyer and researcher at the CRID for the fruitful discussions and her precious advices.

[1] Directive 2002/58/EC concerning the processing of personal data and the protection of privacy in the electronic communications sectors.

[2] See the still in discussion proposal for a Directive of the EU Parliament and of the Council amending directive 2002/22/EC on universal service and users' rights relating to electronic communications networks, Directive 2002/58/EC concerning the processing of personal data and the protection of privacy in the electronic communications sectors and Regulation (EC) No. 2006/2004 on consumer protection cooperation, 2007/0248. On May 6, 2009 the European Parliament adopted the second reading amendments on the review of the EU 2002 regulatory framework for electronic communications including the review of the E-Privacy Directive (The famous Telecom Package). The amendments under discussion in the course of the Directive's review reflect the compromise reached between Parliament and Council, except for what concerns the refusal by the EU Parliament to endorse a provision legitimizing the French HADOPI system about the fight against illegal copying. A vote, by the telecommunications Council after this second reading by the EU Parliament, is expected in September 2009 and a third reading by the EU Parliament in mid-December 2009.

Y. Poullet (✉)
Research Centre for Information Technology & Law (CRID),
University of Namur, Namur, Belgium
e-mail: yves.poullet@fundp.ac.be

S. Gutwirth et al. (eds.), *Data Protection in a Profiled World*,
DOI 10.1007/978-90-481-8865-9_1, © Springer Science+Business Media B.V. 2010

drafted.[3] The initial one intended to consider privacy as a legal right protecting our intimacy and directly linked with certain specific data, specific places or specific exchanges. It relies on the idea that our home must be viewed as a closed garden where we might express ourselves without being observed or surveyed by unauthorized people. Sensitive data related to our philosophical, political or religious opinions were protected in order to preserve their intimate character, linked with our own constitutional liberties, but also to avoid the risk of discrimination linked to their use by third parties.

This negative conception of privacy defined as a right to opacity or to seclusion has been progressively considered in our Information Society as not being sufficient. The possibility of storing and processing huge numbers of data through computers modifies to a large extent the informational power relationships between companies and administrations, on the one hand, and the individuals and citizens on the other hand, between "the information haves" and the individuals: "the information have nots". This disequilibrium of the balance of the informational powers is furthermore increased by the radical opacity of the functioning of the information systems surrounding the citizens. This mutation of the information society therefore requires new principles which characterize the second generation. As demonstrated through the analysis of the first German Constitutional Court decision consecrating the informational self determination as a new constitutional right, judgement issued in 1983[4], the restoration of the equilibrium has required the enactment of what we might call the data protection principles or what American scholars call the "Fair use of personal information". Self-determination requires that it be ensured. Starting from the first data protection legislation in the early 1970s, the enactment of three main principles has been recently asserted by the quasi constitutional EU Charter on citizens' rights:[5] (1) Privacy needs, for its protection, a regulation covering all personal data irrespective of its nature or its intrinsic content. (2) Privacy protection implies, in the dialogue between data subjects and data controllers, the assertion; regarding the former, of new rights in order to ensure the transparency of the processing and, regarding the latter, certain limits (legitimacy of the processing and

---

[3] See A. Rouvroy and Y. Poullet, "The Right to Informational Self-determination and the Value of Self-development: Reassessing the Importance of Privacy for Democracy", in *Reinventing Data Protection,* eds. S. Gutwirth et al. (Dordrecht: Springer, 2009), 65 ff. we have developed extensively this idea of third generation in Y. Poullet, « Pour une troisième génération de réglementation de protection des données », in *Défis du droit à la protection à la vie privée*, coll. Cahiers du Centre de Recherches Informatique et Droit, 31 (Bruxelles: Bruylant, 2008), 25–70.

[4] G. Karlsruhe, B.Verf. December 15, 1983, *EuGRZ* (1983): 171 ff. See E.H. Riedl, "New Bearings in German Data Protection", *Human Rights Law Journal* 5 (1) (1984): 67 ff.; H. Burkert, « Le jugement du Tribunal Constitutionnel fédéral allemand sur le recensement démographique et ses conséquences », *Dr. Inf.* (1985): 8 ff. See also, E. Brouwer, *"Digital Borders and Real Rights"* (Nijmegen: Wolf Legal Pub, 2007), 501.

[5] The Charter of Fundamental Right of the European Union (2000/C 364/01) in its Article 7, § 1 reasserts the existence of the right to private and family life, home and communication, whereas Article 8 of the same Charter raises the protection of personal data to the status of a fundamental right.

the proportionality of their content) and certain obligations, like the obligation to a secure processing. (3) Furthermore, privacy protection requires the existence of a data protection authority viewed both as a "balance keeper" between the two main actors and ensuring a certain social control of the development of our information society. In other words, this second generation intends to substitute the negative approach of the first generation with a more positive approach grounded on the creation of the conditions of an equilibrated dialogue between two categories of actors and guaranteeing a societal control on this dialogue.

Do we need a new generation of privacy legislation, what we call a third generation? Everybody agrees that these last years the tremendous development of Information and Communication Technologies (ICT) radically modified our way of life, our habits and behaviours. ICT are ubiquitous and are increasingly functioning as autonomic systems able to learn from the data they are collecting and retrieving in unsuspected ways.[6]

The development of information technology can be described chronologically along three evolutions.[7] First, might be pointed out, in reference to Moore's law, the constant growth of the capacity of computers, user terminals and the communication infrastructure to which is added the seemingly limitless capacity of computer analysis. Second, we have the Internet revolution, which we can look at in three ways: the convergence of the network around a single interoperable platform, the appearance of the "semantic web" and Web 2.0 and, lastly, the changes in identification and authentication techniques. Third, there is a still more profound change linked to the emergence of ambient intelligence which uses technology and the network to put that technology into our everyday life, the things around us, the places we go, the body we inhabit. One of the main arguments for the deployment of "ambient intelligence systems" is the possibility to contextualize and personalize the environment according to the supposed needs or wishes of the users. In order to achieve this goal, these systems have to collect and manage large amounts of personal data and to set up dynamically statistical profiles. These data are often *collected and merged without the subject's notice*, based on different technical devices such as cookies, IP addresses or RFID tags playing a role of "silent and continuous trackers" of the users' habits. These systems raise obvious questions regarding personal data protection and *question one of its key principles, informed consent.* But they also raise controversies about empowerment and capabilities.[8] These controversies concern the self-determination of the individuals and their capabilities to build their own past and present personality and social life by personal learning, seclusion and reflexive

[6] Among others, see R. Bronsword, *"Rights, Regulation and the Technological Revolution"* (Oxford: Oxford Univ. Press, 2008) and the suggestive article written by J. Cohen, "Examined Lives: Informational Privacy and the Subject as Object", *Stanford Law Review*, 52 (2000): 1373 ff.

[7] About these different aspects, read our article, Y. Poullet, "Data Protection Legislation: What's at Stake for Our Society and Our Democracy?", *Computer Law & Security Report* 25 (2009): 211 ff.

[8] L. Introna and H. Nissenbaum, "Shaping the Web: Why the Politics of Search Engines Matters", *The Information Society* 16 (3) (2000): 169–86.

experiences and the shaping of their proper history and images. With these systems, the personal and social experiences are to some extent perverted by external silent rationalities and logics characterized by their opacity and fuzziness which do not allow individuals to impact on the "informational image" compiled on themselves, nor on the interpretation thereof. To some extent, these systems question the vitality and the diversity of our society because *they foster both individualism and social conformity and therefore undermine our democracies.*[9]

In our societies, the Internet user is both confronted with the "Big Brother" of the Orwell novel, a person who gathers information and can decide everything faced with an evermore transparent Internet user, and living in a world described by the Kafka trial,[10] where a person is defying a machine, the totally obscure and illogical functioning of which prevents him from anticipating the consequences of the acts he decides.

---

[9] P. De Hert and S. Gutwirth, "Privacy, Data Protection and Law Enforcement. Opacity of the Individuals and Transparency of the Power", in *Privacy and the Criminal Law,* eds. E. Claes, A. Duff, and S. Gutwirth (Antwerpen: Interscientia, 2006), 74, express it quite correctly: *"Never does an individual have an absolute control over an aspect of his or her privacy. If individuals do have freedom to organise life as they please, this will only remain self-evident up to the point that it causes social or inter-subjective friction. At that stage, the rights, freedoms and interests of others, as well as the prerogatives of the authorities come into play. The friction, tension areas and conflicts create the need for a careful balancing of the rights and interests that give privacy its meaning and relevance. That shows clearly, although quintessential for a democratic constitutional state, because it refers to liberty, privacy is a relational, contextual and per se social notion which only requires substance when it clashes with other private or public interests"*. The link between protection of privacy and the defence of our democracy is asserted by many authors. See notably, J. Habermas, *"Between Facts and Norms"* (Cambridge, MA: MIT Press, 1996); P.M. Schwartz and W.M. Treanor, "The New Privacy", *Michigan Law Review* 101 (2003): 216; James E. Flemming, "Securing Deliberative Autonomy", *Stanford Law Review* 48 (1) (1995): 1–71, arguing that the bedrock structure of deliberative autonomy secures basic liberties that are significant preconditions for persons' ability to deliberate about and make certain fundamental decisions affecting their destiny, identity, or way of life. On deliberative democracy, see James E. Flemming, "Securing Deliberative Democracy", *Fordham Law Review* 72 (2004): 1435.

[10] The contrasts between the visions of Orwell and Kafka are very well described in the book of D.J. Solove, *"The Digital Person: Technology and Privacy in the Information Age"* (New York: New York Univ. Press, 2004), 7 ff.: *"The dominant metaphor for modern invasions of Privacy is Big Brother... Big Brother oppresses its citizens, purges, dissenters, and spies everyone in their homes. The result is a cold, drab grey world with hardly any space for love, joy, original thinking, spontaneity or creativity. It is a society under total control. Although the metaphor has proven quite useful for a number of privacy problems, it only partially captures the problems of digital dossiers. Big Brother envisions a centralized authoritarian power that aims for absolute control, but the digital dossiers constructed by business aren't controlled by a central power, and their goal is not to oppress us but to get us to buy new products and services". "The trial captures an individual's sense of helplessness, frustration and vulnerability when a large bureaucratic organization has control over a vast dossier of details about one's life...The problem is not simply a loss of control over personal information nor is there a diabolical motive or plan for domination as we describe it by the Big Brother... The problem is a bureaucratic process that is uncontrolled".*

Let us recall the dangers which arise:

- From an imbalance of the respective powers[11] of those responsible for data processing on the one hand, and the persons concerned on the other. This imbalance can lead to all kinds of discriminations;
- From "de-contextualisation":[12] where data circulating on the web is "issued" by people concerned with a precise objective, or in a particular context. The exchanges of data of all kinds and the possibilities to use search engines with any key words engender the risk of being judged "out of context";
- From the obscurity[13] of the functioning as much of terminals (cookies, RFID) as infrastructures (see "distributed agents" localised throughout information systems such as those known as being of "ambient intelligence"). This opacity carries the fear of unsolicited and unwanted information processing, and the motivation henceforth is to conform to a behaviour believed to be expected in these new invisible places of surveillance;

---

[11] D.J. Solove, "Privacy and Power: Computer Data Bases and Metaphors for Information Privacy", *Stanford Law Review* 53 (6) (2001): 1393 ff.

[12] The importance of the respect of the context, that is to say the zone of confidence in which personal data is transmitted by the concerned individual has been remarkably highlighted by H. Nissenbaum, ("Privacy as Contextual Integrity", *Washington Law Review* 79 2004: 150 et s.). The author asserts: *"the freedom from scrutiny and zones of 'relative insularity' are necessary conditions for formulating goals, values, conceptions of self, and principles of action because they provide venues in which people are free to experiment, act and decide without giving account to others or being fearful of retribution".*

[13] The dangers resulting from the lack of transparency and threatening our information societies for citizens; where they cannot know exactly how the information systems work, which data are collected, where data processing takes place and by whom, were underlined in 1983 by the well known constitutional judegment in the case of census (Bundesverfassungsgerichtshof, December 15, 1983, *EuGRZ* (1983): 171 et s.). The temptation of citizens is thus to behave in the way they think is expected by society and not to dare expressing themselves freely what is harmful to our democracies: *"The possibility of inspection and of gaining influence have increased to a degree hitherto unknown, and may influence the individuals' behaviour by the psychological pressure exerted by public interests. Even under certain conditions of modern information processing technology, individual self-determination presupposes that the individuals left with the freedom of decision about actions to be taken or to be omitted, including the possibility to follow that decision in practice. If someone cannot predict with sufficient certainty which information about himself in certain areas is known to his social milieu and cannot estimate sufficiently the knowledge of parties to whom communication may be possibly be made, he is crucially inhibited in his freedom to plan or to decide freely and without being subject to any pressure influence. If someone is uncertain whether deviant behaviour is noted down and stored permanent as information, or is applied or passed, he will try not to attract attention by such behaviour. If he reckons that participation in an assembly or a citizens' initiative will be registered officially and that personal risks might result from it, he may possibly renounce the exercise of his respective rights. This would not only impact his chances of development but would have also impact the common good ("Gemeinwohl"), because self-determination is an elementary functional condition of a free democratic society based on its citizen's capacity to act and to cooperate."*

- From reductionism:[14] more and more, collected data concerning events, even the most trivial in our lives, are multiplied, and information systems analyse us via this data which reduces our choices and in general human beings, even our personalities, to "profiles", created in line with conceptions having defined objectives by those who use such data, even directly by the technological system. In "ambient intelligence" systems where man is put on the network with all the paraphernalia of his surroundings, he becomes, at the heart of the network, a communicating object among others, of which some will provoke this or that reaction;
- From the blotting out of the distinction between the public sphere and the private sphere.[15] Man, lost in the crowd, can be followed, can be traced. Inversely, even in his home, doubly locked in, he can be seen via the GMS (global monitoring system), in his pocket the RFID which he can carry, via his use of interactive TV, and his computer connected to Internet; spied, followed and his intimate secrets pierced. We will come back to this point. The protection of the physical dwelling place, an inviolable place, would traditionally seem, and is in the eyes of the law, as something fundamental for the development of the personality of the individual. Now this notion also finds itself in question in the light of current technological developments.

Could all these new features and the involved privacy risks be adequately addressed by our current data protection legislation? Definitively Data Protection Authorities particularly are trying, in certain cases, through audacious reasoning, to demonstrate that Directive 95/46 on data protection might bring solutions to these new challenges, but certain of their assertions raise legal objections from the courts and create doubts which might prejudice the market and, at the same time, the protection of the citizens. Perhaps it might be recalled that the Directive was enacted before the explosion of the Internet. In 2002, the Directive concerning the processing of personal data and the protection of privacy in the electronic communications sectors, known now as the E-Privacy Directive, was adopted. Definitively the Internet applications were at this moment quite different from those developed since then. For instance, RFIDs were at their birth and social networks remained confidential. Nevertheless, several of these E-Privacy Directive provisions are enlarging our privacy protection in certain important directions which in our opinion have to be considered now in order to redefine our human liberties' protection in this ubiquitous and still more invasive information society.

In this contribution, we will consider the three main extensions suggested by the E-Privacy Directive. The first one is linked with the concept of data. Is personal

---

[14] The danger of « reductionism » is analysed by J. Rosen, *"The Unwanted Gaze: The Destruction of Privacy in America"* (2000) quoted by D.J. Solove, *ibidem*, 424: *"Privacy protects us from being misdefined and judged out of context in a world of short attention spans, a world in which information can easily be confused with knowledge"*.

[15] On this classic distinction and its radical calling into question J.A. Eichbaum, "Towards an Autonomy Based Theory of Constitutional Privacy: Beyond the Ideology of Familial Privacy", *Harvard Civil Rights—Civil Liberties Review* 14 (1979): 361–84. On this point, read also, D.J. Solove, "Conceptualizing Privacy", *California Law Review* 90 (2002): Especially 1138 and 39.

data in the sense of the definition given by the Directive 95/46 still adequate? The second one takes into consideration the fact that the dialogue between data subjects and data controllers has now become interactive and is ensured by the functioning of terminals more and more multifunctional and ubiquitous, and by infrastructures increasingly complex and at the same time interoperable and convergent. The regulation of their functioning appears as a condition for the protection of our privacy. This second point leads onto take into consideration new actors and new objects. The Directive reduces the data protection debate to a regulation of the data subjects and the data controllers. The E-Privacy Directive suggests the need of regulating not only these two actors, but also the infrastructure and the terminals placed between them. This infrastructure and these terminals are indeed ensuring not only their dialogue but also a lot of other possibilities for other parties to introduce themselves into this dialogue, to create new ones or, simply, to be aware of these dialogues. We conclude with the consideration, that we definitively need to extend privacy debates to a reflection on questioning our information society on very fundamental values such as, Human dignity and liberty. Without this enlargement it must be feared that we will loose the essential. Data protection legislation is only a tool at the service of our dignity and liberties and not a value as such.

1.1 Is Personal Data the Adequate Concept?

Data protection legislation covers the protection of all personal data. The definition of personal data contained in Directive 95/46/EC (henceforth "the Data Protection Directive" or "the Directive") reads as follows:

> Personal data shall mean any information relating to an identified or identifiable natural person ("data subject"); an identifiable person is one who can be identified, directly or indirectly, in particular by reference to an identification number or to one or more factors specific to his physical, physiological, mental, economic, cultural or social identity.

It is quite obvious that the concept encompasses a lot of information regardless of its format, its nature (sound, text or image), its sensitivity, its subjective or objective character, etc. The scope is very broad and Article 29 Working Party clearly asserted, on the basis of the Directive's Recital 26, that any information which might be referred to an individual—including by having recourse to a third party—must be considered as personal. So, notwithstanding divergent judicial interpretation[16] including by the highest Courts,[17] IP addresses even if they are purely temporary

---

[16] See the Durant case in the UK, where a plate identification number was not considered as a personal data.

[17] Two recent decisions of the French Highest Court (Cour de cassation, May 1, 2007 and April 27, 2007) have clearly asserted that IP addresses were not personal data: *"Cette série de chiffres (ne constituent) en rien une donnée indirectement nominative à la personne dans la mesure où elle ne se rapporte qu'à une machine et non à l'individu qui utilise cette machine"* et *« l'adresse IP ne (permettait aps d'identifier le ou les personnes qui ont utilisé cet ordinateur puisque seule l'autor-*

attributed have been considered as personal data insofar as it would be possible for the person collecting that information to retrieve a possessor at a certain time through the intervention of his or her Internet access provider.

Directive 2002/58/EC envisages the regulation of two specific categories of data, traffic data and location data, as follows:

> Traffic data means any data processed for the purpose of the conveyance of a communication on an electronic communications network or for the billing thereof; Location data means any data processed in an electronic communications network, indicating the geographic position of the terminal equipment of a user of a publicly available electronic communications service.

It has to be underlined that these two categories of data are defined without reference to the central concept of personal data used within the Directive 95/46/EC to fix the scope of application of data protection legislation. As regards the notion itself, traffic data is defined by reference to the purpose for which it is processed: this is any data processed for the purpose of the conveyance of a communication on an electronic communications network (such as the phone number calling or being called, e-mail addresses, IP address of the sender and of the receiver, etc.) or for the billing thereof (such as for the duration of the communication, size of the e-mail sent, phone number calling, etc.). They include data supplied by the sender (URL, e-mail address of the recipient, etc.) as well as data generated by the traffic. According to Recital 15, *"traffic data may, inter alia, consist of data referring to the routing, duration, time or volume of a communication, to the protocol used, to the location of the terminal equipment of the sender or recipient, to the network on which the communication originates or terminates, to the beginning, end or duration of a connection. They may also consist of the format in which the communication is conveyed by the network"*. The same remarks might be addressed to the concept of location data. In other words, the authors of Directive 2002/58/EC consider that these categories must be regulated[18] in any case, notwithstanding the nature of personal data due to its specificities and the risks linked to its uses.[19] This assumption leads to the discussion on the notion of personal data as the key concept for defining the scope of our data protection legislation.

---

ité légitime pour poursuivre l'enquête (police ou gendarmerie) peut obtenir du fournisseur d'accès l'identité de l'utilisateur ». More cautious, was the decision issued by the same court on January 13, 2009. About these discussions, see Y. Defraigne and A.M. Escoffier, *« La vie privée à l'heure des mémoires numériques », Rapport d'information, Commission des lois* 441 (2008–2009), available here www.senat.fr.

[18] See Articles 6 and 9 about the severe limits imposed on public communications services as regards the processing of these data and the EU Directive on data retention, which regulates strictly the retention (which data, for which duration, …) of these data.

[19] *"The reference to the definitions provided by the Data Protection Directive is logical in light of art. 1(1) since the provisions of the Directive are intended to complement and particularize the provisions of the Data Protection Directive's. The definitions provided in art. 2 of the Data Protection Directive relate to key concepts of the application of data protection legislation such as 'personal data', 'processing of personal data', 'controller' or 'processor'. However, the Directive makes rather limited use of these key concepts and more generally relies on specific proper concepts that are not based on these definitions. For instance, the Directive uses the terms 'traffic data' in arts. 6 and 9, 'location data' in art. 9 or 'information' in art. 5(3) which data or information are not necessarily 'personal data' per se"*.

1.1.1 New Kinds of Sensitive Data in Our Modern Networks: Identifiers and Contact Data

Indeed, in the context of the present functioning of Internet's application, different remarks have to be proposed as regards this central concept of personal data. The first one does take into consideration the fact that traffic and location data, which are strictly regulated by the E-Privacy Directive, are different in their nature from traditional sensitive data in the sense of Directive 95/46/EC. Traditionally, the personal data in mind were what we might call *"bibliographical data"*. It means data directly linked with past or present events of individuals' lives: their home address, their health problems, the shopping basket, their precise location at a certain moment, etc. We are used to classifying these data according to their sensitivity and, on that basis, to distinguish the applicable rules. As regards this category of data, the ubiquitous character of information systems, coupled with the fact that storage capacity is increasing tremendously and is cheaper and cheaper, induces the collection of more and more trivial data and instantaneous slices of our lives. The risk is no longer linked with the very nature of the data but with the multiplication of the data collected and cross-matched permitting the definition of individual profiles.

Apart from this first category of data, the Internet (r)evolution leads to take fully into account two new kinds of data. The **first** one might be described as *identifiers* or, more precisely, as "matching identifiers", since these data have as main role to permit the crossing of data belonging to various databases in order, notably, to profile the individual behind the data collected. Another remarkable evolution on the internet has come from the availability and use of identification and authentication methods of users. These methods allow users to identify themselves and to be identified or, together with identity management systems, to allow access to informational resources or services. Beyond this, it is also possible to identify users with certainty and thereby add or deduce new information about them drawing on sources from all sites over the web with no concern for any border limitations.[20] These "digital identities" are a kind of metadata that allow the cross-referencing of individuals' information available on different databases, in other words as matching identifiers. We need to underline the dangers of using the same digital identity in several areas of our online life. It is clear that, most often, the same identification method or access key is used in different databases with as a result that our identity can be cross-referenced more easily. We know for example that in certain countries, the national registration number is stored in all governmental databases. This increases the possibility of cross-referencing the information and thus, enhances the power of the state in regards vis-à-vis the citizen. From that point of view, these

---

[20] On that point, M. Rundle, "International Personal Data Protection and Digital Identity Management tools" (paper presented at the Identity Mashup Conference, Harvard Law School, June 20, 2006), available at the SSRN paper collection: http://papers.ssrn.com/abstract or at the Berckman Center for Internet and Society Research Publication Series web site (Research publication No. 2006, June 2006–06) available at: http://cyber.law.harvard.edu/publications. From the same author, M.C. Rundle and P. Trevithick, "Interoperability in the New Digital Identity Infrastructure", (paper published at Social Science Research Network, February 13, 2007), available on the web site http://papers.ssrn.com/sol3/papers.cfm?abstract._id=962701.

matching identifiers might be considered as quite sensitive data even if they are not always linked with an identified or identifiable individual, but with an object.[21] Overall, the sharing of this identifying data by those who collect it raises the question of how to handle correctly the data within the given context.

Finally, let us examine more closely the evolution of the nature of these digital identities. The primary digital identifiers are directly connected to a person, name, address, mobile phone number, password or electronic signature; the secondary identifiers are indirect but are based on known information concerning the individual. Cookies, IP addresses or RFID tag numbers, while not necessarily known to the individual, they are associated with a site or object with which the person is connected; these ID techniques are mastered and understood by the people or businesses that place them there. With biometric identification technology (iris, fingerprints, voice) identity and identifiability are reduced from a flesh and blood reality, to just "data". Here we note a certain evolution, as biometric information can concern an exterior physical trait or look or, more deeply, the genetic level of the individual. In the latter case, this genetic information can be used to follow the individual from cradle to grave.[22] Contrary to other identification and identifiability data, these particular data cannot be controlled or erased by the person concerned.[23]

Another kind of data seems more and more relevant in our information society. **Contact data** is used in order to allow data controllers to enter into contact with data subjects. On that point it might be interesting to underline how mobile phones will be more and more used in connection with ambient intelligence systems to send advertising messages but also, at their customers' request, service links for determining their precise location. So, contact data authorizes its data processor to make immediate decisions for the person identified or not by this contact data.

To be complete, it must be added that these three categories are not separated, but that certain overlapping might exist. So, data like an e-mail address or a RFID tag number belongs to all three categories of data: bibliographical, contact and matching data since it might reveal our name, but also serve as an identifier, and finally it may be used to send messages to the individual in possession of the e-mail address or the RFID tag. What becomes obvious in our modern societies is that the data of the two last categories must be considered in many contexts as sensitive, since as regards the "matching identifiers" they permit to a large scale to aggregate data belonging to the same individuals and thus to "profile" them very precisely. So, an RFID tag embedded into the employee's clothes allows the retrieval of the different

---

[21] On that point, read J.M. Dinant, "The Concepts of Identity and Identifiability: Both a Legal and Technical Deadlock for Protecting Human Beings in the Information Society?", in *Reinventing Data Protection*, eds. S. Gutwirth et al. (Dordrecht: Springer, 2009).

[22] A. Ceyhan, "Technologization of Security: Management of Uncertainty and Risk in the Age of Biometrics", *Surveillance and Society* 5 (2) (2008): 102–23.

[23] About the very specific peculiarity of biometric data and the risks linked with their uses, read C. Priens, "Biometric Technology Law. Making Your Body Identify for Us: Legal Implications of Biometric Technologies", *Computer Law & Security Review* 14 (1998): 159 ff. A. Cavoukian and A. Stoianov, "Biometric Encryption: A Positive-Sum. Technology that Achieves Strong Authentication, Security and Privacy" (Information and Privacy Commissioner/Ontario, March 2007).

movements of this employee during his or her stay on the company's premises. The stable IP v.6 address linked with a terminal device will facilitate the tracing of the internet user through their different visits of websites. As regards contact data, now we underline that through these data controllers, immediate and appropriate decisions vis-à-vis the person so targeted can be taken. Let us take an example. A person who has at a certain moment attempted to fraud an e-ticketing system thanks to an RFID system, might be automatically recognised the day after by the tag reader and see the door automatically blocked.

1.1.2 IP Address, Cookies, Data Generated by RFID, Always "Personal Data"? Why Regulate Them Anyway?

The second remark comes back to our initial surprise when considering the definition of traffic and location data under Directive 2002/58/EC. We noticed that these definitions do not refer to the concept of personal data even if they are regulated by strict prohibitions regarding certain processing.[24] We know that some question[25]

---

[24] Article 6 of the E-Privacy Directive as regards traffic data provides:

1. *Traffic data relating to subscribers and users processed and stored by the provider of a public communications network or publicly available electronic communications service must be erased or made anonymous when it is no longer needed for the purpose of the transmission of a communication without prejudice to paragraphs 2, 3 and 5 of this Article and Article 15(1).*
2. *Traffic data necessary for the purposes of subscriber billing and interconnection payments may be processed. Such processing is permissible only up to the end of the period during which the bill may lawfully be challenged or payment pursued.*
3. *For the purpose of marketing electronic communications services or for the provision of value added services, the provider of a publicly available electronic communications service may process the data referred to in paragraph 1 to the extent and for the duration necessary for such services or marketing, if the subscriber or user to whom the data relate has given his/her consent. Users or subscribers shall be given the possibility to withdraw their consent for the processing of traffic data at any time.*

Article 9 provides as regards the location data: *"Where location data other than traffic data, relating to users or subscribers of public communications networks or publicly available electronic communications services, can be processed, such data may only be processed when they are made anonymous, or with the consent of the users or subscribers to the extent and for the duration necessary for the provision of a value added service."*

In the new version of the directive presently debated, the authors have foreseen an additional purpose legitimizing the processing of location or traffic data. The public communications service operator might also process the data for their own internal security needs.

See also Directive 2006/24/EC on Data Retention, which explicitly regulates the storage of traffic and location data.

[25] The Article 29 Working Party echoes these doubts present in the E-Privacy Directive revision by repeating that, under its opinion, IP address must be considered as personal data. The Working Party 29 recalls that, in most cases—including cases with dynamic IP address allocation—the necessary data will be available to identify the user(s) of the IP address. The Working Party noted in its WP 136 that *"... unless the Internet Service Provider is in a position to distinguish with absolute certainty that the data correspond to users thatcannot be identified, it will have to treat all*

marks surround the assertion that IP addresses are automatically personal data, since the possibility for websites collecting these IP addresses to retrieve the person behind the data from the Internet access provider will meet his refusal insofar, precisely under Directive 2002/58/EC, it is strictly forbidden for him to communicate that kind of information to a third party. Other doubts have been raised about the nature of cookies as personal data, since cookies definitively identify a terminal (or a session opened into a terminal), but not an individual as such, even if it is quite clear that in certain cases the number and quality of the data collected through cookies might reveal what Article 2 of Directive 95/46/EC calls *"one or more factors specific to his physical, physiological, mental, economic, cultural or social identity"*.

Let us take another example. In a large supermarket, a customer is walking along the shelves with his or her trolley equipped with both a RFID tag (sender and reader) and a small video screen. Combined with the presence of products equipped also with RFID tags, the RFID system reveals at each moment the products purchased by the customer, as well as his or her precise location in the store, and is able to send the appropriate advertisement according to this data: *"Hello, Yves, I suggest you to buy this kind of wine today sold at reduced price which is perfect to accompany the cheese and the vegetables you have bought today"*. It is quite clear that, on the contrary, when the RFID is embedded in the shopping card, the store has no indication as regards the person who is conducting the trolley and does not need this knowledge in order to select the "adequate" advertisement but definitively, as it is the case with cookies, the information system can make decisions geared towards the individual.

In its famous opinion on the concept of personal data,[26] Article 29 of the Working Party makes a distinction between data related to individuals on the basis of their content, of their purpose and of the result of their processing. The last category seems to match with the problem at stake. We quote the Working Party: *"Despite the absence of a 'content' or 'purpose' element, data can be considered to 'relate' to an individual because their use is likely to have an impact on a certain person's rights and interests, taking into account all the circumstances surrounding the precise case. It should be noted that it is not necessary that the potential result be a major impact. It is sufficient if the individual may be treated differently from other persons as a result of the processing of such data"*. This third category does represent a shift as regards the notion of personal data since it does not refer to the nature of the data, as it was the case under Directive 95/46/EC, but to the potential impact that the use of collected data might have on an unidentifiable individual through the characteristics of the information system in use by the individual. So what is at stake is no longer the data but the technical possibility to contact a person X in order to have

---

IP information as personal data, to be on the safe side...". These considerations will apply equally to search engine operators (WP 148). See again the strong emphasis put on this point in the WP 159 dated from February 10, 2009 on the last version proposed by the EU Council of Ministers.

[26] "Working Paper 4/2007 on the Concept of Personal Data, WP 136", (June 20, 2007).

an impact on his or her rights or interests. To definitively identify a person is not anymore a prerequisite for data processing affecting him or her.[27] A single identifier and a contact point are sufficient.[28] That possibility might create discrimination or abusive surveillance that violate our privacy in the broad sense of this concept.[29] However, do we need to regulate these possible privacy violations through data protection legislation without there being any possibility of applying all the provisions of that legislation, particularly those related to the right of access considered as a key element by Article 8 of the EU Charter on Fundamental Rights?[30]

Our opinion does not lead to avoiding any principles/prescriptions enshrined in data protection principles/rules/laws (one "principles" needs to be changed—for clarity), but rather to deducing these applicable principles directly from privacy protection requirements. So the principles of proportionality, both regarding processing and content, and that of fair collection; meaning for the least that information on data collection and the infrastructure in place, have to be provided even if they are not collecting personal data since their use might impact the rights or interests of individuals. That final assertion must be correlated with the existence of profiling methods which until now are not taken into consideration by our data protection legislation and, in our opinion, would have to be subject to specific regulation, as we now explain.

---

27 Concerning the use of location data and all the possibilities linked with the use of location data and data mining methods, read F. Gianotti and D. Pedreschi, eds., *"Mobility, Data Mining and Privacy"* (Dordrecht: Springer, 2007).

28 On that point, read J.M. Dinant, "The Concepts of Identity and Identifiability: Both a Legal and Technical Deadlock for Protecting Human Beings in the Information Society?", in *Reinventing Data Protection*, eds. S. Gutwirth et al., (Dordrecht: Springer, 2009).

29 Article 8 asserts the three major elements of any data protection legislation based on the European model:

1. *Everyone has the right to the protection of personal data concerning him or her.*
2. *Such data must be processed fairly for specified purposes and on the basis of the consent of the person concerned or some other legitimate basis laid down by law. Everyone has the right of access to data which has been collected concerning him or her, and the right to have it rectified.*
3. *Compliance with these rules shall be subject to control by an independent authority.*

30 *"Humans will, in an Ambient Intelligent Environment, be surrounded by intelligent interfaces supported by computing and networking technology that is embedded in everyday objects such as furniture, clothes, vehicles, road ad smart materials-even particles of decorative substances like paint. AmI implies a seamless environment of computing advanced networking technology and specific interfaces. This environment should be aware of the specific characteristics of human presence and personalities; adapt to the needs of the user; be capable of responding intelligently to spoken or gestured indications of desire; and even result in systems that are capable of engaging in intelligent dialog. AmI should be relaxing and enjoyable for the citizen, and not involve a steep learning curve"* (IST Advisory Group's Report, *"Ambient Intelligence: From Vision to Reality. For Participation in Society and Business"* (2003), ftp://ftp.cordis.europa.eu/pub/ist/docs/istag).

1.1.3 New Data to be Protected: The Profiles

Computers, information and communication technologies, often in conjunction with other unknown capturing capacities; such as communication and processing of information relating to the interactions of individuals with their environment,[31] whether physical or digital, allow for the large-scale collection of anonymous or personal data. We can talk about "ubiquitous" computing in as much as the terminals can be placed anywhere and note everything we do in our daily lives, our movements, our hesitations, or what we choose to eat. Next, this is a technology that is largely invisible in two ways ("Calm Technology"): it operates in a largely hidden way (we do not know what information is collected, when or for whom), but also, as a natural extension of an activity or movement (a door opens and the computer comes on) assisting us in our choice of activities. Finally, this technology learns. These systems often adapt their operations based on feedback from their users. We might speak also about "ambient intelligence technologies" which tend to associate the virtual and real worlds. This is done in the space created in the network where there is dialogue between objects, and between objects and people, this is in the real world, the territory held by ICT. As a consequence, a large amount of data relating to the personal circumstances, social contacts and activities of the user can be accessed in the working memory and on the storage media of such systems. If this data, even made anonymous or coded, is collected and evaluated by third parties, it can be highly illuminating as to the personality of the user, and may even make it possible through sophisticated statistical inferences to form a profile. These profiling operations[32] are supported by the existence of vast data warehouses, which are utilized in an increasingly effective and targeted manner by calculation, comparison and statistical correlation software. When the profiles are applied to an individual known or unknown, they create the possibility to make decisions geared towards these individuals.

The risks[33] linked with these activities might be identified as follows. First, the process results in attributing certain characteristics to an individual derived from the probability (dogma of statistical truth) that he or she belongs to a group and not from data communicated or collected about him or her. Second, the process is to a large extent unknown for the individual, who might never imagine the logic behind the decision taken towards him or her. Third, the use of profiling for detecting potential

[31] This collection may use in particular the processing of traffic data and user queries on the Internet, the recording of consumer purchasing habits and activity, the processing of geo-location data concerning mobile telephone users, the data collected by video surveillance cameras and by RFID systems, foreshadowing the "Internet of things", and finally by biometric systems.

[32] About these profiling practices and the need to regulate them, J.M. Dinant et al., *"Profiling and Data Protection"*, Report Addressed to the Convention 108 Consultative Committee (September 2008), available on the Council of Europe website.

[33] On these risks, read M. Hildebrant and S. Gutwirth eds., *"Profiling the European Citizen"* (Dordrecht: Springer, 2008). See also, A. Rouvroy, "Privacy, Data Protection, and the Unprecedented Challenges of Ambient Intelligence", *Studies in Law, Ethics and Technology* (2008), available at http://works.bepress.com/antoinette-rouvroy//2.

infringers induces a reversal of the burden of the proof. Fourth, it creates some risks of discrimination, and even threats to social justice, since certain consequences are attached to the meaning of the profile. Amazon's "adaptive pricing" system is often quoted in that perspective. This system adapts prices on the basis of certain *a priori* characteristics of the detected profile of the customers. Opportunities are so offered to the processor to have an automated judgment by considering not the individual but the profile that person belongs to. *"Profiling burdens those in the proxy class when the social meaning of the profile expresses denigration of the group defined by the proxy trait but the persons in the proxy group need to prove either that they are actually injured psychologically by the stigmatizing meaning or that they individually interpret the social meaning of the profile denigrates those in the proxy class. This requires them to show that the reasonable person familiar with our culture and traditions would understand the practice to have this meaning".*[34]

In another context,[35] we have demonstrated that Article 15 of the Data Protection Directive applies only to certain profiling systems. Article 15 grants everyone *"a right not to be subject to a decision which produces legal effects concerning him or significantly and which is based only on automated processing of data intended to evaluate certain personal aspects relating to him".*[36] Definitively, this article is not applicable to profiling systems as most of them do not affect our legal rights and have no significant consequences. Furthermore, it is not applicable to functioning systems that do not identify or make people identifiable. Nevertheless, we do consider that liberties would be jeopardized if there were no regulation at all regarding these methods of processing.[37] Privacy is an issue which goes well beyond data protection. This concept means to provide the conditions of informational self determination. In our ubiquitous information society functioning on opaque profiling systems notably with ambient intelligence systems, privacy ought to mean equality of arms, due process and imposes that the person to whom profiling systems are applied to must be aware of the existence of these systems. They must have knowledge of their logic and must have the possibility to contest the accuracy and the applicability of these profiles. Privacy, except in cases where there are other

[34] D. Hellman, "Classification and Fair Treatment: An Essay on the Moral and Legal Permissibility of Profiling", *(Univ. of Maryland School of Law, Working Research Paper No. 2003–04)*, available at http://www.ssrn.com/abstract=456460.

[35] In the context of the works done by the Council of Europe about profiling and privacy, J.M. Dinant et al., *"Profiling and Data Protection"*, Report Addressed to the Convention 108 Consultative Committee (September 2008), available on the Council of Europe website. See in the same sense, M. Hildebrandt, "Profiling and the Identity of the European Citizen", in *Profiling the European Citizen,* eds. Hildebrandt & Gutwirth (Dordrecht: Springer, 2008), 303–393.

[36] This article needs to be interpreted in regard of Article 12 about the right of access. This article provides that the data subject has the right to obtain from the data controller the logic involved into any automatic system referred to in Article 15(1).

[37] See the Recommendations in preparation by the Council of Europe on that issue.

prominent public or private interests, implies in our opinion the right not to be profiled.[38]

1.2 New Objects and New Actors to be Regulated?

The E-Privacy Directive is also quite revolutionary in another aspect. It contains the basis for regulating objects which were not covered by the previous Directive 95/46/EC. The protection of human dignity and fundamental rights in the framework of the new applications deployed in the context of the Information Society can be effective if and only if all the stakeholders, such as; producers, designers and developers of software or information systems for electronic communications terminal equipment, profile designers, internet access providers and information society service providers could also technically contribute to ensuring the privacy and the data protection friendly deployment of electronic communications and information society services users' profiles. This assertion might be derived from different provisions under the E-Privacy Directive. The first ones concern the integrity of the terminal equipment.[39] Article 5.3 enacts: *"Member States shall ensure that the use of electronic communications networks to store information or to gain access to information stored in the terminal equipment of a subscriber or user is only allowed on condition that the subscriber or user concerned is provided with clear and comprehensive information in accordance with Directive 95/46/EC, inter alia about the purposes of the processing, and is offered the right to refuse such processing by the data controller. This shall not prevent any technical storage or access for the sole purpose of carrying out or facilitating the transmission of a communication over an electronic communications network, or as strictly necessary in order to provide an Information Society service explicitly requested by the subscriber or user".*

Article 14.2 grants the European Commission the competence to impose standards on terminal equipment manufacturers when their functioning does not comply with privacy requirements: *"Where required, measures may be adopted to ensure*

---

[38] A. Rouvroy, « Réinventer l'art d'oublier et de se faire oublier dans la société de l'information? », in *La sécurité de l'individu numérisé: Réflexions prospectives et internationales* (2008), Paris, L'Harmattan, 240–78.

[39] The notion of "terminal equipment" is quite broad. The term "telecommunications terminal equipment" (in this paper referred to as "terminal equipment") is defined in the *European Directive on telecommunications* (European Parliament and Council Directive 1999/5/EC of March 9, 1999, concerning terminal equipment, *Official Journal* L091 (April 4, 1999): 10 ff.) *terminal equipment as "a product enabling communication or a relevant component thereof which is intended to be connected directly or indirectly by any means whatsoever to interfaces of public telecommunications networks (that is to say, telecommunications networks used wholly or partly for the provision of publicly available telecommunications services)".* This broad definition includes not only personal computers, or other typical user terminals such as telephones (mobile or fixed), faxes, but equally RFID, chip cards, and tomorrow, "intelligent molecules" implanted in people themselves.

that terminal equipment is constructed in a way that is compatible with the right of users to protect and control the use of their personal data, in accordance with Directive 1999/5/EC and Council Decision 87/95/EEC of 22 December 1986 on standardisation in the field of information technology and communications".[40]

These two provisions illustrate the enlargement of data protection legislation. Directive 95/46/EC does only take into account the relationship between data controller and data subjects and has no consideration at all about the technical features embedded into the functioning of our modern networks and the risks linked with them. This functioning leads to new privacy threats, for instance through invisible hyperlinks, cookies or spyware, the automated generation of identifiers or transclusive[41] links like those provided by Google analytics. The intervention of untrusted third parties during the communication sessions between data subjects and data controllers are another reality we definitively ought to consider. Progressively, the Data Protection Authorities became conscious of these threats entailed by Internet communications hardware and software. In its Recommendation 1/99,[42] Article 29 of the Working Party has clearly established the principle that software and hardware industry products should provide the necessary tools to comply with EU data protection rules.

This assertion will progressively be extended through different steps. The first one is the support the EU Commission will give to Privacy Enhancing Technologies (PETs). The second one might be characterized by the increasing demand of Data Protection Authorities to impose certain liability on terminal equipment manufacturers and information systems designers, as the RFID case illustrates. The third step might be derived directly from Article 5.3 of the E-Privacy Directive, which considers our terminal equipment as a kind of virtual "domicile" to be protected like a physical one. A recent German Constitutional Court decision will give us the opportunity to interpret in a quite revolutionary way Article 8 of the Council of Europe Convention.

---

40 Decision as last amended by the 1994 Act of Accession, *Official Journal* L36/31 (February 7, 1987).

41 *"Transclusion is the inclusion of part of a document into another document by reference. For example, an article about a country might include a chart or a paragraph describing that country's agricultural exports from a different article about agriculture. Rather than copying the included data and storing it in two places, a transclusion embodies* modular design, *by allowing it to be stored only once (and perhaps corrected and updated if the link type supported that) and viewed in different contexts. The reference also serves to link both articles."* (definition taken from Wikipedia encyclopaedia (http://www.en.wikipedia.org/)).

42 Directive 1999/5/EC of March 9, 1999 on Radio equipment and telecommunications terminal equipment and the mutual recognition of their conformity, *Official Journal* L91 (7 April, 1999): 10–28.

1.2.1 EU Commission's Support to PETs

As we know, PETs[43] include all kinds of information and communication technologies that strengthen the protection of individuals' private lives by an information system that prevents unnecessary or unlawful processing of personal data, or by offering tools and controls to enhance the individual's control over his/her personal data. A recent report distinguishes different kinds of PETs: *"PET can be used to detach identification details from the other data stored about the person. The link between the identification details and the other personal details can only be restored with the use of specific tooling. Another option offered by PET is to prevent the registration of personal details altogether, for instance, once the identity has been verified. Software can also be used to enforce the condition that personal data are always disclosed to third parties in compliance with the prevailing privacy policies"*.[44]

As progressively asserted, PETs should be part of the architecture of the information system, right from the start. In this phase, the functional design is further elaborated and detailed in a more technical sense. An important aspect is that the technical design of the PETs option must be integrated in the complete technical design of the information system. Repeatedly, it has been considered that the PETs option is, after all, not a separate component that can be added; therefore, the technical design of PETs cannot be separated from the technical architecture of the entire information system.

By its recommendation dated from May 2, 2007, *"the Commission expects that wider use of PETs would improve the protection of privacy as well as help fulfil the data protection rules. The use of PETs would be complementary to the existing legal framework and enforcement mechanisms. In fact the intervention of different actors in the data processing and the existence of the different national jurisdictions involved could make enforcement of the legal framework difficult"*.[45]

---

[43] Directorate of Public Sector Innovation and Information Policy (DIIOS), *"Privacy-Enhancing Technologies-White Paper for Decision-Makers"*, Written for the Dutch Ministry of the Interior and Kingdom Relations (2004). This paper distinguishes different kinds of PETs: *"From a functional perspective, it is not difficult to implement PET. With the aid of PET, it is possible to protect information about a person, such as identity and personal details. PET comprises all the technological controls for guaranteeing privacy. For instance, PET can be used to detach identification details from the other data stored about the person. The link between the identification details and the other personal details can only be restored with the use of specific tooling. Another option offered by PET is to prevent the registration of personal details altogether, for instance, once the identity has been verified. Software can also be used to enforce the condition that personal data are always disclosed to third parties in compliance with the prevailing privacy policies."* See also, J.J. Borking and C. Raab, "Laws, PETS and Other Technologies for Privacy Protection", *Journal of Information, Law and Technology* 1 (February 2001), available at: http://elj.warwick.ac.uk/jilt:01-1:borking.html

[44] DIIOS, *White Paper.*

[45] On that point, see also the Working Party 29's Opinion 2/2008 on the E-Privacy Directive issued May 15, 2008 (No. 150): *"The Working Party 29 advocates the application of the principle of data minimisation and the deployment of Privacy Enhancing Technologies by data controllers. The Working Party calls upon European legislators to make provision for a reinforcement of said*

As regards the terminal, broadly defined by the EU regulation, as any equipment connected to the public network and that are able to enter into dialogue with the latter (RFID tags, mobiles, etc.), no specific obligation has been imposed on them in order to make them privacy compliant. It is quite noticeable that, notwithstanding repeated calls from the Data Protection Authorities for a better cooperation with standardisation bodies,[46] and, overall, the existence of Article 14.3 quoted above, the Commission has never taken any initiative to impose technical standards on terminal equipment manufacturers in order to ensure their privacy compliance. Certain authors are analysing that situation as a lack of courage at a time when the EU Commission does not want to prejudice European companies and their competition potential in front of the rest of the world by imposing on them additional charges. This EU position might be criticized for two reasons. First, it is the positive duty for our states, including EU authorities, to protect human rights through all means. Second, from an economic point of view, it might be of some interest for our market to develop labelled privacy equipment, which might meet also the interest of the rest of the world. In our opinion, the privacy option definitively/definitely does represent an opportunity to impose on the global market European standards and products.

1.2.2 Towards a Liability of Terminal Equipments Producers and Information System Designers: The RFID Case

The recent European debates regarding RFID chips lead to certain conclusions regarding the responsibilities of terminal manufacturers and suppliers of RFID systems, and more specifically on the Commission Recommendation of May 12, 2009[47] on the implementation of privacy and data protection principles in applica-

---

principle, by reiterating Recitals 9 and 30 of the ePrivacy Directive in a new paragraph in Article 1 of this Directive."

46 See as regards this concern, the Article 29 Working "Party Opinion 1/2002 on the CEN/ISSS Report on Privacy Standardisation in Europe", WP 57 (May 30, 2002). See also, the International Conference of data protection Commissioners expresses its strong support to the development of an effective and universally accepted international privacy technology standard and make available to ISO its expertise for the development of such standard … Final resolution of the 26 International Conference on Privacy and Personal data protection (Wroclaw, September 14, 2004), Resolution on a draft ISO Privacy standards read also, the CEN/ISSS secretariat Final Report. *"Initiatives on Privacy Standardisation in Europe"*, (February 13, 2002), Brussels, available at http://ec.europa.eu/enterprise/ict/policy/standards/ipse_finalreport.pdf.

About the importance of these private standardisation bodies, such as W3C or IETF, read P. Trudel et al., *"Droit du cyberespace"* (Montréal: Themis, 1997), Book. 3 and the critiques addressed to that privatisation, M.A. Froomkin, "Habermas@discourse.net: Towards a Critical Theory of Cyberspace", *Harvard Law Review* 116 (1996): 800 ff.

47 C (2009) 3200 Final. It must be also underlined that the draft E-privacy directive still in discussion provides that the directive provisions (Article 3: *Services concerned*) are applicable to devices like RFID when they are connected to publicly available communications networks or

tions supported by radio-frequency identification. These conclusions concern the infrastructures of the collection and transmission systems, the data generated by RFID terminals, the databases themselves and the analysis on which the ongoing decisions are based. It was essential that the European debate enlarge/extend the basic protection of data to include the infrastructures and terminals.

How can the data be properly protected if technical solutions do not take into account present-day constraints and do not transpose them efficiently into regulation? For instance, regarding the case of RFID again, do we agree with the Article 29 Working Party[48] and with the EU Commission Recommendations that a person carrying a chip should be duly informed[49] about the presence of these tags and be able to deactivate them easily, and that transmissions should be protected cryptographically? This approach, called "Privacy by Design",[50] is based on some early thinking in the area first framed in French law in 1978 and recalled by the Recital 2 of the EU Directive 95/46: *"Information technology should be at the service of every citizen. Its development shall take place in the context of international co-operation. It shall not violate human identity, human rights, privacy, or individual or public liberties"*. Based on this text, Data Protection Authorities have consistently confirmed the principle that the responsibility for protecting the data of any users lies with the suppliers of terminal equipment and those creating the infrastructures, as they are responsible for the risk they are creating.

In that context and precisely to measure the risks linked with the dissemination of RFID and its use, the RFID Commission's recommendations are going a step ahead by imposing on the operators[51] an obligation to *"conduct systematically an*

---

make use of electronic communications services as a basic infrastructure: *"This directive shall apply to the processing of personal data in connection with the provisions of publicly available communications services in public communications networks in the Community, including public communications networks supporting data collection and identification devices"*.

[48] "Working Paper on the Questions of Data Protection Posed by RFID Technology WP 105", (January 19, 2005), available on the European Commission website: http://www.ec.europa.eu/justice_home/fsj/privacy/docs/wpdocs/2005/wp105_fr.pdf.

[49] The Recommendation refers to a sign which has to be developed by the European standardisation body (CEN).

[50] As asserted by Anne Cavioukan, DPA Commissioner from Ontario (Canada) in its introductory remarks to the Privacy Guidelines for RFID Information Systems available on the web site: http://www.ipc.on.ca.: *"Privacy and Security must be built in from the Outset: At the design Stage"*. Examples of privacy by design include the road per-use payment system proposed in De Jonge and Jacobs "Privacy-Friendly Electronic Traffic Pricing via Commits", in *Proceedings of the Workshop of Formal Aspects of Securiy and Trust (FAST 2008)*, Lecture Notes in Computer Science, vol. 5491, (Berlin: Springer, 2008) in which the car journeys are not sent to a central server for fee computation but kept on the on board computer (and still auditable in case of dispute). Another illustration of the approach is the ambient intelligence architecture put forward in Le Métayer "A Formal Privacy Management Framework", in *Proceedings of the Workshop of Formal Aspects of Securiy and Trust (FAST 2008)*, Lecture Notes in Computer Science, vol. 5491, (Berlin: Springer, 2008), 162–76) which involves "privacy agents" in charge of managing and protecting personal data.

[51] The 'operator' is defined by the Commission Recommendation as *"the natural or legal person, public authority, agency, or any other body, which alone or jointly with others, determines the*

assessment of the applications, implementation for the protection of privacy ***and***[52] *data protection, including whether the application could be used to monitor an individual. The level of detail of the assessment should be appropriate to the privacy risks possibly associated with the application; take appropriate technical and organisational measures to ensure the protection of personal data* ***and*** *privacy; designate a person or group of persons responsible for a continuous assessment…; make available the assessment to the competent authority at least six weeks before the deployment of the application; (...)"*. This obligation to produce a 'Technology Assessment' on privacy risks[53] and to make this assessment publicly and individually available constitutes, in our opinion, the first regulatory assertion of the necessity to take fully into account, as of the early stage of conception of equipment, the privacy risks linked with the deployment of information systems. It is quite interesting to see how this obligation will be enlarged to all invasive and ubiquitous technologies which will characterize our future information society. It must be noted that furthermore the Recommendations plead for awareness-raising actions and for research and development with respect to the introduction of 'security and privacy by design' at an early stage of RFID applications. We will come back on this point in the conclusions but we do insist about the importance on these points in the context of a large societal debate.[54]

1.2.3 Terminal Equipment as a Virtual Home?

Let us come back to Article 5.3 of the E-Privacy Directive. This provision forbids, to a large extent, intrusions in the terminal equipments including RFID tags.[55] More specifically, intrusions are strictly regulated even if Recital 25 recognizes certain legitimate uses of some of these devices such as, for instance, the installation of

purposes and means of operating an application, including controllers of personal data using on RFID application". It must be underlined again that this concept designates a category of persons broader than the 'data controllers' and might definitively target RFID information systems or RFID terminal producers.

52 We underline. See our reflection in our conclusions.

53 On *"Privacy Impact Assessment"*, see R. Clarke, "Privacy Impact Assessment: Its Origins and Development", *Computer Law & Security Review* 25 (2009): 123 ff. This article provides in two appendices a list of exemplars of PIA documents and references to guidelines describing different PIA methodologies.

54 On that point, we would like to pinpoint R. Brownsword's approach: *"Potentially however even this degree of plurality could be destabilizing. It is critical, therefore, that members of a community of rights not only agree on the general shape of their ethical commitments but also agree upon the processes that will employed to resolve their disagreements. In other words, the community of rights needs to develop a political-legal framework orientated towards the Community's basic ethics, that facilitates the provisional settlement of the Community's differences."* (in *Rights, Regulation and the Technological Revolution* (New York: Oxford Univ. Press, 2008), 292).

55 About intrusive software, read: http://www.clubic.com/actualite-21463-phishing-et-spyware-les-menaces-pesantes-de-2005.html.

cookies on a user's hard disk in order to facilitate the provision of services or to verify the user's identity or capacity to conclude transactions. It is clearly stated that the use of these mechanisms might be justified on the grounds of legitimate purposes, for example, a session (not a permanent) cookie placed on the terminal equipment during the connection with a website offering travel services in order to be sure that if the connection is interrupted the user does not need to restate all the information already given. Recital 25 points out the fact that *"access to specific website content might be conditional on the well informed acceptance of a cookie or similar device, if it is used for a legitimate purpose"*. Therefore, portals that offer access to multiple websites might invoke avoidance of charges as a reason to condition the offering of services to a prior installation of cookies. The draft of the revised Directive[56] adds that restrictions are also available when the intrusion is permitted by a device connected (e.g. through a CD Rom reader) at a certain moment to the terminals and not only through the connection to the network.

Certain additional conditions are established by Article 5.3 to allow the use of such devices. First, it is provided that users have to be informed clearly and precisely about the purposes of the data generated by the devices introduced into their terminal equipment in such a way to be sure that they are aware of that intrusion and of its nature and purpose. This provision is a clear application of the right to be informed enacted by the Data Protection Directive, as expressly asserted by Recital 25. It implies that the name of the data controller and the purposes of the processing must also be provided. This consequence is important insofar as many tracking devices are introduced by third parties (cyber marketing companies) in the context of invisible hyperlinks between them and the information society services called on by the internet user. It should be emphasized that, by doing so, the Directive recognizes that cookies are personal data, a point that has on occasion been contested in the past.[57] The processing of data generated through these devices is subject to the other principles of the Data Protection Directive. For example, the duration of the placement of a cookie might be limited to the period justified by the legitimate purpose. This consideration is important insofar as, in many cases, cookies are placed for very long periods of time (20–30 years). Second, users have no opt-in right as requested by privacy advocates, but rather an opt-out right, or, in other words, the

---

[56] See the amendments proposed to the Article 5.3 and so commented: *"Software that surreptitiously monitors actions of the user and/or subverts operations of the user's terminal equipment for the benefit of a third party poses serious threat to users' privacy. A high and equal level of protection of the private sphere of users needs to be ensured, regardless of whether unwanted spying programmes are inadvertently downloaded via electronic communications or are delivered and installed in software distributed on other external data storage media, such as CDs, CD-Roms or USB keys."*

[57] In our opinion it is far from being legally founded that cookies have to be considered per se as 'personal data', since that information refers to equipment and not to an individual except through other data linked to the cookies. It is quite interesting to underline that speaking about cookies and other spyware Article 5.3 of Directive 2002/58 speaks about 'information' (broader concept) and not about 'personal data'. See already the comments made about the qualification of IP addresses as 'personal data', supra No. 11.

right to refuse to have a tracking device placed on their terminal equipment, except in two cases carefully specified in the provision. Recital 25 underlines the obligation to offer this right to refuse through user-friendly methods. Finally, according to the same recital, *"the information and right to refuse may be offered once for the use of devices during the same connection and also covering any further use that may be made of those devices during subsequent connections"*.

Our main concern is not to describe more extensively these provisions but, starting from the recitals of the E-Privacy Directive and a recent German Constitutional Court decision dated from February the 27th 2009,[58] to suggest new privacy principles as regards the functioning of our terminal equipments. Indeed, Recital 24 does suggest an interesting comparison between the terminal equipment of a user and a private sphere similar to the domicile requiring protection under the European Convention for the Protection of Human Rights and fundamental freedoms. Any intrusion into the electronic domicile through spyware, web bugs, hidden identifiers like cookies or other similar devices, ought to be considered a violation of the private electronic space (virtual domicile), that could even be viewed as a form of hacking punished by criminal provisions. The provision clearly focuses on protection against intrusion mechanisms irrespective of the fact that personal data are processed or not through these mechanisms. The German Constitutional Court decision[59] addresses the problem of intrusion into the terminal equipment by Law enforcement authorities. In the case at stake, the recourse was taken against a lander's legislation (Westphalia) allowing the police to make surveillance of suspected people at distance by introducing spyware in their computers. This intrusion is severely condemned by the judges who enact a new constitutional right directly derived from the Dignity and the right to self development enacted by the Article 1 and 2 of the German Constitution. As expressly asserted, *"the general right of personality (Article 2.1 in conjunction with Article 1.1 of the Basic Law (Grundgesetz—GG)) encompasses the fundamental right to the guarantee of the confidentiality and integrity of information technology systems"*.

This new right implies that "the secret infiltration of an information technology system by means of which the use of the system can be monitored and its storage media can be read is constitutionally only permissible if factual indications exist of a concrete danger to a predominantly important legal interest". In the instant case, under the constitutional judges' opinion, the encroachments are not constitutionally

---

[58] BVerfG, 1 BvR 370/07 vom February 27, 2008, *Absatz-Nr.* (2008): 1–267, http://www.bverfg.de/entscheidungen/rs20080227_1bvr037007.html. About this decision, see G. Hornung, "Ein neues Gründrecht", *Computer und Recht* (2008): 299 ff. and G. Hornung and C. Schnabel, "Data Protection in Germany II: Recent Decisions on On-line Searching of Computers, Automatic Number Plate Recognition and Data Retention", *Computer Law & Security Review* 25 (2009): 114 ff. See also on that decision, in the present book the contribution signed by R. Bendrath, G. Hornung, and A. Pfitzmann, "Surveillance in Germany: Strategies and Counterstrategies".

[59] About that judgement, read, P. De Hert, K. de Vries, and S. Gutwirth, "La limitation des « perquisitions en ligne » par un renouvellement des droits fondamentaux, note sous Cour constitutionnelle allemande 27 février 2008", *Revue du Droit des Technologies de l'Informatique*, 34 (2009): 87–93.

justified: § 5.2 no. 11 sentence 1 alternative 2 of the North Rhine-Westphalia Constitution Protection Act does not comply with the principle of the clarity of provisions, the requirements of the principle of proportionality are not met and the provision does not contain any sufficient precautions to protect the core area of private life. The principles stated in this decision might be applied to any kind of intrusion by third parties, public or private ones into a private information system. The reasoning of the judges has to be underlined. First, they recognize the increasing importance of the use of information systems in the daily life of the individuals and their growing role in the development of their personality: "The performance of information technology systems and their significance for the development of personality increase further if such systems are networked with one another. This is increasingly becoming the norm, in particular because of the increased use of the Internet by large groups of the population". Second, that interconnection creates new risks in two ways. The first one has already been enunciated. It consists in the possibility due to the large amount of data exchanged through the networks for third parties known or unknown by the information systems user to profile an individual. The second risk is enunciated as follows: "the networking of the system opens to third parties a technical access facility which can be used in order to spy on or manipulate data kept on the system. The individual cannot detect such access at all in some cases, or at least can only prevent it to a restricted degree".[60] As a consequence, the Court does consider that "a need for protection that is relevant to the fundamental rights perspective emerges from the significance of the use of information technology systems for the development of the personality and from endangerments of the personality linked with this use. The individual relies on the state respecting the expectations of the integrity and confidentiality of such systems which are justified with regard to the unhindered development of the personality."

This legitimate expectation of not being observed through opaque systems of surveillance has to be ensured both by the secrecy of communications right—the modern translation of the traditional secrecy of postal correspondence asserted by the Article 8 of the European Convention of Human Rights—but also by a new right to confidentiality and integrity of information systems, which more or less translates in our modern Information Society the right of inviolability of the home enacted also by the same Council of Europe Convention's provision, although *"the interests protected by this traditional fundamental right are constituted by the spatial sphere in which private life takes place"*. This new right is indeed independent of all precise physical location and is not limited, as the traditional one, to a physical

[60] The Court enumerates different reasons why technical protection against these intrusions are not sufficient to protect citizens: *"Information technology systems have now reached such a degree of complexity that effective social or technical self-protection leads to considerable difficulties and may be beyond the ability of at least the average user. Technical self-protection may also entail considerable effort or result in the loss of the functionality of the protected system. Many possibilities of self-protection—such as encryption or the concealment of sensitive data—are also largely ineffective if third parties have been able to infiltrate the system on which the data has been stored. Finally, it is not possible in view of the speed of the development of information technology to reliably forecast the technical means which users may have to protect themselves in future"*.

space,[61] but its enactment does correspond to the same philosophy as the inviolability of the home.

According to Konvitz, the essence of privacy is *"the claim that there is a sphere of space that has not been dedicated to public use of control"*.[62] And indeed, the notions of "private and family life" have been interpreted extensively by the ECHR. The right to privacy protects individuals against invasions of privacy by public authorities or, through the Convention's *horizontal effect*, by other individuals. According to the Strasbourg jurisprudence, the state is not merely under the obligation to abstain from interfering with individuals' privacy, but has also to provide individuals with the material conditions needed to allow them to effectively enjoy their right to private life. *"The fundamental right-related protection of the expectation of confidentiality and integrity exists regardless of whether access to the information technology system can be achieved easily or only with considerable effort. An expectation of confidentiality and integrity to be recognised from the fundamental rights perspective however only exists insofar as the person concerned uses the information technology system as his or her own, and hence may presume according to the circumstances that he or she alone or together with others entitled to use it disposes of the information technology system in a self-determined manner"*.[63]

1.2.4 Conclusions of Sect. 1.2

All these considerations plead for an assertion of a new privacy right: the right to a privacy compliant terminal with a transparent and mastered functioning by its user. That new right encompasses different facets, such as the right to have at disposal a terminal programmed by default to minimize the data sent and received to the strict minimum needed for achieving the purposes pursued by its user. This first facet, includes data minimization; that the data generated, stored and transmitted by the terminal will be reduced to what is technically necessary for ensuring the telecommunication services used. The transparent functioning of the terminal equipment imposes that the terminal may not initiate a communication unless required by the user to do so, or unless it is strictly necessary for the adequate functioning of the communication networks or services (suppression of data chattering). The user ought to know what is entering into, and what is going out from his or her terminal.

---

[61] *"The encroachment may take place regardless of location, so that space-oriented protection is unable to avert the specific endangerment of the information technology system. Insofar as the infiltration uses the connection of the computer concerned to form a computer network, it leaves spatial privacy provided by delimitation of the dwelling unaffected. The location of the system is in many cases of no interest for the investigation measure, and frequently will not be recognisable even for the authority. This applies in particular to mobile information technology systems such as laptops, Personal Digital Assistants (PDAs) or mobile telephones."*

[62] K. Konvitz, "Privacy and the Law: A Philosophical Prelude", *Law and Contemporary Problems* 31 (1966): 272, 279–80.

[63] *Copland v. U.K.*, 62617/00 (ECHR, April 3, 2007).

In this way, the user should be able to know, through a clear and easy method, the extent to which his computer chatters on about him, what information is sent or received, who is doing his sending and receiving, and what use will be made of this information. To this end, a data log would seem to be a technique that is both appropriate and relatively easy to implement. Terminal equipment's interfaces must clearly and permanently indicate if its user is currently identified or identifiable by another party. In order to minimize the risk linked with common identifiers and contact points, it would be desirable that the identifiers generated by the terminal would be both as least permanent as possible and, if possible, independent from each other, as regards the different data controllers. The rights of the user not to be submitted to unsolicited communications and advertisements, to refuse any intrusion into his or her terminal and finally to have the means to personally audit the privacy compliant functioning of his or her terminal are other facets that ensure citizens' right of self-determination.

1.3 Final Conclusions

Until now, the predominant view, at least in Europe, is to consider privacy as the most adequate and relevant concept to ensure an appropriate protection of human dignity and, fundamental rights and liberties. Privacy is seen as a pre-condition not only for the self-development of human beings but also for their ability to take an active role as citizens. However, one must admit that the concept of privacy is subject to a variety of interpretations and its protection is more and more difficult to ensure in the new information and communication era. In fact, the challenge posed by new technologies is more serious than the weakening the effectiveness of privacy protection instruments: we have reached a stage where *new technologies call into question the very foundations of privacy* and ultimately the position of the subject in the new information era. On that issue, our reflections have demonstrated two things. The first one is that the development of technologies has lead to privacy challenges that our traditional data protection legislation is unable to face if we do not enlarge our considerations in regards to the values which are enacted by the privacy concept. It is quite interesting to see how the German Constitutional Court repeatedly refers directly to the Dignity and self-development principles to justify the recognition of new rights. Definitively, (personal) data protection in the sense of Article 8 of the EU Charter on fundamental rights does not exhaust the privacy values. Last year we already criticized the risk we take by distinguishing, as does the EU Charter, the right to privacy from the right to data protection without seeing that the second one is just a tool for ensuring the first one. If we are not doing that, we will be unable to cover the risks linked with profiling activities and the use of non-personal data. We will be unable to ground regulations of operators which are not data controllers and thus not under the obligations imposed by Directive 95/46/EC, and we will miss what is fundamental, that is the regulation of the infrastructure and of terminal equipment. In respect to these two aspects, the E-Privacy Directive currently in course of revision, indicates the right way by not hesitating to propose new objects, new data and new actors to be regulated. Moreover, as an indication of the need to come back to the very fundamental roots and values of privacy, it is not astonishing that our reflections have led us to come back to an interpretation of the wording used in 1950 when we have spoken about electronic communication as correspondence and home as "virtual" home designating so our terminal equipments.

If Technology is viewed as the major challenge for our privacy, it might also be the solution. The role of technology must be reassessed and *new research efforts should be devoted in computer science to the design of future "privacy aware systems"*. With traditional Privacy Enhancing Tools (PETs), technologies are used to enhance "user empowerment", for example by providing means to ensure that the subject can hide his personal data (or encrypt them) or by offering guarantees for the express consent of the user through computer facilities such as software agents. But technologies might also be used in direct or indirect relationships with law, either by enforcing or facilitating the compliance of controllers with their legal commitments, by developing a policy for the standardisation of terminal equipments which takes into consideration privacy requirements, by providing auditing techniques for labelling authorities, by facilitating the attribution of liabilities in case of litigation and, finally, in relationships with social usages, by defining architectures for reinforcing negotiation or for adopting collective privacy statements, notably in the context of Web 2.0 platforms, what we call P5P (Peer to Peer Platforms for Privacy Preferences).

In conclusion, we see that the law cannot attempt to solve all the problems. As far as data protection is concerned, the law must look to other methods of regulation, more particularly to the place of regulation through the technology itself. As we noted in the conclusions of the Miauce Report:[64] *"Time has come for the law to also seek the help of technology to ensure that the same instruments aimed at observing persons and events (for purposes ranging from safety or security, to marketing and entertainment; through technologies involving observation and/or interaction and/or profiling) do not disproportionately and illegitimately deny individuals' adequate protection of their fundamental rights and liberties"*. The above-described RFID case has demonstrated the importance to assign new duties and obligations for terminal equipment providers, the obligation to conduct a 'privacy technology assessment' and a new role for the state; i.e. a duty to create the conditions for a public debate on the technologies and their impact on our citizenship. One major question we have to address considering the way in which our society is definitively and deeply transformed by all these surrounding technological applications and their inherent normativities[65] is how to *conciliate the individualistic approach*

[64] M. Cornelis et al., *"Miauce, Deliverable D5.1.2. Ethical, Legal and Social Issues"*, available online on the Miauce website, www.miauce.org.

[65] On the comparison between legal and technological normativities, read M. Hidebrandt, "Legal and Technological Normativities: More (and Less) Than Two Sisters", *Techné* 12(3) (2008): 169 ff.

inherent to human rights and their collective dimension in a democratic state.[66] Along the same lines, one may analyse to what extent democracy is at stake when we are speaking about privacy protection. On that point, perhaps the *parallel with environmental law* (precaution principle, multi-stakeholders' discussion, governance, need for technology assessment) would be appropriate. How far can this comparison be pushed forward? How to ground this parallelism? And what practical lessons can be drawn for privacy protection? There are many questions to be solved rapidly if we want to renew in an appropriate way our reflections on Privacy in our modern information society.[67] Furthermore, it remains within the tasks of the law, through an operation of qualification, to delineate what exactly, among the new technological architectures, must be considered as pertaining to the "public space", or as "basic goods" so essential for the "capacitation" of citizens, which, as such, must not be exclusively at least regulated by private actors.[68]

---

[66] The same problematic is explored in V. Mayer-Schônberger, "Demystifying Lessig", *Wisconsin Law Report* 4 (2009): 714 ff.

[67] Certain arguments have been proposed in Y. Poullet and A. Rouvroy, "General Introductory Report", in *Ethical Aspects of the Information Society*, Conference Organized Jointly by UNESCO and Council of Europe, Strasbourg (November 15, 2007), text available on the UNESCO website.

[68] On that point see precisely the European Parliament resolution condemning the French HADOPI system which introduced the possibility in case of repeated illegal copying to block the access of the Internet user.

Chapter 2
Some Caveats on Profiling

Serge Gutwirth and Mireille Hildebrandt

2.1 Introduction

In this chapter we endeavor to expose the singularity of profiling techniques, data mining or knowledge discovery in databases. Pursuant to this, we point at a number of caveats that are linked to the specifics of profiling. Those caveats pertain to issues related to dependence, privacy, data protection, fairness (non-discrimination), due process, auditability and transparency of the profilers and knowledge asymmetries. This chapter reiterates and builds further upon some of the findings of our research on profiling we presented in a volume we co-edited: *Profiling the European Citizen. Cross-disciplinary Perspectives,* which brought together leading experts in the domains of computer science, law and philosophy. We thank these authors, members of the EU funded consortium on the Future of Identity in the Information Society (FIDIS), for their joint effort to compose a handbook on a subject that is mostly discussed from singular disciplinary perspectives (Hildebrandt & Gutwirth 2008).

2.2 What Is It with Profiling?

Profiling can pertain to one individual person, to a group or groups of persons, but also to animals, to objects and to relations between all those. It can be used, on the one hand, to classify, describe and analyze what happened, which is not particularly new or problematic. This type of retrieval of stored information is called a query. In such cases profiling permits a structuration of what was already known. On the

S. Gutwirth (✉)
Center for Law, Science, Technology & Society (LSTS), Vrije Universiteit Brussel, Pleinlaan 2, 1050 Brussels, Belgium
e-mail: serge.gutwirth@vub.ac.be

M. Hildebrandt
Center for Law, Science, Technology & Society (LSTS), Vrije Universiteit Brussel, Pleinlaan 2, 1050 Brussels, Belgium

Erasmus University Rotterdam, 3000 DR, Rotterdam, The Netherlands

S. Gutwirth et al. (eds.), *Data Protection in a Profiled World,*
DOI 10.1007/978-90-481-8865-9_2, © Springer Science+Business Media B.V. 2010

other hand—and this is what we target in this contribution—profiling is used to cluster data in such way that information is inferred, and predictions or expectations can be proposed. Such profiling activity thus *produces* a particular sort of knowledge, by means of the process known as knowledge discovery in databases (KDD). The knowledge produced is *non-representational*: it does not represent a current state of affairs. Profiles are patterns resulting of a probabilistic processing of data. They do not describe reality, but are detected in databases by the aggregation, mining and cleansing of data. They are based on correlations that cannot be equated with causes or reasons, without further inquiry. Taken to a more abstract level, by mining of machine-readable data, profiling leads to the identification of patterns in data of the past which can develop into probabilistic knowledge about individuals, groups of humans and non-humans in the present and in the future. In a way, our view of present and future is then shaped by what the data mining makes visible. This is why we think that profiling is a productive type of knowledge: it tends to create the "reality" it infers from past occurrences.

However, even if the profiling process shows that a pattern occurs every time some conditions are met, one cannot be 100% sure it will happen today and tomorrow as well. Based on its experience, an animal may associate a situation with a danger as a result of the recognition of a certain pattern and act consistently, even if the situation, in reality, is not a dangerous one: the bad human smell and the shuffling footsteps were not those of a bloodthirsty hunter, but those of a sweet animal rights observer. The example demonstrates that profiling is not a new phenomenon, but that it is as old as life. It is a kind of knowledge that has always supported the behaviour of living beings and humans. It might well be that the insight that we often 'intuitively know something' before we 'understand' it, can be explained by the role profiling spontaneously plays in our minds (Gutwirth and De Hert 2008).

2.3 From Measurement to Detection

Although profiling in the sense of pattern recognition is nothing very new, it is however important to acknowledge the profound difference between the autonomic profiling that is characteristic of all living beings, and the type of machine profiling that is now proliferating. In recent decades profiling capacities have grown exponentially as a result of both the advances in technology and the increasing availability of readily processable data and traces.

The use and convergence of the web, mobile phones, electronic financial systems, biometric identification systems, RFIDs, GPS, ambient intelligence and so forth, all participate in the automatic generation of data which become available for still more pervasive and powerful data mining and tracking systems. In sum, an enormous and permanently inflating cloud of electronic dust is up for grabs, enabling not only extensive data mining and profiling, but also providing for real-time and autonomic applications which impact upon ongoing actions and their environment. To us these evolutions represent more than mere quantitative changes: they represent a significant qualitative shift compared to more classical statistical approaches that aim at validating or invalidating already proposed correlations believed to be relevant and pertinent to answer preceding questions. These types of 'traditional' correlations are the result of an oriented questioning; they are *measurements*. Today, however, such preceding questions are disappearing. Very differently, the emergence by pure aleatory statistical methods of a correlation has become in itself the pertinent information and will in its turn launch questions and suppositions. Things are going the other way around now: the *detection* of the correlation *is* the information.

Detections, however, are much wider than measurements; they don't have a specific meaning, but they will have an impact if used or applied, and their meaning is produced by their application. In other words, the *qualitative shift* lies in the fact that correlations and profiles get generated before any preceding interest or question. This is why it can be said that humans have become detectable far beyond their control: their actions have become the resources of an extensive, if not unlimited, network of possible profiling devices generating knowledge affecting and impacting upon them (Gutwirth and De Hert 2008).

2.4 A Risky Dependence

Before embarking on the commonly known caveats regarding human rights like privacy, non-discrimination and due process, we like to stress the risks of an increased dependence on data mining technologies. Profiling is a powerful technique that renders visible what is invisible to the naked human eye. This, however, concerns patterns in databases that must not be mistaken for reality. By making visible what is aggregated in the data base, profiling also make invisible what cannot be translated into machine-readable data. In as far as the governance of people and things becomes dependent on these advanced profiling technologies, new risks will emerge in the shadow of the real time models and simulations these technologies make possible. What has been made invisible can grow like weeds. In a salient analysis an information theorist (Ciborra 2004) has explained what he called the duality of risk. He gave the—now ominous—example of financial risk assessments: 'consider recent developments in the ideas of 'democratising finance': by transferring its sophisticated calculus techniques at the level of individual existence so that life choices, change and innovation are devolved to the level of the individual, armed with better knowledge and sophisticated financial tools. This new way of looking at, and practising, finance as a science for managing risk 'democratically' gives digital technologies an overarching importance and a new role. They become 'grid technologies', i.e. an information infrastructure that allows the calculation of indexes and units of accounts, so that risks are quantified and can be traded, pooled and shared on global markets by large numbers of individuals'. Ciborra's conclusion is that 'the more we are able to extend the frontier of (formalised) knowledge thanks to technology, the more dangerous could be the events emerging out of the regions of our ignorance'. This concerns the stability of the financial system, but also the safety supposedly provided by critical infrastructures like the provision of water, electricity and broadband—to name but a few. Just like few of us expected a meltdown of the financial infrastructure, few of us now expect smart technologies based on autonomic profiling technologies to eradicate privacy and autonomy to an extent that returns us to arbitrary rule by a strong state or to vest corporate business enterprise with the capacity to rule our (un)conscious mind by means of sophisticated proactive service provision.

2.5 Privacy, Fairness (Non-discrimination) and Due Process

Indeed, the qualitative shift we described above, demands careful monitoring from the perspective of the democratic constitutional state, because it likely entails a number of threats, such as:

1. the surreptitious influencing, formatting and customisation of individual behaviour, which poses a threat to privacy in the sense of personal autonomy (Gutwirth 2002), coined as the 'autonomy trap' by Zarsky (2002–2003);
2. the sharpening of power inequalities between those that possess the profiles and those that are being profiled, which poses a threat to privacy as personal autonomy as well as fairness and due process, due to the potential manipulation inherent in knowledge asymmetries (Solove 2004);
3. the making of wrong decisions as a result of false positives and false negatives, which poses a threat to fairness in as far as a person is 'judged' on the basis of inaccurate data, and a threat to due process in as far as a person is not aware of the use of group profiles that match her data but do not apply because the profiles are non-distributive (Vedder 1999; Custers 2004);
4. the making of unfair decisions based on correct profiles that allow for unwarranted and invisible discrimination, which poses a threat to non-discrimination as well as due process in as far as categorisations can be used for unjustified but invisible discrimination (Lyon 2002; Gandy 2006);
5. the taking of unmotivated and unilateral decisions about individuals, which poses threats to personal autonomy and due process in as far as such decisions cannot be contested or can be contested only with difficulty (reversal of the *onus probandi*) (Steinbock 2005; Citron 2007).

Interestingly, most authors who write about informational privacy focus on the protection of personal data, which is also the focus of most computer scientists who work on designing privacy enhancing technologies (PETs). With the notable exception of for instance Solove (2004), Rouvroy (2008) and Zarsky (2004) few legal scholars seem to draw conclusions from the kind of privacy threats specifically posed by profiling. Wider implications concern what Marx (2001) has coined the 'murky conceptual waters' between the public and the private, calling attention to what Nissenbaum (2004) has called 'privacy in public'. Profiling affords a type of seamless, pervasive but seemingly non-invasive, real time surveillance across a variety of contexts: online, offline, at the office, in the home, during leisure, on the road, in the hospital and so forth. In speaking of 'privacy in public' Nissenbaum and others suggest that we no longer limit 'privacy' to the sphere of the 'private life', because the anonymity that used to protect us in former days cannot be taken for granted anymore, requiring us to rethink notions like privacy in the digital age.

2.6 Causality and (Criminal) Liability

Next to these threats, profiling is also the precondition for autonomic computing and Ambient Intelligence (Van den Berg 2009), that allows for a new socio-technical infrastructure that 'runs' *autonomically*, that is by taking a number of decisions without human intervention (Kephart and Chess 2003). Autonomic computing will involve distributed intelligence that emerges from networked objects which are in a process of continuous real time machine to machine communication, and it is not clear how, in the case of harm, liability could be attributed to one of the 'nodes' of such networks (Karnow 1996; Hildebrandt 2008a). Decisions taken, then, are not intentional in the traditional sense of the word, and they are not taken by one particular human or even by one particular non-human node. Civil liability can of course be based on a strict liability, but to attribute criminal liability in a case where neither a cause nor blame can be attributed seems highly problematic.

2.7 Who Owns My Data; Who Authors the Profiles I Match with?

Another issue worth mentioning relates to the legal status of profiles: who has what type of rights upon this machine generated knowledge? The debate about intellectual rights in relation to privacy has focused entirely on the idea of attributing some kind of property rights in/to personal data. Whereas some authors have suggested that this will empower individual citizens (Lessig 1999), others declare that due to knowledge asymmetries a market failure will prevent any such empowered (Schwartz 2000; Zarsky 2004). Still others argue that personal data should not be commodified, but treated as inalienable personality rights that should not be traded against trivial advantages (Prins 2006). Concerning the legal status of profiles not much work has been done as yet. If a profile is constructed solely out of an individual's personal data, it is clearly protected as such, at least within the jurisdiction of the Data Protection Directive 95/46 EC. However, the group profiles that are inferred from databases that contain masses of anonymised data, are most probably protected as either trade secrets, or as part of a database that is protected by means of a copyright or the database right sui generis. The software that generates profiles is also protected as part of a trade secret or by means of patent or copyright. Recital 41 of the preamble to the Data Protection Directive 95/46/EC has acknowledged this, stating that any transparency or access rights with regard to the logic of processing must be balanced with the rights of those who generated the profiles. This seems a precarious disposition, suggesting that we cannot have our cake and eat it too—giving with one hand, what is then taken with the other.

Profiling raises the issue of ownership and authorship in relation to personal identity, especially if we take into account that identity is a relational and relative notion, since the construction of an identity requires continuous interactions and negotiations between an individual and his or her direct and indirect environment (cf. Gutwirth 2009). If we are not the "owners" of our identity and in many ways 'co-author' of ourselves in a process of border-negotiations with other people and other things, than what is at stake if these co-authors are invisible profiling machines who can claim copyrights on the profiles that are part of the narrative that constructed our identity?

2.8 Transparency and Anticipation

For this reason a crucial point is indeed that the process of data mining and the ways profiles are built are mostly invisible and uncontrollable for the citizens to which they are applied. Citizens whose data is being mined do not have the means to anticipate what the algorithms will come up with and hence they do not have a clue what knowledge about them exists, how they are categorized and evaluated, and what effects and consequences this entails. For individual citizens to regain some control, access is needed to the profiles applied to them and/or information about how these profiles may affect them. This will require both legal tools (rights to transparency, such as for instance that under Article 12 of the Data Protection Directive 95/46 EC) and technological tools (the means to exercise such rights, for instance creating the possibility to check in real time what kind of profiles are being constructed and applied). Before further exploring this issue, we will first look into the 'traditional' legal instruments to protect privacy and (personal) data, after which we will return to the questions that remain unresolved.

2.9 Privacy and Data Protection

From a legal point of view, profiling makes it necessary to clearly distinguish between privacy on the one hand and data protection on the other (Gutwirth and De Hert 2008).

Privacy is recognized as a fundamental right in different major international legal instruments and in many national constitutions. In short, it protects a number of fundamental political values of democratic constitutional states, such as the freedom of self-determination of individuals, their right to be different, their autonomy to engage in relationships, their freedom of choice, and so on. By default privacy prohibits interferences of the state and private actors in the individuals' autonomy: it shields them off from intrusions, it provides them a certain degree of opacity and invisibility.

The scope and reach of privacy are underdetermined and in the final instance it is up to the judges to decide when privacy interests are at stake and when protection can rightfully be invoked. Legislators can also intervene to protect particular privacy interests, for example through statutory protection of professional secrets, the secrecy of communications or the inviolability of the home.

Data protection is both broader and more specific than the right to privacy. It is broader because data protection also protects other fundamental rights such as the freedom of expression, the freedom of religion and conscience, the free flow of information, the principle of non-discrimination, next to individual liberty and self-determination. But data protection is also more specific than privacy since it *simply and only* applies when "personal data" are "processed". The application of data protection rules does not raise a privacy issue: data protection applies when the statutory conditions are met. By default, and contrary to privacy, data protection rules are not prohibitive, but they organize and control the way personal data is processed: such data can only be legitimately processed if some conditions pertaining to the transparency of the processing, the participation of the data subject and the accountability of the data controller are met.

With regard to profiling, the former entails that data protection law only applies when profiling activities involve personal data. Protection beyond personal data is not foreseen and that actually leaves out the situations wherein profiling techniques make it possible to impact upon a person's behaviour and autonomy *without* rendering this person identifiable, which will happen frequently, particularly in applications of Ambient Intelligence (Schreurs et al. 2008). In such cases privacy interests are still under pressure and privacy protection can be called upon, which significantly implies that the non-applicability of data protection does not mean that there is no existing protection in as far as a privacy interest can be invoked. But this indeed is not to say that there is no need for a better protection, considering especially the invisibility of the profiling process and the ensuing profiles. The problem is also that threats to non-discrimination and due process are not really met in the present legal framework (Schreurs et al. 2008).

That is why we think that profiling calls for a system of protection of individuals against the processing of data that impact upon their behaviour even if those data cannot be considered as personal data. For some authors this implies a shift from the protection of personal data to the protection of data *tout court* (Gutwirth and De Hert 2009). Another option is to shift from an indiscriminate *protection of personal data* to a more specific *protection against (the) unwarranted application of profiles.* To achieve such protection we need to know which of our data (trivial or personal) we want to hide, because they match with profiles we may want to resist (Hildebrandt 2009). Protection of data other than personal data is in fact not a revolutionary step since it can pick up the thread followed by the Directive 2002/58 which, in order to protect privacy, provides for the protection of location and traffic data (which are not necessarily personal data). Similarly, one might also propose a regulation of 'unsolicited adjustments' inspired by the existing regulation of Directive 2002/58 of 'unsolicited communications' or 'spam', providing for an opt-in system: no real-time adjustments of profiles without explicit prior and informed consent of the concerned, would then be the rule (Gonzalez Fuster and Gutwirth 2008).

Considering the new challenges posed by profiling, however, we think that policy makers, lawyers and computer scientists should join forces to explore the possibility of a new legal approach of profiling, focusing on the way profiles can affect our behaviour and decisions, anticipating how the emerging socio-technical infrastructure could articulate legal norms that are more than paper dragons. Such a shift would emphasize the issues of discrimination and manipulation of conduct through the use of profiles, as well as the transparency and controllability of profiles (cf. Dinant et al. 2008).

2.10 From Data Minimisation to Minimal Knowledge Asymmetries?

The focus on data minimisation can be understood as a sensible policy for the time when the collection and aggregation of personal data was the main target of marketing as well as that of public security. With smart applications, however, the target is to collect and aggregate as much data as possible, in order to mine them for relevant patterns that allow the profiler to anticipate future behaviours. The hiding of data in fact diminishes the 'intelligence' of the applications; it seems to be at odds with the paradigm of proactive computing and Ambient Intelligence. Therefore, we believe that in so far as governments and industry invest in smart technological infrastructures, they should focus on reducing the knowledge asymmetries rather than paying lip service to the data minimisation principle. Regulators, as well as industry are keen to applaud data minimisation in combination with users' consent, apparently reconciling extensive data collection with informational self-determination. In a smart environment, however, with a growing asymmetry between those who profile and those who are being profiled, consent has no meaning if it is not coupled with an awareness of the profiles that match one's data. To know which of your data you want to hide you need to know what profile they match; to know if you want programs and profiles automatically adapted to your behaviour, you need to know when and how this happens.

There are serious legal as well as technological drawbacks at this point. From a legal perspective a right of access to the algorithms used to construct relevant profiles faces the trade secret, copyright or patent from the data controller or data processor. Also, providing users with such algorithms would not be of use since it would destroy the hidden complexity that is one of the key features of ubiquitous computing environments. Technically it is hard to imagine how end users could gain access to the data mining processes performed by data processors that are mainly mining other peoples' data. A business model that incorporates sharing data mining algorithms with those who may be impacted by the use of the ensuing profiles, is difficult to imagine. Incompatibility of practices and goals, and contradictory incentives can be invoked against the idea. However, a number of interesting conceptual explorations have already been made, moving the focus from the stage of data collection to that of the implementation of decisions based on data mining operations (Jiang 2002; Nguyen and Mynatt 2002; Zarsky 2004; Weitzner et al. 2007). We think that these initiatives should not merely be left to contingent market incentives. In a constitutional democracy the democratic legislator should set the defaults for fair play, designing smart legal protections into the information and communication infrastructure.

2.11 AmLaw: From Privacy Enhancing Technologies to Transparency Enhancing Tools?

In short, even if data protection law theoretically applies to many facets of profiling, many problems subsist, because profiling techniques remain a technological black box for citizens, making data protection ineffective and unworkable. Whereas data protection demands transparency and controllability, data mining and profiling tend to remain opaque, incomprehensible and evasive. That is why the integration of legal transparency norms into technological devices that can translate, for the citizen, what profiling machines are doing should be given priority. This entails a shift from privacy enhancing technologies that aim to empower users to exercise existing data protection rights, to legal tools articulated in the technology of the digital infrastructure instead of merely articulating them in the 'traditional' technology of the script (Collins and Skover 1992).

Within the FIDIS network a vision of Ambient Law (AmLaw) has been developed in harmonious counterpoint to the vision of Ambient Intelligence (AmI) (Hildebrandt and Koops 2007; Hildebrandt 2008b). The idea behind AmLaw is that instead of using technologies, like for instance PETs, to enforce, implement legal rules or to exercise legal rights, leaving the development and introduction of these technologies to the market, the democratic legislator should intervene and articulate a set of legal opacity and transparency tools for the socio-technical infrastructure they aim to protect against. Waiting for a business-model that aims to reduce knowledge asymmetries while in fact the market provides contrary incentives makes no sense whatsoever. Taking into account the enormous consequences for individual citizens of a potential loss of autonomy, unjustified discrimination and violations of due process, democratic government should step in at an early stage and design legal norms into the communications infrastructure of the information society. AmLaw should program two core standards of constitutional democracy as a default into the emerging infrastructure: first, technological devices that have the capacity to proactively regulate the life of citizens should be made transparent, while citizens should have the tools to create a measure of opacity for their own lives; second, technological devices that have the capacity to proactively rule out certain behaviours should enable users to contest these decisions, if necessary in a court of law.

2.12 Call for Attention

We hope that research into profiling technologies will help to re-visualise what is happening under the sheets of autonomically interacting networks of things and other applications of ambient intelligence, and that it will put profiling on the agenda of policy makers, academics and activists as one of the most powerful and invisible techniques that is shaping our present and our futures.

References

Ciborra, C. 2004. Digital technologies and the duality of risk. Paper 21, ESRC Centre of Analysis of Risk and Regulation. London School of Economics.

Citron, D.K. 2007. Technological due process. *Washington University Law Review* 85: 1249–1313. Also available online at http://papers.ssrn.com/sol3/Papers.cfm?abstract_id=1012360.

Collins, R.K.L., and D.M. Skover 1992. Paratexts. *Stanford Law Review* 44 (1): 509–52.

Custers, B. 2004. *The power of knowledge. Ethical, legal, and technological aspects of data mining and group profiling in epidemiology.* Nijmegen: Wolf Legal Publ.

Dinant, J.-M., C. Lazaro, Y. Poullet, N. Lefever, and A. Rouvroy. 2008. Application of convention 108 to the profiling mechanism. Council of Europe/Crid. (11 January 2008), 35.

Gandy, O. Jr. 2006. Data mining, surveillance and discrimination in the post-9/11 environment. In *The new politics of surveillance and visibility*, eds. K.D. Haggerty and R.V. Ericson, 373–84. Toronto: Univ. Toronto Press.

Gonzalez Fuster G., and S. Gutwirth 2008. Privacy 2.0? *Revue du droit des Technologies de l'Information*, Doctrine 32: 349–59.

Gutwirth, S. 2002. *Privacy and the information age.* Lanham: Rowman & Littlefield Publ.

Gutwirth, S. 2009. Beyond identity? *Identity in the information society*, 1: 122–133

Gutwirth, S, and P. De Hert 2008. Regulating profiling in a democratic constitutional state. In *Profiling the european citizen. Cross-disciplinary perspectives*, eds. M. Hildebrandt and S. Gutwirth, 271–302. Dordrecht: Springer.

Hildebrandt, M. 2008a. A vision of ambient law. In *Regulating technologies*, eds. R. Brownsword and K. Yeung, 175–91. Oxford: Hart.

Hildebrandt, M. 2008b. Ambient intelligence, criminal liability and democracy. *Criminal Law and Philosophy* 2: 163–80.

Hildebrandt, M 2009. Who is profiling who? Invisible visibility. In *Reinventing data protection?*, eds. S. Gutwirth, Y. Poullet, P. De Hert, C. de Terwangne, and S. Nouwt, 239–52. Dordrecht: Springer.

Hildebrandt, M., and B.-J. Koops 2007. *A vision of ambient law.* Brussels: FIDIS.

Hildebrandt, M. and S. Gutwirth (eds) 2008. *Profiling the European citizen. Cross-disciplinary perspectives.* Dordrecht: Springer Science. p.

Jiang, X. 2002. Safeguard privacy in ubiquitous computing with decentralized information spaces: Bridging the technical and the social. *Privacy workshop September 29, 2002.* University of California, Berkeley, Berkeley. Also available online at http://guir.berkeley.edu/pubs/ubicomp2002/privacyworkshop/papers/jiang-privacyworkshop.pdf.

Karnow, C.E.A. 1996. Liability for distributed artificial intelligences. *Berkely Technology Law Journal* 11: 148–204.

Kephart, J.O., and D.M. Chess 2003. The vision of autonomic computing. *Computer* 36: 41–50.

Lessig, L. 1999. *Code and other laws of cyberspace.* New York: Basic Books.

Lyon, D., ed. 2002. *Surveillance as social sorting. Privacy, risk and digital discrimination.* New York: Routledge.

Marx, G.T. 2001. Murky conceptual waters: The public and the private. *Ethics and Information Technology* 3: 157–69.

Nguyen, D.H., and E.D. Mynatt 2002. Privacy mirrors: Understanding and shaping socio-technical ubiquitous computing systems. Atlanta: Georgia Institute of Technology.

Nissenbaum, H. 2004. Privacy as contextual integrity. *Washington Law Review* 79: 101–40.

Prins, C. 2006. When personal data, behavior and virtual identities become a commodity: Would a property rights approach matter? *SCRIPTSed* 3 (4): 270–303.

Rouvroy, A. 2008. Privacy, data protection, and the unprecedented challenges of ambient intelligence. *Studies in Law, Ethics and Technology* 2 (1): 1–51.

Schreurs, W., M. Hildebrandt, E. Kindt, and M. Vanfleteren. 2008. Cogitas, ergo sum. The role of data protection law and non-discrimination law in group profiling in the private sector. In

Profiling the european citizen. Cross-disciplinary perspectives, eds. M. Hildebrandt and S. Gutwirth. 241–70. Dordrecht: Springer.

Schwartz, P.M. 2000. Beyond lessig's code for internet privacy: Cyberspace filters, privacy-control and fair information practices. *Wisconsin Law Review* 2000: 743–88.

Solove, D.J. 2004. *The digital person. Technology and privacy in the information age.* New York: New York Univ. Press.

Steinbock, D.J. 2005. Data matching, data mining and due process. *Georgia Law Review* 40 (1): 1–84.

Van Den Berg, B. 2009. *The situated self. Identity in a world of ambient intelligence.* Rotterdam: Erasmus Univ. Rotterdam.

Vedder, A. 1999. KDD: The challenge to individualism. *Ethics and Information Technology* 1: 275–81.

Weitzner, D.J., H. Abelson et al. 2007. *Information accountability. Computer Science and Artificial Intelligence Laboratory Technical Report.* Cambridge, MIT.

Zarsky, T.Z. 2002–2003. Mine your own business!: Making the case for the implications of the data mining or personal information in the Forum of Public Opinion. *Yale Journal of Law & Technology* 5 (4): 17–47.

Zarsky, T.Z. 2004. Desperately seeking solutions: Using implementation-based solutions for the troubles of information privacy in the Age of data mining and the internet society. *Maine Law Review* 56 (1): 14–59.

Chapter 3
Levelling up: Data Privacy and the European Court of Human Rights

Gordon Nardell QC

3.1 The Background

Telephone calls between the UK and Ireland are carried by microwave between a telecommunications tower near Chester, northwest England, and another in Wales. The line of sight crosses a uranium enrichment plant at Capenhurst, Cheshire. In 1999, Channel 4 and journalist Duncan Campbell revealed that in the late 1980s, with the Northern Ireland conflict still in full flow, the UK Ministry of Defence built a 50 metre high "electronic test facility" at the plant and used it to intercept large numbers of these calls.

In the 1984 *Malone* judgment,[1] the European Court of Human Rights[2] criticised the UK for lacking any legislative framework governing telephone interception. It found a violation of Article 8 of the European Convention of Human Rights (ECHR). In response, the UK enacted the Interception of Communications Act 1985 (IOCA). Following the Channel 4 revelations the NGO, Liberty, was concerned that conversations with its sister organisation ICCL and another NGO, British–Irish Rights Watch, had been routinely monitored through Capenhurst. The calls included confidential discussions between lawyers about current cases related to the conflict. In 2000 the NGOs complained to the Court that the IOCA regime for international calls failed to meet the standards for protection of privacy required by Article 8. They had to wait until July 2008 for a decision. But their patience was rewarded: in *Liberty and others v. UK*[3] the Court found a violation of Article 8.

In England and Wales the police can take fingerprints and a DNA sample from anyone arrested for a recordable offence. The prints and DNA are retained even

[1] Ser. A no. 82.

[2] In this chapter, "the Court".

[3] (2008) 48 EHRR 1 Chamber judgment of 1 July 2008.

G. Nardell QC (✉)
39 Essex Street Chambers, London, UK
e-mail: gordon.nardell@39essex.com

S. Gutwirth et al. (eds.), *Data Protection in a Profiled World*,
DOI 10.1007/978-90-481-8865-9_3, © Springer Science+Business Media B.V. 2010

if the person is not charged with an offence or is charged but acquitted. A unique profile derived from the sample is added to the searchable national DNA database, held on the Police National Computer. The profile is retained indefinitely and remains accessible for between 5 and 35 years. A request to remove a profile from the database can only be granted in "exceptional" circumstances.[4] As at December 2008, the database contained profiles of some four million people or 7% of the UK population (the equivalent figure for the United States is 0.5%.).[5] In *S. and Marper v. UK*[6] the practice was challenged by two individuals, charged but not convicted—one aged 11 at the time of arrest. The Court found violations of Article 8 in relation to both fingerprints and DNA. The UK Government is now consulting on a new regime.

These two cases concern law and practice in the UK. But the Court's thinking is significant in the wider context of public policy trends in data and communications privacy. Much of the European agenda—including the Data Retention Directive[7]—has followed the shift in official attitudes, in the wake of 9/11, accelerated by the terrorist attacks in London in July 2005. The UK Government has sought to enhance its security and intelligence capability with a steady stream of measures for increasingly comprehensive information-gathering, storage and access. Taking the past 12 months alone, Government initiatives—over and above transposition of the Data Retention Directive into domestic law—include a reported proposal to create a central database of retained communications data, an idea since modified following widespread adverse comment;[8] a press statement by the interception agency, GCHQ,[9] ominously titled "Mastering the internet"; and provisions in the Coroners and Justice Bill which (had they too not been shelved for the time being) would have abandoned the long-standing principle that data collected by one arm of the

---

[4] The power to take and retain fingerprints and samples is contained in Police and Criminal Evidence Act 1984 ("PACE"), ss. 62–64. "Recordable" offences are those designated as such by ministerial regulations (PACE, ss. 27 and 118). They include a wide range of offences, many of them trivial and punishable only by a modest fine. The detailed provisions governing the practice of retention and destruction of records are contained not in legislation but in the "Retention Guidelines for Nominal Records on the Police National Computer 2006", prepared by the Association of Chief Police Officers in England and Wales. An Appendix to the Guidelines describes "exceptional" cases as "rare by definition", giving as examples cases where the original arrest or sampling was unlawful or where it is established beyond doubt that no offence existed.

[5] Margolis Adrienne, "Getting the Balance Right on DNA." *International Bar News* (December 2008) [37].

[6] 30562/04, Grand Chamber judgment of 4 December 2008.

[7] 2006/24/EC. In *Ireland v. European Parliament*, Case C-301/06 (Judgment 10 February 2009), the ECJ accepted that the Directive had been validly adopted under Article 95 EC.

[8] See Home Office consultation document, April 2009, "Protecting the Public in a Changing Communications Environment" (Cm 7586), http://www.homeoffice.gov.uk/documents/cons-2009-communications-data. The document, describing proposals for an Interception Modernisation Programme, proudly reminds the reader that the Data Retention Directive was adopted during the UK's EU Presidency.

[9] Government Communications Headquarters.

State for one purpose should not be generally available to other branches of Government for other purposes.

Any expansion of State power in this area implies a corresponding retreat in personal privacy. Even if Parliament and Government are relaxed about that shift, one might expect the domestic judiciary to be rather less so. In a 1991 case, *Marcel v. Metropolitan Police Commissioner*[10] the Vice-Chancellor, Sir Nicolas Browne-Wilkinson, was alarmed at the idea of government mining for information about the individual in a centralised pool of accumulated data:

> (The) public interest in confidentiality as such is immensely increased when the information in question has been obtained by a public authority using compulsory powers. There are today numerous agencies of the state upon which, no doubt for good reason, Parliament has conferred the power compulsorily to obtain information and documents from the private citizen. If this information is not communicated to others but is known to, and used by, only the agency which is given the statutory power to obtain it, no great harm is done. But if the information obtained by the police, the Inland Revenue, the social security offices, the health service and other agencies were to be gathered together in one file, the freedom of the individual would be gravely at risk. The dossier of private information is the badge of the totalitarian state. … The courts should be at least as astute to protect the public interest in freedom from abuse of power as in protecting the public interest in the exercise of such powers.

That case was decided some 9 years before the ECHR became directly applicable in UK domestic law.[11] Ironically, more recent decisions of the courts reflect apparent judicial acceptance of the swing away from the individual's right to privacy towards the State's right to know. The tribunal which heard parallel domestic proceedings in the *Liberty and others* case resulted in IOCA's successor, the Regulation of Investigatory Powers Act 2000 (RIPA), receiving a clean bill of health.[12] In the domestic litigation that preceded *S. and Marper*, the English courts went as far as to deny that Article 8 was even *applicable* to retention of fingerprints and DNA—let alone violated.[13]

The overall result is that on the plane of European politics, standards of privacy protection have been allowed to sink to the lowest level. This is precisely why *Liberty* and *S. & Marper* are of such interest. As we will see, the Court was not prepared to adopt a lowest common denominator approach to privacy protection in Europe. To appreciate this aspect of the Court's thinking, we need to take a short diversion into the principles that apply in Article 8 cases.

---

[10] (1992) Ch. 225 at 240 (a decision of the English High Court.

[11] Human Rights Act 1998, in force 2 October 2000.

[12] *Rulings of the Tribunal on Preliminary Issues of Law*, IPT/01/62, 9 December 2004, http://www.ipt-uk.com/docs/IPT_01_62.pdf.

[13] *R. v. Chief Constable of South Yorkshire Police, ex parte Marper*, (2004) 1 WLR 2196.

3.2 Legality, Necessity, Secrecy

Article 8(1) of the European Convention on Human Rights (ECHR) confers the right to respect for private life, family life, home and correspondence. The Court has given these expressions a generous interpretation. Together, "private life" and "correspondence" provide legal protection for almost any attribute or behaviour that defines the individual's identity as a human being, including the expectation of keeping interpersonal communications away from the State's prying eyes. But this right is far from absolute. Article 8(2) allows a public authority to interfere so long as the measures it takes are "in accordance with the law" and "necessary in a democratic society" in pursuance of a wide range of "legitimate aims", including prevention of crime and disorder and protection of the rights of others. So, key to the effectiveness of Article 8 in protecting privacy rights is the Court's approach to the open-textured concepts of legality and necessity.

The general principles applied by the Court have been around for some years and are well known to most lawyers and many policy-makers. A measure is "in accordance with the law" if the source of legal authority for the State's action is "foreseeable" and "accessible".[14] The law conferring discretionary power on a State body has to be precise enough, and sufficiently made known to the public, to enable the individual to understand what the State can do and when.[15] To put it crudely, the citizen with whose rights the State interferes is entitled to ask: "why me?"

A measure is not "necessary in a democratic society" unless shown to respond to a "pressing social need", supported by "relevant and sufficient reasons" and "proportionate to the legitimate aim pursued". It must also be subject to sufficient safeguards—checks, restraints, opportunities for scrutiny—to protect the individual from abuse. States have a "margin of appreciation" in deciding which measures are appropriate to local circumstances. But the Court dislikes "blanket" measures that apply indiscriminately to a large class of people, since these prevent a case-by-case assessment of the need for an interference: a one-size-fits-all approach to human rights needs compelling justification.[16]

The European Court accepts that the modern State is entitled to undertake covert surveillance. But there is a judicial dilemma: on the one hand, clandestine activity by officials poses obvious risks of abuse. On the other, the individual target of surveillance cannot be entitled to know "why me" in a literal sense. The essence of an undercover investigation is precisely the secrecy of what the State knows or suspects so as to justify its interest in the target.[17] The solution is to modify the foreseeability and accessibility principles so that the public are entitled to ask "why me?" in an indirect sense. As the Court explained in *Malone*, the law must:

---

[14] *Sunday Times v. UK*, (1979) Ser. A no. 30.

[15] *Goodwin v. UK*, (1996) 22 EHRR 123, para. 31.

[16] *Handyside v. UK*, (1976) Ser. A no. 24; *Connors v. UK*, (2005) 40 EHRR 9; *Hirst v. UK (No. 2)*, (2006) 42 EHRR 41.

[17] *Klass v. Germany*, (1978) 2 EHRR 214.

> Give citizens an adequate indication as to the circumstances in which and the conditions on which public authorities are empowered to resort to this secret and potentially dangerous interference with the right to respect of private life and correspondence.[18]

The problem in *Malone* was that domestic law effectively contained *no* provision authorising police interception of telephony. However, what is the Court's attitude where the complaint is that the law makes *some* provision but *not enough* to provide an "adequate indication" of the State's powers? The answer is illustrated by a series of cases dealing (like *Malone*) with phone tapping in criminal investigations. This line of authority began with *Kruslin and Huvig v. France*[19] and has been gradually refined, so that in *AEIH and Ekimdzhien v. Bulgaria*,[20] the Court was able to state the following requirements:

> [75] In view of the risk of abuse intrinsic to any system of secret surveillance, such measures must be based on a law that is particularly precise. It is essential to have clear, detailed rules on the subject, especially as the technology available for use is continually becoming more sophisticated...
> [76] ...the Court has developed the following minimum safeguards that should be set out in statute law to avoid abuses: the nature of the offences which may give rise to an interception order; a definition of the categories of people liable to have their communications monitored; a limit on the duration of such monitoring; the procedure to be followed for examining, using and storing the data obtained; the precautions to be taken when communicating the data to other parties; and the circumstances in which data obtained may or must be erased or the records destroyed....
> [77] In addition, in the context of secret measures of surveillance by public authorities, because of the lack of public scrutiny and the risk of misuse of power, the domestic law must provide some protection against arbitrary interference with Article 8 rights... The Court must be satisfied that there exist adequate and effective guarantees against abuse. This assessment depends on all the circumstances of the case, such as the nature, scope and duration of the possible measures, the grounds required for ordering them, the authorities competent to permit, carry out and supervise them, and the kind of remedy provided by the national law

Thus, safeguards occupy the crossover region between legality and necessity: the Court is looking for adequate procedures, checks and oversight mechanisms, and these must be integral to the published framework of law under which the State acts.

3.3 Legality: The Liberty Case

Given these clear statements of principle, what was the problem? The answer is that while insisting on high standards of legal precision in cases about secret *investigative* techniques, the Court and former Commission took a much more relaxed approach to covert activity undertaken for more general security purposes.

[18] *Malone v. UK*, (1984) Ser. A no. 82, para. 67.

[19] (1990) 12 EHRR 547.

[20] 62540/00, Judgment of 28 June 2007.

In *Christie v. UK*[21] the Commission declared manifestly ill-founded an Article 8 complaint by a trade union official who believed the Government was using IOCA powers to monitor fax communications with eastern European counterparts. Earlier Commission decisions took a similar approach to security vetting of public service broadcast officials[22] and the security services' practice of indefinite retention of information gained from surveillance.[23]

The *Liberty* case challenged this distinction. At the centre of the case lay the contrast within IOCA between the highly targeted system regulating interception of domestic calls and the much looser system for calls to or from the UK. Internal calls could not be monitored unless a senior minister issued a warrant, which had to relate to a specific individual or communications address. So, the law made clear that authorisation was linked to suspicion against a specific target. The system for external calls was superficially similar, also involving a warrant issued by a minister. But this time the warrant, accompanied by a ministerial certificate, covered an entire class of calls. Potentially a single warrant could authorise interception of every single external call initiated or terminating in the UK. The resulting mass of intercept product was then subjected to a multi-stage process of "filtering", "minimisation" and "dissemination": the items of interest to the authorities were drawn from the pool using searching techniques, and those items were then passed on to the relevant agencies.

Thus the most significant interference with privacy—the human examination of material relating to identifiable individuals—took place at the post-interception stage. In other words the real sting of the system lay in the *data-mining exercise* that followed the interception itself; and by that stage of the process, the statutory provisions about warrants became irrelevant. The legislation dealt with post-interception processes in the most cursory terms. IOCA imposed a bare duty on the Secretary of State to make "arrangements" in relation to these processes. The arrangements themselves were unpublished.

In the Strasbourg proceedings, the UK Government argued that domestic and external communications were sufficiently different to justify the contrasting provisions. It also argued, relying on *Christie*, that the need to maintain operational secrecy, especially where national security was at stake, entitled it to keep the detailed "arrangements" secret. Nevertheless, the Government submitted a lengthy witness statement from an official, describing—so far as he was able within the constraints of national security—the operating procedures for the post-interception steps. This explained (among other things) how officials were supervised, how functions were separated between staff teams, and how access to intercept product was restricted. But the problem remained that at the time the interception took place, there had been no information whatsoever in the public domain describing the regulation of the authorities' powers to select material from the intercept pool and subsequently disclose, use and retain it.

---

[21] (1994) 78A DR 119.

[22] *Hilton v. UK*, (1988) 57 DR 108.

[23] *Hewitt and Harman v. UK (No. 2)*, Comm. Rep 1.9.93.

Addressing these issues, the Court pointed out that its approach had "evolved" since *Christie*,[24] and there should no longer be a distinction in the way the principles of foreseeability and accessibility apply to measures "targeted at specific individuals" on the one hand and "general programmes of surveillance" on the other. It held that the broad scope of a certificated warrant meant that "the legal discretion granted to the executive for the physical capture of external communications was … virtually unfettered."[25]

Against that background, and most importantly of all, the Court rejected the Government's argument that the efficacy of covert operations would be compromised by publication of information about the regulation of post-interception steps. In particular it pointed to its earlier decision in *Weber & Saravia v. Germany*.[26] In *Weber* the Court rejected a complaint that interception under the German G10 Act failed the "in accordance with the law" test. But it did so precisely because the legislation (which by this time had been successively refined and revised by the BVerfG and federal legislature) regulated every stage of the interception and post-interception process in explicit detail. Its provisions governed the way individual communications were selected from the pool of "strategic intercept" product; how selected material could be disclosed among the various State agencies; the use each agency could properly make of the material; and the retention or destruction of the material. At each stage there were meticulous requirements for review, verification and record-keeping.[27]

The contrast with the IOCA regime could hardly be greater. The Court's view, put simply, was that if Germany could operate an effective system of covert operations governed by precise and accessible legal provisions, then so too could the UK. IOCA failed to "set out in a form accessible to the public any indication of the procedure to be followed for selecting for examination, sharing, storing and destroying intercepted material".[28] So interception and subsequent processing of external communications under IOCA was not "in accordance with the law" and thus violated Article 8.

3.4 Necessity and Proportionality: The S. and Marper Case

The Court in *S. and Marper* could well have chosen to focus on the "in accordance with the law" issue. All the significant detail about operation of the DNA and fingerprint databases—from the arrangements about who could access the data, for what

[24] Judgment, para. 63.

[25] *Ibid.*, para. 64.

[26] 54934/00, decision of 29 June 2006.

[27] *Liberty and others* judgment, para. 68; and see *Weber* decision paras. 32–61.

[28] *Liberty and others* judgment, para. 69.

purpose and for how long, to the criteria for removal of profiles—was contained in non-statutory internal guidance.[29] The Court made the point that the foreseeability and accessibility principles applied equally to retention of personal profiling data as it did to covert monitoring:

> ...it is as essential, in this context, as in telephone tapping, secret surveillance and covert intelligence-gathering, to have clear, detailed rules governing the scope and application of measures, as well as minimum safeguards concerning, *inter alia*, duration, storage, usage, access of third parties, procedures for preserving the integrity and confidentiality of data and procedures for its destruction, thus providing sufficient guarantees against the risk of abuse and arbitrariness.[30]

It agreed that parts of the material were "worded in rather general terms and may give rise to extensive interpretation".[31] But it decided that that these questions were better considered as part of the "broader issue" of whether the interference was necessary in a democratic society. On that issue, the evidence[32] was stark. The UK regime was significantly out of step with practice in other Council of Europe Member States. All others (including Scotland, a separate jurisdiction within the UK) operated DNA databases under some or all of the following constraints:

- Profiles could be retained only from those *convicted* of *defined categories* of *serious offence*;
- Profiles could be retained from persons outside that class, but *only in defined circumstances*, e.g. where an unconvicted individual remains under suspicion.
- Profiles could be retained only for *limited periods of time*, with additional *discretion to destroy/delete early* (i.e. before expiry of the maximum time limit) if no longer required.[33]

Against that background, the Court was "struck by the blanket and indiscriminate nature" of the UK legislation, which authorised permanent retention of personal data regardless of the nature and gravity of the suspected offence and regardless of the suspect's age. The State's margin of appreciation was "restricted" where a "particularly important facet of an individual's existence or identity", such as genetic information, was at stake. The "stigmatisation" of unconvicted individuals by assimilation to convicted persons was "of particular concern" to the Court, and the practice of retaining personal data from unconvicted minors was "especially harmful". The Government's statistical evidence on the supposed usefulness of DNA evidence in subsequent criminal investigations failed to persuade the Court that indefinite retention of data from unconvicted individuals was necessary or proportionate. The Court concluded that UK database rules for both DNA data and fingerprints failed the necessity test and violated Article 8.[34]

---

[29] Above, note 4.

[30] Judgment, para. 99, citing *Liberty and others* with approval.

[31] *Ibid.*

[32] Much of it submitted by Liberty as intervener.

[33] Judgment, paras. 45–49.

[34] Judgment paras. 102, 119, 122–125.

3.5 Where Does It Leave Us?

In each of these cases, the Court declined to lower European standards of data protection to fit UK policy. Instead, as regards both the extent of published information about the machinery of covert data-gathering, and the substantive scope of the State's powers to obtain and keep important data about the individual, the Court insisted that the UK level up.

Within the UK, IOCA is long gone, replaced in 2000 by RIPA. RIPA largely replicates the architecture of IOCA, subjecting the processing of external intercept product to unpublished "arrangements". But the difference—and this may be the key to achieving compliance with Article 8—is that RIPA provides for publication of an official Code of Practice. It should be relatively simple for the Government to amend the current Code by adding an outline of the machinery that regulates filtering, selection, disclosure and destruction of intercept product. The Government recently consulted on revisions to the RIPA Codes, but unfortunately shows no sign of making amendments (or indeed doing anything else) to comply with the *Liberty* judgment. Transparency may be legally easy to achieve, but the UK authorities seem to find it culturally difficult. As regards DNA, the Government has published proposals for a revised retention regime. But, at present, these fall well short of meeting the *S. and Marper* criticisms.

What about the implications for wider European law and policy? The Convention and Strasbourg judgments are not, of course, directly binding on EU institutions. But, at the Community level, they tend to shape the attitude of the European Court of Justice, and they can also form a basis for domestic challenges to national implementing legislation. So the *Liberty* and *S. and Marper* judgments should give Community policy makers pause for thought on several levels.

Perhaps the most obvious source of conflict, given the current direction of Community policy towards generalised requirements to store communications information, is the Court's evident disdain in *S. and Marper* for blanket, indiscriminate measures. The Court emphasised in its judgment the heightened importance of safeguards where sensitive data about individuals are subject to automated processing: the retained data must be "relevant and not excessive" and "protected from misuse and abuse".[35] Given the sheer width of the UK DNA database, the Court found it unnecessary to deal specifically with the adequacy of safeguards in the processing arrangements.[36] But it is hard to see how legislative measures requiring ISPs and phone networks to retain an undifferentiated mass of data about citizens' communications for periods of months or years could pass the necessity test where no attempt is made to limit the pool of retained data to those genuinely believed to be of interest to the authorities for legitimate public protection purposes. These must inevitably be regarded either as "blanket" measures or as involving retention of data beyond the "relevant and not excessive".

[35] Para. 103.

[36] Para. 125.

It is no answer to say that what is retained is merely communications *data* rather than content. In *Malone* the Court held that the same principles applied to telephone metering data as to the calls themselves.[37] That is quite logical once you recall that Article 8 is not about communications in the abstract but as an aspect of private life. Information about who called whom, when, for how long, etc. enables authorities to build up a vivid picture of an individual's activities and associations. Likewise information about e-mail "to" and "from" addresses, and IP addresses of web sites visited. Developments such as social networking and cloud computing have further blurred the distinction between data and content.

The *Liberty* judgment, meanwhile, is an important reminder of the need to ensure that the rules for operating the data-gathering and processing regime are sufficiently clear and placed in the public domain. That is especially important for the down-stream end of any data-gathering exercise, when the assembled material is mined for terms or patterns of potential interest to the authorities. Even if the legislation covers the initial gathering and retention of data, it is essential to ensure that the *subsequent* treatment of the material is regulated by clear, precise and published rules that demonstrably protect against "misuse and abuse".[38] The example of the German G10 Act shows that the right place for those rules is on the face of the statute book. It may be permissible in principle for the rules to appear in some other instrument, such as official guidance or a statement of practice. But the risk with such non-legislative material is that, as in *Malone*, the public cannot tell "with any reasonable certainty what elements of the powers … are contained in legal rules and what elements remain in the discretion of the executive."[39]

It will be interesting to see how the Community legislature and the Member States manage the clash between the policy direction of EU Governments on the one hand and Strasbourg's emphasis on universally high standards of transparency and justification on the other. Nothing in the Court's recent judgments precludes effective measures to protect the public and its democratic institutions against the threat of terrorism or other serious crime. What the Convention requires are intelligence and investigatory powers that are properly focused on the source of danger and that operate in accordance with basic concepts of the rule of law. Far from compromising the defence of our democracy, levelling up to these high standards across Europe immeasurably strengthens it.

[37] Paras. 85–87.

[38] *S. and Marper* judgment, para. 103.

[39] *Malone* judgment, para. 79.

Chapter 4
Responding to the Inevitable Outcomes of Profiling: Recent Lessons from Consumer Financial Markets, and Beyond

Tal Zarsky

4.1 Preface

Data profiling practices in today's information age take many shapes and have many faces. They generate both public intrigue and concern, which in many cases make their way to the media and from there, to relevant regulators. These latter entities, in turn, struggle in search of a proper regulatory response to the complicated issues set before them. Profiling presents a policy challenge which is indeed frequently invoked and discussed. However, both the harms it presents and the way in which it should be resolved are extremely difficult to conceptualize. The challenge of regulators and scholars grappling with these issues is three-fold: they (a) must generate a helpful taxonomy for understanding and addressing the various practices and their potential problems. They must also (b) establish which issues could be resolved by internal and external market pressures, as well as indirect regulatory pressures, and which issues require direct regulatory scrutiny and intervention. Finally, and most importantly, they must (c) formulate (or recommend) regulatory responses at the distinct junctures they deem necessary. In this short paper I attempt to draw out a brief strategic response to these questions, while relying on previous work (Zarsky 2002–2003, 2004). My analysis will focus on the first two elements, while providing merely initial intuitions towards overall solutions. In doing so, I will strive to account for the technological, market and legal developments of the most recent years.

My analysis is set within the confines of a limited context—that of profiling, data aggregation and the subsequent data analysis and data mining carried out by the consumer-oriented financial services sector, with a special focus on practices that allow for the targeting of specific consumers. I also make a short detour to the

---

Senior Lecturer, University of Haifa—Faculty of Law. I thank the organizers of the CPDP2009 conference for their invitation to speak and for the participants for their insightful feedback. I especially thank Mireille Hildebrandt, Serge Gutwirth and Paul de Hert for their insights. I also thank Aner Rabinovitz for his excellent assistance in research.

T. Zarsky (✉)
Faculty of Law, University of Haifa, Mt. Carmel, Haifa, Israel
e mail: tzarsky@law.haifa.ac.il

S. Gutwirth et al. (eds.), *Data Protection in a Profiled World*,
DOI 10.1007/978-90-481-8865-9_4,

realm of media and entertainment service providers. By "targeting" I refer to the entities' ability to engage in interactions with specific consumers (facilitated mostly, yet certainly not exclusively, by the internet) which has been greatly enhanced in recent years by novel interfaces and business models, as well as by advances in both computer and social sciences (for recent examples, see Baker 2008). During these targeted interactions, firms rely upon and take advantage of the data and knowledge they previously collected, which is specific to the relevant individual, with whom they are now interacting directly and exclusively. The ability to meet the technical challenges targeting presents leads to exciting business opportunities for entities providing financial services (as well as others). Yet it also introduces concerns and challenges.

The chapter proceeds along three sections. In Sect. 4.2, I briefly draw out a three-part analysis of profiling, which will prove constructive (so I hope) in addressing a variety of instances where a policy response to profiling practices is contemplated and perhaps even needed. This analysis provides a basic flow chart for identifying several forms of problems associated with the collection, analysis and usage of personal information, and reasons for regulatory intervention (as well as where such intervention should be withheld). Generally, I explain (while relying on earlier work) that the key to understanding such harms and solutions lies in the actual *uses* of the knowledge derived from the profile. I advocate this strategy, as opposed to merely focusing on the creation of the profile (or the *collection* stage), which generates the majority of legal and public attention. In addition, I argue that we need not focus on data subjects' ability to control future forms of *analysis* of data pertaining to them (including data mining processes), for a variety of reasons. This leads us to the *usage* stage—which in itself presents unique challenges. These challenges are mapped out using a four-factor structure.

In Sect. 4.3, I present four test cases, "ripped from the headlines" of the international press. These test cases allow me to demonstrate how the taxonomy and categories I draw out in Sect. 4.2 can forward our understanding of privacy concerns and our ability to identify the specific instances which require regulatory intervention (note that this segment does not focus on providing solutions—these are partially provided later). Three stories address consumer financial services—a sector which has been through recent turmoil which is only sharpening the issues at hand. I provide an additional test case from the somewhat different realm of media services to add both clarity and complexity to the analysis. The examples serve an additional important purpose: they strengthen the assertions made in Sect. 4.2, as to the importance of focusing regulatory efforts on the usage stage, and the relevance of the four-factor structure offered, while demonstrating how it could be applied.

I conclude, in Sect. 4.4, by addressing some possible solutions which should be developed in future academic work and regulatory debate, while distinguishing among the different problems and concerns previously addressed.

Before proceeding, I must clarify that the main contribution of this chapter is not necessarily in the broader legal concepts and analysis it sets forth (for a similar taxonomy, see Solove 2008). The chapter's main contribution is three-fold; first, by using the examples set out in Sect. 4.3, I strive to strengthen an assertion I have made several times in the past—that profiling concerns might be best addressed at the point where the data is used, rather than before. I find reinstating this argument (and presenting it with additional clarity and to a broader audience) important, especially since it is quite different than the common approach in the EU. Second, I use the examples mentioned to elucidate and reinforce the analytic framework drawn out in Sect. 4.2. The examples, in turn, prove helpful in reshaping and refining the theoretical models so that they indeed comply with these most recent challenges. Finally, I use these new examples for the mapping of some solutions to the questions they raise, which could be addressed in other contexts as well.

Thus, the chapter applies a somewhat different analytic move than the one usually used in jurisprudential reasoning. Rather than promoting a normative theory after looking at the development of *case law*—I draw out a theory looking at cases of a different kind—technological and business reports that indicate a shift towards a new environment that requires some legal adjustments. In many fast paced markets, I believe this latter form of inquiry should at times be preferred. I also concede that the study here presented is not empirical in its nature; I cannot argue that the events referred to in the news reports quoted bellow occur with a greater frequency than others. However, I do believe these reports indicate both public interest and concerns regarding these forms of profiling (these are major publications, after all), and thus might challenge various regulators in the near future. This study also does not examine the philosophical meanings and importance of *privacy, profiling* or *personal information* as concepts. For that, I rely upon accepted notions of these concepts in EU and US scholarship, and other learned articles presented throughout this volume.

4.2 Rethinking the Regulation of Profiling: In a Nutshell

The key to understanding the harms of profiling, as well as the way to solve them, requires a close examination of the actual *uses* of the knowledge derived from them. To make this point, I must walk the readers through several conceptual steps. First, I must acquaint them with my understanding of the flow of personal information (Sect. 4.2.1), which includes the stages of data collection, analysis and use. Then (Sect. 4.2.2), I explain why focusing our analytic vigor on solving the concerns of profiling by regulating and limiting the collection stage is unwise. This is due to the fact that collection is in many cases inevitable or invaluable (or both). In Sect. 4.2.3., I make a similar argument for the subsequent "analysis" stage. Finally, in Sect. 4.2.4, I explain that the challenge of confronting the potential detrimental aspects of profiling require us to examine the various uses while applying four analytic factors. These help establish whether and to what extent regulators must intervene in the flow of personal information.

4.2.1 A Brief Introduction to the Flow of Personal Information

For the sake of simplicity, I refer to the practices of targeting and profiling through a reoccurring three-tier process, which includes the stage of *collection, analysis*, and *usage* of such data. By *collection* I refer to the point where the information included in the relevant individual profile is gathered and effectively stored (or warehoused). Both normative and philosophical arguments call for the limitation of collection practices. Furthermore, both specific laws and privacy torts protect individuals from unauthorized collection efforts (see Zarsky 2004). Collection could take various forms; it could be done directly from the data subjects, with or without their consent; it could be collected through third parties, and it could be carried out in the open, or on the data subjects' or collectors' (virtual or actual) property. However, one specific context generates a great deal of difficulty and traction—instances where information is collected directly from the data subject, after he conceded to such collection—yet the extent of his understanding of what data was collected, how it might be analyzed and how it would be used, is questionable. This is the realm upon which our analysis will focus.

Collection (and the subsequent storage of the data) is followed by data *analysis*. Here the database, which includes the profiles of many individuals, is analyzed in search of knowledge which might prove helpful to the relevant firms. In many instances, the analysis points to potential uses which were not apparent at the time of collection. This is especially made possible by using data mining techniques, which apply sophisticated computing algorithms to reveal hidden patterns and clusters in the data (Zarsky 2002–2003).

The practices here described are both technically possible and economically viable for many firms. Yet the "processing" of personal data is an issue extensively regulated in the EU Data Protection Directive, as well as elsewhere in EU and US law. Among other issues, the EU Directive requires collectors to limit their analysis to the initial reason cited when analyzing personal data (sometimes referred to as "purpose specification" or the "finality principle") (Article 6(B)). This limitation could (to a certain extent) be circumvented by receiving advance consent to future analyses of the collected data, or broadly interpreting the purposes of the initial collection *ex post*.

The two stages mentioned lead to the actual *usage* of the knowledge derived from the data analysis—a process which could lead to various benefits to the parties involved. Yet hand in hand with the promises of this process, dangers to the data subject loom. Errors in the database or the process could lead to unfair treatment. Private information apparent from the database analysis could lead to the subjects' embarrassment, potential abuse and even blackmail. Less radical (yet more common) outcomes result of the additional insights firms have into their users conduct and behavior. These generate an interesting information imbalance among the parties involved—where at times the firms "know" their consumers better than the consumers know themselves! Thus, the information could be used to discriminate among the targeted users while relying on a variety of factors and strategies—indications of the ability to pay, higher switching costs, higher information and opportunity costs, and more. Finally, such knowledge could potentially allow the targeting firms (especially in the realms of marketing and advertising) to use their insights into the individuals' preferences and previous actions to unfairly manipulate them.

All these issues raise potential problems, which might require regulatory action. However, as I explain below, distinguishing between instances which mandate intervention and those that do not is quite a difficult task. To do so, I introduce several factors for consideration, with an overall sense of caution; over-regulation has detriments and inefficiencies of its own, which are best avoided, especially in dynamic markets.

Finally, it should be noted that the flow of personal information does not cease at the point of usage, but continues in an everlasting cycle. The firms interacting with the consumers record (or "collect") their reaction to the targeted messages, analyze these reaction and accordingly change their future data uses. Thus, the information flow facilitates a feedback loop between firms and consumers that could lead to both vast benefits and detriments—elements which would be demonstrated in the examples below.

4.2.2 The Limits and Troubles of Regulating Data Collection

Although most of the doctrinal and philosophical emphasis in privacy law and policy is on the first and essential "collection" stage, this strategy is in my opinion flawed—especially in the contexts to be explored below. This is because data collection (or the creation of the profile) is in many cases inevitable. In today's markets (as in all the examples provided below), profiles are a product of ongoing relationships between firms and consumers and are collected as part of the regular course of business. In these cases, the collection is both important to all parties, and consented to by the data subjects. The profiles serve as an important tool in maintaining the relationship between these parties, as well carrying out the firms' internal tasks. In many cases consumers openly concede to such collection—either because they choose to do so—or that they do not have a choice (note that I do not refer to acts of coercion, but to the fact that the service will not be provided without agreeing to such collection).

Either way, these forms of profiles are here to stay—and are a key component in the concerns I will address shortly. Given the fact that a vast portion of our lives is carried out as an interaction with firms (such as banks, vendors and content providers) the extent and effects of these almost inevitable profiling practices will be substantial. Thus, we should strive to find solutions which assume their existence, and deal with their aftermath.

4.2.3 The Limits and Troubles of Regulating Data Analysis

A similar argument can be made with regard to the subsequent "analysis" stage. In other words, recognizing and enforcing the data subjects' right to control the ways in which data pertaining to them is subsequently analyzed by others is, in my opinion, not necessarily the proper manner to protect against privacy-related concerns. Nor would such enforcement do much to limit the fears and problematic outcomes of profiling. Setting forth these two arguments might indeed surprise and even upset European readers—as the "processing" of information is a notion extensively addressed in EU law. Indeed, restrictions of the ability to use personal information for a task which is different from the one originally designated at the time of collection (or "Secondary Use")—is a controversial regulatory element which distinguishes among privacy laws and attitudes on both sides of the Atlantic. As opposed to the EU position stated above, US laws restrict secondary uses in only limited and specific contexts (Zarsky 2004; Swire and Litan 1998). The European position is grounded in rationales of autonomy and control. Yet the US position could be strongly advocated as well. The firms' ability to engage in secondary use allows them to optimally utilize the information at their disposal, in ways that are in many cases to the benefit of consumers and the overall market (Cate 2001). For that reason, there are strong arguments to limit the restriction of secondary use, which in my opinion have a great deal of merit. Accepting these arguments should lead to the loosening of limitations on analysis, and "pushing" the regulation of profiling down the information flow, towards the stage of actual *use*.

Yet even readers who choose to maintain their devotion to the powerful analytical concepts limiting analysis, could be convinced that this regulatory strategy will have limited success in overcoming the challenges of profiling. This is due to the fact that this strategy is difficult to both define and enforce (with the exception of simple instances of blatant misuse). Understanding and establishing after the fact which pieces of data were used, for which task and to what extent within the organizational framework, is very difficult for the regulator standing outside the firm and peering inward. This task is greatly complicated if consent has been provided for some secondary uses (as it usually is), but not others. Here, courts will be required to examine complaints that the firms' have exceeded their initial usage mandate and will be asked to interpret the meaning and extent of said authorization. These complaints, when rolled to the doorstep of courts, will lead to uncertainty at a crucial juncture of the information (and actual) economy.

Furthermore (and similarly to the argument presented above), secondary use could be easily circumvented (and often is) by establishing user consent, especially in the instances (mentioned above) where the profile is an outcome of an ongoing relationship between firms and consumers (Cate 2006). The fact that such consent would usually be given in the context of a contract of adhesion, need not mean that it should be rendered moot by courts after the fact. Rather, it would mean that again courts would be required to figure out what would be the optimal arrangement at every juncture—and given the vast benefits of secondary use there is no guarantee they will find for the data subjects and prohibit the secondary use of data.

4.2.4 Regulating Profiling by Addressing Uses: Possibilities, Factors and Limits

As indicated above, our analysis leads to the conclusion that we must approach the subsequent uses of profiles in various commercial settings to examine whether they lead to specific detriments, and thereafter proceed to initiate a regulatory response.

Yet here I advocate a cautious approach as well. I recognize that the knowledge the information analysis produces, when held solely by one side to the transaction, can generate a potential power imbalance between the parties involved (namely the firms as opposed to the consumers/data subjects). However, this potential will not always materialize into the abuse of such power.

To work through this issue, I hereby offer a four-factor test which would be applied throughout the paper (and thus elucidating elements which might seem too abstract at this juncture: (1) whether the usage at hand is beneficial (and to whom), (2) whether the detriments here addressed could be resolved by applying existing consumer protections rules (or at least doctrines), (3) whether potential detriments could be mitigated by market and social forces, and (perhaps most importantly) (4) whether the uses allow firms to manipulate their users' preferences unfairly. When the answer to questions (2) and (3) are negative (and (1) is indecisive), specific regulatory steps must be put in place. When question (4) is answered affirmatively, formulating the regulatory response is especially challenging, as it requires us to distinguish between fair and unfair attempts to affect the consumers' tastes and preferences. I will now briefly elaborate upon these elements while leaving some elaboration to be carried out below, when addressing concrete examples.

In terms of factor (1), in some instances, the knowledge is applied in a manner that is beneficial to some or all parties. The analysis will allow markets to produce optimal outcomes and usage would prove beneficial to firms and consumers alike (regardless of the initial negative visceral feeling the dynamic might invoke) by lowering search and information costs. In other instances, the uses of the analysis will not benefit all, but still a vast segment of the population will gain, even when firms exercise "price discrimination" (a notion I extensively address elsewhere (Zarsky 2002–2003)).

As we move to factor (2), I must note that in many other situations, however, these actions generate risks and problems—yet these could be resolved by applying existing legal rules and doctrines, especially from the field of consumer protection. For instance, that would be the case in some of the instances where the profile is used to unfairly discriminate, generates market failures or when it leads to an erroneous outcome or one that is socially unacceptable. In addition, consumer protection doctrines provide tools for mitigating power and information gaps among parties. These power and information gaps are at times precisely the outcome of the consumer profile analysis carried out by firms.

Here, existing laws and doctrines should be applied to resolve these problems. For instance, at times these processes allow firms to deny service to "weaker" consumers and users—or plainly ignore them—because they prove to be unattractive customers. This dynamic could be remedied (when mandated to do so by policy considerations) by requiring firms to serve all consumers equally or at least provide these consumers with a minimal level of service. In other instances, the usage of profiling will allow for overcharging a specific set of consumers/users because the firms' analysis indicates the firms' ability to do so. The analysis will point to these indications while establishing data subjects' ability to pay, the fact that there is an information asymmetry between them and the firms, or perhaps that high switching costs impede upon the consumers' ability to explore other options. In some of these instances consumer protection law will (or could) intervene on behalf of these consumers. It could do so by requiring the firms to disclose information or even refrain from the problematic pricing techniques mentioned. Clearly specific forms of consumer protection rules might be needed, as the data analysis process generates novel forms of information and power gaps, and because targeting creates new opportunities for abuse. However, on a conceptual level, the targeting practices and the outcomes here described do not generate a serious conceptual challenge (as the tools and their theoretical foundations are already available).

Factor (3) refers to a crucial point that might (again) be unpopular with European readers. Here I argue that in some cases, market and other social forces can potentially curb adverse actions launched by firms as part of the profiling process. Thus, those concerned with the problematic outcomes of profiling need not prod governments to take specific actions. Below I will present several examples of such dynamics, which provide interesting outcomes in instances where the profiling practices clearly upset the firm's clients. Exercising restraint and refraining from regulatory intervention unless definitely needed should be the strategy of choice in realms which involve fast-paced and ever changing markets. One must remember that taking regulatory actions might lead to problematic and inefficient outcomes of their own, as regulation could be overreaching, captured by interest holders or plainly wrong.

The key to these economic and social dynamics is that in competitive markets, in theory at least, firms should be reluctant to offend their customers by using their profiles in ways which seem unsuitable. In the internet age, where negative information travels quickly via blogs, social networks and other new media forms, this dynamic should be even more powerful (Gurak 1999). One could also argue that the lack of competition among firms need not limit the chilling effect of negative reputation when abusing consumer profiles, while relying on Alfred Hirschman's powerful arguments stated in "Exit, Voice and Loyalty" (Hirschman 1970). According to this argument, even in monopolistic or concentrated markets, the fear of governmental intervention which would be motivated by constituents' complaints (hence "voice") might also suffice. It would keep firms from abusing their power and taking advantage of potential power and information gaps. Google's careful conduct regarding the usage of personal information and its powerful search platform could prove to be a case and point.

Yet market and social forces cannot always be relied upon. They will not be in play when the firms' actions (when using consumer profiles) are subtle and ambiguous, or when the detriments are unapparent. These are indeed the instances where even the most devoted *homos economicus* would agree that legal intervention is mandated. This, therefore, is a central caveat to the non-intervention approach, and a key point to the analysis in its entirety: there are specific uses stemming from the analysis of personal data, which are harmful to consumers and society, which will not be covered by other legal doctrine, and which will not be resolved by market forces. These are the instances which academics must single out, and governments must regulate.

Beyond these three factors, factor (4) focuses on even deeper concerns. These manifest when the profile is used to gain insights to the users' current state of mind and future behavior, and on this basis, applied to manipulate the data subject. These instances, where the individual's autonomy comes under attack, are hard to define and call for delicate distinctions. They require us to establish whether the data is used to reveal "true" user preferences, or applied to cause users to stray from these preferences, and lead them to prefer short term gains. They require us to decide whether the consumer has reached an autonomous decision, or has been unfairly manipulated into adopting a new position. These notions, which indeed sound abstract and seem unclear, will be demonstrated while referring to the examples below.

While I have indicated above the differences in both law and thought between US and EU law regarding profiling practices, I believe they will both concur that intervention is needed at the specific juncture here addressed. From the philosophical (and somewhat European) perspective, the conduct here described should be limited as it allows for the treatment of individuals as means to achieve specific ends. This is as opposed to treating them with dignity, as autonomous agents. From the market-based approach, such conduct will not achieve an overall optimal outcome but one that would be tilted towards the interests of the commercial firms (that also act as data aggregators and analyzers), and thus has adverse outcomes for the market in its entirety. Market forces will presumably fail in countering these problematic practices, as they fail to counter inefficient credence qualities in products (Parisi 2004). The detriments of these actions to consumers' welfare would only be exposed at a later time and after the negative effects played out. Even if consumers do eventually learn to overcome such manipulations, their learning period would be quite long. In the meantime, however, they would be disadvantaged in a variety of settings, which indeed require regulatory intervention. Therefore, all will agree that regulatory intervention is required. Yet the challenges of identifying these instances (which we will attend to in Sect. 4.3) and formulating proper responses (which we will begin to approach in Sect. 4.4) are substantial.

To *summarize* this section, I believe that both academic rigor and regulatory attention must focus on a specific subset of the analytic puzzle that profiling presents; where personal data usage takes place, existing consumer protection laws and markets are unhelpful, and where manipulation might be afoot. I surely concede that the structure above may seem complex and abstract. Therefore, in what follows, I will show how recent developments provide strong evidence that the concerns and questions I am raising are far from theoretical and academic. In doing so I will also further illuminate some of the distinctions and categories drawn out above.

4.3 A Tale of Four Data Miners

In this section I strive to demonstrate the way in which the taxonomy drawn out above can be applied. In addition, I demonstrate the accuracy and relevance of the analytical steps mentioned, while relying on four recent reports of profiling, data analysis and subsequent use. These reports, I will argue, also strengthen the underlying assertions of the previous section—our regulatory attention must focus on the third, usage step. Furthermore, it must focus within it on a specific sub-category which relates to instances where data subjects might be subject to various forms of manipulation.

The first three stories are to a certain extent a timeline of the recent economic crisis. First, there is a story of banks relying on the analysis of profiles to offer their clients specially tailored and attractive (or perhaps merely "attractive") loans, which meet their customers' taste with amazing precision. Second, we learn of credit card companies that "fire" their clients when they begin to show behavioral traits which the firms' analysis associates with the prospect of defaulting on payments (as opposed to actual defaults). Third, we learn of financial institutes which make use of the personal information they have amassed about their clients to construct tailored strategies for getting them to cover their debt. Our final story shifts to the content market, and pertains to *Netflix* and its new technological and business models, which strive to provide their users with movie recommendations that are premised on their previous selections.

As we will see, these four stories can be broken down into several sub-groups. Clearly the first three differ from the last one in several ways: The former address the financial industry, while the latter addresses media and entertainment. Thus, the information used by the former is of transactional and monetary nature, while the latter relies on data pertaining to personal tastes and preferences. Both forms of information provide a great deal of insight to the individual's inner thoughts, yet are routinely held by third parties. But perhaps most importantly, the former three stories generate a strong visceral feeling of unease (to say the least) when examining the actions taken on the basis of the data analysis. The last story generates a much calmer (not to say, sympathetic) response. I will focus on these distinctions below and try to decipher the reasons for these differences in attitude, while pointing to other forms of categorization. More importantly, I will show how every one of these stories fits within the taxonomy and analysis offered in Sect. 4.2, and therefore focus our attention to specific contexts within the broader profiling debate. At times I will identify specific harms to the individual's will and autonomy. In others cases I will emphasize information and power asymmetries—all of which might mandate specific regulatory intervention.

(A) I start with a *New York Times* report (Stone 2008) of the usage of profiling and data mining by banks, credit card issuers and mortgage brokers (as well as intermediaries working to forward their objectives). These entities closely scrutinized the financial data at their disposal as well as data available through public records and purchased on the secondary market. According to the mentioned report, these entities use insights gained through this analysis, termed "predictive modeling", to predict what the consumers' next financial move or need might be, and when it will be taking place. They then contact their clients and provide them with enticing offers (by mail, phone or direct contact) at exactly the right time and place. Some customers have been quoted to say: *"I can't believe you just called me. How did you know we were just getting ready to do that?"* The information the financial entities collected has informed them when and how to pressurize their consumers into undertaking various loans. The remainder of the article proceeds to describe how many of these loans turned out to indeed be "too good to be true"—and thus led to negative outcomes for the customers, the banks and the economy in general (yet not necessarily for the brokers initially selling these loans who received hefty underwriting bonuses). The insights the profiling practices gave mortgage brokers and others into the inner lives and needs of potential lenders has assumedly assisted them in selling financial products the lenders couldn't really afford or understand. One can clearly imagine how these practices are linked to the overall recent financial crisis, which was fueled by defaults on loans which should have never been given. Though, to be fair, there are numerous other factors in play[1] (and thus pinning the entire crisis on these ruthless lending practices would be inaccurate and improper).

This story provides, in my opinion, a powerful example of how the three-part analysis drawn out above points us to a specific subset of concerns which focus on the stage of data usage. I now quickly work through these stages to demonstrate. *First,* rules focusing on the limiting of collection and the creation of profiles would do little to mitigate the problems here discussed. Although some of the information used in this process came from external sources, much of it came from the ongoing relationship between banks and clients—a database which would be formulated in any event. *Second,* limits on analysis or "secondary use" of data will also probably fail to provide the needed protection in this context. Banks and financial institutions reserve the right to analyze the personal/financial information they collect so to offer their clients deals they deem appropriate. While consumers usually concede to these practices while signing an extensive and often incomprehensible agreement with their bank, there is little real reason to believe that most clients would truly object to such provisions, even if laid out to them clearly. These practices could indeed generate vast benefits to clients if applied fairly (Staten and Cate 2003). This leads us to focus our inquiry on the third stage of data use.

Here I turn to examine the four factors mentioned above. First, I note that these practices have their advantages (as a tool that better matches risks and rewards among consumers and firms within this industry). However, it is unclear (or actually unlikely) that the benefits of these analyses and uses are fairly distributed among the various consumers in this market. Second (and third), we must examine the ability of social and market forces to resolve these issues on their own, as well as whether relevant consumer protection rules might provide a sufficient remedy. Indeed, the article itself mentions several ways in which these forces caused firms to scale back on these strategies. It indicates that banks shied away from blatantly referring to personal information in their solicitations in a way which would cause clients to feel uncomfortable or applying practices that are clearly harmful to their customers, from fear of negative publicity. These and similar findings should lead to limiting

[1] There are plenty of entities to share the blame with—investment banks grouping bad debt together and selling it to unsuspecting clients, rating agencies, regulators and of course incautious investors and their advisers—and even the lenders themselves who should have exercised much more caution and restraint.

the role of regulators in this context. In other words, responding to the voiced questions is a complex task with mixed outcomes.

Further delving into this matter (and approaching the fourth factor mentioned—that of unfair manipulation), leads to the conclusion that it is quite difficult to figure out what the banks have done wrong. What more, at times they were (as mentioned) met by enthusiastic consumers who noted that the offers set forth were a perfect match with their preferences (or at least that is what they initially thought). Thus, the story presents an analytic and regulatory challenge—to what extent should these practices be regulated or even prohibited—if they comply with the overall consumer protection laws pertaining to this setting (namely, rules regulating loans such as usury laws and disclosure requirements). This is the same challenge we mentioned above (when presenting the forth analytic factor of the analysis)—establishing when the banks' practices stop providing the consumer with what they wanted and start "pushing" consumers in a direction that the bank suggests. These, in their essence, are the real challenges of profiling and privacy.

It should also be noted that this context could lead to a flurry of additional consumer-related problems which were not addressed in this report; consumers not receiving favorable terms for their loans when marked as potentially ill-informed (and thus could be potentially taken advantage of); consumers not being cleared for loans at all, given other problematic traits on their records or being turned down because of errors in the database and the process (which market forces fail to cure). These problems resemble instances which can be covered by the concepts of consumer protection law mentioned above (if the regulator finds these steps necessary—and it indeed does by applying a breadth of banking and credit related laws). I will touch upon similar cases in the next example.

(B) The second story, which was reported in the New York Times and other publications in early 2009 (Lieber 2009) follows the credit card industry into the recent years of financial turmoil. It reveals an alarming practice that several US card issuers have adopted—"firing" their cardholders when they believed that their default is near (as opposed to terminating their credit lines once they began to fall back on their actual payments). Perhaps the issue that raised the most concern was the way the issuers deduced defaults were inevitable. This was done through the sophisticated analysis of transactional history of card holders which eventually defaulted, and later applying the rules the data revealed, again through the use of "predictive modeling," to the broader pool of card users. This analysis allows American Express (as well as others) to pinpoint establishments, forms and times of transactions which are indicative of a looming default. To avoid the actual defaults (and thus to limit their potential exposure), the card companies acted defensively and limited the "suspicious" card holder's credit line (in accordance to its right to do so, based on the initial agreement with the card holder).

The report indicates a mixed outcome. It appears that in view of these media reports, some firms have scaled back on these practices and stated that they will refrain from limiting credit on the basis of the specific venue where the card was used, while others are carrying them out more subtly (for examples, see Dehigg 2009). There is little doubt, however, that these stories are merely the beginning of a new trend of assessing and hedging risks by card issuers, as well as a cat-and-mouse game between them, card holders, businesses (whose role I will introduce shortly) and regulators.

Fitting this story and the process it describes into the three-part analysis addressed above leads to interesting results and insights regarding profiling concerns. First, again the underlying data collection process (the formation of the profile) is probably inevitable. The credit card business evolves around handling the transactional information of its customers. While it is true that there are potential models for carrying out the process of clearing transactions without maintaining the databases here addressed (such as by using e-cash, (Chaum 1992)), those have failed to gain substantial traction. Second, the analysis and data mining enabling the practice discussed in this example is also very hard to block, on both a practical and a normative level. Practically speaking, it is fair to assume that card issuers will *always* demand that they be allowed to analyze transaction-related data to maintain creditworthiness, as this matter stands at the center of their business model. It does not seem reasonable or efficient that card issuers (as well as other card holders, for that matter) assume the risk of default by clients without the ability to hedge their risks while tracking their consumer actions, especially in a tight economy. In addition, it is unlikely that consumers (or courts and regulators for the matter) will choose to restrict the usage of the databases held by the credit card issuers to mere billing activity (strictly defined). Analyses of credit card information greatly benefits consumers by protecting them from credit card fraud and allowing the firms to provide them with occasional discounts.

At this point, many readers would remain unconvinced, and argue that this story is precisely an example of regulation that should focus on the "analysis" stage. Namely, that (as the article itself suggests) consumers would demand that specific factors, such as the name of the store, or the identity of the product purchased would not be taken into account throughout the analysis of "predictive defaults" (and regulators should assure these demands are met). Yet I believe that this context actually presents an example as to the limitations of the regulation of analysis—which would here prove to be both meaningless and almost unenforceable. It would prove meaningless because data mining analysis allows these firms to conduct an array of analyses while relying on an abundance of other factors (some of which were mentioned in the news report) such as the timing, number, size and location of transactions—as well as the interactions among these factors. Any one of these factors can raise a flurry of privacy-related issues—while blocking one factor as opposed to another would do little to avoid them. The "name of establishment" factor happened to gain public traction because it is easy to grasp (and other reasons addressed below). These limitations are also to a certain extent unenforceable, as it is quite difficult to limit firms from using information at their disposal.

Therefore, the response to this issue as well is best resolved by examining the actual uses of the data—which leads to the *third* element of our analytic framework—and the four factors we mentioned (which I would now examine). First, one must address the beneficial outcomes of these practices. These practices have their advantages (as a tool that allows for a better match of risks and rewards among consumers and firms within this industry). The fear that this process is tainted and will lead to errors of various kinds is substantial, but could be possibly met by rules which will prohibit the error-ridden processes (although such rules would be quite difficult to enforce). The process might have additional negative effects—such as a cross-subsidy between sophisticated consumers (who understand the ways in which the process can be "gamed" and the issuers are led to believe the users' finances are sound) and non sophisticated consumers. In addition, it might generate negative externalities, by motivating consumers to refrain from using their credit cards when engaging in transactions which might indicate potential defaults. Obviously, all these elements must be reviewed prior to limiting these practices (although many of these problems exist in today's legal and business setting as well).

In addition, one must wonder whether the issues at hand can be covered by consumer protection concepts applied to this specific context. I would carefully argue that consumer protection laws might provide a partial response. On the most basic level these rules might set out a framework that provides a minimal level of access to credit—regardless of the users' specific traits. In addition, such rules can map out which forms of information can and cannot be used in this context (as the US credit laws do)—although, as mentioned, such rules suffer severe shortcomings. More specifically to this context (and given the shortcomings of relying on the steps mentioned alone), such rules could take aim at knowledge asymmetries between consumers and card issuers *regarding the chances for default*—gaps which result from the inevitable process of profiling and analysis of personal information described above. In other words, consumers should be informed what the chances of their default are—and perhaps what they can do about it (although such information might not always be available). In addition, if consumers are unable to control the way information is gathered and used and cannot really understand why they were marked as "default risks," they should be provided with the opportunity to correct this impression. In other words, the problem at hand is caused by profiling, yet it can be partially resolved through concepts taken from the realm of consumer protection (as opposed to the previous example). As mentioned, however, some of these information asymmetries will be very hard to correct. Yet resolving *all* information asymmetries might not be an important policy objective. The practices have at least some utility. While it is true they generate concern and an overall negative response—that might be resolved through the workings of the market and social pressures on the relevant firms (which I now examine).

Next, we must examine the ability of social and market forces to resolve these issues on their own. The article demonstrates several ways in which these forces indeed caused the firms to scale back their aggressive strategies, and thus perhaps limiting the role of regulators. However, relying upon market pressures to protect card holders in this context is, in my opinion, insufficient and the display of market forces transpiring in the report above is somewhat deceiving. The economic forces which "protected" consumers at one juncture would not necessarily be in play at another. For instance, singling out specific establishments of credit card use as an indication of potential default was an especially foolish strategy for the card issuers—since they are directly compensated by these vendors and have little interest in angering them directly. However, when card issuers will turn to more subtle and elaborate elements, consumers will be left to their "own devices" and might be unable to convince the issuers to refrain from such conduct. Even when taking into account the competitive market for credit cards, one must only look to the recent calls to overhaul the credit card industry's regulatory framework to understand that markets forces cannot resolve various concerns generated in this context and consumer protection rules would be needed.

To conclude the analysis of this example, I turn to the last factor. This example, I believe, does not consist of a situation in which consumers are manipulated on the basis of the additional insights into their inner persona that the data analysis reveals. Nonetheless, the knowledge of these practices generates a strong visceral response with many consumers (as the news reports clearly indicate)—a reason for closely looking at the practice at hand—though an insufficient reason (on its own) for applying new forms of regulation to the data flow of personal information. In sum, while this example seems almost as aggravating as the previous one—the strategy for dealing with it must be quite different. It calls for closing the information gap between the credit card issues and holders—a task that scholars and the recent American administration are indeed tackling with vigor at this time. Specific forms of regulation addressing the usage stage directly seem as a feasible response.

(C) Our next story presents us with the next stage of financial activity which transpired in view of the looming financial crisis. Here we examine yet another New York Times news report which addresses the most recent application of profiling and analysis of personal information—assistance in debt collection (Duhigg 2009). According to this report, credit card companies (or the collection agencies they employ) work through the personal data concerning the debtor which is at their disposal, to map out the best psychological strategy for convincing him or her to pay them the maximum amount possible out of the sum they owe. For instance, they analyze the debtors' behavior and come up with ways to deepen the relationship between the consumers and the relevant financial firms—and in that way strengthen the debtor's commitment to pay their bills. On the basis of this information some debtors are offered steep discounts on their bills, while others are not—but in exchange are offered kind and encouraging words, or maybe a scolding for not "living up to their word". The article shows at least anecdotal evidence of the success of these strategies.

What should be the regulatory response to these practices, which are enabled by the extensive profiling and subsequent targeting carried out by credit card companies, collection agencies and other entities? To respond I apply the three-tier test offered above. *First,* it is again apparent that the collection of the information, though problematic, is inevitable. The data in play is collected during the ongoing operations of the credit card issuers (billing) and the collection agencies (such as recording when and where the debtor answers the phone). It is very difficult (on various levels—as discussed above) to restrict the creation of such data sets. *Second,* the analysis and mining of such information is again difficult to block both positively and normatively. Even if recognizing a data subject's right to control the secondary uses of information after the time of collection, credit card issuers will maintain their right to analyze all data at their disposal to assure payment in full. Consumers will most likely agree, perhaps because they will have no choice, and perhaps because of well documented biases which lead them to underestimate the chances they will default and thus be subject to such analysis. Normatively, it makes perfect sense that firms should be allowed to analyze the information at their disposal to find debtors and convince them to pay in full (as these are sums the card users actually owe). The challenge, again, seems to be drawing the line between legitimate and illegitimate practices, which lead us to the *third* tier of the information flow and our analysis.

Confronting the usage of personal information at this context is again a thorny task—and I move to apply the four factors discussed. The use of such information (in the way here described) does convey some benefits to society in general—having debtors pay in full (or at least as much as possible) leads to a fair distribution of resources between consumers who pay their bills and those whom refrain from doing so. However, there are vast detriments. Again this process might lead to an unwanted cross subsidy between assertive and sophisticated consumers (for instance, those who know to demand and insist that the card issuer slash their debt at least in half, or else they will declare bankruptcy and the issuer will remain with nothing) and others—not necessarily an ideal policy objective or a fair outcome. But above all, the story *seems* unfair—yet finding the proper paradigm for articulating this negative feeling is challenging. We will try and uncover it below.

When considering the practices here described, it is hard to see how they could be curbed by market and social forces. As mentioned above, the actions of collection agents at the time of default are hardly issues consumers consider at the time of acquiring a card (and thus signing the service contract) given the non-salience of the matter and the debtors' inability to properly understand the risk involved (Korobkin 2003). In addition, it is hard to believe that the limited voices of these defaulting debtors will move regulators to action. To that, one must add the fact that the dynamics described above are almost always hard to decipher; debtors might never know they could have gotten away with less, or were "sweet-talked" into paying their bills. They might indeed discover these factors at a much later stage, but even then be too ashamed to act upon these matters.

Consumer protection rules might curb some concerns, yet not others in this context. Existing laws might limit the access collectors have to their debtor, as well as the forms of threats and pressures they can apply. In addition, some of the problems here addressed indeed result from information and power asymmetries among the parties, and could be resolved by closing these gaps. Thus, this context might call for a specific set of disclosures: For instance, collectors might be required to indicate the average percentage of the overall debt that debtors usually pay at this juncture, as well as present fairly what are the debtor's rights.

However, as with the first example, the disparities in power and information only tell part of the story. It appears that the situation at hand calls for a specific set of considerations, given the card issuers'-turned collectors' ability to try and manipulate their customers (the forth factor in our analysis). Here again the collectors can take advantage of the insights they have gained into the personality traits of the data subjects, so to influence them to pay in full. In view of these practices, debtors might opt to pay, even if this might conflict with their "real" preferences and long term goals. For that reason, this story illuminates a particularly troubling side of profiling, and calls for a specific solution to this challenge, which goes beyond the notions of consumer protection. This is what distinguishes the current example from the previous (second) one. We will touch upon measures to resolve this issue, below.

(D) Our final story is very different. Here I am referring to a recent article, in which the New York Times' technology reporter describes (at length and with some admiration) the extensive profiling practices of *Netflix,* the internet based DVD-rental firm (Thompson 2008). Netflix closely examines and analyzes the tastes and previous consumption patterns of its customers,[2] and makes recommendations as to which DVDs they might find desirable.[3] This has been found to be easier said than done in view of the complexity of predicting content tastes and preferences. Netflix has even chosen to offer a One Million US Dollar prize ("The Netflix Challenge") to programmers who would assist it in improving the algorithm used for matching movie recommendations to specific individuals, above a certain threshold.

While the overall sense of this project seems mostly positive, it is still worth examining through the same analytic lenses the other examples were put through. I begin with the three-part information flow. In this example as well, we witness the *collection* of information within a close relationship between service provider and customer—a collection process which would be hard to restrict. Thereafter, the example refers to the *analysis* of information (through the use of data mining), which is probably acceptable and thus cannot be blocked due to the consent of users at the time of collection, and the overall value is generates. Note that at this juncture these two conclusions (regarding the collection and analysis) might be open to debate, especially in the EU context; unlike the financial setting it seems quite possible for this media firm to operate without retaining historical record data, or analyzing it at a later time (but by merely offering DVD rentals at the consumers' requests). It is also quite apparent to the regulator watching from aside that personal information is put to use for the recommendation process. Thus, regulatory authorities could relatively easily enforce a restriction to analyze information for this task (as well as punish violators of such a restriction) if it deems these processes as unacceptable to consumers. Therefore, this example actually shows that in a regime which strives to tightly restrict secondary use—the

[2] For the moment, it appears Netflix merely relies on the previous films ordered when making recommendations and the consumers' satisfaction with them, while not taking into account the age, gender, location, etc. of the patron. According to the article, Netflix officials actually don't find this form of information very helpful for the recommendation task.

[3] While on its face this example is not connected to the financial crisis, one is tempted to note some incidental links—for instance that the financial downtown has presumably been quite good for firms like Netflix, as consumers scale back their spending and choose to save on entertainment, while deciding to enjoy more evenings at home, accompanied by the entertainment Netflix and others provide.

somewhat innocuous analysis carried by Netflix is likely to be stifled. This is as opposed to the very problematic analyses drawn out in the examples mentioned above—which are very likely to be permitted. I see this as yet additional evidence to the unsuitability of coping with profiling concerns by restricting collection and secondary use.

I now move to address the third stage of information usage (under the assumption that the analysis and secondary use of the data has been permitted in this case by law and/or contract). As before, I here examine the four factors—starting with the question as to whether the process benefits the parties involved. A powerful recommendation mechanism benefits Netflix (though somewhat indirectly, as I explain below), as it strengthens the appeal of its service to both existing and prospective patrons given the sheer size of their inventory (over 100,000 movies). Such applications might even be rendered a "must" for firms that service the "long tail" of products and options which online vendors can provide. With this tool in hand, Netflix is able to distinguish itself in the competitive market of content distribution (which includes video rental stores, broadcasters and other new and unique online ventures). In addition, it appears that these processes are helpful to the consumer as well (I am setting aside for the moment the somewhat social/educational discussion as to whether watching more TV and movies is indeed ever in the benefit of the end-user); recommendations—if they are good—cut search costs for consumers and provide them with what they want in less time.

It should be noted that the process can generate some detriments; users might be aggravated by the prospect that their media preferences (that certainly give a great deal of insight to their personal preferences, personality and many aspects of their lives) are held by a third party they might not trust (though applying pseudonymity is not very difficult, thus minimizing this problem). They might also be annoyed by recommendations that are wrong, offended by recommendations they find insulting, or even appalled by the accuracy of Netflix's ability to "guess" what they would be interested in next. I believe, however, that these detriments could be resolved in part by market forces (thus addressing the third element of our analysis, above) as well as by technical and business solutions. Netflix competes with a broad array of content services, and will clearly try and keep its consumers happy. I further believe that those detriments which cannot be resolved are a relatively small price we all must pay for the conveniences of modern life (although others might disagree).

The databases constructed and applied in this example indeed generate potential power and information gaps between consumers and the firm. However, in terms of our analysis of the usage stage, there are, at this time at least, limited issues which require consumer protection. One issue that indeed requires regulatory intervention (which indeed exists in the EU context and to some extent in the US) pertains to *data security*—the duty of the entities controlling the database to hold it in a secure manner which would protect it from both internal and external attacks. Although this issue goes beyond the reach of this paper, it should be noted that Netflix has allowed for an alarming security lapse to take place (even though it probably acted in good faith; Lemos 2007)—which compromised sensitive information of many of its users. However, existing rules pertaining to data security in the online realm should prove sufficient in resolving this concern. Obviously, additional consumer related concerns might arise with possible changes in the Netflix business model, and regulators should keep their eyes open towards such changes (as I will demonstrate below).

This all leads to the final stage of our analysis—whether Netflix could and indeed might use its knowledge resources to manipulate its consumers—and the regulatory implications of such abilities. The news reports regarding Netflix, as well as the overall public opinion regarding the matter are overall positive and indicate no traces of such fears or actual practices. On its face, therefore, the concerns voiced when addressing our first and third examples above seem irrelevant. Yet these examples do present similar traits—a recommendation system premised on knowledge derived from an ongoing relationship between the relevant parties. How can we explain the difference—and introduce it into our model? How would we know when concerns of potential manipulation arise? Are the differences in the attitudes towards these examples and firms a result of good/bad PR—or are there substantial reasons for this disparity?

I would suggest that the key to the different treatment and response towards the previous examples and the Netflix story is not premised on law, but might result from the different business models applied. Netflix gains only indirectly from the improvement of its recommendation process. At this point, Netflix's business model is premised on a fixed monthly price, whatever the number of rentals. Thus, Netflix's most profitable clients are probably those who sign up for the service, yet use it irregularly. The recommendation system seems to render benefits to the customers, and indirectly to the Netflix brand. The financial institutions mentioned in examples (A) through (C), however, benefit directly from every additional transaction their recommendation systems leads to. This indeed motivates them to manipulate, and it generates fears that such manipulations are in place (and thus potentially triggering a regulatory response).

Yet even though the Netflix story does not generate concerns or visceral responses, these might not be too far away. Online content vendors such as Amazon.com or iTunes offer elaborate recommendation mechanisms. However, unlike Netflix, they both benefit directly from a sound recommendation which would potentially induce a prospective consumer to engage in additional transactions and thus increase their revenue and profit. The regulatory intervention (if any) such dynamics require are again one of the key challenges in confronting profiling practices. As I previously explained, here we must address the blurring line between tools which *give* consumer what they want—and *tell* consumers what that is. These issues go beyond our current understanding of both privacy and consumer protection law. Yet they are the key challenge of these fields today. Thus, the analysis of this example, in accordance to the four-factor taxonomy mentioned, shows that the Netflix example can quite quickly generate the serious concerns of manipulative conduct addressed above, should Netflix choose to alter its business model, ever so slightly!

4.4 Some Conclusions and Summing Up

As I explained above, profiling practices challenge legal thinkers and policy makers by generating novel situations, with privacy and autonomy-related problems that are hard to establish and conceptualize. However, identifying the problematic junctures and fitting them into taxonomies only takes us halfway towards resolving the situation at hand. I conclude this chapter by drawing out initial and general strategies to overcome the problems and challenges discussed in the previous sections.

At first, even though the emphasis of this chapter was on the final usage stage, at times regulatory solutions are called for at the earlier stages of *collection* and *analysis.* Many of such solutions are already in place, and prohibit the collection of especially sensitive bits of information. In addition, at times, prohibitions on forms of analyses which have great potential for abuse and user agitation are mandated—and even US law has introduced limitations on the analysis of medical data for later commercial use.[4]

Yet, the most delicate issues pertain to the firms' use of personal information to either take advantage of information asymmetries or to manipulate consumers, while using the insights they gain to the consumers' inner thought processes, preferences and vulnerabilities. Throughout this chapter I provide initial responses to deal with the information asymmetries (mostly through consumer protection law and concepts), while merely indicating the existence of manipulation. Dealing with this latter issue will require at least two stages. At first, a comparative analysis which will involve law, technology, business and mainly the social sciences (with an emphasis on psychology) must be launched. This study must strive to establish empirically the actual and potential effects of using consumer profiles vis-à-vis the consumers' preferences, willpower and behavior. The findings of these studies will be crucial for framing the next policy moves.

The next step would be mapping out the policy options for dealing with these matters. Here, categorizing the issue at hand as one which resembles "undue influence" and "unfair manipulation" will prove very helpful, as it will guide us towards a specific set of regulatory responses, which are premised on existing doctrines. Here we can partially rely upon legal doctrine applied elsewhere, where the law strives to shield individuals from the overreaching hand of those trying to unfairly influence them. In some instances, laws *distance* those attempting to manipulate from their perspective victims (as in Election law at the time of the elections). In others, laws provide individuals with *cool off periods* to rethink a transaction when subjected to powerful influences (such as in door-to-door sales). In yet other instances, the law mandates *transparency* and full disclosure of potential motivations and other information when approaching individuals (such as in advertising and promotions—both in print and over the air). Finally, in extreme situations, the law *prohibits* the potentially manipulative communications all together (such as in advertising to minors and other specific contexts).

---

[4] For a recent ruling on this issue, see *IMS Health, Inc.v. Ayotte,* 550 F.3d 42, (1st Cir. 2008).

The real challenge for policy makers in the context of information privacy and data protection in the years to come would be matching each of these remedies to the specific incidents of personal information usage. This must be done on the basis of the analysis presented here (which requires further elaboration), a deep understanding of the harms the data usage causes and the empirical findings yet to come. These issues will clearly provide much work and food for thought for scholars and regulators. Returning to the examples presented above (specifically to those which I suspected as demonstrating unfairly manipulative practices), I would argue that Example (A) would call for "cool off" periods (which would allow consumers to contemplate the offers of the banks) and even prohibition of some transactions. Example (C) will call for greater transparency in the collection process. It should also call for "distancing" the debtor and the collector who might try and contact him or her at times of vulnerability. Yet much additional analysis must be carried out prior to the formulation of policy at this juncture.

The challenges mapped out within this short chapter are great. To overcome the challenges of profiling, I practically call for the erection of several conceptual bridges among almost foreign concepts; I call for the meshing of the American notions of privacy protection (or lack thereof) with the European understanding of Data Protection (and its limits). I also call for connecting the American themes and concepts of market solutions with the European ideas of regulatory intervention, while protecting the individual's autonomy. Finally, I draw upon the laws of consumer protection to answer for the troubles of data aggregation. These are extremely difficult tasks, yet I believe we must apply a great deal of ingenuity to handle the complexities we face in the realm of law and technology. The advent of technology and business practices presents intriguing challenges to legal experts. At times, we worry of technology running amok and leaving law staggering behind. In other cases, it is the law that quickly reacts to the new technological challenges, but in the process slows and limits innovation. Navigating clear of these problematic options to the shores of fair and optimal outcomes is an almost impossible challenge—but of course we must not be too timid to try.

References

Baker, Stephen. 2008. *The numerati.* New York: Houghton Mifflin Harcourt.

Cate, Fred H. 2001. *Privacy in perspective.* Washington, DC: AEI Press.

Cate, Fred H. 2006. The failure of fair information practice principles. In *Consumer Protection in the Age of the Information Economy,* ed. J.K. Winn, 358. Williston: Ashgate.

Chaum, David. 1992. Achieving electronic privacy. *Scientific American* 267: 96–101.

Duhigg, Charles. 2009. What does your credit-card company know about you? *New York Times Magazine*.

Gurak, Laura J. 1999. *Persuasion and privacy in cyberspace.* New Haven, CT: Yale Univ. Press.

Hirschman, Albert O. 1970. *Exit, voice and loyalty.* Cambridge, MA: Harvard Univ. Press.

Korobkin, Russel B. 2003. Bounded rationality, standard form contracts, and unconscionability, *University of Chicago Law Review* 70: 1203–1295.

Lemos, Robert. 2007. Researchers reverse Netflix anonymization. *Security Focus* (December 4).

Lieber, Ron. 2009. American Express kept a (very) watchful eye on charges. *New York Times*.
Parisi, Francesco. 2004. The harmonization of legal warranties in european sales law: An economic analysis. *American Journal of Comparative Law* 52 (2): 403–431.
Staten, Michael E., and Fred H. Cate. 2003. The impact of opt-in privacy rules on retail credit markets: A case study of MBNA. *Duke Law Journal* 52: 745–786.
Solove, Daniel J. 2008. *Understanding privacy.* Cambridge, MA: Harvard Univ. Press.
Stone, Brad. 2008. Banks mine data and woo troubled borrowers. *New York Times*.
Swire, Peter S., and Robert E. Litan, 1998. *None of your business* Washington, DC: Brookings Institution Press.
Thompson, Clive. 2008. If you liked this, you're sure to love that. *New York Times,* November 23, 2008.
Zarsky, Tal Z. 2002–2003. Mine your own business! Making the case for the implications of the data mining of personal information in the forum of public opinion. *Yale Journal of Law and Technology* 5: 1–57.
Zarsky, Tal Z. 2004. Desperately seeking solutions: Using implementation-based solutions for the troubles of information privacy in the age of data mining and the internet society. *Maine Law Review* 56 (1): 22,28.

Part II
Specific Issues: Security Breaches, Unsolicited Adjustments, Facebook, Surveillance and Electronic Voting

Chapter 5
The Emerging European Union Security Breach Legal Framework: The 2002/58 ePrivacy Directive and Beyond

Rosa Barcelo and Peter Traung

Hardly a day goes by without a new press report of a security breach resulting in the loss of thousands, perhaps millions, of records. People are potentially exposed to identity theft, financial loss and reputational damage when databases are hacked or suffer malfunctions disclosing such sensitive information as credit card numbers, financial account numbers, passwords or health related data.

Yet, up until now when these incidents occur, under EU legislation there is no explicit obligation to inform affected individuals and authorities. This is about to change. The revised ePrivacy Directive, as amended through the so called Citizens' Rights Directive,[1] sets forth an obligation for ISPs and telcos to notify affected individuals and authorities of security breaches leading to the compromise of personal data.[2]

This paper analyses the security breach notification framework established under the revised ePrivacy Directive. The paper first looks at the need for a breach noti-

Rosa Barcelo is legal adviser at the office of the European Data Protection Supervisor (EDPS). Peter Traung is an administrator at the Committee on Industry, Research and Energy of the European Parliament. Both authors were involved in the legislative process leading to the data breach notification rules discussed here. The views in this paper are personal to the authors and do not represent the views of either the European Parliament or the EDPS.

[1] Directive 2009/136/EC of the European Parliament and of the Council of 25 November 2009 amending Directive 2002/22/EC on universal service and users' rights relating to electronic communications networks and services, Directive 2002/58/EC concerning the processing of personal data and the protection of privacy in the electronic communications sector and Regulation (EC) No. 2006/2004 on cooperation between national authorities responsible for the enforcement of consumer protection laws.

[2] The new rules will have to be transposed into national law by the 27 Member States by 25 May 2011.

P. Traung (✉)
European Parliament
Committee on Industry, Research and Energy (ITRE),
ATR 00K035
DD: +32-(0)2-284 31 05
Mobile: +32-(0)477-33 02 54
e-mail: peter.traung@europarl.europa.eu

S. Gutwirth et al. (eds.), *Data Protection in a Profiled World*,
DOI 10.1007/978-90-481-8865-9_5,

fication requirement, as well as the principles and purposes underpinning the new EU security breach notification framework. Second, it analyses the main elements of the new EU provisions, including (1) the scope of the obligation to notify, (2) the notification criteria, timing, content and means of providing notice, and (3) the enforcement provisions. The paper also undertakes to compare this new framework with current breach notification requirements in the US. The last section discusses the future steps, including the expected forthcoming implementing measures complementing the present framework.

The paper shows that the emerging EU security breach framework strikes an appropriate balance between the protection of individuals' rights and the obligations imposed on entities and authorities.

5.1 Introduction

5.1.1 The EU Security Breach Legal Framework: The Background

On 13 November 2007, the European Commission adopted a proposal for a Directive *amending* Directive 2002/58 concerning the processing of personal data and the protection of privacy in the electronic communications sector (hereinafter 'Commission's Proposal').[3] Directive 2002/58 is often referred to, also in this paper, as the ePrivacy Directive. As further described below under Sect. 5.1.2, the Directive was finally adopted by Council on 26 October 2009.

The Commission proposal amending the ePrivacy Directive put forward, for the first time in the EU, a mandatory security breach notification framework. In general terms, mandatory data breach notification simply involves the holder of personal data notifying the person to whom the data belongs, and the relevant authorities, of security breaches leading to the accidental or unlawful destruction, loss, alteration or unauthorized disclosure of that data.

While the Data Protection[4] and ePrivacy Directives contain security requirements, an explicit obligation to report security breaches to authorities and inform individuals has so far not existed.[5]

[3] COM (2007) 698 final ("Citizens' Rights Directive") which in addition to the ePrivacy Directive also includes proposed changes to Directive 2002/22/EC on universal service and users' rights relating to electronic communications networks and Regulation (EC) No. 2006/2004 on consumer protection cooperation. While the proposal contained amendments also to two other Directives, for simplicity we will refer directly to the ePrivacy Directive, not the Citizens' Rights Directive.

[4] Directive 95/46/EC of the European Parliament and of the Council of 24 October 1995 on the protection of individuals with regard to the processing of personal data and on the free movement of such data.

[5] Article 4 of the ePrivacy Directive includes an obligation to notify subscribers in cases of *risk* of a breach of the security of the network: *"In case of a particular risk of a breach of the security of*

At EU Member State level, up until newly no Member State has passed personal data breach notification laws. But following recent events there, Germany adopted a federal data breach notification law.[6] Also, Spain has a system which has been referred to as a "notification 'like structure'[7] without, however, being sufficiently 'like'" to actually require notification.

This situation contrasts with that of the United States. Since 2003, when California introduced the first law on the subject, 44 additional US states have adopted security breach notification laws of varying complexity.[8] At federal level, various attempts to introduce a security breach notification law have so far been unsuccessful. The latest proposal is a bill to introduce a "Data Accountability and Trust Act".[9] Section 3(a) of that bill provides that any person engaged in interstate trade and who own or possesses electronic personal data shall notify a breach to individuals, if the breach led to an unauthorised third person acquiring the data, and also to the Federal Trade Commission.

5.1.2 The Review of the ePrivacy Directive

The Commission's proposal to amend the ePrivacy Directive was adopted as part of the "the telecoms package", intending to update the entire EU telecoms regulatory framework.[10]

---

the network, the provider of a publicly available electronic communications service must inform the subscribers concerning such risk and, where the risk lies outside the scope of the measures to be taken by the service provider, of any possible remedies, including an indication of the likely costs involved."

[6] For an overview of the German law, see e.g. Hunton & Williams, *"Germany Adopts Stricter Data Protection Law: Serious Impact on Business Compliance"*, http://www.hunton.com/files/tbl_s10News/FileUpload44/16482/germany_adopts_stricter_data_protection_law.pdf.

[7] Stewart Dresner and Amy Norcup, *"Data Breach Notification Laws in Europe"*, Report on Privacy Laws & Business, (8 May 2009), 14 f.

[8] Situation as of 27 July 2009. The laws can be found here: http://www.ncsl.org/programs/lis/cip/priv/breachlaws.htm.

[9] The bill can be found here: http://frwebgate.access.gpo.gov/cgi-bin/getdoc.cgi?dbname=111_cong_bills&docid=f:h2221ih.txt.pdf. The bill would also introduce requirements for those owning or possessing data to establish policies and procedures regarding information security practices for the treatment and protection of personal information. As regards the effect on state law, the bill provides that it *"supersedes any provision of a statute, regulation or rule of a State ... with respect to those entities covered by ... this Act"*. Later proposals are pending, see e.g. http://threatpost.com/en_us/blogs/two-data-breach-notification-bills-advance-senate-110609, but not addressed here.

[10] The proposals forming the telecoms package as well as the impact assessment and other relevant documentation can be found here: http://ec.europa.eu/information_society/policy/ecomm/library/proposals/index_en.htm.

On 6 May 2009, the European Parliament voted in second reading to adopt the ePrivacy Directive.[11] The vote was cast on an agreement between the European Parliament and Council on the texts of the telecoms package, including the ePrivacy Directive. Had the European Parliament fully endorsed the agreement reached with Council, the telecoms package as a whole would have become law. That did not happen. While the European Parliament adopted the ePrivacy Directive with the changes agreed to with Council, another part of the agreement however, an aspect of the Framework Directive, was rejected.[12]

Council referred the Framework Directive to conciliation and discussions regarding the one outstanding aspect of that Directive were successfully concluded on 5 November 2009, subject to approval by the European Parliament in plenary. In the meantime, given that there was no disagreement between Council and the European Parliament regarding the ePrivacy Directive, Council adopted the ePrivacy Directive on 26 October 2009. The Member States will therefore have to implement the revised ePrivacy Directive in their national laws by mid-2011. We hereafter refer to the new security breach provisions as **'the revised ePrivacy Directive'** or, in general, the **'EU security breach framework'**.[13]

5.1.3 An Overview of the Security Breach Framework Under the Revised ePrivacy Directive

Before engaging in a more detailed analysis of the new framework resulting from the revised ePrivacy Directive, it may be useful to provide a brief overview of its main provisions.

Pursuant to the revised ePrivacy Directive, security breaches leading to the accidental or unlawful destruction, loss, alteration, unauthorized disclosure of or access to personal data (collectively designated as **'compromised data'**), must be notified to affected individuals and to national regulatory authorities (**'authorities'**).

---

[11] The relevant documents produced by the European Parliament, Council and Commission during the legislative process can be found here: http://www.europarl.europa.eu/oeil/file.jsp?id=5563642, here: http://www.europarl.europa.eu/oeil/file.jsp?id=5563972 and here: http://www.europarl.europa.eu/oeil/file.jsp?id=5563982.

[12] The European Parliament reinstated the so-called Amendment 138, which refers to three strikes approach schemes.

[13] While the changes to the ePrivacy Directive are introduced through the separate Citizen's Rights Directive, to facilitate understanding this paper as mentioned, refers directly to the ePrivacy Directive where possible. References to **Articles** therefore are to, and follow the numbering of that Directive unless otherwise stated. References herein to **recitals** are to recitals to the Citizens' Rights Directive, unless otherwise stated. The text of the Citizen's Rights Directive as adopted by the European Parliament on 6 May 2009, which includes the Commission declaration referred to under Sect. 5.8.3 below, can be found here: http://www.europarl.ep.ec/sides/getDoc.do?pubRef=-//EP//TEXT±TA±P6-TA-2009-0360±0±DOC±XML±V0//EN&language=EN. The final text is available here: http://eurlex.europa.eu/JOIndex.do?year=2009&serie=L&textfield2=337&Submit=Search&_submit=Search&ihmlang=en.

The obligation to notify security breaches has two distinct parts. First, it includes an obligation to notify affected *individuals* when the breach is likely to adversely affect their personal data and privacy. An express exception to this obligation applies when the provider has *"implemented appropriate technical protection measures"*, rendering the data concerned by the breach unintelligible to any unauthorised person. Second, it includes an obligation to notify *authorities* which applies without exception.

Accordingly, the *threshold* over which notification to affected individuals is mandatory is when the breach is *likely to adversely affect* their privacy and personal data. The threshold is usually referred to as the 'standard' or 'trigger' for the notification.

Two additional elements must be considered: First, the definitions of 'data breach' and 'personal data'. As further developed below, both definitions are broad, which is likely to lead to many situations being caught by the scope of the obligations. Second, the types of entities bound by the obligation (**'covered entities'**). Under the revised text of the ePrivacy Directive, in principle, the covered entities are providers of communication services, which include ISPs and telecom providers. As described below, a wider coverage is envisaged in the near future.

5.2 Purposes and Existing Data Protection Principles Underpinning the New EU Security Breach Framework

5.2.1 Preventing and Minimising Adverse Effects for Individuals

The notification of security breaches makes individuals aware of the risks they face when their personal data are compromised and helps them to take the necessary measures to mitigate such risks. Indeed, the basic and most self evident ***purpose*** of the data breach notification framework is to enable individuals whose data has been compromised to take action against the effects of a breach, whether those effects are economic or not. For example, when alerted of breaches affecting their financial information, individuals will (or must) be able, among other things, to change passwords or cancel their accounts.

The revised ePrivacy Directive explicitly refers to this purpose as the justification for the security breach provisions. Indeed, Recital 59 explains that security breach notification reduces the adverse effects associated to breaches. In particular, it refers to economic loss, which for example, could happen following a breach of credit card and bank account related information. It also refers to social harm which could result, for example, from breaches of health, sexual or other sensitive types of information. Recital 61 confirms this reasoning: *"A personal data breach may, if not addressed in an adequate and timely manner, result in substantial economic loss and social harm, including identity fraud, to the subscriber or individual concerned. Therefore, as soon as the provider of publicly available electronic communications services becomes aware that such a breach has occurred, it should notify the...subscribers or individuals whose data and privacy could be adversely affected by such breaches...without delay in order to allow them to take the necessary precautions."*[14]

The notification of security breaches is not intended to and cannot solve *all* problems resulting from such incidents (i.e., completely safeguard against financial loss, much less against possible reputation damage if the data has been made publicly available). However, the obligation is meant to enable individuals to minimise, to the extent possible, the negative consequences that derive from them.

Whereas alerting and enabling affected individuals to react and take action to minimise the effects of security breaches is clearly the main objective of the EU mandatory security breach legislation, that framework has other important effects that contribute to compliance with existing data protection and privacy principles and overall protection of personal data. Compliance with those principles may not have been the primary effect or purpose sought through the security breach provisions, however, this does not minimise the importance of these ancillary effects. A description of the data protection principles which are reinforced as a result of the new requirements follows below.

5.2.2 The Security Principle

Article 17 of the Data Protection Directive requires a data controller to put in place measures to avoid any accidental or unlawful destruction, loss or alteration, against any unauthorised disclosure or access and against any other forms of unlawful processing, including with respect to transmission of data over a network.[15] This is mirrored in the ePrivacy Directive, which i.a. requires providers of communications services to take appropriate measures to safeguard security at a level appropriate to the risk presented (i.e., the risk that would materialise if the data is lost or other-

[14] At a high level, the Commission impact assessment, SEC (2007) 1472, indicates the following advantages and disadvantages on p. 115: *"On the other hand, notification to individuals on occasions where their personal data had been compromised could potentially discourage certain groups from using new technologies altogether or limit their use to the absolute minimum. However, this possible negative effect could be counter-balanced by the experience of empowerment and 'being in control', at least with respect to personal data."*

[15] *"Member States shall provide that the controller must implement appropriate technical and organizational measures to protect personal data against accidental or unlawful destruction or accidental loss, alteration, unauthorized disclosure or access, in particular where the processing involves the transmission of data over a network, and against all other unlawful forms of processing. Having regard to the state of the art and the cost of their implementation, such measures shall ensure a level of security appropriate to the risks represented by the processing and the nature of the data to be protected."*

wise compromised).[16] Breaches of these provisions can be sanctioned pursuant to Chap. 3 of the Data Protection Directive.

The revised ePrivacy Directive has added additional security provisions, applying to providers of communication services.[17] Furthermore, a new Chapter IIIA of the Framework Directive introduces requirements regarding security and integrity of networks and services.

The introduction of security breach notification requirements is likely to lead to improved data security practices. Mandatory breach notification means that security breaches are frequently reported in the news, resulting in reputation damage to covered entities, particularly in cases of repeated breaches. Furthermore, economic costs derived from security breaches may be high.[18] In addition to direct costs, a security breach may require hiring lawyers, auditors and accounting firms, as well as adding customer support resources. The potential for lost productivity is also important.

Clearly, in order to avoid both the reputation and economic costs derived from security breaches, covered entities can be expected to implement stronger security measures to protect personal information and prevent breaches. This means that they will increase their investment in security and also pay closer attention to their internal administrative and organisational measures towards the protection of personal data. By doing so, they are working towards reinforcing compliance with the security principle.

---

[16] Article 4(1): *"The provider of a publicly available electronic communications service must take appropriate technical and organisational measures to safeguard security of its services, if necessary in conjunction with the provider of the public communications network with respect to network security. Having regard to the state of the art and the cost of their implementation, these measures shall ensure a level of security appropriate to the risk presented."*

[17] The text added to the ePrivacy Directive reads: *"Without prejudice to Directive 95/46/EC, the measures referred to in paragraph 1 shall at least: ensure that personal data can be accessed only by authorised personnel for legally authorised purposes;—protect personal data stored or transmitted against accidental or unlawful destruction, accidental loss or alteration, and unauthorised or unlawful storage, processing, access or disclosure; and—ensure the implementation of a security policy with respect to the processing of personal data."* The new provisions in the Framework Directive (Directive 2002/21/EC of the European Parliament and of the Council of 7 March 2002 on a common regulatory framework for electronic communications networks and services) require providers to notify the authorities of any breach of security or integrity having a significant impact on the operation of the network or services.

[18] Cost estimates relating to 2007, while difficult to interpret, are USD 197 for the US and GBP 47 for the UK, in both cases per record compromised (*2007 Annual Study: U.S. Cost of a Data Breach* and *2007 Annual Study: U.K. Cost of a Data Breach*, published by PGP and Symantec for the US and PGP and Vontu for the UK, both based on research by the Ponemon Institute). The Ponemon Institute also indicate the average cost of a data breach in Germany in 2008 as EUR 112 per record compromised, http://www.pgp.com/insight/newsroom/press_releases/2008_annual_study_germany_cost_of_data_breach.html. For the UK and Germany, these estimates of course do not take into account a mandatory breach notification requirement. The New York State Consumer Protection Board's *Business Privacy Guide* (October 2008) indicates an average cost for the provider of each breach incident of USD 192. The Commission's Impact Assessment does not attempt to particularise costs.

5.2.3 The Data Minimisation Principle

Article 6(1)(b) of the Data Protection Directive requires that processing be limited to the purpose originally notified to the data subject. This principle has contributed to the concept of data minimisation, also expressed in Article 6(1)(c), meaning that the processing of personal data must be restricted to the minimum necessary.

Security breach legislation is likely to contribute to the implementation of this principle. This is because collecting and maintaining large volumes of information increases the likelihood of security breaches and the inherent legal liability and the reputation damage that come with them. Entities will realise that a way to diminish such risk is by implementing a strict minimisation policy requiring either discarding information that may not be absolutely necessary or simply abstaining from collecting such information.

5.2.4 The Information Principle

EU data protection law requires that data processing is fair, among other things meaning that the individual must be able to know about the facts and circumstances related to the processing of her/his data. This information principle is expressed in Articles 10–11 of the Data Protection Directive and also covers transfers of data to third parties. Recital 39 of the same Directive elaborates on the individual's right to be informed when data about him/her is disclosed to third parties, even if such disclosure was not envisaged at first.

The revised ePrivacy Directive explicitly refers to the general interest of individuals to know about their data as an explanation that justifies the mandatory security breach obligation. Recital 59 states: *"... the notification of security breaches reflects a general interest of citizens in being informed of security failures which could result in their personal data being lost or otherwise compromised, as well as of available or advisable precautions that they could take in order to minimise the possible economic loss or social harm that could result from such failures. The interest of users in being notified is clearly not limited to the electronic communications sector ..."*

The above reflects the importance of the individual's right to information about the use of his or her personal data. The security breach notification provisions are a logical consequence of the application of this principle. Insofar as data controllers are obliged to notify voluntary transfers of personal data, it should follow that also involuntary data disclosures must be notified to the data subject.[19]

---

[19] This could be viewed as an argument for a data breach notification obligation already being imposed by the information principle as laid down in existing EU data protection law.

5.2.5 The Accountability Principle

Under EU data protection law, including the ePrivacy Directive and the Data Protection Directive, natural and legal persons who process personal data are accountable towards individuals and authorities for the protection and appropriate use of that data.

Accountability extends to a variety of obligations such as those described in the sections above as well as giving access to information, ensuring that the data is accurate, etc. The obligation to notify security breaches builds upon these existing obligations. In fact, it enhances the accountability of those bound by the obligation to notify. First, it does so because the notification in itself entails an assumption of responsibility regarding the personal information that has been compromised. By notifying authorities and individuals, entities become more answerable for their actions in connection with their processing of personal data. Second, security breaches enhance accountability by compelling entities that process personal data to be more diligent in the way they handle the data, which entails increased application of state of the art administrative, technical, and physical safeguards in order to protect the information.

The purpose of mandatory notification of security breaches does not seem to include punishing the entities that suffered the breach, as may be the case in the United States.[20] This is because existing EU data protection legislation already provides sanctions for violation of the mandatory data protection rules, including the security provisions. Therefore, there is no need to shoehorn the mandatory notification of security breach notification into pursuing an already met objective. However, it is likely that in the context of examining the facts and circumstances related to a particular personal data breach, authorities will also review compliance with other data protection obligations such as the security provisions. This could lead to the imposition of sanctions if violation of such provisions is uncovered. If mandatory breach notification serves the purpose of punishing entities for lack of security (or for breach of other provisions), these entities could be dissuaded from reporting the breach to authorities and that would be a counterproductive outcome of the new provisions.

[20] See P.M. Schwartz and E.J. Janger, "Notification of Data Security Breaches", *Michigan Law Review* 105 (March 2007): 913, 916 *"... seek to punish the breached entity and protect consumers ..."*. The aim of punishing the breached entity may be dominant, idem p. 957: *"Notification letters have the potential to (1) create a credible threat of negative costs or other punishments for the firm..."* and 917: *"...notification serves another, often overlooked function: it can help ... consumers ... mitigate the harm caused by a leak"*. The federal bill discussed above under Sect. 5.1.1 states that its purpose is *"to protect consumers by requiring reasonable security policies...to protect personal information, and to provide for nationwide notice in the event of a security breach"*.

5.3 Elements of the EU Security Breach Notification Framework

In analysing the security breach notification provisions, there are four critical points to consider, further discussed in Sects. 5.4–5.7.

- First, their *scope*. This requires an analysis of the definition of security breach as well as of the covered entities;
- Second, the *standard* that triggers the obligation to notify and its exceptions;
- Third, the means of providing *notice*, the timing and the content of the notice, and
- Fourth, the *enforcement* provisions.

5.4 Scope of the EU Security Breach Notification Framework

The scope of the data breach notification provisions follows from a combination of the definition of personal data breach and from the definition of covered entities, as discussed below.

5.4.1 Entities Obliged to Notify: Covered Entities

Article 4(3) subparagraph 1: *"In the case of a personal data breach, the provider of publicly available electronic communications services shall ... notify ..."*

Pursuant to Article 4(3) subparagraph 1 the entities obliged to notify security breaches are limited to providers of electronic communication services. In order to understand the practical implications of this, the following remarks are relevant.

First, electronic communications services are defined in Article 2 of the Framework Directive. They cover services normally provided for remuneration that consists wholly or mainly in the conveyance of signals on an electronic network. The definition excludes provision of content and also of information society services, which do not consist wholly or mainly in the conveyance of signals on electronic communications networks.

Second, in practice the above means that the core of entities covered by the mandatory security breach notification obligation only includes providers of communications and Internet access, excluding for instance providers of hosting services or Web 2.0 platform providers.

Third, independently of the above, the outer boundaries of the definition of electronic communications service are not clear. Whereas providers of telephony (including VoIP) service and Internet access are clearly covered, it is uncertain whether providers of certain other, similar, services are included as well. Indeed, various

Directives in the communications area indicate that services such as "electronic mail conveyance" or "Web email" (which may be something different than "electronic mail conveyance") are covered. But this does not seem crystal clear. [21]

Fourth, the criterion "publicly available" is not defined but is in broad terms met if the service is available to the public at large.[22]

Fifth, in this context, it may be of interest to note that the terms "data controller" and "data processor", concepts that are defined and central to the Data Protection Directive, are not used in the security breach notification provisions. This would seem to support the view that providers of communications services are obligated to notify independently of whether they are data controllers or data processors.[23]

5.4.2 The Application to Information Society Services and Beyond

Recital 59: *"Community law imposes duties on data controllers regarding the processing of personal data, including an obligation to implement appropriate technical and organisational protection measures against, for example, loss of data. The data breach notification requirements contained in Directive 2002/58/EC (Directive on privacy and electronic communications) provide a structure for notifying the competent authorities and individuals concerned when personal data has nevertheless been compromised. Those notification requirements are limited to security breaches which occur in the electronic communications sector. However, the notification of security breaches reflects the general interest of citizens in being informed of security failures which could result in their personal data being lost or otherwise compromised, as well as of available or advisable precautions that they could take in order to minimise the possible economic loss or social harm that could result from such failures. The interest of users in being notified is clearly not limited to the electronic communications sector, and therefore explicit, mandatory notification requirements applicable to all sectors should be introduced at Community level as a matter of priority ..."*

---

[21] See Recital 10 to the Framework Directive, Recital 6 and 16 to the ePrivacy Directive and Recital 13 to Directive 2006/24/EC on the retention of data generated or processed in connection with the provision of publicly available electronic communications services or of public communications networks and amending Directive 2002/58/EC. Eleni Kosta and Peggy Valcke, "Retaining the Data Retention Directive", *Computer Law and Security Report* 22 (2006):, 374, discuss problems relating to the definition of electronic communications services, in particular in relation to webmail.

[22] Compare Recital 55. See also the elaborate analysis in Ofcom's Regulation of VoIP Services, paragraphs A.5.39–45: http://www.ofcom.org.uk/consult/condocs/voipregulation/voipstatement/voipstatement.pdf.

[23] Compare the distinction made in Recital 47 of the Data Protection Directive. That recital establishes that the controller for traffic data relating to an email is the provider whereas the controller with respect to the content of the same email is the sender.

The issue whether to limit the scope of the security breach notification breach to providers of communication services and ISPs or extend it was far from uncontroversial. The European Parliament took the view that at least providers of information society services such as on-line banks, on-line retailers, on-line health providers etc., should also be covered.

During the legislative process, the EDPS and the Working Party 29[24] voiced their support for the European Parliament's position.[25]

The Commission, supporting the Council, consistently opposed such an extension of the scope, on the basis, as expressed in the Commission's amended proposal of 6 November 2008, that *"the inclusion of providers of information society services goes beyond the current scope of the regulatory framework ... and is accordingly deleted"*[26]—that is, the overall scope of the Directive is meant to regulate providers of communications and access only. However, this formal rationale is undermined substantially by the existence of other sections in the ePrivacy Directive that have a broader application.

Furthermore, the type of information commonly held by providers of information society services may partly be identical to that held by providers of communications services and may frequently contain additional and more sensitive information. Individuals can be as likely, or more, to suffer harm from the undue disclosure of bank-account details as from the disclosure of, for example, their telephone bills. Thus, the sensitivity of the information compromised weighs heavily in favour of including at least providers of information society services in the obligation to notify.

In sum, citizens' expectations for a much broader application of data breach notification are clearly not met with the current scope of the revised ePrivacy Directive.[27] From a user perspective, it does not matter whether personal data are lost by a provider of communications services or by someone else.

---

[24] Working Party 29 was set up under Article 29 of Directive 95/46/EC. It is an independent European advisory body on data protection and privacy. Its tasks are described in Article 30 of the Data Protection Directive and Article 15 of the ePrivacy Directive.

[25] EDPS Second opinion of 9 January 2009 on the review of Directive 2002/58/EC concerning the processing of personal data and the protection of privacy in the electronic communications sector (Directive on privacy and electronic communications, *Official Journal* C128 (06 June 2009): 28); Working Party 29 opinion 2/2008 on the review of the Directive 2002/58/EC on privacy and electronic communications (ePrivacy Directive), adopted on 15 May 2008. The issue of a broader scope was raised by the EDPS in his first opinion of 10 April 2008, *Official Journal* C181 (18 July 2008): 1. The EDPS opinions are available here: http://www.edps.europa.eu/EDPSWEB/edps/site/mySite/pid/82 and the Working Party 29 opinions here: http://ec.europa.eu/justice_home/fsj/privacy/workinggroup/wpdocs/2009_en.htm.

[26] COM (2008)723 final, p. 17.

[27] The Commission impact assessment, see footnote 15, reports on p. 115 that 64% of Europeans responded positively to the proposition that they would like to be informed "in all circumstances" if their personal data (such as name, address and credit card details) were lost. The question asked was not limited to telecom providers: "Companies like telecom providers collect personal data such as name, address and credit card details. In case any of your personal data was lost, stolen or altered in any way, would you like to be informed or not?", *Special Eurobarometer 274, E-com-*

Whereas this limitation of the scope of the ePrivacy Directive is regrettable, the discussions on the issue resulted in Recital 59 recognising the importance of security breach across sectors, and announcing that *"explicit, mandatory notification requirements applicable to all sectors should be introduced at Community level as a matter of priority"* as well as in a declaration by the Commission that it would promptly initiate preparatory work to extend mandatory security breach notification in other areas. This is discussed below under Sect. 5.8. For the time being however, the situation is that of a limited scope.

5.4.3 Definition of 'Personal Data Breach'

Article 2(h): *"'personal data breach' means a breach of security leading to the accidental or unlawful destruction, loss, alteration, unauthorised disclosure of, or access to, personal data transmitted, stored or otherwise processed in connection with the provision of a publicly available electronic communications service in the Community."*

Whereas, as described above, the type of covered entities concerned by the obligation is very limited indeed, the scope of the definition of personal data breach is broad. The following points illustrate its reach.

First, under Article 2(h) of the revised ePrivacy Directive, in order for a security breach to occur, it must include "personal data". Personal data is defined broadly in the Data Protection Directive, and does not relate specifically to e.g. data which may cause economic loss if compromised.[28] For example, traffic data, i.e., data relating to the conveyance of a communication or the billing thereof, is covered to the extent it relates to an identified or identifiable natural person and therefore constitutes personal data.[29] This has to be put in contrast with the situation in the United States where the federal bill referred to under Sect. 5.1.1 follows the approach of state security breach laws in containing a closed list of personal information which,

munications household survey, July 2006, http://ec.europa.eu/information_society/policy/ecomm/library/ext_studies/index_en.htm.

[28] Article 2(a) of the Data Protection Directive: *"any information relating to an identified or identifiable natural person ('data subject'); an identifiable person is one who can be identified, directly or indirectly, in particular by reference to an identification number or to one or more factors specific to his physical, physiological, mental, economic, cultural or social identity"*. The issue as to whether and when e.g. IP addresses are personal data is discussed at length elsewhere and not addressed here. See generally on the concept of personal data e.g. Working Party 29 opinion 4/2007 and specifically with respect to IP addresses, Peter J. Hustinx, "Protection des données à caractère personnel en ligne: la question des adresses", *Légicom* 42 (1) (2009): 1–9.

[29] Compare, for a more limited approach, the type of data covered by the US bill referred to under Sect 5.1.1 above, namely personal information consisting of name, address or phone number in combination with e.g. a social security number or other additional identifier.

if compromised, triggers notification. If the compromised information does not contain the items of the list, notification is not necessary.[30]

Second, under Article 2(h), a data breach occurs not only in cases of unauthorised disclosure or unauthorised access to personal data but also in cases of simple accidental destruction or alteration which is not followed (or very unlikely to be followed) by unauthorised access.[31]

Third, Article 2(h) is blind as to the medium carrying the personal data: a data breach involves not only personal data in electronic form but also personal data in any other form.

Fourth, it is sufficient that the breach occurs *in connection with* the provision of a communications service. In this regard, it can be assumed that a data breach occurring while, for example, personal data is being processed by an external data processor would be covered.[32]

Furthermore, in the case of data transmitted in a chain involving both publicly available and non-publicly available services, "in connection with" could also mean that data compromised through the non-public leg of the transmission would be covered.

5.5 The Threshold Triggering the Obligation to Notify

5.5.1 Description of the Threshold

Article 4(3) subparagraph 1: *"In the case of a personal data breach, the provider of publicly available electronic communications services shall...notify the personal data breach to the competent national authority."*

Article 4(3) subparagraph 2: *"When the personal data breach is likely to adversely affect the personal data or privacy ... the provider shall also notify the subscriber or individual of the breach... without undue delay."*

One of the most relevant questions in the context of mandatory breach notification is when, in which circumstances, covered entities are obliged to notify personal data breaches to authorities and affected individuals.

[30] See, regarding state laws, Lisa J. Sotto and Aaron P. Simpson, "A How to Guide to Information Security Breaches", *Privacy and Security Law Report* 6 (14) (2007): 559–62.

[31] The US bill referred to above requires unauthorized acquisition of the personal information. A US commentator argues against the application of mandatory notification in circumstances where the data merely *could* have been accessed, even if there is no evidence that they have been. See Fred H. Cate, *"Information Security Breaches. Looking Back & Thinking Ahead"*, The Centre for Information Policy Leadership (2008), 5.

[32] The revised ePrivacy Directive does not contain provisions requiring a data processor to notify the covered entity in case of data breach. Although the obligation to notify does not arise until the breach is known by the covered entity, it might still want to consider including such a requirement in its contract with the processor.

5.5.1.1 Notification to Authorities

Pursuant to Article 4(3) subparagraph 1, notification to authorities is due every time there is a data breach leading to the compromise of personal data. There are no exceptions to the rule. This means that every single personal data breach, as defined under Article 2(h) is to be notified to the authorities.

The Working Party 29, concerned about the additional workload on the authorities, suggested that they should only be notified if the threshold of adverse effect is reached.[33] The practical implication for the authorities however depends on what action, if any, they are obliged to take on notification of security breach. If they can not apply a selective policy, but have to open proceedings every single time that they receive a notification, the Member States may have to increase their resources.[34]

Independently of the above, in practice the fear of additional workload coming from security breach notifications may be somewhat exaggerated. This is because, for the time being, the limited scope of application of the security breach provisions will serve to minimised any additional workload on the authorities. Indeed, while the security breach provisions remain limited to providers of communications services, the risk of notification overload is unlikely to materialise.

5.5.1.2 Notification to Individuals

Notification to individuals is due when the breach is *likely to adversely affect* their personal data and privacy. We will further comment on that issue under Sect. 5.5.2 below.

This standard alleviates the otherwise perceived problem of over-notification. Indeed, during the legislative procedure it was suggested that an obligation to send notices whenever personal data has been compromised, in other words without any limitations, would lead to over-notification and 'notice fatigue', which could result in desensitization.[35]

On the basis of the information principle discussed at Sect. 5.2.4 above, it may be argued that individuals are entitled to know about breaches independently of their effects. On the other hand, if individuals were to receive breach notices even in those situations where there are no adverse effects, harm or distress, they may end up ignoring notices in those instances where they may actually need to take steps to protect themselves. The standard of adverse effect is meant to strike the right balance in providing meaningful notice without undermining the right to be informed.

---

[33] Opinion 1/2009 of 10 February 2009: http://ec.europa.eu/justice_home/fsj/privacy/docs/wpdocs/2009/wp159_en.pdf.

[34] As regards the action required by the authorities, see Sect. 5.7.2 below.

[35] See e.g. the second EDPS opinion referenced in footnote 25, at §§ 35 and ff.

5.5.2 "Likely to Adversely Affect the Personal Data and Privacy"

Article 4(3) subparagraph 2: *"When the personal data breach is likely to adversely affect the personal data or privacy of a subscriber or individual, the provider shall also notify ..."*

Article 4(3) subparagraph 4: *"Without prejudice to the provider's obligation to notify subscribers and individuals concerned, if the provider has not already notified the subscriber or individual of the personal data breach, the competent national authority, having considered the likely adverse effects of the breach, may require it to do so."*

Recital 61: *"... Therefore, as soon as the provider of publicly available electronic communications services becomes aware that such a breach has occurred, it should notify the breach to the competent national authority. The subscribers or individuals whose data and privacy could be adversely affected by the breach should be notified without delay in order to allow them to take the necessary precautions. A breach should be considered as adversely affecting the data or privacy of a subscriber or individual where it could result in, for example, identity theft or fraud, physical harm, significant humiliation or damage to reputation in connection with the provision of publicly available communications services in the Community ...."*

The concept of 'adverse effect' used in the above provisions is not new in EU data protection law. Indeed, Article 17 of the Data Protection Directive uses the same concept to exempt from notification to the authorities data processing operations that are unlikely to affect adversely the rights and freedoms of data subjects. Despite the previous use of this concept, covered entities may, in many instances, be uncertain as to whether they have to notify. The discussion below addresses how the concept of adverse effects should be understood in the context of breach notification.

First, whereas no definition of adverse effect is given in the ePrivacy Directive, Recital 61 gives some examples of where adverse effect is always at hand. They include identity theft or fraud, physical harm and significant humiliation or damage to reputation. In the light of these examples, it can be assumed that adverse effect goes beyond purely economic harm to encompass also other effects such as reputation damage, which are very common in the context of data protection.

Second, the concept of adverse effect is a flexible one, allowing for, and requiring, a global evaluation of the relevant facts in each particular case, including of the possible unauthorised use of the personal data.[36]

---

[36] Such a global assessment may for example conclude that there is no likelihood of adverse effect if a password-secured laptop (see footnote 39 below re adequacy of password protection as a technological protection measure) has been stolen but quickly recovered and investigation shows that the information was not accessed. Compare guidelines issued by the New Zealand Privacy Commissioner available here: http://www.privacy.org.nz/privacy-breach-guidelines-2/. P.M. Schwartz and E.J. Janger, op. cit. 937 ff, quote an example from 2005, where a courier service lost a backup tape containing personal data for around two million persons. The tape was found after one month,

Third, in assessing whether the obligation to notify exists, it will also be necessary to assess whether the necessary *likelihood* that the adverse effect will happen is met. However, the determination of the degree of probability of adverse effect is not an exact science. Such determination should be made taking all relevant aspects into account, and against the overall purposes of the EU data protection legislation, namely to ensure protection of fundamental rights and freedoms. Thus, in principle, a risk in the form of a mere probability that the personal data and privacy of individuals could be adversely affected should suffice.[37]

Fourth, a relevant question in this context is who must decide whether the threshold for notification is met and whether notification to individuals is due. The solution reflected in the revised ePrivacy Directive strikes a balance which involves, on the one hand, enabling covered entities to make the decision, on the other, giving authorities the possibility to overrule the finding of a covered entity if it is deemed to be erroneous.

The above is expressed in Article 4(3) subparagraph 2 according to which it is primarily for the covered entities to make the determination of whether a breach is likely to cause adverse effects. This is an efficient approach as covered entities are likely to be in possession (at least more than authorities) of all relevant facts and circumstances surrounding the breach, and therefore are in a better position to evaluate whether there is a likelihood of adverse effect or not.

At the same time, it follows from Article 4(3) subparagraph 4 that authorities are empowered to overrule a finding by the covered entity that there is no likelihood of adverse effect. The possibility of intervention by an authority serves both to protect the individuals concerned by the breach and to allow for the development of a harmonised approach to when notification is necessary. Ultimately of course, determining if a likelihood of adverse effect is at hand will be a matter for the courts.

5.5.3 *Exceptions Relating to Technological Protection Measures and Law Enforcement*

Article 4(3) subparagraph 3: *"Notification of a personal data breach to a subscriber or individual concerned shall not be required if the provider has demonstrated to the satisfaction of the competent authority that it has implemented appropriate tech-*

---

and no third party had gained access to it. As the EU rules do not allow a delay in notification lasting for one month, notification would have had to be given.

[37] Compare ECJ judgment of 7 September 2004 in case C-127/02 regarding the Habitats Directive. The Court found that a requirement of "likely to have a significant effect" means that a "mere probability", "probability" or "risk" is enough, and that the requirement, in light of the precautionary principle applicable in environmental law, is met "if it cannot be excluded on the basis of objective information" that there will be significant effects. See also the interesting discussion in the AG Kokott opinion at par 61–74. It is submitted that the purpose of the EU data protection legislation to protect fundamental rights and freedoms would lead to a similar conclusion in the current context as the precautionary principle did in the case.

nological protection measures, and that those measures were applied to the data concerned by the security breach. Such technological protection measures shall render the data unintelligible to any person who is not authorised to access it."

Recital 64: *"In setting detailed rules concerning the format and procedures applicable to the notification of personal data breaches, due consideration should be given to the circumstances of the breach, including whether or not personal data had been protected by appropriate technical protection measures, effectively limiting the likelihood of identity fraud or other forms of misuse. Moreover, such rules and procedures should take into account the legitimate interests of law enforcement authorities in cases where early disclosure could unnecessarily hamper the investigation of the circumstances of a breach."*

Article 4(3) subparagraph 3 exempts from the obligation to notify when appropriate technological protection measures render the data unintelligible have been implemented. As usual in Community law, the provision is neutral with respect to the type of technology used. It can be of any kind as long as it renders the data useless.[38] As to the conditions for the application of this exemption, the following is relevant:

First, the exemption for technological protection measures, rendering the compromised data useless for any unauthorised person, is not an automatic safe harbour. It obviates the need for notification only if (1) the covered entity has received the *approval* of the authority for the measures applied, and (2) those measures were *actually applied.*

It should be possible for an authority to pre-approve technological protection measures (supported by any relevant organisational measures) that they find appropriate, subject to periodic re-evaluation and respecting the principle of technological neutrality.[39] However, the covered entity would still have to notify the authority, and demonstrate that such measures had actually been implemented with respect to any compromised data. If the authority is in doubt as to whether the technological protections measures actually were applied, or if, for example, the use of recent technology means that a formerly approved method can be bypassed, it can order the covered entity to notify.

Second, the technological protection measures must render the data unintelligible to any non-authorised person. This requirement is absolute—protection meas-

[38] Albeit in a different context, a definition of technological protection measures, and effectiveness of such measures, can be found in Article 6(3) of Directive 2001/29/EC on the harmonisation of certain aspects of copyright and related rights in the information society. For the purpose of that Directive, such measures are defined, somewhat edited for relevance in our context, as *"any technology, device or component that, in the normal course of its operation, is designed to prevent or restrict acts ... which are not authorised ... Technological measures shall be deemed 'effective' where the use ... is controlled ... through application of an access control or protection process, such as encryption, scrambling or other transformation ... which achieves the protection objective."*

[39] It may be expected that systems relying on password protection, if and to the extent they can be considered technological protection measures at all, will not easily be approved by the authorities, given the frequent lack of security around passwords.

ures which only make access more difficult or which can be compromised in other ways do not meet the standard.[40]

In addition to the above, a particular exception is mentioned in Recital 64, namely that the legitimate interests of law enforcement authorities should be taken into account in those cases where early notification could unnecessarily hamper the investigation of the breach.

5.6 Means of Providing Notice, Timing and Content

5.6.1 Means of Providing Notice

Article 4(3) subparagraph 1: *"In the case of a personal data breach, the provider... shall...notify the personal data breach to the competent national authority."*

Article 4(3) subparagraph 2: *"When the personal data breach is likely to adversely affect the personal data and privacy of a subscriber or individual, the provider shall also notify the subscriber or individual ..."*

Apart from notification to the authority, the rule is that any affected individual, whether a subscriber or not, whose personal data is likely to be adversely affected by the breach shall be notified. The Directive says little about how this notification should be given. Below follow some thoughts on this issue.

First, notification must obviously be made in an effective manner, i.e., in the way most likely to promptly and reliably reach the individuals concerned, while not imposing an unnecessary burden on the covered entity. If email addresses are known, depending on the circumstances of the case, notification by email may be acceptable.

Second, an interesting question is how to notify in those cases where no contact details are known, or when obtaining such contact details would be particularly cumbersome. Under these circumstances, it may be acceptable, with the approval of the authorities, to notify indirectly, for example, publishing a notice addressed to the public in general in major newspapers.

A notice on the website of the covered entity might also be considered in addition or as an ultimate a fall-back solution. Notification to subscribers in their invoices would rarely meet the requirement to notify without undue delay, and would not reach other individuals concerned.

---

[40] Appropriate encryption could be an adequate technological protection measure, assuming that any key is not lost together with the data. Depending possibly on the character of the personal data concerned, the encryption should be state-of-the-art. As an example, the former encryption standard DES was approved as a US federal standard in 1977 but became defunct in 1998, when various advances in hardware, software etc enabled the encryption to be broken in 56 hours, see Mccafftey, *"Encrypt It"*, http://msdn.microsoft.com/en-us/magazine/cc164055.aspx. The US federal bill referred to under Sect. 5.1.1 above requires that encryption must include appropriate management and safeguards of encryption keys to protect the integrity of the encryption.

Third, as to the applicable national law, *ex* Article 4.1(a) of the Data Protection Directive, it can be argued that notification should be given to the authority in the Member State in which the provider is established. Individuals should be notified pursuant to the same national law. Where it is known that individuals resident in other Member States are affected, that authority should as a matter of good practice liaise with the other authorities involved, in order to take their views into account when deciding whether to require notification to individuals (in cases where it has not already been done).

Finally, as discussed under Sect. 5.6.3 below, the authorities may—and should—issue instructions as to how notification shall be made.

5.6.2 Timing of the Notification

Article 4(3) subparagraphs 1–2: *"... without undue delay ..."*

Recital 61: *"... as soon as the provider ... becomes aware that ... a breach has occurred...the subscribers or individuals whose data and privacy could be adversely affected by the breach should be notified without delay in order to allow them to take the necessary precautions ...."*

Once it has been determined that notification to individuals is required, the next step is to actually send the notifications.

First, notification shall be given *"without undue delay"* after discovery of the breach. As is the case for "likelihood" and "adverse effect", without undue delay is a flexible concept allowing for and requiring an evaluation in accordance with the circumstances in each individual case.

Second, broadly, the guiding principle is that the notification must be given in such time as to enable the individual to mitigate the adverse effects of the breach. If all relevant facts surrounding the breach are immediately apparent, there is no reason for any delay, and notification should be given immediately.

The purpose of enabling individuals to take mitigating action against possible loss flowing from the breach also means that without undue delay implies a shorter interval in relation to notification to an individual than with respect to notification to the authority.

Third, despite the above, before serving the notice to individuals, in some cases, particularly in criminal investigations, covered entities may have to take into account instructions of law enforcement agencies. Such agencies may require delaying the notification if they perceive that notifying could affect or prevent the criminal investigation.

Fourth, in some cases, it may also be necessary to delay notification until the security of the system has been restored. Any delay should not exceed the minimum required to patch the security problem by the swiftest means available.

Finally, in those cases where the covered entity does not consider there to be a need for individuals to be notified, it would nevertheless clearly be in its interest to establish contact with the authority as promptly as possible. If the authority is inclined to require notification to individuals, the covered entity should proceed to notify immediately as it otherwise risks breaching the time limit.

5.6.3 Content of the Notification

Article 4(3) subparagraph 5: *"The notification to the subscriber or individual shall at least describe the nature of the personal data breach and the contact points where more information can be obtained, and shall recommend measures to mitigate the possible adverse effects of the personal data breach. The notification to the competent national authority shall, in addition, describe the consequences of, and the measures proposed or taken by the provider to address, the personal data breach."*

Article 4(4): *"Subject to any technical implementing measures adopted under paragraph 5, the competent national authorities may adopt guidelines and, where necessary, issue instructions concerning the circumstances in which providers are required to notify personal data breaches, the format of such notification and the manner in which the notification is to be made …."*

The content of the notification represents a balancing of the need for notification to be given promptly and effectively, to enable individuals to take appropriate action to mitigate risks, and to provide meaningful information to the authorities.[41] In drafting notifications, the following rules of thumb should be considered.

First, in all circumstances, the information to be provided in the notice should be as brief and clear as possible, to enable all those concerned to quickly understand the risk.

Second, individuals should not be requested to call the covered entity's call centre to learn the circumstances of the breach and actions to take. The reading of the notification should be sufficient for them to understand the risks at stake and the recommended protective measures.

Third, the covered entity is responsible for recommending effective mitigating measures, but should not be required to recommend every theoretically possible measure, or measures that could only be applied by those with particular competences.

If the measures recommended are ineffective, and there is no rectification given by the covered entity in time for those concerned to mitigate the risk, the covered entity could be held liable.

Fourth, in order for the notification to be effective, risks of confusion with spam or junk mail must be avoided. Also to avoid confusion, the notification should not

[41] The language/-s of the notification should be the same as those normally used by the provider to communicate with its customers.

be allowed to contain offers from the covered entity to sign up for additional services offered by it or on its behalf.[42]

Authorities should draw up standard formats of notifications to ensure that the notifications are effective. As further developed below, the ePrivacy Directive provides for technical implementing measures at EU level to harmonise the basic content of notifications (see Sect. 5.8.2). However, the covered entities are responsible for making sure that the content of the notification is effective under the circumstances in each individual case.

5.7 Enforcement of the Provisions

5.7.1 Audit and Other Tools Available to the Authorities

Article 4(4): *"... the competent national authorities ... shall ... be able to audit whether providers have complied with their notification obligations ... and shall impose appropriate sanctions in the event of a failure to do so."*

Recital 58: *"The competent national authorities should ... have the necessary means to perform their duties, including comprehensive and reliable data about security incidents that have led to the personal data of individuals being compromised. They should monitor measures taken and disseminate best practices among providers of publicly available electronic communications services. Providers should therefore maintain an inventory of personal data breaches to enable further analysis and evaluation by the competent national authorities."*

Article 28(3) of the Data Protection Directive provides for a minimal set of powers which must be conferred to authorities. Articles 4(4) and Article 15a of the revised ePrivacy Directive complement such powers as follows:

First, the overall policing of the ePrivacy Directive is strengthened substantially by the new Article 15a which complements Article 28(3) of the Data Protection Directive. Among other things, Article 15a gives authorities powers to order cessation of infringements and obliges Member States to ensure that the authorities have all investigative powers and resources to monitor compliance.

Second, authorities are given the right and obligation to monitor covered entities' compliance with their reporting obligations. Indeed, on receipt of a notification of a security breach in which the covered entity has decided that notification to individuals is not required, authorities have the power to overrule this decision.

Third, authorities have a right to audit concerned entities; this may happen before or following the notification of a security breach. For example, authorities may

---

[42] See further P.M. Schwartz and E.J. Janger, op. cit. 951 ff, regarding fuzzy notification letters, mentioning examples of breached entities including offers for credit monitoring and identity theft insurance in notification letters.

carry out an audit having heard of the breach via a complaint or through the press. Alternatively, they can audit following receipt of a security breach notification.

Fourth, covered entities must maintain an inventory of breaches sufficient for the authorities to verify compliance with their notification obligations. This obligation will assist authorities in conducting their audits.

Fifth, authorities can impose appropriate sanctions in cases of non-compliance. What constitutes an appropriate sanction depends on national law, provided always that they meet Community law requirements of being effective, proportionate and dissuasive.

Finally, the authorities could also make use of the fact that every data breach has to be notified to them to regularly assemble and publish detailed statistics of data breaches.

5.7.2 Selective to be Effective

It is important for authorities to be able to set their own priorities and to have freedom of choice in terms of how they operate as regulators. Authorities have in the context of the so called London initiative underlined the need for them to be able to use their powers and resources in a selective and pragmatic manner, enabling them to concentrate on serious cases and main risks facing individuals.

In the context of mandatory reporting of security breaches, the ability to select and prioritise would enable authorities to focus their investigative efforts on those areas that are felt to be more sensitive or on entities that are perceived to be particularly at risk.

Furthermore, in the cases of mandatory reporting of security breaches, as outlined in Sect. 5.5.1.1 above, if a selective approach is not allowed, taking into account that covered entities are obliged to report *all* breaches to authorities, the supervision and enforcement as a whole could be seriously jeopardised. This is particularly true if a similar standard applies to security breaches in areas other than the communications sector.

Arguably, the revised ePrivacy Directive is ambiguous whether a selective approach is allowed. Whereas in order to carry out their monitoring obligations it does appear necessary for the authorities to engage in a cursory examination of each notification, it is uncertain whether an in-depth examination of each case will also have to be performed. The better view is that the authorities are not positively obliged to review each notification in detail, only to consider the likely adverse effects before ordering the covered entity to notify. Ultimately, this will depend on implementing measures and Member States' laws.

As mentioned above, the authorities are empowered to issue instructions as to the format of the notifications, which would help in highlighting those cases that may require a more thorough examination from the authority.

5.7.3 Damages

Notification as such does not exclude any other remedies available under national law, such as damages.[43] Notification, properly done, would however serve to protect the covered entity by allowing the individuals concerned to mitigate the risks involved and therefore their potential loss.[44]

As the requirement to notify individuals is separate from the requirement to notify authorities, notification to an authority only does not exclude liability for the covered entity in case individuals should have been notified, regardless of whether the authority subsequently orders notification to the individual or not.

5.8 The Next Steps

5.8.1 Technical Implementing Measures Through Comitology

Article 4(5): *"In order to ensure consistency in implementation of the measures referred to in paragraphs 2, 3 and 4, the Commission may, following consultation with the European Network and Information Security Agency (ENISA), the Working Party on the Protection of Individuals with regard to the Processing of Personal Data established by Article 29 of Directive 95/46/EC and the European Data Protection Supervisor, adopt technical implementing measures concerning the circumstances, format and procedures applicable to the information and notification requirements referred to in this Article. When adopting such measures, the Commission shall involve all relevant stakeholders particularly in order to be informed of the best available technical and economic means of implementation …."*

Recital 63: *"Provision should be made for the adoption of technical implementing measures concerning the circumstances, format and procedures applicable to information and notification requirements in order to achieve an adequate level of privacy protection and security of personal data transmitted or processed in connection with the use of electronic communications networks in the internal market."*

Recital 64: *"In setting detailed rules concerning the format and procedures applicable to the notification of personal data breaches, due consideration should be given to the circumstances of the breach, including whether or not personal data had been protected by appropriate technical protection measures, effectively limit-*

---

[43] The Data Protection Directive provides that every person shall have a right to a judicial remedy for any breach of the rights guaranteed in relation to processing (Article 22), and that any person who has suffered damage shall be entitled to receive compensation (Article 23).

[44] For the US, P.M. Schwartz and E.J. Janger, op cit. 925, note that only three states provide a private right of action for individuals whose information has been breached.

ing the likelihood of identity fraud or other forms of misuse. Moreover, such rules and procedures should take into account the legitimate interests of law enforcement authorities in cases where early disclosure could unnecessarily hamper the investigation of the circumstances of a breach."

Article 4(5) of the revised ePrivacy Directive empowers the Commission to adopt technical implementing measures, i.e., detailed measures on security breach notification, through a comitology procedure.[45] This empowerment is justified in order to ensure consistent implementation and application of the security breach legal framework. Consistent implementation works towards ensuring that individuals across the Community enjoy an equally high level of protection and that covered entities are not burdened with diverging notification requirements.

Before adopting technical implementing measures, the Commission must engage in a broad consultation, in which ENISA, the EDPS and the Working Party 29 must be consulted. Furthermore, the consultation must also include other "relevant stakeholders", particularly in order to inform of the best available technical and economic means of implementation.

5.8.2 Areas/Subjects Covered by Comitology

As usual, the revised ePrivacy Directive enables the Commission to adopt implementing measures in defined areas. These areas cover the circumstances, the format and the procedures applicable to the information and notification requirements. Special emphasis is put on the need to take into account whether the data has been protected with appropriate technical protection measures as well as the interests of law enforcement agencies.

Throughout this article some examples have been given of the items that could be further developed through technical implementing measures within the margins given to the Commission. Among others, the following could be addressed:

1. The determination of certain personal information, which due to its sensitivity, if compromised, would inevitably constitute "adverse effects" in the sense of Article 4(3) subparagraph 2 (over and above the cases identified in Recital 61 as always involving adverse effect);
2. Setting up a standard EU format with at least headlines to be addressed in a notification, e.g. description of the breach, the effects, and the measures taken/proposed, in order to help authorities to carry out the assessment of the breach in the context of their supervisory powers;

[45] Comitology involves the adoption of technical implementing measures through a committee of Member State representatives chaired by the Commission. For the ePrivacy Directive, the so called regulatory procedure with scrutiny applies, meaning that the European Parliament, as well as Council, can oppose measures proposed by the Commission. See further http://europa.eu/scadplus/glossary/comitology_en.htm.

3. Possibly, to the extent it can be deemed included in "information and notification requirements", setting forth the procedure to follow in case of a data breach. This could include, for example, requiring more concrete deadlines for notification of the breach to the authorities, including to law enforcement authorities. It could also require concrete procedural steps which may include, for example, a request for covered entities to restate the security of the system, enlist forensic investigators in order to ascertain the facts and circumstances surrounding the breach, etc;
4. Determination of the allowed modalities for serving notices to individuals, with guidance as to whether and in which cases email and telephone notification are permitted;
5. Cases where notification to individuals via newspapers will be allowed (for example, if addresses are not known to the covered entity), and
6. Determination of the specific technical measures which, if applied, would exempt from notification.

5.8.3 Towards the Application of a Security Breach Notification Scheme Across Sectors

5.8.3.1 Future Legislative Proposal

It appears foreseeable for the Commission to put forward, in a relatively short time span, legislative proposals that would complement the EU security breach legal framework created in the context of the ePrivacy Directive. In particular, these legislative measures would have as a main purpose to extend the scope of application of the mandatory security breach rules to other sectors, including any legal or physical entity holding personal data. The reasons that justify this expectation are threefold.

First, Recital 59 of the revised text of the ePrivacy Directive explicitly calls on the Commission to propose, as a matter of priority, mandatory notification requirements applicable to all sectors.

Second, the Commission made a declaration, which was accepted by the European Parliament and Council, committing itself to promptly start work to develop an appropriate proposal for data breach notification rules of general applicability, i.e., covering anyone holding someone else's personal data.[46]

[46] Commission declaration on data breach notification, included in the text adopted by the European Parliament on 6 May 2009: "The Commission takes note of the will of the European Parliament that an obligation to notify personal data breaches should not be limited to the electronic communications sector but also apply to entities such as providers of information society services. Such an approach would be fully aligned with the overall public policy goal of enhancing the protection of EU citizens' personal data, and their ability to take action in the event of such data being compromised. In this context, the Commission wishes to reaffirm its view, as stated in the course of the negotiations on the reform of the Regulatory Framework, that the obligation for providers

Third, the Commission, in particular the Directorate General responsible for the Data Protection Directive is currently engaged in an exercise to look at new challenges for privacy taking into account new technologies and globalisation issues. In this context, the Commission has undertaken to examine the extent to which the Data Protection Directive may need to be amended in order to cope with these challenges. Legislation on security breach applying across sectors fits perfectly in this exercise. Furthermore, the Commission has informally recognised that security breach notification is part of this review exercise.

In this context, if the Commission were to propose security breach legislation across sectors, an interesting question is the extent to which it would be appropriate for the underlying rules to divert from those of the ePrivacy Directive.

5.8.3.2 Interim Soft Law Application

Recital 59: "*... Pending a review to be carried out by the Commission of all relevant Community legislation in this field, the Commission, in consultation with the European Data Protection Supervisor, should take appropriate steps without delay to encourage the application throughout the Community of the principles embodied in the data breach notification rules contained in Directive 2002/58/EC (Directive on privacy and electronic communications), regardless of the sector, or the type, of data concerned.*"

Commission declaration: "*... In addition, the Commission will consult with the European Data Protection Supervisor on the potential for the application, with immediate effect, in other sectors of the principles embodied in the data breach notification rules in Directive 2002/58/EC, regardless of the sector or type of data concerned.*"

The development of data breach notification rules of general applicability is likely to take a number of years. Pending their adoption, pursuant to Recital 59 of the revised ePrivacy Directive and the Commission declaration, the Commission, after consulting the EDPS, should carry out the necessary actions to stimulate immediate application across all sectors of data breach notification rules based on the principles contained in the revised ePrivacy Directive.

In order to implement the above, the Commission could, for example, issue a Recommendation which would put forward best practices on security breach across sectors to be enforced by authorities.

---

of publicly available electronic communications services to notify personal data breaches makes it appropriate to extend the debate to generally applicable breach notification requirements. The Commission will, therefore, without delay initiate the appropriate preparatory work, including consultation with stakeholders, with a view to presenting proposals in this area, as appropriate, by the end of 2011 …."

5.9 Conclusions

The obligations to inform individuals and authorities of security breaches are perfect building blocks upon the existing data protection legal framework. Yet, regrettably, it has taken too long for the EU to enact an explicit notification requirement. On the bright side, the long wait has finally resulted in a commendable mandatory security breach legal framework.

The emerging EU security breach legal framework strikes an appropriate balance between the protection of individuals' rights, including their rights to personal data and privacy, and the obligations imposed on covered entities. At the same time, this is a framework with real "teeth," as it is backed by meaningful enforcement provisions, which provide authorities with sufficient powers of investigation and sanction in the event of non-compliance.

Embedded in the security breach legal framework, is a system of checks and balances designed to maintain a proper balance between the different interests at stake. For example, the definition of personal data breach is broad in scope, requiring notice for the compromise of any type of personal data, independent of the media on which it is stored and whether there has been an unauthorized access. On the other hand, the obligation to notify affected individuals exists only when the personal data breach is likely to adversely affect their personal data and privacy.

Another example is the exemption from notification when the covered entity can demonstrate that the compromised information was protected with appropriate technological protection measures such as encryption. As has been proven in other jurisdictions this type of exception has served a critical role in enhancing data security. On the other hand, this is not a free ride insofar as entities still are required to demonstrate to the authorities that they have properly implemented such technologies (i.e., it is not a *per se* exception).

A number of relevant aspects, critical for the successful application of the rules, must be adopted by way of technical implementing measures by the Commission in consultation with stakeholders. To this end, an EU standard template could be developed for notification to the authorities as well as a harmonized EU approach in terms of the methods of providing notice to affected individuals.

The new breach notification system certainly has some shortcomings. The key one is its limited scope of application, which at present covers only breaches in connection with data held by providers of communications and ISPs. This despite the clear case during the legislative debate for a wider scope of application to include on-line banks, hospitals, public authorities, etc. As a result, the Commission promised to present proposals to broaden the scope of application of the security breach provisions in not too long.

Thus, this is not the end of the story, and it may only be a temporary shortcoming. Hopefully, the Commission, as a part of its on-going activities in the context of the review of the Data Protection Directive, will soon put forward, as promised, appropriate proposals for an extension of the mandatory security breach provisions across sectors.

Chapter 6
From Unsolicited Communications to Unsolicited Adjustments

Redefining a Key Mechanism for Privacy Protection

Gloria González Fuster, Serge Gutwirth and Paul de Hert

6.1 Protecting the Individual in front of Technology

The right to respect for private life recognises in arguably rather general, vague terms the right of individuals to be protected against unjustified, disproportional or arbitrary interferences in their private and family life, their home and their correspondence. Article 8 of the European Convention for the Protection of Human Rights and Fundamental Freedoms (ECHR) of 4 November 1950 is written in such terms,[1] but fails to define how the mentioned private and family lives, home or correspondence should be understood.[2] Neither does it explain what is exactly meant by interferences with them. It is the judiciary and the legislator who have

[1] Article 8 of the ECHR: *"(1) Everyone has the right to respect for his private and family life, his home and his correspondence. (2) There shall be no interference by a public authority with the exercise of this right except such as is in accordance with the law and is necessary in a democratic society in the interests of national security, public safety or the economic well-being of the country, for the prevention of disorder or crime, for the protection of health or morals, or for the protection of the rights and freedoms of others".*

[2] It will be noted that Article 8 of the ECHR does not mention the term 'privacy', but refers to the right of respect for one's private life. This notion, which has been developed over the years by the European Court of Human Rights in an activist fashion, has an open and evolving nature: thus, it has been judged that it may be not only impossible, but also useless to define it (F. Rigaux, *"La protection de la vie privée et des autres biens de la personnalité"* (Bruxelles: Bruylant, 1990), 725). The notion is related to, but not fully coincidental with the notions of 'privacy' as conceived by American or British legal frameworks. The notion of 'privacy' has been extensively debated from different perspectives (see, notably: F.D. Schoeman, ed., *"Philosophical Dimensions of Privacy: An Anthology"* (Cambridge: Cambridge Univ. Press, 1984) and should in any case also be considered as referring to a plurality of values (on the relation between both notions, see, among others: M. Hildebrandt, "Profiling and the Identity of the European Citizen", in *Profiling the European Citizen: Cross-Disciplinary Perspectives*, eds. M. Hildebrandt and S. Gutwirth, 303–43 (New York: Springer, 2008b).

G. González Fuster (✉)
Research Group on Law, Science, Technology & Society (LSTS),
Vrije Universiteit Brussel (VUB), Brussel, Belgium
e-mail: gloria.gonzalez.fuster@vub.ac.be

S. Gutwirth et al. (eds.), *Data Protection in a Profiled World*,
DOI 10.1007/978-90-481-8865-9_6,

been working out, over the years, the interpretation of the content of the right, eventually distilling and constructing a series of much more concrete legal instruments and concepts through which it is to be applied and guarded.

One of the major challenges of such translation of the right into more easily applicable legal tools has consisted in the taking into account of technological developments. Since the 1960s, and especially during the 1970s, it has been felt that, for the right to respect for private life to offer sufficient guarantees for the individual in front of such developments, special attention needed to be granted to the automated processing of personal data.[3] This notably lead to the adoption of the Convention for the Protection of Individuals with regard to Automatic Processing of Personal Data of 1981,[4] as well as of many other legal instruments focusing on the regulation of the processing of personal data.[5] The vitality of this approach has been so strong that the protection of personal data progressively became a model for privacy protection, and even managed to establish itself in some legal frameworks as a *sui generis* right,[6] parallel to the right to privacy.[7]

Automated processing of personal data is not, however, the only technological development which has triggered a need to come up with new or updated legal notions in the name of the right to respect for private life. And not all of such new mechanisms came to life through the prism of personal data protection.[8] One of

[3] S. Gutwirth, *"Privacy and the Information Age"* (Lanham: Rowman & Littlefield Publ., 2002), 16–20 and 83–108.

[4] Convention for the Protection of Individuals with regard to Automatic Processing of Personal Data, Strasbourg, 28/1/1981 (Convention No. 108), and Additional Protocol to the Convention for the Protection of Individuals with regard to Automatic Processing of Personal Data regarding supervisory authorities and transborder data flows, Strasbourg, 8/12/2001.

[5] See, notably: OECD-Guidelines on the Transborder Flows of Personal Data, Paris, 23 September 1980 (via www.oecd.org) and the Directive 95/46/EC of the European Parliament and Council of 24 October 1995 on the protection of individuals with regard to the processing of personal data and on the free movement of such data, *Official Journal* L281 (23.11.1995): 31–50.

[6] See, in this sense: D. Korff, *"The Legal Framework: An Analysis of the "Constitutional" European Approach to Issues of Data Protection and Law Enforcement"*, UK Information Commissioner Study Project: Privacy & Law Enforcement, Foundation for Information Policy Research (FIPR).

[7] Cf. P. De Hert and S. Gutwirth, "Privacy, Data Protection and Law Enforcement. Opacity of the Individual and Transparency of Power", in *Privacy and the Criminal Law*, eds. E. Claes, A. Duff, and S. Gutwirth, 61–104 (Antwerp: Intersentia, 2006) and P. De Hert. and S. Gutwirth, "European Data Protection's Constitutional Project. Its Problematic Recognition in Strasbourg and Luxembourg", in *Reinventing Data Protection?* eds. S. Gutwirth et al., 3–44 (Dordrecht: Springer, 2006). The impact of the progressive emancipation of the right to the protection of personal data, both on its very content and on the content of the right to privacy, is still to be fully assessed. Such an assessment would in particular need to take into account the complexity of the EU system for the protection of fundamental rights, in which different levels of protection (the Council of Europe, the EU and the national legal frameworks) coexist and influence each other.

[8] For example, the judiciary and the legislator were forced to rethink how to ensure the confidentiality of communications with the advent of the telephone, with the European Court of Human Rights eventually taking the view that the numbers dialled are an integral element in the communications made by telephone (*Malone v. The United Kingdom*, n 8691/79 A n 95, § 84 (European

these mechanisms, unrelated to the processing of personal data, is the regulation of so-called unsolicited communications.

6.2 The Regulation of Unsolicited Communications

The European Union (EU) has been dealing with unsolicited communications and related practices for more than a decade. A chronology of this phenomenon could take 1997 as a starting point, and in particular the Directive 97/7/EC on the protection of consumers in respect to distance contracts.[9] With explicitly reference to Article 8 of the ECHR, Directive 97/7/EC considered that the right to privacy of the consumer should be recognised, particularly as regards certain particularly intrusive means of communication.[10] Thus, it established several restrictions on the use of certain means of distance communication, and, concretely, it required the prior consent of the consumer for the use of automated calling systems without human intervention and fax as a means of distance communication for the conclusion of a contract between the consumer and the supplier.[11]

Directive 97/66/EC concerning the processing of personal data and the protection of privacy in the telecommunications sector,[12] also of 1997, contained equivalent provisions to be applied to unsolicited calls and faxes. With the aim of providing safeguards for all subscribers of telecommunication services against intrusion into their privacy by means of unsolicited calls and faxes,[13] Article 12 established an opt-in regime for the use of any automated calling machines without human intervention, including faxes, for purposes of direct marketing.

Directive 2000/31/EC on certain legal aspects of information society services, in particular electronic commerce, in the Internal Market ('Directive on electronic commerce')[14] of 2000 was the first Directive to explicitly refer to a now very common type of unsolicited communications: e-mail ('spam').[15] Observing that

---

Court of Human Rights, 2 August 1984) and consequently inspiring regulation from this perspective.

[9] Directive 97/7/EC of the European Parliament and of the Council of 20 May 1997 on the Protection of Consumers in respect of distance contracts, *Official Journal* L144 (4.6.1997): 19–27. See also: Lodewijk F. Asscher and Sjo Anne Hoogcarspel, *"Regulating Spam: A European Perspective After the Adoption of the E-Privacy Directive"* (The Hague: T.M.C. Asser Press, 2006), 20.

[10] Recital (17) of Directive 97/7/EC.

[11] Article 10(1) of Directive 97/7/EC.

[12] Directive 97/66/EC of the European Parliament and of the Council of 15 December 1997 concerning the processing of personal data and the protection of privacy in the telecommunications sector, *Official Journal* L24 (30.1.1998): 1–8.

[13] Recital (22) of Directive 97/66/EC.

[14] Directive 2000/31/EC of the European Parliament and of the Council of 8 June 2000 on certain legal aspects of information society services, in particular electronic commerce, in the Internal Market ('Directive on electronic commerce'), *Official Journal* L178, (4.6.1997): 1–16.

[15] L. F. Asscher and S. A. Hoogcarspel (2006), op. cit., 21.

the sending of unsolicited commercial communications by e-mail may be undesirable for consumers and information society service providers and may disrupt the smooth functioning of interactive networks,[16] Directive 2000/31/EC introduced specific provisions to protect users form unsolicited commercial communications by e-mail.[17]

Directive 2002/58/EC, concerning the processing of personal data and the protection of privacy in the electronic communications sector[18] deals in detail with unsolicited communications. Its Recital 40 reasons that safeguards must be provided for individuals against intrusion of their privacy by unsolicited communications for direct marketing purposes, in particular by means of automated calling machines, faxes, and e-mails, including SMS messages. This is so, it is clarified, because these forms of unsolicited commercial communications are relatively easy and cheap to send, and may impose a burden or cost on the recipient.[19] Consequently, Article 13 of the Directive establishes that the use of automated calling systems without human intervention, of faxes or of e-mail for the purposes of direct marketing may only be allowed in respect of subscribers who have given their prior consent ('opt-in').[20]

Overall, these different provisions seem to respond to two common concerns deserving particular attention. First, they are based on the careful observation of constant technological and marketing developments, and have no vocation of technological neutrality[21] whatsoever. Their evolution proves that special care has been taken to keep continuously updating them, for instance by clarifying that their scope

[16] Recital (30) of Directive 2000/31/EC.

[17] Article 7 of Directive 2000/31/EC.

[18] Directive 2002/58/EC of the European Parliament and of the Council of 12 July 2002 concerning the processing of personal data and the protection of privacy in the electronic communications sector (Directive on privacy and electronic communications), *Official Journal* L201 (31.7.2002): 37–47. Directive 2002/58/EC replaced Directive 97/66/EC.

[19] Directive 2002/58/EC, Recital (40).

[20] Directive 2002/58/EC, Article 13(1). Notwithstanding this general rule, Article 13(2) established that where a natural or legal person obtains from its customers their electronic contact details for electronic mail, in the context of the sale of a product or a service, in accordance with Directive 95/46/EC, the same person may use these details for direct marketing of its own similar products or services provided that customers clearly and distinctly are given the opportunity to object, free of charge and in an easy manner, to such use. It shall be noted that, although Article 13 aims at harmonising the conditions under which electronic communications can be used for marketing purposes, there is a general understanding that some of the concepts it uses appear to be subject to differences of interpretation in EU Member States (Article 29 Data Protection Working Party 2004, *Opinion 5/2004 on Unsolicited Communications for Marketing Purposes Under Article 13 of Directive 2002/58/EC*, WP 90, Brussels, 27 February, 2).

[21] Which can be understood as the will to adopt regulation applicable regardless of technological change. On technological neutrality, see: B.J. Koops, "Should ICT Regulation Be Technology-Neutral?" in *Starting Points for ICT Regulation. Deconstructing Prevalent Policy One-Liners*, eds. B.J. Koops et al., 77–108 (The Hague: T.M.C. Asser Press, 2006). As an example of a policy document arguing in favour of technological neutrality, see, for instance: Organisation for Economic Co-operation and Development (OECD), *"RFID Radio Frequency Identification: OECD Policy Guidance: A Focus on Information Security and Privacy Applications, Impacts and Country Initiatives"*, OECD Digital Economy Papers, No. 150 (2008, 6).

of application covers the latest advances of the time, be it faxes, e-mails, or SMS messages. Second, the interest protected by the regulation of unsolicited communications is definitely a notion of 'privacy' unlinked to the protection of personal data.[22] What is at stake are not the conditions related to the possible processing of personal data required to perform the communication, but a much broader privacy-interest to which the unsolicited communication is in any case felt to constitute an undesired intrusion or interference.

But how can this 'privacy-interest', protected by this mechanism, be conceptually framed? Directive 97/7/EC alludes to the right to privacy of the consumer; Directive 97/66/EC mentions the privacy of the subscriber; Directive 2000/31/EC aspires to broadly protect the user; Directive 2002/58/EC refers extensively to the privacy of individuals.[23] The nature of these provisions allow to envision such a privacy as an interference-free space to which individuals are entitled to, and to which they should not be obliged to renounce even if they choose to subscribe to a telecommunications network, or to use information society services. In this sense, the regulation of unsolicited communications is not concerned with persevering a private space from all external interferences, but more precisely with safeguarding the possibility of enjoying such space needed for the building up of our personality, by limiting unrequested and undesired interferences. From this point of view, autonomy (rather than seclusion) lies at the core of the legislator's privacy concerns.[24]

It this perspective, the mechanism can be related to a more global, and possibly currently emerging right of privacy of the consumer, or right of the consumer to be (relatively) left alone[25] and to be protected against unwanted and unasked attempts

---

[22] This should not be interpreted as implying that other provisions contained in the Directives dealing with the regulation of unsolicited communications are not designed to develop the protection of personal data. Directive 2002/58/EC, for instance, is indeed partially concerned with 'particularising' the protection granted by Directive 95/46/EC (see Article 1(2) of Directive 2002/58/EC: *"The provisions of this Directive particularise and complement Directive 95/46/EC for the purposes mentioned in paragraph 1"*).

[23] Even though it is not exclusively concerned with the protection of natural persons, but also with the protection of legal persons (see, notably, Recitals (12) and (45) and Article 1(2) of Directive 2002/58/EC).

[24] Thus demonstrating the relevance of relying on a notion of privacy as a concept serving a multiplicity of values (see note 2). See also: A. Rouvroy and Poullet, "The Right to Informational Self-Determination and the Value of Self-Development: Reassessing the Importance of Privacy for Democracy", in *Reinventing Data Protection?* eds. S. Gutwirth et al. 45–76 (Dordrecht: Springer, 2009).

[25] See, for instance: Múgica S. Cavanillas, "Dos derechos emergentes del consumidor: a no ser molestado y a una interacción informativa". *Revista general de legislación y jurisprudencia* 2 (2008): 175–93. The connections between consumer law and privacy protection have been increasingly explored during the past years, especially as privacy has been positioned as a key element of consumer confidence in the digital environment (see, for instance: Y. Poullet, "Les aspects juridiques des systèmes d'information". *Lex Electronica* 10 (3) (2006): 15, also available online at http://www.lex-electronica.org/articles/v10-3/poullet.htm; F. Alleweldt et al., *"Consumer Confidence in the Digital Environment"*, Briefing Note, European Parliament, PE382.173 p. 11), but much more could be certainly be done to reinforce them, in particular by reinforcing the effectiveness of privacy protection through consumer law mechanisms.

to influence and steer the consumer's behaviour. This right is believed to inspire not only the regulation of unsolicited communications, but also the establishment of minimum rules and standards on television advertising, for instance as established already in 1989 by the Directive 89/552/EC on the coordination of certain provisions concerning the pursuit of television broadcasting activities.[26] Directive 89/552/EC stated that such rules and standards were essential in order to ensure that the interests of consumers as television viewers are fully and properly protected,[27] and similar provisions were later to be found in Directive 97/36/EC, of 1997,[28] or in the 2007 'Audiovisual Media Services Directive'.[29] The rationale behind this type of provisions is that, although advertising might have its advantages, it needs to be regulated so it does not have a detrimental effect on the enjoyment of television by its viewers.[30]

6.3 The Shift Towards Unsolicited Adjustments

If the interest protected by the regulation of unsolicited communications is still to be effectively preserved in the future, it is crucial to keep adequately updating it. This is true not only because technical developments are continuously taking place, and unsolicited communications come regularly in new forms and shapes, but also because marketing practices are evolving. The evolution does not affect solely the technical nature of communications. It is more radical and profound. To better grasp its proportions, we should consider both current presaging practices and progress expected in the long term. We will start with the latter.

---

[26] Council Directive 89/552/EEC of 3 October 1989 on the coordination of certain provisions laid down by Law, Regulation Or Administrative Action in Member States concerning the pursuit of television broadcasting activities, *Official Journal of the European Communities* L298 (17.10.1989): 23–30.

[27] See Article 11 of Directive 89/552/EEC.

[28] Directive 97/36/EC of the European Parliament and of the Council of 30 June 1997 amending Council Directive 89/552/EEC on the coordination of certain provisions laid down by law, regulation or administrative action in Member States concerning the pursuit of television broadcasting activities, *Official Journal of the European Communities* L202 (30.7.1997): 60–70.

[29] Directive 2007/65/EC of the European Parliament and of the Council of 11 December 2007 amending Council Directive 89/552/EEC on the coordination of certain provisions laid down by law, regulation or administrative action in Member States concerning the pursuit of television broadcasting activities, *Official Journal of the European Communities* L332 (18.12.2007): 27–45.

[30] The intention here is thus not to preserve the privacy of individuals against the risks of television consumption, but to make sure that individuals can access television programmes without suffering the burden of excessive advertising. For an understanding of television as a force marking the destruction of privacy by taking individuals away from their private intensions, see: Mills C. Wright, *"The Power Elite"* (New York: Oxford Univ. Press, 1956, 2000), 314.

6.3.1 *Upcoming Practices*

Prospective developments in this area are delineated by the upcoming 'ubiquitous computing' and 'ambient intelligence' scenarios. This is a future in which objects are interconnected and communicate with each other, while also being able to interact with individuals. This is a future in which the on-line world meets the off-line world, and everything potentially reaches the on-line status. Devices, embedded in the environment and furnished with sensors, are context-aware; they react to changes by adapting their behaviour, and are even able to anticipate them.[31] This is the time of 'smart' homes, in which 'smart' kitchens are equipped with 'smart' freezers keeping track of daily consumption to timely suggest purchasing milk before it goes off, or are even programmed to automatically order it from a selected store.

According to the examples put forward by companies investing in this field, 'smart' objects would seem to respond to some sort of neutral, almost philanthropic interests, always advising what is genuinely the best for the individual based on factual information virtuously collected and some mysteriously unprejudiced guidance. Nevertheless, there is no reason why this should occur entirely this way. If the on-line world is really going to meet the off-line world, online marketing practices, and, in particular, online behavioural advertising are not to disappear, but to turn pervasive. Marketing practices based on predictive data mining and consumer profiling, now pullulating on the Internet, are to be rolled out through the 'smart' freezers, in our private ('smart') kitchens, across our private ('smart') homes.

It appears extremely difficult to determine what should be considered as an 'unsolicited communication' in this kind of context. Actually, it is already highly laborious to decide what should be designated in these future scenarios as a 'communication', as most of the messages conveyed from object to object, and even from objects to individuals, would fail to qualify as communications in a traditional, legal sense.[32] Might a 'smart' freezer announcing on its door that there is no milk left inside, be considered as a communication? Would it be doing so if it simultaneously sent an SMS to the householder? What about if every time the door is opened and there is almost no milk left, a jingle informs about discount prices on milk at a nearby store? What if the freezer suddenly offers the possibility to directly purchase more milk from a new, unknown but 'recommended' brand by simply touching an icon? And if all these practices are not really communications, what are they? Are they simple functionalities of the object, just like any other? Are they decisions the freezer 'smartly' takes on its own?

Linguists have been discussing for decades about the thin line separating mere statements, which purely inform, to performative utterances, which do not only

---

[31] About "ambient intelligence" techniques and impacts, read Wright et al., *"Safeguards in a World of Ambient Intelligence"* (Dordrecht: Springer, 2008); and M. Hildebrandt, "Profiling and the Rule of Law", *Identity in Information Society (IDIS)* 1 (1) (2008a): 6.

[32] For instance, Directive 2002/58/EC defines 'communication' as *"any information exchanged or conveyed between a finite number of parties by means of a publicly available electronic communications service"* (Article 2(d)).

comment about reality, but change reality. They eventually even questioned whether such a thin line existed at all, as in a sense all utterances have an impact on reality. Marketing practices in upcoming 'ubiquitous computing' and 'ambient intelligence' scenarios might be better understood by acknowledging that the key issue with them is not whether they constitute a mere communication, an actual decision, or an adaptation facilitating a decision by the individual. What should be clear is that a series of practices, not restricted to our current idea of what a 'communication' is, can constitute invasive practices, just as unsolicited communications do now. They can be thus viewed as falling under a wider category of 'adjustments' or automatic adaptations of software or devices to be described as unsolicited adjustments, and deserving ad hoc regulation.[33]

6.3.2 Present Problematic Practices

The discussion of future scenarios should not lead the reader to believe that this style of practices are not being developed and implemented right now. Some applications used in contemporary computers or 'smart' phones already tend to follow the same logic, by systematically privileging the direct adaptation of their behaviour, or features, instead of sending communications to the users to invite them to envisage such adaptations. It is the case, for instance, when devices seem to take the initiative to connect with a specific service, to download a particular file or software, or to re-tailor the user's preferences. But we should now consider another type of example, apparently very distant but ultimately fully pertinent.

This example takes us outside the private space of the home, to the indubitably public space of public transport. More concretely, it takes us to the Parisian metro, where the deployment of a new type of digital interactive advertisement screens caused much controversy, and notable indignation by the civil society, in the spring of 2009.[34] The digital screens, to be installed in the corridors of the Paris underground, were labelled as 'spying' monitors: looking like simple screens, they actually hid two cameras and an electronic system allowing to count the number of persons passing by, to measure for how long they looked at the screen and to analyse their reactions in order to detect which element of the image had caught their attention. The system was also capable, in principle, to provide information about the age and gender of people walking by.

---

[33] Cf. González Fuster G. and S. Gutwirth, "Privacy 2.0?" *Revue du droit des Technologies de l'Information*, Doctrine 32 (2008): 357–59.

[34] Five French NGOs (Résistance à l'agression publicitaire, Souriez vous êtes filmés, Big Brother Awards, Robin des toits and Le Publiphobe) introduced a complaint against the companies responsible for the advertisement in the Parisian underground because of the mentioned screens. For the official press release dated from April 22, 2009 see: http://bigbrotherawards.eu.org/Ecrans-de-pub-interactifs-la-RATP-et.html.

All the screens were equipped with Bluetooth technology, and the company responsible for them[35] had originally planned to allow for the sending of messages via Bluetooth to the mobile phones of all passers-by. This idea, however, was strongly opposed by the French authority responsible for the monitoring of compliance with privacy and data protection legislation.[36] In the name of the regulation of unsolicited communications, the authority considered that the practice would be unlawful, as the consent of the subscriber was needed before the communication was sent, and without such prior consent no communication for marketing purposes was possible. The Bluetooth functionality was eventually deactivated.

It soon appeared that there was little more that the French authority could do in this case, and its reaction[37] might be considered illustrative of some hesitations and inadequacies of the existing legal framework for privacy protection in Europe. Facing an operative screen already in place, the authority assessed that the device in question was simply measuring the screens' audience, by measuring the number of passers-by looking at it and for how long they did so. As the images were not recorded, transmitted or visible to anybody,[38] it concluded that provisions related to CCTV[39] were not applicable. The authority argued, nevertheless, that the screens might be viewed as personal data processing equipments, because, although they stored only the mentioned statistical information, in order to obtain it they were processing images that included identifiable faces, to be qualified as personal data, thus triggering the applicability of data protection provisions. If this argument were considered valid, then the screens would have to comply with data protection legislation. However, it would suffice to the company to claim that the faces were blurred and not related to identifiable persons not to have to comply with any data protection legislation, and it is clear that the company has no particular interest in identifying anybody, as identifying the passers-by does not provide any added value. The weakness of the protection offered is consequently obvious.

This weakness becomes much more worrying when we take into account all the functions that this type of advertisement screens are in principle designed to perform. Another company active in the same market,[40] for instance, offers very similar performances but promises to announcers using its so-called 'dynamic advertisement networks' real time information on the number of viewers attracted, the exact distance they were at, and their demographic profile.[41] If the demographic profile is obtained in real time, the next logical step for any announcer should be to adapt

---

35 Called Majority Report.

36 Commission nationale de l'informatique et des libertés (CNIL).

37 For its press release, see: http://www.cnil.fr/index.php?id=2538&tx_ttnews[backPid]=17&-tx ttnews[swords]=Recommandation%20de%20la%20CNIL&tx_ttnews[tt_news] =440&cHash=b9249cf46d

38 And as the actual determination of the age and gender of audience was not being operated in that particular case.

39 Closed-circuit television.

40 Named Quividi.

41 See: http://www.quividi.com/fr/message_targeting.html

the content of the advertisement showed on the monitor taking into account such information, also in real time, for enhanced targeting. If tempted to do so, current provisions on unsolicited communications would not be an obstacle, as they would not apply to this kind of advertising. It certainly can appear to be totally inconsistent to pretend, on the one hand, that because of privacy protection announcers cannot send messages via Bluetooth to the mobile phones of passers-by even if they are walking around by their Bluetooth device knowingly activated. But also allow, on the other hand, the same announcers to freely and systematically scrutinize all passers-by without their knowledge, to try to guess their age and gender and, that based on this information, to furtively adapt the content of their advertisements, and force passers-by to endure all this process and the resulting adapted advertisement even if they just want to use the public transport and are not even carrying on any electronic device at all. Unfortunately, the existing regulation dealing with unsolicited communications backs up this kind of paradoxical outcome.

6.3.3 The (Other) Limits of Current Legislation

One might think that, despite the limitations of the present regulation of unsolicited communications, other legal mechanisms are already in place to effectively guarantee the right to respect for private life of individuals in front of the described developments. This is not exactly the case. The deficiencies of personal data protection in these situations have already been coined.[42] Provisions on personal data protection do not apply when personal data is not processed, and there is actually no need to process data obviously falling under the traditional notion of 'personal data',[43] to perform a communication or adjustment constituting an intrusion of the privacy of the individual. This configures the greatest weakness of traditional data protection in this field.[44]

Online behavioural advertising[45] is already highlighting this crucial flaw of data protection, and unsurprisingly much of the legal discussion surrounding the issue

---

[42] See, notably: L. A. Bygrave, *"Data Protection Law: Approaching Its Rationale, Logic and Limits"* (The Hague: Kluwer Law International, 2002); Y. Poullet, "Pour une troisième génération de réglementations de protection des données" *Jusletter*, also available online at http://jusletter.weblaw.ch/article/de/_4213; and, in relation to profiling in particular, M. Hildebrandt and S. Gutwirth (2008b), op. cit.

[43] Defined as "any information relating to an identified or identifiable natural person ('data subject')" in Directive 95/46/EC (Article 2(a)).

[44] These observations are not meant to suggest that the current problems faced by personal data protection law are insurmountable. Many efforts have been deployed to refine and reinforce data protection law, and they should certainly be backed up.

[45] For the moment, regulated mainly through self-regulation efforts. See, for instance: International Advertising Bureau (IAB), *"Good Practice Principles for Online Behavioural Advertising"* (2009); Federal Trade Commission, *"FTC Report: Self-Regulatory Principles for Online Behavioral Advertising"* (February 2009). Online behavioural advertising practices can also be instructive

has focused on whether the data used is personal data or not. Online behavioural advertising relies on the processing of user-specific data collected while monitoring the on-line conduct of individuals, but companies executing it will tend to contest that this data relates to identified or identifiable persons, thus maintaining that data protection provisions are not applicable. As a response to such a strategy, and as far as online behavioural advertising is concerned, there is still the possibility to argue that the practice also affects another mechanism of privacy protection, which is unrelated to personal data: the right to confidentiality of communications. Indeed, online behavioural advertising will generally be undertaken intercepting, monitoring and even altering communications that, in the name of the right to confidentiality of communications, might deserve to be kept free from any interference.

This argument, however, would not apply when behavioural advertising is no longer deployed on-line, but off-line, and when the conduct monitored does not consist of any communication activities but relates, for instance, to milk consumption in the private space of the home. In that case, it is true, we could try to invoke still another mechanism for privacy protection, which is the protection of the home. But that mechanism would no longer be applicable when we consider the example of the 'spying' screens in the corridors of the underground.

A last relevant possibility is, when unsolicited adjustments are based on profiling, the regulation of automated decision-making. Existing regulation, nonetheless, would not guarantee any effective protection, as provisions[46] are generally concerned with decisions that per se produce legal effects or significantly affect individuals, which would not be the case with the majority of unsolicited adjustments. Altogether, it appears that at the moment no concrete legal tool ensures effectively the interests of the individual in front of the described developments.

6.4 Concluding Remarks

This contribution has argued in favour of widening the protection currently granted through the regulation of unsolicited communications via the new notion of 'unsolicited adjustments'. We have shown that the evolving nature of communications and, more generally, of marketing practices, urgently requires a rethinking of the existing legal mechanisms. Otherwise, current developments will continue to benefit from the existing legal loopholes and, slowly but surely, tend to design a world in which objects that are supposedly there in order to assist and guide, in practice

from the perspective of the regulation of unsolicited adjustments because of the innovative and sometimes subtle ways in which marketing practices sometimes take place, for instance by embedding product endorsements or blurring distinctions between advertising and editorial contents (The Public Voice, *"Fuelling Creativity, Ensuring Consumer and Privacy Protection, Building Confidence and Benefiting from Convergence"*, Civil Society Background Paper, (2008), 24).

[46] Such as Article 15 of Directive 95/46/EC.

secretly track individuals, to surreptitiously adapt their performances based on undisclosed criteria.

In our description of unsolicited communications, we have highlighted that the interest protected by their regulation and related provisions appears to be the privacy of the individual, sometimes envisaged as a 'consumer', as a 'subscriber' or as a 'user'. Although such privacy of the individual is never described or defined, its preservation is envisaged as an aspect of the right to respect for private life. Thereby, the mechanism ultimately serves the very same goals pursued by Article 8 of the ECHR, which are certainly not limited to the mere insurance of a sheltered space in which individuals can (relatively) peacefully watch television, receive solicited phone calls or electronically purchase products just for the sake of it. Fundamentally, the mechanism is intended to guarantee such privacy of the consumer,[47] of the subscriber, of the user and, in general, of the individual or citizen as an instrument favouring self-development and personal autonomy, and ultimately, as all privacy-related legal tools, his or her freedom.

References

Alleweldt, F., F. Anna, and A. Merle. 2007. *Consumer confidence in the digital environment.* Briefing note, European Parliament, PE382.173.

Article 29 Data Protection Working Party. 2004. *Opinion 5/2004 on unsolicited communications for marketing purposes under Article 13 of Directive 2002/58/EC.* WP 90. Brussels, 27 February.

Asscher, L.F., and S.A. Hoogcarspel. 2006. *Regulating spam: A European perspective after the adoption of the E-Privacy directive.* The Hague: T.M.C. Asser Press.

Bygrave, L.A. 2002. *Data protection law: Approaching its rationale, logic and limits.* The Hague: Kluwer Law International.

Cavanillas Múgica, S. 2008. Dos derechos emergentes del consumidor: A no ser molestado y a una interacción informativa. *Revista general de legislación y jurisprudencia* 2: 175–93.

De Hert, P., and S. Gutwirth. 2006. Privacy, data protection and law enforcement. Opacity of the individual and transparency of powe. In *Privacy and the criminal law*, eds. E. Claes, A. Duff, and S. Gutwirth, 60–104. Oxford: Intersentia.

De Hert, P., and S. Gutwirth. 2009. European data protection's constitutional project. Its problematic recognition in Strasbourg and Luxembourg. In *Reinventing data protection?* eds. S. Gutwirth, Y. Poullet, P. De Hert, and C. de Terwangne, 3–44. Dordrecht: Springer.

Federal Trade Commission. 2009. *FTC report: Self-regulatory principles for online behavioral advertising.* FTC, February.

[47] This approach would be fully consistent with Sunstein's very important analysis of the possible negative impact on citizenship of excessive consumer choice (Cass R. Sunstein *"Republic.com 2.0"* (Princeton, PA: Princeton Univ. Press, 2007), 136). Unregulated unsolicited adjustments would not serve consumer choice, but could, on the contrary, tend to eradicate it by replacing it by the absolute impossibility of the choice for consumers, and the imposition on them of a certain vision of reality, predetermined by third parties. This imposition could have the same negative impact on citizenship as excessive consumer choice, or, possibly, even worse effects. Only by preserving the possibility for individuals to be released from these practices and confronted with the unexpected and the presumably unwanted can their ability to chose be ensured.

González Fuster, G., and S. Gutwirth. 2008. Privacy 2.0? *Revue du droit des Technologies de l'Information, Doctrine*, 32: 349–59.
Gutwirth, Serge. 2002. *Privacy and the information age.* Lanham: Rowman & Littlefield Publ.
Hildebrandt, M. 2008a. Profiling and the rule of law. *Identity in Information Society (IDIS)* 1 (1): 55–70.
Hildebrandt, M. 2008b. Profiling and the identity of the European citizen. In *Profiling the European citizen: Cross-disciplinary perspectives*, eds. M. Hildebrandt and S. Gutwirth, 303–43. *Profiling the European Citizen: Cross-Disciplinary Perspectives* New York: Springer.
International Advertising Bureau (IAB). 2009. *Good practice principles online behavioural advertising.*
Koops, B.J. 2006. Should ICT regulation be technology-neutral? In *Starting points for ICT regulation. Deconstructing prevalent policy one-liners*, eds. B.J. Koops, M. Lips, C. Prins, and M. Schellekens, 77–108. The Hague: T.M.C. Asser Press.
Korff, D. 2004. *The legal framework: an analysis of the "constitutional" European approach to issues of data protection and law enforcement.* UK Information Commissioner Study Project: Privacy & Law Enforcement, Foundation for Information Policy Research (FIPR).
Organisation for Economic Co-operation and Development (OECD). 2008. RFID radio frequency identification: OECD policy guidance: A focus on information security and privacy applications, impacts and country initiatives. Paper presented at the meeting of the OECD Ministeriel, Seoul (OECD Digital Economy Papers, No. 150).
Poullet, Y. 2006. Les aspects juridiques des systèmes d'information. *Lex Electronica* 10 (3). Also available online at http://www.lex-electronica.org/articles/ v10-3/poullet.htm.
Rigaux, F. 1990. *La protection de la vie privée et des autres biens de la personnalité.* Brussels: Bruylant.
Rouvroy, A., and Poullet, Y. 2009. The right to informational self-determination and the value of self-development: Reassessing the importance of privacy for democracy. In *Reinventing data protection?* eds. S. Gutwirth, Y. Poullet, P. De Hert, and C. de Terwangne, 45–76. Dordrecht: Springer.
Schoeman, F.D. ed. 1984. *Philosophical dimensions of privacy: An anthology.* Cambridge: Cambridge Univ. Press.
Sunstein, Cass R. 2007. *Republic.com 2.0.* Princeton, PA: Princeton Univ. Press.
The Public Voice. 2008. Civil society background Paper: Fuelling creativity, ensuring consumer and privacy protection, building confidence and benefiting from convergence. Paper presented at the meeting of the OECD Ministeriel, Seoul.
Wright, D., S. Gutwirth, M. Friedewald, Y. Punie, and E. Vildjiounaite, eds. 2008. *Safeguards in a world of ambient intelligence.* Dordrecht: Springer Science.
Wright Mills, C. 1956, 2000. *The power elite.* New York: Oxford Univ. Press.

Chapter 7
Facebook and Risks of "De-contextualization" of Information

Franck Dumortier

7.1 Introduction

Participation in online social networking sites (hereafter "OSNS") is continuously growing these recent years, with the number of users multiplying at an exponential rate. For instance, while Facebook's international audience totalled 20 million users in April 2007, that number had increased to 200 million 2 years later with an average of 250,000 new registrations per day since January 2007. The "active proportion" of Facebook's audience is also impressive: according to statistics published on the website, more than 100 million users log on to Facebook at least once a day while more than 20 million users update their statuses at least once each day.[1] Founded in February 2004, Facebook develops technologies that *"facilitate the sharing of information through a social graph, the digital mapping of people's real-world social connections"*.[2] To rely on danah boyd's[3] definition, Facebook is thus a "social network site" in the sense that it is a *"web-based service that allows individuals to (1) construct a public or semi-public profile within a bounded system, (2) articulate a list of other users with whom they share a connection, and (3) view and traverse their list of connections and those made by others within the system"*.[4] Moreover, the main characteristic of a site like Facebook is to connect participants' profiles to their public identities, using real names and other real-world identification signs

[1] See detailed statistics on Facebook's website, http://www.facebook.com/press/info.php?timeline.

[2] *Ibidem.*

[3] danah boyd does not capitalize her name.

[4] Boyd, D., and N. Ellison. 2007. Social network sites: Definition, history, and scholarship. *Journal of Computer-Mediated Communication* 13 (1) Article 11., http://jcmc.indiana.edu/vol13/issue1/boyd.ellison.html. Boyd and Ellison use "social *network* site" rather than "social *networking* site" because "participants are not necessarily 'networking' or looking to meet new people; instead, they are primarily communicating with people who are already a part of their extended social network".

F. Dumortier (✉)
Research Centre for Information Technology & Law (CRID),
University of Namur—FUNDP, Namur, Belgium
e-mail: franck.dumortier@fundp.ac.be

S. Gutwirth et al. (eds.), *Data Protection in a Profiled World*,
DOI 10.1007/978-90-481-8865-9_7,

such as pictures, videos or e-mail addresses in order to enable interaction and communication between real-world subjects. Therefore, Facebook is a thousand miles away from pseudonymous chat rooms and cannot purely be considered as a playground for "virtual bodies" in which identities are flexible and disconnected from "real-world bodies". In fact, there is almost nothing "virtual" in sites like Facebook. Not only is the provision of accurate and current information from the users encouraged, it is even required by the terms of use. Indeed, Facebook imposes its users to *"provide their real names and information"*, to keep their *"contact information accurate and up-to-date"* and prohibits them to *"provide any false personal information"*.[5] These requirements, along with the service's mission of organizing the real social life of its members, provides important incentives for users to publish only real and valid information about themselves. Statistics speak for themselves: already in 2005, 89% of the Facebook profiles used real names whereas 61% of the profiles contained images which were suitable for direct identification.[6]

According to Facebook's statistics, more than 850 million photos and more than eight million videos are uploaded each month. Also, more than one billion content pieces (web links, news stories, blog posts, notes, photos, etc.) are shared each week. Given the widespread use and sharing of personal information deemed to be accurate and up-to-date, important privacy threats can derive from interactions on Facebook, the main one being the risk of "de-contextualization" of the information being provided by the participants. According to me, this "de-contextualization" threat is due to three major characteristics of Facebook: (1) the simplification of social relations, (2) the large dissemination of information and (3) the network globalization and normalization effects of Facebook. The risk of "de-contextualization" not only threatens the right to data protection, i.e. the right to control the informational identity a Human being projects in a certain context. More fundamentally it threatens the right to privacy as a Human right: the right of the Human being to be a multiple and relational self without unjustified discrimination.

In Sect. 7.2, I examine the various characteristics of Facebook which imply a risk of "de-contextualization" of the circulating information. Section 7.3 exposes why this de-contextualization phenomenon threatens both the rights to privacy and to data protection. Finally, I argue that protecting privacy and data protection on Facebook must focus not merely on remedies and penalties for aggrieved individuals but on shaping an architecture to govern the multi-contextual data flows on the site. Given the importance of the "de-contextualization" threat, the architecture of Facebook must be build in such a way that it prevents any interference with both rights to privacy and to data protection when such interference is not strictly necessary in a democratic state.

---

5 See Facebook's "Statement of Rights and Responsibilities", http://fr-fr.facebook.com/terms.php.

6 Gross, R., and A. Acquisti. 2005. Information revelation and privacy in online social networks. In *Proceedings of the 2005 ACM Workshop on Privacy in the Electronic Society*, 77. New York, ACM.

7.2 The Risks of De-contextualization Deriving from Interactions on Facebook

In this paper I use the term "de-contextualization" to conceptualize what happens when behaviours or information are used in another context from that for which they were intended. As Nissembaum argues, the de-contextualization phenomenon arises when individuals do not respect contextual norms of distribution and appropriateness.[7] For example, when a behaviour appropriate with a close friend in a bar is conducted in public or at work it violates contextual norms of appropriateness. In the same way, if my boss comes to know about information that was originally intended for my girlfriend it violates contextual norms of distribution. The problematic thing about these contextual norms is that they can't precisely be defined since these derive from personal sensations about how information should circulate in the physical world, or should I say in the "offline world". Indeed, both norms of appropriateness and distribution presume a certain situational environment because the way information is divulged depends on very granular properties of that environment such as its architectural, temporal and inter-subjective characteristics.[8] As an example, I would not behave in the same way with my boss in a bar at 10 pm than I would do at 8 am at work, neither would I disclose the same information at 10 pm in the same bar with my boss if my mother comes to join us. In the physical world, contextual norms of distribution and appropriateness are thus based on something typically Human: feelings.

However, as I explain in the next sections, Facebook has a completely different design than the physical world, and its architectural, temporal and inter-subjective properties can potentially create an asymmetry between users' "feelings" and the way information can be propagated. Therefore, the use of the concept of "de-contextualization" is particularly interesting in the case of Facebook since it is an environment *"where worlds collide, where norms get caught in the crossfire between communities, where the walls that separate social situations come crashing down"*.[9]

In the next sections I argue that the de-contextualization threat on Facebook is due to three of its major characteristics: (1) the simplification of social relations, (2) the large information dissemination and (3) Facebook's globalization and normalisation effects.

---

[7] See Nissenbaum, H. 2004. Privacy as contextual integrity. *Washington Law Review* 79 (1). http://ssrn.com/abstract=534622.

[8] This idea was also formulated by Peterson. C. 2009. In *Saving face: The privacy architecture of facebook* (Draft for comments—Spring), The Selected Works of Chris Peterson, (2009) 9, Available at http://works.bepress.com/cpeterson/1.

[9] See Peterson, C. 2009. *Saving face: The privacy architecture of facebook.* (Draft for comments—Spring), *op.cit*, abstract.

7.2.1 The Simplification of Social Relations on OSNS

According to statistics published on Facebook, an average user has 120 "friends" on the site. This means that when a user updates his profile (by uploading a picture or a video, modifying his religious or political preferences, or by changing his relational status), posts a message on a "wall" or answers a quiz, this information is, by default and on average, available to more than one hundred persons with whom the user entertains different kinds of relationships. Indeed, connections of a user on Facebook can be as diverse as family members, colleagues, lovers, real friends, bar acquaintances, old schoolmates or even unknown people. Social network theorists have discussed the relevance of relations of different depths and strengths in a person's social network.[10] Noteworthy is the fact that the application of social network theory to information disclosure highlights significant differences between the offline and the online scenarios. In the offline world, the relation between information divulgation and a person's social network is traditionally multi-faceted: *"In certain occasions we want information about ourselves to be known only in a small circle of close friends, and not by strangers. In other instances, we are willing to reveal personal information to anonymous strangers, but not to those who know us better".*[11] Hence, on offline social networks, people develop and maintain ties that could aproximatively be defined as weak or strong ties, but in reality these ties are extremely diverse depending on inter-subjective, temporal and contextual. factors. Online social networks, on the other side, reduce these complex nuanced connections to very simplistic binary relations: "Friend or not".[12] Observing online social networks, danah boyd notes that *"there is no way to determine what metric was used or what the role or weight of the relationship is. While some people are willing to indicate anyone as Friends, and others stick to a conservative definition, most users tend to list anyone who they know and do not actively dislike. This often means that people are indicated as Friends even though the user does not particularly know or trust the person".*[13]

Increasingly, Facebook users thus tend to list as *"Friends"* anyone they do not actively hate[14] and share with these connections an incredible amount of data which

---

[10] See e.g., Granovetter, M. 1973. The strength of weak ties. *American Journal of Sociology* 78: 1360–1380. See also Granoetter, M. 1983. The strength of weak ties: A network theory revisited. *Sociological Theory* 1: 201–233. The privacy relevance of this theory has been highlighted by Strahilevitz. See Strahileviez, L.J. 2005. A social networks theory of privacy. *University of Chicago Law Review* 72: 919. Originally cited by Gross, R., and A. Acquisti. 2005. Information revelation and privacy in online social networks. In *Proceedings of the 2005 ACM Workshop on Privacy in the Electronic Society*, 81. New York, ACM.

[11] Gross, R., and A. Acquisti. 2005. Information revelation and privacy in online social networks. In *Proceedings of the 2005 ACM Workshop on Privacy in the Electronic Society*, 81. New York, ACM.

[12] *Ibidem.*

[13] Boyd D. 2004. Friendster and publicly articulated social networking. in *Conference on Human Factors and Computing Systems (CHI 2004)*, April 24–29, 2. Vienna: ACM, April 24–29.

[14] Note that Hatebook.org, the exact opposite version of Facebook, defines itself as *"an anti-social utility that disconnects you from all the things you hate".*

can potentially be inappropriate in Facebook's *heterotopical*[15] context. Let's take for example a Facebook user who has 100 "Friends": 4 of them being family members, 16 "close friends", 1 lover, 4 ex-lovers, 30 old school mates, 30 acquaintances (from different contexts), 14 work colleagues and his boss. Now imagine that our user installs a third party application on Facebook to answer a funny "Are you alcoholic?" quiz and at the same time sets his "relationship status" to single. There is no doubt that the combination of these information will have a different meaning for his friends and lover than for his colleagues, his boss or his mother. From these observations derives a threat of de-contextualization: the difficulty for a multi-faceted self to contextually curtail the information he wants to share to "Friends" of different contexts. Simply said, answering a "What's your favourite sexual position?" quiz can certainly provide interesting information to my girlfriend but is surely not *appropriate* for any of my colleagues.

With this regard, the "Friend Lists" feature provided by Facebook which enables users to organize friends into different categories is a start. The tool allows them to include and exclude groups of friends from being able to see parts of their profile and content. In our example, an aware user could group each type of "friends" into different categories he predefines and grant them different sets of permissions to information such as pictures, videos, status, messages, etc. However, by making the problem of limiting access to certain information easier by adding more specific control, Facebook also introduced more complexity and conceptual overhead for users: they now have to "categorize" their "friends". This is precisely why the "Friends Lists" feature can't be considered as accurately mimicking the way in which we all limit access to certain personal information to specific friends in the real world. Indeed, the feature looks much more like how a system administrator might set up permissions to computer resources than how information divulgation processes happen in everyday life: "labelling" friends and creating "Friend Lists" doesn't happen consciously in the offline world.

The simplification of social relations on OSNS thus induces a first threat of de-contextualization of information given that the binaryc relationships on these sites can lead to breaches of contextual norms of appropriateness or norms of distribution: information divulgation will never be as granular in the online world as it is in the offline world.

7.2.2 *The Large Information Dissemination Implied by Interactions on Facebook*

Not only does the simplification of social relations on Facebook induce a threat to de-contextualization, so does the way in which information can potentially be largely disseminated along the social graph. In offline scenarios, it is exceptionally unlikely that information about a person will be interesting beyond two degrees of

---

[15] For more details about Facebook as a heterotopical space, see Sect. 2.1, p. 11.

information. In such scenarios, Duncan Watts notes that *"anyone more distant than a friend of a friend is, for all intents and purposes, a stranger ... Anything more than two degrees might as well be a thousand"*.[16] In other words, at least in the pre-Facebook era, no one much cared about those people who were removed from us by more than two links. Strahilevitz illustrates this perfectly in the following quote:

> Extra-marital affairs are fascinating events. That said, no self-respecting person would go to a cocktail party and tell a private story about a friend of a friend of a friend who is having an adulterous affair with someone unknown to the speaker and listener. It is only if the speaker or listener know who the adulterers are, or if the details of the affair are particularly sordid, humorous, or memorable that the information is likely to get disseminated further through the social network. And by the time the information makes it through this chain, it seems likely that the participants' names would have dropped out of the story. "[17]

Thus, when dealing with events described via word-of-mouth, someone should have a "reasonable expectation of contextual integrity" beyond two links in a social network. This rule of thumb appears to hold less strongly when one moves away from offline communications and interacts on online network services such as Facebook, and this for five main reasons.

First, dissemination of information along the social graph is encouraged by the presence of a visible network of friends on every participant's profile. Whereas in the real-world, friends can spend years without knowing that they share a mutual friend, on Facebook they can very easily find out which common friends they share. Such a list also makes it easier for anyone to know which are the friends of a friend of a friend of his. Moreover, each profile of the list of friends of a friend can be "shared" and commented on the users profile. As an example, I could go through my connection list, pick out one of my friends, look at his friends then to the friends of his friends and finally publish the limited profile of one of them on my profile with a disgracious comment that can then again be shared and commented further trough the social graphs of my own "friends".

Second, Facebook is constituted by a large number of networks, and users are incited to join them in order to meet and make "friends" with other people. The biggest of these networks are the so-called "geographic networks", the Belgian one bringing more than 780,000 people together. Having joined such a network, a user can then "classify" users of a same network on the basis of criteria such as gender, age, relationship status, interests and political views. Moreover, depending on the target's privacy settings, users can then access parts or the entirety of friends of friends of friends' profiles.[18]

---

[16] Watts, D.J. 2003. *Six degrees: the science of a connected age*, 299–300. New York: Norton.

[17] L.J. Strahilevitz, *op.cit*, 47.

[18] According to the article *Facebook Security Fails Again* published on IT-ONLINE, in 2007, the IT security and control firm Sophos revealed that members involuntarily exposed their personal data to millions of strangers, at risk of identity theft. The security company chosed randomly 200 users in the London Facebook network, which is the largest geographic network on the site, with more than 1.2 million members, and found that a staggering 75% allowed their profiles to be viewed by any other member, regardless of whether or not they had agreed to be friends. The reason of this unwanted divulgation of information was that even if you had previously set up your pri-

Another factor that can potentially cause broad information divulgation is the "tagging" feature proposed by Facebook. A tag is a keyword, often the real-name of a participant associated with or assigned to a piece of information (a picture, a video clip, etc.), thus describing the item and enabling keyword-based classification and search of information. When associated with a picture or a video, a tag directly provides a link to the represented user's profile. Here comes the classic Facebook problem: you don't login to the site for a few hours 1 day and photos (or other information) of the moment are suddenly posted for all friends of a friend to view, not just your close friends who shared the moment with you. Indeed, Facebook didn't create a default privacy setting that would allow users to approve or deny photo tags before they can appear on the site.[19]

A fourth worry for unwanted dissemination of information derives from "Facebook Platform for Mobile". According to Facebook's statistics, *"there are currently more than 30 million active users accessing Facebook through their mobile devices. People that use Facebook on their mobile devices are almost 50% more active on Facebook than non-mobile users"*.[20] The biggest privacy threat of such a feature derives from the ubiquity of mobile devices that can potentially let online information enter into the offline world anytime, anywhere and anyplace. Indeed, privacy settings don't matter in the offline world: with his mobile, one of my real-world friends could easily show me the complete Facebook profile of one of his "friends" whom I completely don't know just because one of his/her characteristics were interesting in the context of our personal discussion.

Finally, the introduction of third-party applications on Facebook has opened users' personal data up to an increasingly large group of developers and marketers. According to a 2007 review[21] of the top 150 Facebook applications, nearly 91% had access to unnecessary personal data. Given the recreational nature of many top applications today, this statistic has probably not changed drastically. Users have become accustomed to authorizing even simple applications and do not know what data will be used and to whom it will be transferred prior to authorizing an application. "We're Related" is one such third-party application that has been the source of these concerns. According to one report, this application, which claims 15 million active users each month, seeks to identify and link family members who are already on the network, even if they are only distantly related: *"New users are asked to*

---

vacy settings to ensure that only friends could view your information, joining a network automatically opened your profile to every other member of the network. It is only in 2009 that Facebook changed the default privacy settings for geographical networks to avoid unwanted open profiles.

[19] There is a possibility to indirectly restrict the visibility of the tagged photos by first visiting your profile privacy page and modify the setting next to "Photos Tagged of You", select the option which says "Customize …", select the option "Only Me" and then "None of My Networks". If you would like to make tagged photos visible to certain users you can choose to add them in the box under the "Some Friends" option. In the box that displays after you select "Some Friends" you can type either individual friends or friend lists.

[20] See Facebook statistics on http://www.facebook.com/press/info.php?statistics.

[21] A. Felt, and D. Evans. 2008. *Privacy protection for social networkin APIs.* W2SP, May 2008, available at http://www.cs.virginia.edu/felt/privacybyproxy.pdf.

give a blanket approval to let the application 'pull your profile information, photos, your friends' info and other content that it requires to work'. The application then appears to give itself the power to release this information to anyone else on Facebook—even if users have set stricter privacy settings to limit access to their personal data".[22] However, as indicated in Facebook's user terms, the company does not consider itself responsible for inaccurate privacy practices of third party applications developers.[23]

Combined together, these five factors induce a risk of unwanted dissemination of data going beyond the "reasonable expectations of contextual integrity" of Facebook users since important information exchanged with their "friends" can potentially propagate much further than two links of information.

In the next section, I argue that this de-contextualization threat can potentially be increased by Facebook's globalization and normalization effects.

7.2.3 The Globalization and Normalization Effects of Facebook

Everyone has experienced the increasing pressure from connections to finally get with the program and join the network. This can partly be explained by the fact that when someone registers on Facebook, the site invites the new user to *"find out which of (his) email contacts are on Facebook"*. Facebook then asks users for their email address and password for many of the major providers of webmail services (Yahoo, Hotmail, Gmail, etc.). Facebook then logs on to the e-mail account, and downloads all the contacts from there.[24] The user is then given the option of inviting all of their contacts to join Facebook. By default, all of the contacts are pre-selected: the default behaviour is thus to send messages to all of one's contacts inviting them to become friends on Facebook.

Incentives to be on the program become even more concrete when one examines the "tagging" feature proposed by Facebook. A problematic element about that feature is that even people who did not register on the network can be tagged (thus possibly by so-called friends, complete strangers or even enemies). Of course, the right of access and the right to rectification/deletion can be used if someone wants to remove a particular tag about himself, but therefore he has to first register on Facebook. This is what we could call the globalization effect of Facebook: without

---

[22] See R. Waters, 2009. Facebook applications raise privacy fears. *Financial times online*, available at http://www.ft.com/cms/s/0/2a58acfa-5c35-11de-aea3-00144feabdc0.html.

[23] See Facebook's Platform Application Terms of Use: *"When you install a Developer Application, you understand that such Developer Application has not been approved, endorsed, or reviewed in any manner by Facebook, and we are not responsible for your use of or inability to use any Developer Applications, including without limitation the content, accuracy, or reliability of such Developer Application and the privacy practices or other policies of the Developer. YOU USE SUCH DEVELOPER APPLICATIONS AT YOUR OWN RISK"*. Available at http://developers.facebook.com/user_terms.php.

[24] See http://epic.org/privacy/facebook/

being on the program, someone can already be a data object defined by pictures and articles. Without even knowing it and without being able to react, someone can already be a well-documented widely disseminated discussion topic. To become a real data subject, the data object has first to register on Facebook before being able to exercise his data protection rights. To become active actors in the control over their informational identity, people become obliged to register on the program.

Given the impressive growth of Facebook (314% in the last year), the service is increasingly becoming an everyday communication tool with for example 21% of the Belgian population being registered.[25] Paradoxically, it thus becomes increasingly more abnormal not to be on Facebook than the contrary. This is what we could call the normalization effect of Facebook: a future where employers will ask themselves the question: *"why is Mr X not on Facebook? That's strange ... has he something to hide?"* is maybe not so far.

Having now described the three main characteristics of Facebook leading to a risk of de-contextualization of personal information, in the next section I analyze the consequences of such a threat on the respect of the rights to privacy and to data protection.

7.3 Consequences of the Threat of De-contextualization on the Rights to Privacy and to Data Protection

The three characteristics of Facebook that I exposed—(1) simplification of social relations, (2) wide dissemination of information and (3) globalization and normalization effects—can potentially lead to important risks of de-contextualization of information. Such a threat of de-contextualization of personal information on Facebook can potentially affect both the right to privacy and the right to data protection of the service's users.

The links between both rights have already been seriously examined by influential authors.[26] For the purposes of our discussion, let us simply take as a starting point the mere fact that the right to privacy is traditionally seen as a "Human right" recognised to Human beings whereas the "rights to data protection" are provided to "data subjects" by the most significant legal instruments at the European level. Indeed, where privacy and the ECHR are all about Humans, Directive 95/46 cares about data subjects. *Why?* The question could seem somewhat simplistic or trivial, but understanding from such an angle the respective meanings of both rights to

---

[25] See statistics on http://katrin-mathis.de/wp-mu/thesis/.

[26] Gutwirth and De Hert, for example, discussed the distinction by viewing the right to privacy as being a kind of *"tool of opacity"* whereas, according to the authors, the right to data protection would be a *"tool of transparency"*. See Gutwirth S., and P. De Hert 2006. Privacy, data protection and law enforcement. Opacity of the individual and transparency of power. In *Privacy and the criminal law*, eds. E. Claes, A. Duff, and S. Gutwirth, 61–104. Antwerp: Intersentia.

privacy and to data protection can, I think, help us to understand in which way de-contextualization of information threatens both rights.

7.3.1 Consequences of the Threat of De-contextualization on Privacy as a Right of the Human Being

Recalling that privacy is a right provided to Human beings can appear to be trivial, however the term "Human" is extremely ambiguous and has known an extraordinary historical and philosophical evolution. In order to properly introduce this topic and to avoid unnecessary discussions, let us only acknowledge that a Human being cannot be reduced to a body nor to a physical person. Of course, Human rights should ideally be conferred to all bodies having Human specifications as defined by anatomy, but, historically, there is no doubt that lawyers were also influenced by philosophical conceptions of the "inner self" when designing the Human rights framework. As an example, Article 1 of the Universal Declaration of Human Rights defines the Human as being *"endowed with reason and conscience"*, recalling a very Kantian point of view according to which the definitive characteristic of the Human self was its capacity for reason. Reason, according to Kant, allowed the self to understand and order the world with certainty. In consequence, the Kantian self was conceived as an identity pole of coherent subjectivity, standing above the stream of changing experience. However, increasingly in the twentieth century, the liberal modernist notion of the self as a unitary, stable, and transparent individual has come under heavy criticism. Indeed, many postmodern and late modern theories of the self asserted that it is fractured and multiple. According to these, the self is an illusory notion constructed as static and unitary, but in reality completely fluid.[27] Evolution of these reflections lead to conceptions of the Human being as a *"multiple-self"*[28] which is relational, inter-subjective and context-dependent. Goffman's nuanced idea of a *"cosmopolitan person"* perfectly reflects the philosophical debate between unification and fragmentation of the modern self which is constantly evolving in a plurality of contexts. According to him,

> In many modern settings, individuals are caught up in a variety of differing encounters … each of which may call for different forms of appropriate' behaviour … As the individual leaves one encounter and enters another, he sensitively adjusts the 'presentation of self' in

---

[27] See, e.g., Ewing, K.P. 1990. The illusion of wholeness: Culture, self, and the experience of inconsistency. *Ethos* 18 (3) 251–278 (arguing that people "project multiple, inconsistent self-representations that are context-dependent and may shift rapidly"); Harris, A.P. 1996. Foreword: The unbearable lightness of identity. *Berkeley Women's Law Journal* 11: 207–211 (arguing that the problem with any general theory of identity "is that 'identity itself' has little substance"); Wicke, J. 1991. Postmodern identity and the legal subject. *University of Colorado Law Review* 62: 455–463 (noting that a postmodern conception of identity recognizes the self as fragmented and captures "its fissuring by the myriad social discourses which construct it").

[28] See, e.g., Elster, J. 1986. *The multiple self.* Studies in Rationality and Social Change. Cambridge, MA: Cambridge Univ. Press.

> relation to whatever is demanded of a particular situation. Such a view is often thought to imply that an individual has as many selves as there are divergent contexts of interaction … Yet again it would not be correct to see contextual diversity as simply and inevitably promoting the fragmentation of the self, let alone its disintegration into multiple 'selves'. It can just as well, at least in many circumstances, promote an integration of self … A person may make use of diversity in order to create a distinctive self-identity which positively incorporates elements from different settings into an integrated narrative. Thus a cosmopolitan person is one precisely who draws strength from being at home in a variety of contexts.[29]

Behind the postmodern dilemma between unification and fragmentation of the self, important for the purposes of our discussion is the fact that Human beings are increasingly conceived as contextual selves constantly reinventing themselves, adopting different roles, postures and attitudes in a complex open network of networks. Taking into account this conceptual evolution of the Human self towards a contextual self, it is then interesting to analyze the evolution of the meaning of his right to privacy.

Since its acceptance as the *"right to be left alone"*,[30] the right to privacy has known significant developments. Interestingly, the European Court of Human Rights has asserted that it would be too restrictive to limit the notion of "private life" to an "inner circle" in which the individual may live his own personal life as he chooses and to exclude entirely the outside world not encompassed within that circle: *"Respect for private life must also comprise to a certain degree the right to establish and develop relationships with other Human beings"*.[31] Privacy is now obviously conceived as a phenomenon that regards the relationships between a self and its environment/other selves. As Fried observes,

> Privacy is not just one possible means among others to insure some other value, but that it is necessarily related to ends and relations of the most fundamental sort: respect, love, friendship and trust. Privacy is not merely a good technique for furthering these fundamental relations; rather without privacy they are simply inconceivable. They require a context of privacy or the possibility of privacy for their existence.[32]

Furthermore, as *"people have, and it is important that they maintain, different relationships with different people"*,[33] relationships between selves are by nature extremely contextual. Therefore Nissenbaum asserted that the definitive value to be protected by the right to privacy is the "contextual integrity"[34] of a given contextual-self having different behaviors and sharing different information depending on the context in which he's evolving. With this regard, Rachels notes that:

---

[29] Goffman, cited in Giddens, A. 1991. *Modernity and self-identity: Self and society in the late modern age.* Stanford: Stanford Univ. Press.

[30] Warren, S.D., and L.D. Brandeis, 1890. *The right to privacy. Harvard Law Review* 4 (5): 193–220.

[31] See e.g. *Niemietz v. Germany*, A 251-B, § 29 (ECHR, 16 décembre 1992).

[32] Fried, C. 1968. Privacy. *Yale Law Journal* 77: 475–93.

[33] Schoeman, F. 1984. Privacy and intimate information. In *Philosophical Dimensions of Privacy: An Anthology*, 403–408. Cambridge, MA: Cambridge Univ. Press.

[34] H. Nissenbaum, *op.cit.*

> (T)here is a close connection between our ability to control who has access to us and to information about us, and our ability to create and maintain different sorts of social relationships with different people … privacy is necessary if we are to maintain the variety of social relationships with other people that we want to have and that is why it is important to us.[35]

In a similar way, Agre defined the right to privacy as *"the freedom from unreasonable constraints on the construction of one's own identity"*.[36] Given that someone's identity-building is increasingly conceived as a progressive autonomic and narrative integration of different elements deriving from a contextual diversity, many authors tend to consider the right to privacy as a "right to self-determination" which is a major precondition for individual autonomy.[37] In other words, as relations with others are essential to the construction of an individual's personality, the right to privacy also encourages self-development[38] by protecting a diversity of contextualized relations from unreasonable intrusions or leaks. In such a perspective, the right to privacy can be conceived as a "right to self-determination of the contextual self" which guarantees him the possibility to act and communicate the way he *contextually* wants to without having to fear unreasonable *de-contextualization* of behaviors or information.

Let us imagine a 45 year old father working as a bank employee, who is politically involved in a left-wing anti-militarist party, who goes hunting with his friends on Saturday, goes with his family to church every Sunday and loves to analyze *Playboy* each Monday with a few colleagues during the morning break. Some might think that some of these context-dependent self-representations are inconsistent or incompatible between them. Others can easily imagine how inappropriate a behavior or an information from one of these contexts could appear in some of the others. But, more fundamentally, everyone will agree that none of these contexts or situations are *in se* illegal or harming. Here's precisely what the right to privacy is all about: showing respect for individual autonomy, even if someone's inter-contextual identity-building could seem incoherent to some of us. In this perspective, the right to privacy is not only an important precondition for individual autonomy but more generally for the persistence of a vivid democracy. Antoinette Rouvroy provides one of the best-informed versions of this claim:

> The right to privacy guarantees the possibility for the subject to think differently from the majority and to revise his first order preferences. Thus, privacy is a condition for the existence of 'subjects' capable of participating in a deliberative democracy. As a consequence, privacy also protects lawful, but unpopular, lifestyles against social pressures to conform to dominant social norms. Privacy as freedom from unreasonable constraints in the construc-

---

[35] James, J. 1975. Why privacy is important. *Philosophy and Public Affairs* 4 (4): 323–333.

[36] Agre, P.E., and M. Rotenberg, eds., *Technology and privacy. The new landscape*, 3. Cambridge, MA: MIT Press.

[37] See e.g., Rouvroy, A., and Y. Poullet, 2009. The right to informational self-determination and the value of self-development. Reassessing the importance of privacy for democracy. In *Reinventing Data Protection*, eds. S. Gutwirth, P. De Hert, and Y. Poullet. Dordrecht: Springer.

[38] See *Odièvre v. France* (ECHR, 13 February 2003), where the Court acknowledged that the right to privacy (Article 8 of the European Convention on Human Rights) protects, among other interests, the right to personal development.

> tion of one's identity, serves to prevent or combat the "tyranny of the majority". The right to privacy and the right not to be discriminated against have in common that they protect the opportunities, for individuals, to experiment a diversity of non-conventional ways of life. Privacy is itself a tool for preventing invidious discriminations and prejudices.[39]

The right to privacy can thus be conceptualized as a right to contextual integrity preserving the possibility for anyone to build his own identity through differentiated relationships. The aim of such a "right to difference" is to ensure multiplicity, creation, novelty and invention in a democratic society and to avoid immobility or sterile heavy normalization. That's why de-contextualization of personal information can be considered as one of the main threats to the right to privacy.

Such a threat of de-contextualization is particularly present in the case of Facebook which is a platform of collapsed contexts. Indeed, the service merges every possible relationship into one single social space: friendship, politics, work, love, etc. arc all mixed together in a unique environment. Therefore Facebook can be seen as what Foucault calls an heterotopia. According to the philosopher,

> Heterotopias are counter-sites, a kind of effectively enacted utopia in which the real sites, all the other real sites that can be found within the culture, are simultaneously represented, contested, and inverted. Places of this kind are outside of all places, even though it may be possible to indicate their location in reality.[40]

This definition, applied to Facebook, reveals all its accuracy. Indeed, Facebook's servers are situated somewhere in the US, making it possible to indicate their location in reality. Moreover, just as heterotopias, Facebook is *"capable of juxtaposing in a single real place several spaces, several sites that are in themselves incompatible"*.[41] In this sense, Facebook can be considered as being outside of all places. Indeed, whereas in the physical world, doors separate rooms, walls muffle sound, curtains block spying eyes, where the volume of our voices during a conversation can be modulated depending on the sensitivity of the content and who is in earshot, the "de-contextualizing" architecture of Facebook is above space, and therefore makes it much more difficult to tailor our presentation to fit different situations.[42] Therefore Facebook's heterotopical architecture can potentially create an asymmetry between a user's imagined audience and a user's actual audience, simply because the platform lacks a separation of spaces. By this, the service makes it much more difficult for users to evaluate which contextual norms of appropriateness or distribution they should expect respect for when divulgating information on the site.

Here's where the phenomenon of de-contextualization on Facebook threatens the right to privacy: it threatens the possibility of the Human being to act as a contextual and relational self and prevents him to build his own identity trough differenti-

---

[39] Rouvroy, A. 2008. Privacy, data protection, and the unprecedented challenges of ambient intelligence. *Studies in Ethics, Law, and Technology* 2 (1): 34.

[40] Foucault, M. 1967. Of other spaces. *Heterotopias*. http://foucault.info/documents/heteroTopia/foucault.heteroTopia.en.html.

[41] *Ibidem*.

[42] The same idea can be found in Peterson, C. 2009. *Saving face: the privacy architecture of facebook*. (Draft for comments—Spring), *op.cit*, 9 and 35.

ated relationships. By this, Facebook can also cause important discriminations and prejudices.

7.3.2 Consequences of the Threat of De-contextualization on Data Protection as a Right of Data Subjects

The de-contextualization phenomenon on Facebook not only threatens the right to privacy of Human beings but also the right to data protection of "data subjects". Indeed, whereas the right to privacy cares about Human beings, the most important data protection instruments create rights for "data subjects". Directive 95/46 defines a "data subject" as an identified or identifiable natural person and an "identifiable person" as one who can be identified, directly or indirectly, in particular by reference to an identification number or to one or more factors specific to his physical, physiological, mental, economic, cultural or social identity. A "subject of data" is thus being conceived as someone who can be identified by reference to one or more factors specific to *one aspect* of his identity. Therefore Agre defines the right to data protection as *"the right to control over an aspect of the identity one projects to the world".*[43] Interestingly the right to data protection can thus be seen as a mean of control on a *partial* projection of someone's "identity", which as already mentioned is extremely *contextual* and *relational.*

For this reason, I believe that the right to data protection can be conceptualized as a right provided to "dividuals". Registered since the first Noah Webster's Dictionary (1828) until today, the term "dividual" means *"divided, shared, or participated in, in common with others".* The Random House Unabridged Dictionary gives the following meanings: (1) divisible or divided; (2) separate, distinct; (3) distributed, shared. Hence the English word "dividual" contains both the meanings of "shared" and "divided", basic characteristics of *contextual relationships* in which "differentiated" content is "shared" depending on who someone communicates to. Also, the term "dividual" has been used by Deleuze in his description of societies of control, *"which no longer operate by confining people but through continuous control and instant communication".*[44] For Deleuze, contemporary society caused a generalized crisis where spaces of enclosure mould people into data *"dividuals".* According to the philosopher;

> The disciplinary societies have two poles: the signature that designates the individual, and the number or administrative numeration that indicates his or her position within a mass. In the societies of control, on the other hand, what is important is no longer either a signature or a number, but a code: the code is a password, while on the other hand disciplinary societies are regulated by watchwords (as much from the point of view of integration as from

[43] Agre, P.E., and M. Rotenberg, eds., *Technology and privacy. The new landscape*, 3. Cambridge, MA: MIT Press.

[44] Deleuze, G. 1992. *Postscript on the societies of control.* 3–7, October_59, Winter Cambridge, MA: MIT Press. available on http://www.spunk.org/texts/misc/sp000962.txt.

> that of resistance). The numerical language of control is made of codes that mark access to information, or reject it. We no longer find ourselves dealing with the mass/individual pair. Individuals have become "dividuals" and masses, samples, data, markets, or banks.[45]

As the quote illustrates, one of the characteristics of the societies of control is the emergence of "dividuals" conceived as *"physically embodied human subjects that are endlessly divisible and reducible to data representations via the modern technologies of control, like computer-based systems"*.[46] Via the data collected on us, the technologies of control can separate who we are and what we are from our physical selves.[47] The data become the representations of ourselves within the web of social relations; the data are the signifiers of our preferences and habits. Borrowing from Laudon, such can be called our "data images":[48] since we are not physically present, we are threatened to be reduced to our documented interests and behaviours. As Williams notes, *"complex processes of self-determination are thereby threatened to be reified by a few formulae in some electronic storage facility. The separation of ourselves from our representations highlights a second aspect of our dividuality. As data, we are classifiable in diverse ways: we are sorted into different categories, and can be evaluated for different purposes. Our divisibility hence becomes the basis for our classifiability into salient, useful, and even profitable categories for third parties that manipulate the data"*.[49] Thirdly and fundamentally, given the divisibility of our data images into various contexts of representation, "contextual dividuals" are increasingly threatened by the risk of de-contextualization. Indeed, given the extreme fluidity of electronic data, information collected in one situational context can increasingly be re-used in another, sometimes in a very inappropriate way.

Taking into account these various threats resulting from our increasing divisibility, I argue that European data protection regulation was designed to provide "dividuals" with the means to control the informational image they project in their "dividual context" by enacting general data protection principles and procuring rights to "data subjects". In other words, "data subjects" can be seen as empowered "dividuals" having legal means to challenge any de-contextualization of the information processed about them. Concrete examples of their means of empowerment as regards their contextual informational image can be found in Directive 95/46. First and foremost, Article 6 impose data to be processed *"for specified, explicit and legitimate purposes and may not further be processed in a way incompatible with those purposes"*. In a certain sense, the purpose limitation principle ties adequate protection for personal data to informational norms of specific contexts, requiring

---

45 *Ibidem.*

46 Williams, R.W. 2005. Politics and self in the age of digital re(pro)ducibility. *Fast Capitalism* 1 (1). available on http://www.uta.edu/huma/agger/fastcapitalism/1_1/williams.html

47 See Poster, M. 1990. *The mode of information, poststructuralism and social context.* Cambridge, UK: Polity Press.

48 See Kenneth, L. 1986. *The dossier society: Value choices in the design of national information systems.* New York: Columbia Univ. Press.

49 Williams, R.W., *op.cit.*

from data controllers that the data should not be further *distributed* when this new flow does not respect the contextual norms. The same article of the Directive also require data to be *"adequate, relevant and not excessive in relation to the purposes for which they are collected and/or further processed"*, demanding that information gathering and dissemination be *appropriate* to that context and obey the governing norms of information within it. These two principles of the European Directive (purpose limitation and data quality) can thus be interpreted as a consecration of Helen Nissenbaum's theory, according to which *"a normative account of privacy in terms of contextual integrity asserts that a privacy violation has occurred when either contextual norms of appropriateness or norms of distribution have been breached"*.[50] In consequence, the rights of information, access, rectification and opposition can be seen as legal means of empowerment provided to "contextual dividuals" for challenging every breach of contextual norms (of appropriateness or distribution) by data controllers.

In summary, whereas the right to privacy guarantees the Human being the possibility to be multi-faceted and to act contextually differently in order to ensure the perseverance of a vivid and deliberative democracy, the right to data protection can be seen as a tool to empower "contextual dividuals" with the means to ensure the contextual integrity of their informational image.

Conceptualizing the right to data protection as a right of "contextual dividuals" can, I think, help us understand why the de-contextualization phenomenon is so particularly harming for our data protection rights on a site like Facebook. Indeed, one of the prime effects of heterotopical environments such as Facebook is to artificially *recompose* the individuals. Quoting Foucault,

> The individual is not to be conceived as a sort of elementary nucleus, a primitive atom, a multiple and inert material on which power comes to fasten or against which it happens to strike, and in so doing crushes or subdues individuals. In fact, it is already one of the prime effects of power that certain bodies, certain gestures, certain discourses, certain desires come to be identified and constituted as individuals. The individual, that is, is not the vis-a-vis of power; it is I believe, one of its prime effects.[51]

In a similar way, on Facebook, *"personal information a user posts online, combined with data outlining the users actions and interactions with other people, can create a rich profile of that person's interests and activities"*.[52] The multi-contextual collation of all of my and my friends' contributions can thus easily paint an *individual* picture of me. Hence, by merging every possible contexts into one single informational environment, Facebook negates the existence of our dividualities, and by consequence denies our rights as dividuals.

In other words, the purpose described on Facebook's main page—*"Facebook helps you connect and share with the people in your life"*—is far too broad to deter-

[50] Nissenbaum, H. 2004 Privacy as contextual integrity. *Washington Law Review* 79 (1): 138.

[51] Foucault, M. 1980 Body/power. In *Foucault on power/knowledge: selected interviews and other writings 1972–1977*, ed. C. Gordon, 91. London: Harvester Press.

[52] Article 29 Working Party, Opinion 5/2009 on online social networking, 12 June 2009, p. 4.

mine which data are adequate, relevant and not excessive in relation with that purpose. If Facebook's architecture destroys contextual integrity, it is because the most fundamental characteristics of its design directly conflicts with norms of distribution and appropriateness. Indeed, global multi-contextuality cannot be concealed with a right to data protection because when the purpose of a service is defined as "everything" then all data can be considered as adequate, relevant and not excessive and every further distribution can be considered as compatible.

7.4 Conclusion

The de-contextualization phenomenon on Facebook certainly constitutes a major threat to both rights to privacy and to data protection. European regulators share a similar point of view. Indeed, in its recent opinion "on online social networking", the Article 29 Working Party stressed that one of its key concerns was *"the dissemination and use of information available on SNS for other secondary, unintended purposes"*.[53] To prevent de-contextualization of information on OSNS, the Working Party advocates *"robust security and privacy-friendly default settings"*[54] but also wants to increase users' responsibilities by imposing them duties of a data controller when the OSNS is used as *"a collaboration platform for an association or a company"*, when the OSNS is mainly used *"as a platform to advance commercial, political or charitable goals"*, when *"access to profile information extends beyond self-selected contacts"* or when *"the data is indexable by search engines"*. Moreover, according to the Working Party, *"a high number of contacts could be an indication that the household exception does not apply and therefore that the user would be considered a data controller"*.[55]

Given that only 20% of users ever touch their privacy settings,[56] I certainly believe that strong default privacy settings would constitute a first guarantee against de-contextualization. This being said, I have more doubts as regards the Working Party's second proposal. Indeed, raising the users' responsibilities with the hope that less de-contextualization will arise supposes high levels of awareness and knowledge from users. However, awareness of data protection rights and duties amongst citizens seems to stay quite low. Indeed, according to a recent Eurobarometer, *"despite drastic technological changes occurring in the last two decades, the level of concern*

[53] Article 29 Working Party, Opinion 5/2009 on online social networking, 12 June 2009, p. 3.

[54] *Ibidem.*

[55] *Ibidem*, p. 4.

[56] According to Facebook CPO Chris Kelly, only 20% of users ever touch their privacy settings. See. Stross Randall, "When Everyone's a Friend, Is Anything Private?", *The New York Times*, March 7, 2009, available at http://www.nytimes.com/2009/03/08/business/08digi.html.

about data protection hasn't practically changed".[57] The highest levels of awareness of the existence of Data protection rights were in Poland (43%), followed by Latvia (38%), France and Hungary (both 35%). Less than one in five citizens in Sweden (16%) and Austria (18%) said they were aware of the legal possibilities they have in order to control the use of their own personal data.[58]

For this reason, and because it is important for the ECHR *"to be interpreted and applied so as to make its safeguards practical and effective, as opposed to theoretical and illusory"*,[59] I sincerely believe that protecting privacy and data protection on Facebook must focus not merely on remedies and penalties for aggrieved individuals but on shaping an architecture to govern the multi-contextual data flows on the site. Given the importance of the "de-contextualization" threat, the architecture of Facebook must be build in such a way that it prevents any interference with both rights to privacy and to data protection when such interference is not strictly "necessary in a democratic state".

To achieve such a goal, European authorities could increase the responsibility of the operators of social networking sites by making them accountable for the design of their sites. Such mechanisms already exist as regards terminal equipment in the electronic communications context. Indeed, according to Article 14(3) of Directive 2002/58, *"where required, measures may be adopted to ensure that terminal equipment is constructed in a way that is compatible with the right of users to protect and control the use of their personal data"*. In the same manner, Article 3(3)(c) of Directive 1999/5 states that *"the Commission may decide that apparatus within certain equipment classes or apparatus of particular types shall be so constructed that they incorporate safeguards to ensure that the personal data and privacy of the user and of the subscriber are protected"*.

In doing so, European authorities could impose less multi-contextual content in OSNS by demanding the operators of such sites to curtail their architecture in accordance with each user's specific intents. As an example, before a user registers on Facebook, a question could be asked such as *"For which purpose do you intend to use Facebook?"* with a list of answers such as "Commercial purpose", "political purpose", "dating purpose", "work relations", "real-world friendship", etc. After having determined more precisely the purpose of each user's registration, Facebook should then collect only adequate, relevant and non-excessive data in relation with that purpose. If a user wants to use the service for multiple purposes, multiple accounts should be encouraged. More generally, Facebook operators should consider carefully *"if they can justify forcing their users to act under their real identity*

[57] See Rapid Press Release *"Eurobarometer survey reveals that EU citizens are not yet fully aware of their rights on data protection"*, IP/08/592, 17 April 2008.

[58] See Eurobarometer, *"Data Protection in the European Union: Citizens' perceptions"*, Analytical report, February 2008, available at http://ec.europa.eu/public_opinion/flash/fl_225_en.pdf.

[59] See *Artico v. Italy*, 37, (ECHR, 13 May 1980), 15–16, § 33, and *Stafford v. the United Kingdom* (GC), 46295/99, § 68 (ECHR 2002-IV).

rather than under a pseudonym".[60] When the specific purpose of use doesn't require the real name, pseudonyms should be encouraged.

Reconstructing places inside Facebook is an absolute necessity for users to evaluate which contextual norms of distribution and appropriateness they can expect. Such a claim is not only useful to respect each user's dividuality as regards his right to data protection. More fundamentally it is essential to allow users to construct their identity as multiple and relational selves and hence to act as Human beings.

[60] Article 29 Working Party, Opinion 5/2009 on online social networking, 12 June 2009, p. 11.

Chapter 8
Surveillance in Germany: Strategies and Counterstrategies

Gerrit Hornung, Ralf Bendrath and Andreas Pfitzmann

8.1 Introduction

In 2008, Germany appeared to be one—if not the—point of culmination as regards the legal, technical and political discussions of new technical surveillance measures. 25 years after its ground breaking population census decision (Bundesverfassungsgericht 1983; see Hornung and Schnabel 2009a; Rouvroy and Poullet 2009), the German Federal Constitutional Court (Bundesverfassungsgericht) delivered three important judgments on governmental surveillance and privacy in less than 2 weeks in early 2008, namely the "online-searching" decision (Bundesverfassungsgericht 2008a, see below), the decision on license plate scanning (Bundesverfassungsgericht 2008b), and the interim injunction to partly stop the enactment of the European data retention directive in Germany (Bundesverfassungsgericht 2008c). In all three cases, the Court ruled against the respective measures (Hornung and Schnabel 2009b), and even established a new "fundamental right to the guarantee of the confidentiality and integrity of information technology systems" (Grundrecht auf Gewährleistung der Vertraulichkeit und Integrität informationstechnischer Systeme) in the online-searching decision.

In parallel Germany has seen the formation of a new civil rights movement campaigning for personal and societal privacy. Under the motto "Freedom not Fear—Stop the surveillance mania!", the largest protest march against surveillance in German history took place in Berlin on 11 October 2008. As there were parallel activities in 15 further countries, privacy promoters in Germany hope for similar developments in Europe and beyond.

At the same time, there are strong promoters of new surveillance measures and new competences for security agencies. The most prominent among them, Federal Minister of the Interior Wolfgang Schäuble, protested after the 11 October demonstration against his portrait being used on hundreds of signs subtitled "Stasi 2.0", referring to the infamous state security service of the former GDR. As the German

G. Hornung (✉)
University of Kassel, Wilhelmshöher Allee 64-66, 34109 Kassel, Germany
e-mail: gerrit.hornung@uni-kassel.de

S. Gutwirth et al. (eds.), *Data Protection in a Profiled World*,
DOI 10.1007/978-90-481-8865-9_8,

Federal Constitutional Court, while demanding high requirements, did not completely rule out new surveillance measures, it remains to be seen which side will prevail in the medium-term.

The aforementioned development can be addressed from very different, albeit deeply connected angels. The legal, technical and social implications have to be analysed in their respective scientific context. The Sect. 8.2 (by *Gerrit Hornung*) analyses the online-searching decision of 27 February 2008, concerning an Act of the Land of Nordrhein-Westfalen authorising the internal intelligence authorities to secretly access information technology systems involving the deployment of technical means. In the reasons given for the judgement, the Court established a new "fundamental right to the guarantee of the confidentiality and integrity of information technology systems", which was violated by the aforementioned provision. The Sect. 8.3 (by *Andreas Pfitzmann*), finds that German politicians usually do not understand information and communication technology (ICT) and therefore, often they do not understand possible uses of ICT they try to regulate. In contrast, the German Federal Constitutional Court did a remarkable job in winter and spring 2008 to decide on regulations of ICT. The Sect. 8.4 (by *Ralf Bendrath*), looks at the growing awareness of privacy risks and the protests which have sparked against data retention in Germany. Organizations and participants used the Internet and web 2.0 tools, which had an impact on the forms of organization, collaboration and action.

8.2 The Online Searching Judgement of February 27th, 2008

The strength of the German constitutional system as regards new technological developments became very visible in the spring of 2008, when the German Federal Constitutional Court delivered three important judgements on privacy (or informational self-determination, as developed by the German federal Constitutional Court in the population census decision) and new surveillance technologies (on the following, see Hornung and Schnabel 2009b). Arguably, the most important of these decisions is the judgement on the online searching of computers, which established a new "fundamental right to the guarantee of the confidentiality and integrity of information technology systems". The birth of this fundamental right led to an ongoing scientific debate in Germany (see, e.g., Böckenförde 2008; Hoffmann-Riem 2008; Hornung 2008; Roggan 2008; Roßnagel and Schnabel 2008), but the decision was also recognised in other countries (see, e.g., Abel and Schafer 2009; De Hert et al. 2009).

8.2.1 Background of the Case

The online-searching case concerned an Act adopted by the state of Nordrhein-Westfalen which authorised the Office for the Protection of the Constitution of the

State (internal intelligence authorities) to, *inter alia*, "secretly access information technology systems through the use of technical means" (on the background, see also Abel and Schafer 2009, p. 107 ff.; Abel 2009, p. 99 ff.). The fact that no further indications were given regarding the mode of access gave rise to speculations on the potential technical approach. Possibilities include one-time online access to the data on the computer, continuous surveillance to tape-record any change of such data, and the observation of further operations (such as keyboard entries or VoIP calls, see Buermeyer 2007).

Most observers had expected the German Federal Constitutional Court to rule against the state of Nordrhein-Westfalen, as the Act suffered from a considerable lack of substantial and procedural privacy safeguards. This impression was fostered in the oral proceedings. Hardly anybody however would have expected the Court to come up with a "new" fundamental right. This right is strictly speaking not a new constitutional right, but a new sub-group of the general personality right (see Hoffmann-Riem 2008, p. 1018 f.). Arguably, the creation of a new right by the Court would have given rise to issues of the separation of powers. In practice however, the future approach of the Court may outweigh the difference between a specific right and a sub-group of the general personality right. As apparent from the development and impact of the right to informational self-determination (another sub-group of the general personality right), the German Federal Constitutional Court does not hesitate to use a non-written fundamental right to severely restrict surveillance activities by state agencies.

8.2.2 Other Fundamental Rights

As to the merits, the German Federal Constitutional Court took the recent developments in the area of information and communication technology as a starting point (Bundesverfassungsgericht 2008a, p. 303 ff.; see Hoffmann-Riem 2008, p. 1010 ff.; Hornung and Schnabel 2009b). Much emphasis is placed on the major role played by these kinds of technology in today's life and their ever increasing influence on the self-development of citizens. As the new technology depends largely on the processing of personal data, it has become obvious that there is a strong need for the protection of privacy. The Court did not consider the existing German system of fundamental rights to be sufficient in this respect. Secrecy of telecommunications, as protected in Article 10 of the Grundgesetz, did not cover online searching of computer systems (see also Abel and Schafer 2009, p. 112 ff.). The Court considered secrecy of telecommunications as being applicable only if the authorities aim at the surveillance of VoIP systems, and the method of the surveillance (e.g., a Trojan horse or similar malware) is technically restricted to the telecommunications, i.e., searching of the system is not possible.

Regarding the sanctity of the home, there was a debate on whether the respective provision of the Grundgesetz (Article 13) applies in the case of the online searching of an IT system which is based in the home of the person affected. While there are solid arguments that this is the case (Hornung 2007, p. 577 f. with further references), the German Federal Constitutional Court (Bundesverfassungsgericht 2008a, p. 309 ff.) responded negatively, arguing that the location of the system is not usually apparent for the authorities, and that the fundamental right in Article 13 of the Grundgesetz has to be construed with regard to the modalities of the access. Lastly, the German Federal Constitutional Court (Bundesverfassungsgericht 2008a, p. 311 ff.) deemed the right to informational self-determination as not covering the peculiarities of IT systems and their relevance for citizens' everyday lives. This last part of the decision has been widely criticized among scientific scholars and may indeed be the weakest part of the judgement. Before the decision, hardly anybody would have doubted that secret online searchings of computers interfere with the right to informational self-determination. Thus, the Court arguably construed a lacuna in the constitutional system of fundamental rights to fill it with the right to the guarantee of the confidentiality and integrity of information technology systems. On the other hand, the political and semantical value of a specific fundamental right for the "information age" should not be underestimated (Abel and Schafer 2009, 122 and ff.).

8.2.3 Content of the "New" Fundamental Right

Having dealt with the other fundamental rights, the Court emphasised what it calls the "loophole-closing guarantee of the general personality right" (Bundesverfassungsgericht 2008a, 313). From there, it was only a small step to the creation of a new sub-group, protecting "IT systems which alone or in their technical networking can contain personal data of the person concerned to such a degree and in such a diversity that access to the system facilitates insight into significant parts of the life of a person or indeed provides a revealing picture of the personality" (Bundesverfassungsgericht 2008a, p. 314). Besides computers, mobile phones, PDAs and similar systems are also included if they "have a large number of functions and can collect and store many kinds of personal data" (see also Abel and Schafer 2009, 120 and ff.). Crucially, it is not decisive whether the system actually stores or processes many kinds of personal data, but whether the system is capable in that respect.

The system will only be protected if, given the concrete circumstances, the person affected can assume that he/she is able to control the system, whether alone or with other authorised persons. Arguably, this also includes online hard drives (Hoffmann-Riem 2008, 1012).

There are two aspects of the new right, namely, the confidentiality and the integrity of the system. The first aspect covers personal data and is thus largely congruent with the right to informational self-determination, although the requirements for interventions are much higher. The second aspect is described by the German Federal Constitutional Court to protect against the unauthorised use of the system regarding its capacities, functions and memory contents. In this respect, it is irrelevant whether personal data of any kind is involved.

8.2.4 *Interferences*

The Court did not consider the fundamental right to be absolute, but specified rather high requirements for any interference by public authorities (on the situation in the UK, see Abel 2009, p. 104). Importantly, these requirements apply to both the police and intelligence agencies. In both cases, there have to be "factual indications of a concrete danger to a predominantly important legal interest. Predominantly important are the life, limb and freedom of the individual or such interests of the public a threat to which affects the basis or continued existence of the state or the basis of human existence." (Bundesverfassungsgericht 2008a, p. 328). The requirement of "factual indications of a concrete danger" had been unknown in traditional German police law. It is arguably placed between the concrete threat itself and the general gathering of information, but there are indications that the Court will require public authorities to firmly establish factual evidence connected to individual persons.

Even if there is such evidence, the interference can only be justified if it is warranted by a judge or a body of equal legal and personal independence (see Hornung and Schnabel 2009b). Furthermore, the legal basis for the measure has to provide safeguards to prevent any infringements of the "core of personal privacy" as developed in the decision on acoustic surveillance of private homes (Bundesverfassungsgericht 2004, p. 311 ff.). In the current case, the German Federal Constitutional Court considered it impossible to analyse the data, in this respect, at the time of collection. According to the technical experts, there are no technical means which would absolutely separate out data belonging to the core of personal privacy from the rest of the information transferred to the authorities. In this situation, the judges demanded that the data is subsequently examined in this respect, and deleted if it pertains to this sphere. However, there are neither indications in the judgement as to the body responsible for the examination, nor to the time within which the examination must take place. The new federal law which allows for the secret searching of IT systems (section 20 k of the Bundeskriminalamtgesetz of 25 December 2008) requires the control of an independent judge. However, the examination itself will be conducted by the federal police, including its data protection officer. This new law has already been challenged before the German Federal Constitutional Court, and it remains to be seen whether the Court considers these safeguards to be sufficient.

8.2.5 *Further Developments*

The opinion of the German Federal Constitutional Court delivers guidelines not only for the online searching of computer systems, but also for other surveillance measures. Hence, the ruling is widely recognised as the most important decision on privacy and constitutional law in Germany within recent years, arguably even since the famous census case of 1983. There are numerous open questions to be addressed in future cases and in the scientific debate (Hornung and Schnabel 2009b; Hornung

2008). These include, *inter alia*, the consequences for open searches of IT systems (Hömig 2009, 210 and ff.), further dimensions of the new fundamental right in regards to the effects between private parties (Roßnagel and Schnabel 2008), and the issue of online searching of IT systems within criminal proceedings, which was not addressed by the Court in the current decision.

On the international plane, it remains open whether other constitutional courts will follow the approach of the German Federal Constitutional Court. Among other factors, this will depend on the role of the court in the respective constitutional systems and the existence of a general personality right or right to privacy which can be developed to address the new challenges in a world of widespread use of IT systems. As the European systems of fundamental rights protection become more and more important, it will be of even more relevance whether the European Court of Human Rights and the European Court of Justice take up the ideas and concerns expressed by the German judges.

8.3 The German Federal Constitutional Court: Closer to ICT and Technology Assessment than German Politicians

German government executives usually do not understand information and communication technology (ICT) well and therefore, often they do not understand possible uses of ICT they try to regulate (and some politicians are even proud of not understanding ICT). So, the German government, e.g., assumes terrorists will connect their computers to the Internet in an insecure fashion so that the German Federal Police can search their hard drives secretly (section 20 k of the Bundeskriminalamtgesetz of 25 December 2008).

In spite of this attitude of the German government, the German Federal Constitutional Court did a remarkable job in Winter and Spring 2008 to decide on regulations of ICT. This section shortly explains why and how.

I admit from the outset that all conclusions are my personal ones based on my own experience in directly interacting with politicians in various roles, e.g., consulting and advising many politicians, three political parties elected to the German Parliament (Bundestag) and several political bodies for more than two decades. I have been an expert witness in parliamentary hearings as well as in trials of the German Federal Constitutional Court dealing with issues described in this section.

8.3.1 Actors and Their Knowledge

For German politicians (at least those of the larger parties), understanding ICT is not "sexy". For them, understanding ICT is as attractive as understanding mathematics and having been a nerd at school. German politicians fear that the electorate would perceive them as too detached if politicians knew much about mathematics and ICT. This would thwart their success in elections, they believe. Nevertheless, German politicians admit that society is on its way to becoming an information society.

So far, it would not be much of a problem, if German politicians drew the consequences of their very limited understanding of the digital space and mainly refrained from trying to regulate it.

In spite of not understanding ICT, German politicians firmly assume that ICT does what it shall do. The more knowledgeable amongst them believe that if ICT systems have some errors or security weaknesses in their first release, these bugs will be fixed soon. Overall German politicians firmly assume that whatever policies they make, these policies can and will be enforced effectively.

So, German politicians act according to this rule: if you lack understanding and experience to rely on, do something and pretend you are certain to do the right things.

Since ICT is not really new (at least for the younger generation), it may well be that the German government has on average better knowledge than society at large, but the German government quite likely has on average less knowledge about ICT than society at large, in particular the younger generation, cf. Fig. 8.1.

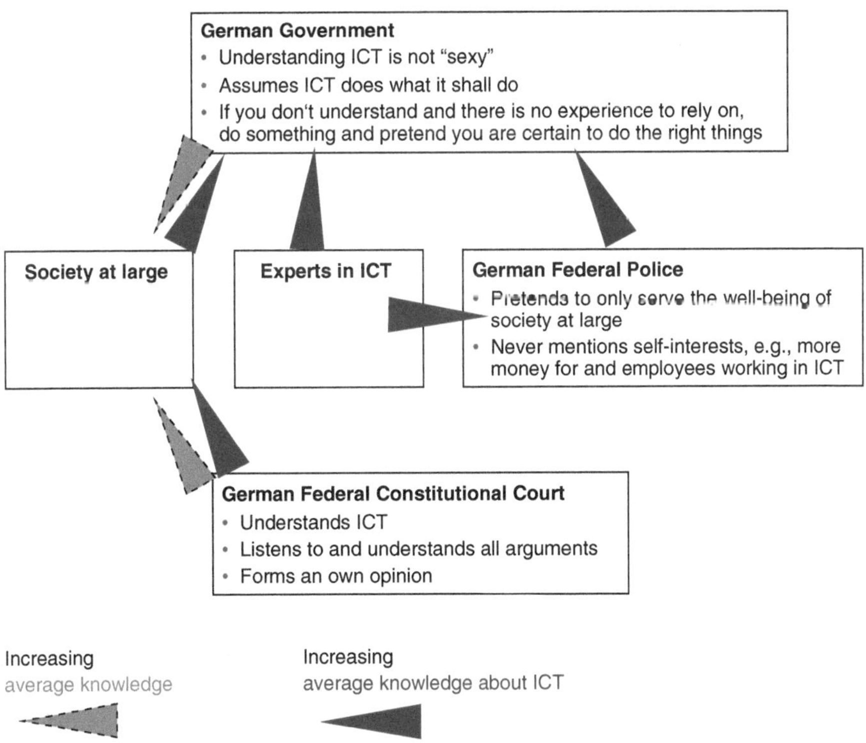

Fig. 8.1 Actors and their knowledge

Let's complete the picture with two more assertions:

Obviously, experts in ICT are on average much more knowledgeable of ICT than even the ICT-interested members of the government.

The German Federal Police has a better understanding of ICT than the German government, but less understanding about ICT than independent experts in ICT, e.g., from academia.

The problem now is that the German government has so little knowledge about ICT that its members do not dare to build up their own opinion on the uses of ICT with respect to surveillance vs. privacy, fighting crime vs. supporting development of society. So they decided to completely rely on the advice given to them by the most knowledgeable governmental bodies. For fighting crime, e.g., this means fully relying on the advice by the German Federal Police. This makes life for politicians as easy as possible, since it avoids being criticized by the police. And it enables German politicians to pretend to do everything which is possible for fighting crime and terrorism as well as providing as much public safety as possible. But of course, the German Federal Police, though pretending to only serve the well-being of society at large, has some self-interests, which are barely mentioned. They include more money and more employees working at the German (Federal) Police in the area of ICT. These usually come along with additional rights and duties. This is a serious downside to our government's approach: more stored data for police and secret services' use does neither mean more security nor more public safety. This is so because foreign secret services as well as organized crime will, quite likely and relatively soon, gain access to these retained data. The same is true for all security loopholes that are not closed as fast as possible due to the interests of, e.g., the German (Federal) Police to further use those loopholes for the online searching of suspects' computers. Furthermore, another downside the government's approach is that it largely ignores citizens' privacy.

To sum up so far: Due to the lack of knowledge of ICT in the German government, society at large is paying with their privacy (and a lot of money, not to completely ignore it) for an uncertain increase in security and public safety. Not a good deal, quite sure. Unavoidable? Probably not, since, first, society at large, meanwhile more knowledgeable about ICT than the German government, will sooner or later elect only politicians into office who are computer-literate, and, second, the German Federal Constitutional Court comes into play.

Over more than two decades, I gave consultancy and advice to many politicians, political parties and political bodies. But I never ever experienced so much interest in understanding ICT as when being expert witness to the German Federal Constitutional Court. Its judges really wanted to understand ICT astonishingly deeply. They really did read the papers I wrote for them—and even more: they read and understood even the papers I recommended to them. For me as a computer expert, it was a unique experience to listen to the court's introductory statements, devoting more than 5 minutes to the fundamental issues of ICT, and having the strong feeling that I myself could not have presented it more clearly. This in complete contrast to listening to leading German politicians, who if not in their first sentence addressing ICT, then in their second sentence reveal their serious misunderstandings of the fundamental properties of ICT.

In the court hearing, the judges listened to all arguments and made sure they understood them. The judges further made sure the experts did discuss their arguments with each other in their presence (and sometimes moderated by the judges or forced by the judges to stick to the point). This is something the German parliamentary system avoids wherever possible. Overall, by the way the judges prepared and organized the court hearing, they ensured to be able to form a valid opinion of their own, taking both the fundamental properties of ICT into account as well as the interests of all parties involved.

Given this distribution of knowledge, what are the strategies of those working unconsciously or consciously against privacy? And what could be appropriate counterstrategies? Overall: How might we arrive at a realistic technology assessment of ICT being a basis for good decisions with regard to the future ICT infrastructure for our society?

8.3.2 Strategies Working Against Privacy and Appropriate Counterstrategies Working Towards Privacy

The main strategy working against privacy is in actors who receive resources for law enforcement, who have self-interests (which are never mentioned), but who are able to pretend that they only serve the well-being of the society at large, as well as being the sole advisors to the government. The main cause for this is that the government is not able to really listen to more than one "expert", since it lacks its own judgement and so no capability to sort out contradictions between "experts".

The counterstrategies are:

- Making sure politicians, including government officials, have to take some ICT training. Not understanding the technological basis of the future society should no longer be acceptable for leaders of any kind. Experts should prepare several courses at the appropriate levels of detail, including basic knowledge to understand the shortcomings of ICT with regard to security. As mentioned, this understanding is an essential precondition to understand that in the foreseeable future, ICT will not just do what it is devised to do—this is a message mainly academia has to spread, since neither German Federal Police nor industry surely have any interests to spread that message.
- German Federal Police should be offered in-depth training in ICT in general and ICT-security in particular. Since it may well be that currently they do not know how bad their proposals actually are with regard to increasing security and public safety.
- In addition, procedures in public hearings, e.g., in the German parliament (Bundestag) should be revised so that not only politicians can ask questions to experts, but that the experts themselves can challenge other experts' statements. This is particularly necessary if some of the "experts" are not independent, but rather officials of governmental bodies, e.g. of the German Federal Police, serving self-interests.

8.3.3 Summing up: Government vs. Court

The knowledge of ICT of the German government is much weaker than the knowledge the German Federal Constitutional Court acquired within a relatively short period of time. So in principle, there is hope that people are able to learn.

Is, what I described, specific to ICT? Probably yes:

- Experience in physical life is not always applicable in the digital space. Therefore, older leading politicians have no basis to decide appropriately in matters regarding the information society.
- Having no knowledge in ICT was socially accepted (and convenient). Hopefully, this is to change quite soon.

Is, what I described, part of a strategy? Maybe it is a strategy of some bureaucrats within government in general and police and secret services in particular. I do not believe it is an explicit strategy of many politicians. With regard to them, it is just an outcome of ignorance.

Is, what I described, an institutional necessity: fight for resources at the cost of freedom? Maybe. And at the moment, we have much more powerful actors who, in their fight for resources, decrease privacy than we have actors who advocate spending resources on privacy protection.

To conclude, appropriate counterstrategies are:

- Government needs training in ICT.
- Making sure that self-interests are disclosed in an open debate.

8.4 The Rise of the Anti-Surveillance Movement 2.0

This section analyzes the new forms of privacy activism that have emerged in Germany around the fight against telecommunications data retention. It provides an explorative case study of the new "activism 2.0" that heavily relies on user-participation, flat hierarchies, and distributed collaborative work as described by authors like Benkler (2006) and Shirky (2008). The case also illustrates some of the challenges connected to these new forms of organizing and political campaigning.

Almost 30 years ago, West Germany already saw the emergence of an active anti-surveillance movement. It mainly fought against the planned nation-wide census, which was seen by many as the entry into the big brother state. Broader issues debated in this context in the 1980s were police surveillance repression against social movements, such as the anti-nuclear movement, the peace movement, the new left, and the squatter community. The 1983 Federal Constitutional Court decision against the census established a new basic right to "informational self-determination" (Bundesverfassungsgericht 1983), but also took the drive out of many of the anti-censorship activists. Together with the integration of the social movements into the parliamentary system of the Federal Republic through the Green party, this took surveillance and data privacy off the streets as well as off the agenda of many groups.

A few years later, the East German opposition that finally led to the fall of the Berlin wall in 1989 was not only a democratic movement, but also was much mobilized by a common rejection of surveillance as a means of dictatorship. A crucial event was the storming of the Stasi headquarters in East Berlin on 15 January 1990, which finally led to the securing of the Stasi archives and the later establishment of the related Federal Agency ("Gauck Commission"). After the German reunification, the concerns of the former opposition groups were largely seen as not necessary anymore.

From late 1990, there was basically no widespread privacy movement anymore in Germany. Only a few NGOs, such as the German Association for Data Protection (DVD), the Computer Scientists for Peace and Social Responsibility (FIfF), the "Verein zur Förderung des öffentlichen bewegten und unbewegten Datenverkehrs e.V." (FoeBuD), the Humanistic Union (HU) and the hacker association Chaos Computer Club (CCC), kept on working on these topics. They tried to fight some of the new surveillance measures, which were introduced as a means in the fight against "organized crime", such as the bugging of private houses, which became known as the "big eavesdropping attack". Too weak for political success, the privacy groups mainly resorted to constitutional challenges of new surveillance laws. Only 10 years later, the German Big Brother Award was born in 2000 and is now in its 10th year.

8.4.1 Data Retention and the Participatory Resistance Against Surveillance

After the events of 9/11 2001, many liberal and left-wing groups as well as the traditional privacy community were feeling a general unease with the new repressive tendencies and surveillance measures. Politically, the anti-terror climate made it hard for them to find much support among the population as well as attention in the media (Bendrath 2001). As a consequence, protest and criticism against many of the supposed anti-terror measures were mainly published and debated in specialized internet forums, but without much political output and even less impact. With the help of this new medium however, the small privacy community was able to exchange news and analyses, stay in touch throughout the dire years, and find new followers among the "internet generation". It took a number of years before a larger opposition against surveillance rose again and finally even placed its concerns high up on the national political agenda.

The turning point was the introduction of the EU data retention directive (EU 2006). Groups like European Digital Rights (EDRi) and Privacy International had tried to fight against the blanket storing of all telecommunications traffic data in the

European Union since 2003, but without much success. When it was finally adopted by the European Parliament on 14 December 2005, German privacy activists immediately knew that it would now hit the national level for transposition into German law. The interesting and extraordinary story of how they successfully organized their protest and activities with the help of new online tools tells us something about the value of the internet for social movements in the information age.

The initiative that later became known as the Working Group on Data Retention ("Arbeitskreis Vorratsdatenspeicherung" or short "AK Vorrat", www.vorratsdatenspeicherung.de) started on the internet itself. Hundreds of readers of the popular IT news service heise.de commented on the article that reported about the European Parliament's decision, expressing their anger and outrage. Many of them understood that this legislative measure for the first time put everybody under surveillance, no matter if there was an initial suspicion or not. They feared that telecommunications traffic was only the beginning and that without large opposition, sooner or later more and more behavioral data of the whole population would be retained and made available to security agencies. Privacy activist Bettina Winsemann (also known as "Twister", who also was one of the complainants in the online-searching decision) from the small group "Stop1984" offered those of them a home on their listserv who wanted to do more than just rail against the decision in some online forum. On the listserv, their feeling of unease and the will "to do something" was facilitated and slowly turned into more organized forms with the help of some more experienced privacy activists. These also organized a first face-to-face meeting of the group at the CCC congress in Berlin 2 weeks later.

AK Vorrat initially had no campaign plan, no money, no staff, no organizational form, and no real infrastructure except for the listserv. It did not even have its name at the beginning. But this lack of resources and fixed structures, interestingly, turned out to be an asset. It forced the activists to set up the infrastructure themselves and to develop the campaign collaboratively and interactively. Someone had a wiki that was used for the first months, others were experienced in graphics design, someone knew a legal expert who had worked on data retention, others were familiar or at least interested in press relations, and so on. With the extremely open set-up of an un-moderated listserv and a wiki, anybody wanting to help could help, in the area of his or her expertise or interest. This created "ownership" and the sense of a community of peers. Through some more popular German blogs, such as netzpolitik.org, word of AK Vorrat spread in the internet community and slowly made it bigger, stronger, and more organized.

The first ideas AK Vorrat's members came up with were focused on mobilizing the wider German internet community through participatory means. They created banners, graphics and widgets (small javascript applets) that others could incorporate in their websites and blogs. They also set up a web portal where anybody could write an open letter which would automatically be sent to the members of the ruling conservative and social democratic parties in the federal parliament. Exactly 1 year after the European Parliament had adopted the data retention directive, AK Vorrat provided a symbolic death notice in traditional design with big black letters and an ark frame, which commemorated the "death of privacy" 12 months before. It was taken up by many bloggers and website owners who put it before their start page. For many months, the press releases were largely ignored by the mainstream media, but were distributed and linked to a growing number of blogs. This, in turn, motivated more internet users to join the group.

The growth of AK Vorrat led to a gradual internal differentiation over time. The activists organized themselves in specialized working groups for design, server maintenance, press work, translations, wiki housekeeping and other areas. After 1 year and with more than 1,000 members on the listserv, the activists also started to set up local chapters. Still, most of the work was coordinated in the wiki (wiki.vorratsdatenspeicherung.de), which made is easy for anybody to set up a local group or coordinate an activity without the need for central discussion or even approval.

8.4.2 From the Internet to the Streets and into Pop Culture

The privacy activists understood early on that if they wanted to be successful, they would have to reach out of the internet community and towards other social groups. They initiated a joint declaration—a manifesto on the dangers of data retention—that was sent to other NGOs for signature. Initially, mainly privacy and legal expert groups as well as some consumer and journalists' organizations signed the declaration, but after a while, groups such as the German AIDS Help, the German Association for Sociology, or the Federal Association of Women Help-Lines also joined. They had understood that their work would also be affected by the blanket retention of telecommunications data.

For the activists, this was not enough. When it was reported that the German Parliament would discuss data retention in late June 2006, they immediately started to organize a street demonstration on the Saturday before. With only about 3 weeks of preparation and mobilization time, only 250 protesters showed up and marched through downtown Berlin. While this demonstration had—foreseeably—no media coverage at all, it showed the activists two things: First, they were not alone, and demonstrations could be a good way of meeting more like-minded people in person. Second, it was easy to do a demonstration if the workload could be distributed through wikis and listservs. As a consequence, AK Vorrat called for and organized more demonstrations over the next year. The second one took place in Bielefeld on the afternoon before the Big Brother Awards ceremony 2006 took place with 350 participants. It was also the first one that had as its motto "Freedom not Fear" ("Freiheit statt Angst"), which expressed the motivation of the privacy activists very well and later became the slogan for internationally coordinated activities. The third demonstration was organized in Frankfurt in April 2007. Here, already 2,000 people showed up on the streets, indicating the growing mobilization for privacy and against surveillance. In order to root privacy better in the population, AK Vorrat also started the platform freiheitsredner.de ("freedom speakers"), where activists could register and indicate their willingness to give talks about surveillance and privacy for school classes, political initiatives and whoever else was interested.

The last push towards a mass movement came in 2007. The Federal Minister of the Interior, Wolfgang Schäuble, had announced a lengthy catalogue of planned new surveillance measures, including the secret online searches of private hard drives through malware, widely known in Germany as the "federal Trojan" (see above). Shortly after this, activists of AK Vorrat were taking part in the first big German-wide blogger and web 2.0 conference, Re:Publica in Berlin. They ran a workshop on activism against surveillance and called for the web-design and web 2.0 communities to come up with creative ideas and campaign elements. An idea was to tag all blog posts related to Schäuble with "Stasi 2.0", a meme that had originally been invented as early as July 2001 in an online forum (NBX 2001). Dirk Adler, co-author of the blog dataloo.de, took part in the workshop at re:publica and came up with a stylized picture of Wolfgang Schäuble and the slogan "Stasi 2.0" in capital letters below it (Adler 2007). This logo became widely known as the "Schäublone" and was extremely popular in the German blogosphere. Adler also sold it on clothing and mugs through a web 2.0 shop at dataloo.spreadshirt.net. He donated part of his revenue to AK Vorrat, and spreadshirt did the same for a couple of months in 2007.

The combination of pop culture coolness, the substantial work of Ak Vorrat and others, and a more and more politicized blogosphere, created a fertile ground for the first large-scale manifestation of the new privacy movement. With the donations from the t-shirt sales, AK Vorrat and a coalition of more than 50 groups and organizations called for another demonstration in Berlin on 22 September 2007. In the end, under a blue sky and a nice autumn sun, 15,000 protestors marched through Berlin and held their final rally right in front of the Brandenburg Gate. From this day it was clear that Germany again had a mass movement against surveillance and for privacy.

8.4.3 Putting Privacy on the Political Agenda

The following year of 2008 can be marked as the year where privacy moved high on the public agenda in Germany. On 1 January, the law on data retention went into effect, which made Germany drop from number one to seven in the country ranking published by Privacy International. At the same day, a constitutional challenge was submitted to the German Federal Constitutional Court. AK Vorrat and its allies again had focused on participatory methods, based on the fact that in Germany, a constitutional challenge does not involve any court fees. Through an online form, they had managed to have more than 34,000 people participate in this case—the largest constitutional complaint ever seen in German history. The paperwork had to be brought to the Federal Constitutional Court in huge moving boxes, which also offered a nice photo opportunity for everyone wanting to demonstrate how many people oppose data retention.

In February, the media reported widely about the Federal Constitutional Court's decision on secret online searches (see above). In March, the Chaos Computer Club published the fingerprint of the Federal Minister of the Interior, Wolfgang Schäuble. This sparked high public attention, made front page news even in the tabloid press, and proved that biometric authentication as introduced in the German passport and identity card is not safe at all. Inspired by the successes, the growing number of privacy activists held a de-central action day in May 2008. Different kinds of activities, like demonstrations, flash mobs, information booths, privacy parties, workshops, and cultural activities took place in all over Germany.

Over the summer, some of the biggest German companies "helped" in raising public awareness of the risks of large data collections. Almost every week, there were reports on a big supermarket chain spying on its employees, on cd-roms with tens of thousands of customer data sets from call centers—including bank account numbers—being sold on the grey market, on the largest German telecommunications provider using retained traffic data for spying on its supervisory board and on high-ranking union members, on an airline using its booking system to spy on critical journalists, on two large universities accidentally making all student data available online, or on a big mobile phone provider "losing" 17 million customer data sets.

The Federal Government, under building public pressure, introduced some small changes for the federal data protection law, but at the same time continued its push for more surveillance measures in the hands of the federal criminal agency (Bundeskriminalamt, BKA). These included the secret online searches the constitutional court had just cut down to very exceptional circumstances a few months earlier. The German public discussed these moves very critically, especially since journalists are exempted from special protections that are given to priests, criminal defense lawyers, and doctors.

Because of the public concern and debate about privacy risks, the call to another mass street protest was even more successful than ever before. The "Freedom not Fear" action day on 11 October was the biggest privacy event in Germany's history. In Berlin, between 50,000 and 70,000 persons protested against data retention and other forms of "surveillance mania". Privacy activists in many cities all over the world participated with very diverse and creative kinds of activities and turned this day into the first international action day "Freedom not Fear". The anti-surveillance protests finally kicked off some serious discussion within the Social Democratic Party (SPD) in a number of the German states. This broke the majority for the law on the federal criminal agency (BKA), in the second chamber (Bundesrat) on the first vote. It only was passed weeks later, after some changes were introduced, and with heavy pressure from leading federal Social Democrats. The new law is still seen as unconstitutional by many legal and privacy experts, and in January 2009 a case was submitted to the Federal Constitutional Court. Related activities are still going on all over Germany, and AK Vorrat is by now only one of the players in this movement—others have been inspired by it, but have started their own activities and actions.

8.4.4 Lessons Learned

The basis of the success of the new privacy movement was its openness. The reliance on open structures and as little hierarchy and central points of control as possible made it easy for anyone to participate and it also created ownership. An additional factor was the maturing of the political German blogosphere, with specialized blogs such as netzpolitik.org being highly successful, but also other, previously non-political blogs slowly becoming politicized. It also has proven very helpful to go offline. Online tools were used to set up local structures and to get the protest offline, onto the streets and into pop culture. The use of creative commons licenses was crucial here, because the "Stasi 2.0" logos as well as other material could therefore be used by anyone. Overall, the (involuntary) founding idea was proven right: "Give people an environment in which they can do what they are good at, and give them tools to coordinate and help each other."

Not all of the success was due to web 2.0, though. Even in times of distributed and nowadays even twitter-based activism, where whole campaigns are glued together by one hashtag, experts are still relevant. If AK Vorrat had not been lucky to get on board such legal experts as Patrick Breyer, who had written his legal dissertation on data retention and was crucial for much of the substantive work, the campaign would never have gotten as far as it went—especially not to the constitutional court. The activism also needed the help of established NGOs for logistics: FoeBuD provided their online shop for the distribution of flyers, posters and other materials; tax-exempt FIfF was donating a bank account and the management of donations and financial contributions.

Of course, such a working environment also creates problems. One lesson quickly learned by the activists was that fluid and open structures create a constant need for discussion about the whole nature of AK Vorrat. Is it a new form of organization? Is it a coalition of established NGOs, many of whom worked inside this new structure? Is it a platform for free-floating activists? Is it a network of like-minded activists? Or is it even all of the above? The activists also had to learn the hard way that decisions and debates about highly political issues (such as the participation of militant left-wing groups in the demonstrations) are hard to hold online and involve a constant danger of escalation and flame-wars. The un-moderated listserv also made it hard to participate for people who are used to more focused and traditional means of communications or who represent more established and formalized organizations such as trade unions. Much of the work of the more experienced privacy activists (including the author Ralf Bendrath) therefore has been in facilitating discussions and leading not by orders, but by listening and moderating. Still, the discussions and internal conflicts have led some activists to turn away from AK Vorrat and set up their own organizations and groups. While this is seen by many activists as a loss of coherence or even as betrayal, in the bigger picture, it can also be interpreted as the growing pains of a maturing social movement. Privacy is on the political agenda again in Germany, and there are no signs of it fading anytime soon.

References

Abel, W. 2009. Agents, trojans and tags: The next generation of investigators. *International Review of Law, Computers & Technology* 23:99–108.

Abel, W., and B. Schafer. 2009. The German Constitutional Court on the right in confidentiality and integrity of information technology systems: A case report on BVerfG. NJW 2008, 822. *SCRIPTed* 6 (1): 106. http://www.law.ed.ac.uk/ahrc/script-ed/vol6-1/abel.asp.

Adler, D. 2007. Stasi 2.0. *dataloo.de*, 14 April. http://www.dataloo.de/stasi-20-525.html.

Bendrath, R. 2001. Wie weiter mit dem Datenschutz? *Telepolis*, 24 October. http://www.heise.de/tp/r4/artikel/9/9903/1.html.

Benkler, Y. 2006. *The wealth of networks. How social production transforms markets and freedom.* New Haven, CT: Yale Univ. Press.

Böckenförde, T. 2008. Auf dem Weg zur elektronischen Privatsphäre. *Juristenzeitung* 63:925–939.

Buermeyer, U. 2007. Die Online-Durchsuchung. *HRR-Strafrecht* 4:154–166. http://www.hrr-strafrecht.de/hrr/archiv/07-04/index.php?sz=8.

Bundesverfassungsgericht. 1983. Decision of 15 December 1983 (1BvR 209, 269, 362, 420, 440, 484/83), decisions. vol. 65, 1–71.

Bundesverfassungsgericht. 2004. Decision of 3 March 2004 (1 BvR 2378/99 and 1 BvR 1084/99), decisions, vol. 109, 279–391. Also available online at http://www.bundesverfassungsgericht.de/entscheidungen/rs20040303_1bvr237898.html.

Bundesverfassungsgericht. 2008a. Decision of 27 Feburary 2008 (1 BvR 370/07 and 1 BvR 595/07), decisions, vol. 120, 274–350. Also available online in English at http://www.bverfg.de/en/decisions/rs20080227_1bvr037007en.html.

Bundesverfassungsgericht. 2008b. Decision of 11 March 2008 (1 BvR 2074/05 and 1 BvR 1254/07), decisions, vol. 120, 378–433. Also available online at http://www.bundesverfassungsgericht.de/entscheidungen/rs20080311_1bvr207405.html.

Bundesverfassungsgericht. 2008c. Decision of 11 March 2008 (1 BvR 256/08). *Europäische Grundrechte Zeitschrift*, 257–265. Also available online at http://www.bundesverfassungsgericht.de/entscheidungen/rs20080311_1bvr025608.html.

De Hert, P., K. de Vries, and S. Gutwirth. 2009. La limitation des 'perquisitions en ligne' par un renouvellement des droit fondamentaux", Note d'observations sur Cour constitutionnelle fédérale allemande, 27 février 2008 (Online Dursuchung). *Revue du droit des Technologies de l'Information, Jurisprudence* 34: 89–92.

EU. 2006. Directive 2006/24/EC of the European Parliament and of the Council of 15 March 2006 on the retention of data generated or processed in connection with the provision of publicly available electronic communications services or of public communications networks and amending Directive 2002/58/EC. *Official Journal* L105 (13/04/2006):54–63.

Hoffmann-Riem, W. 2008. Der grundrechtliche Schutz der Vertraulichkeit und Integrität eigengenutzter informationstechnischer Systeme. *Juristenzeitung* 21:1009–1022.

Hömig, D. 2009. "Neues" Grundrecht, neue Fragen? Zum Urteil des BVerfG zur Online-Durchsuchung, JURA. 207–213.

Hornung, G. 2007. Ermächtigungsgrundlage für die 'Online-Durchsuchung'? *Datenschutz und Datensicherheit* 31: 575–580. Also available online at http://www.uni-kassel.de/fb7/oeff_recht/publikationen/pubOrdner/publikation_2007_hornung_online_durchsuchung.pdf.

Hornung, G. 2008. Ein neues Grundrecht. Der verfassungsrechtliche Schutz der "Vertraulichkeit und Integrität informationstechnischer Systeme". *Computer und Recht* 5:299–306.

Hornung, G., and C. Schnabel. 2009a. Data protection in Germany I: The population census decision and the right to informational self-determination. *Computer Law & Security Review* 25 (1): 84–88.

Hornung, G., and C. Schnabel. 2009b. Data protection in Germany II: Recent decisions on online-searching of computers, automatic number plate recognition and data retention. *Computer Law & Security Review* 25 (2): 115–122.

NBX. 2001. Stasi 2.0. *Comment in Telepolis*, 7 July. http://www.heise.de/tp/foren/S-Stasi-2-0/forum-18164/msg-815528/read/.

Roggan, F., ed. 2008. *Online-Durchsuchungen. Rechtliche und tatsächliche Konsequenzen des BVerfG-Urteils vom 27. Februar 2008.* Berlin: BWV.

Roßnagel, A., and C. Schnabel. 2008. Das Grundrecht auf Gewährleistung der Vertraulichkeit und Integrität informationstechnischer Systeme und sein Einfluss auf das Privatrecht. *Neue Juristische Wochenschrift* 49:3534–3538.

Rouvroy, A., and Y. Poullet. 2009. The right to informational self-determination and the value of self-development. Reassessing the importance of privacy for democracy. In *Reinventing data protection*, eds. S. Gutwirth, Y. Poullet, P. De Hert, de C. Terwangne, S. Nouwt. *New York: Springer*: 45–76.

Shirky, C. 2008. *Here comes everybody: The power of organizing without organizations. New York: Penguin.*

Chapter 9
Verifiability of Electronic Voting: Between Confidence and Trust

Wolter Pieters

9.1 Introduction

In many countries, controversies exist or have existed on the acceptability of electronic forms of voting in elections. These may include both electronic voting machines at polling stations and Internet voting. In the Netherlands, the use of electronic voting machines in elections was discontinued after a pressure group had raised concerns about the secrecy of the ballot and the verifiability of election results. Internet voting experiments were halted as well. The trajectory from the broadcasting of the first findings until the abandonment of the machines was replete with discussions and differences in risk estimation.

In the dynamics of such controversies, trust plays a major role. Do we trust electronic voting machines to accurately count the votes? And, do we trust government measurements of possible secrecy problems due to radiation of the machines? In this chapter, we analyse the importance of trust from the perspective of the Dutch electronic voting controversy. We also address the relation with different types of verifiability in electronic voting. A more extensive overview is found in Pieters (2008).

In Sect. 9.2, we analyse the Dutch electronic voting based on the distinction between confidence and trust, as introduced by the German sociologist Niklas Luhmann. It is argued that the controversy has initiated a transition in the requirements of electronic voting from reliability to trustworthiness. In Sect. 9.3, we show which mechanisms are available to increase the trustworthiness of electronic voting by adding verifiability features. We distinguish between different types of verifiability. In Sect. 9.4, we analyse the trust assumptions of the different forms of verifiability in more detail, and discuss which normative choices need to be made when introducing electronic voting systems. We also investigate how the analysis of trust and verifiability can be applied beyond the context of electronic voting. The last section draws conclusions from the results.

W. Pieters (✉)
EEMCS-DIES, Zilverling building, University of Twente
P.O. Box 217, 7500 AE Enschede, The Netherlands
e-mail: w.pieters@utwente.nl

S. Gutwirth et al. (eds.), *Data Protection in a Profiled World*,
DOI 10.1007/978-90-481-8865-9_9,

9.2 Trust

9.2.1 Good and Bad Trust

In the computing science literature, there seem to exist two different conceptions of trust (Pieters 2006a). On occasion, they even appear in the same article. In a section named "*Increasing* trust" (our italics) in Evans and Paul (2004), the following sentence is found: "One way to *decrease* the trust voters must place in voting machine software is to let voters physically verify that their intent is recorded correctly." (our italics) But was the intent not to *increase* trust? Do we want to increase and decrease trust at the same time? What is happening here?

A similar paradox is found in Randell and Ryan (2006). The authors state that recent cryptographic voting schemes "require only a minimum amount of public trust in voting devices or voting officials." On the same page, they say that their "ultimate goal is an e-voting system that isn't only completely trustworthy—doesn't lose, add, or alter ballots, for example, or violate ballot secrecy—but is also trusted by voters to have these properties." Again, are we aiming for a minimum or a maximum amount of trust?

Apparently, computing scientists stem from a tradition in which minimising trust is the standard. "In computer security literature in general, the term is used to denote that something must be trusted (…). That is, something trusted is something that the users are necessarily dependent on." (Nikander and Karvonen 2001) Because we *must* trust certain parts of the system for the whole system to be verifiably correct according to the computing science models, we wish to minimise the size of the parts we have to trust, thus minimising trust itself. However, from a psychological perspective, or even a marketing perspective, it is desirable that users trust the *whole* system. Maximising trust seems to lead to more fluent interaction between the user and the system, and is therefore desirable. In Nikander (2001), Matt Blaze says: "I've always wanted trust, as a security person, to be a very simple thing: I distrust something if it's allowed to violate my security; something that's trusted is something that I don't have to worry about and if it is broken, I am broken. So I want as little trust in the system as possible, and so security people are worried about minimising trust and now suddenly we have this new set of semantics that are concerned with maximising trust, and I'm terribly confused."

Apparently, two different definitions of trust have to be distinguished (cf. Nikander and Karvonen 2001):

- trust as something that is *bad,* something that people establish because they *have to, not* because the system is trustworthy;
- trust as something that is *good,* something that people establish because they *want to,* because the system *is* trustworthy.

In order to understand the origins of this difference, we need to explain which concepts lie behind the interpretation of trust as bad and good, respectively. We use an analogy here with a discussion in political science, where the situation with respect to the concept of freedom is similar to the situation presented here with respect to security. In political science, there is a well-known distinction between *negative freedom* and *positive freedom*. Negative freedom means the absence of interference by others; positive freedom means the opportunity for people to pursue their own goals in a meaningful way.[1] We see a parallel here with two possible concepts of safety and security, namely a negative and a positive one:

- negative safety/security: absence of everything that is unsafe/insecure;
- positive safety/security: opportunity to engage in meaningful trust relations.

When people use a negative concept of security, trust has to be minimised, since it denotes a dependence on (possibly) insecure systems. By removing everything that is insecure—thus increasing security—trust defined in this way can indeed be minimised, just as constraints imposed by others have to be minimised to increase negative freedom. In a setting where security is defined positively, however, trust suddenly forms an essential precondition for security, because security then requires the possibility to engage in trust relations. This is precisely the approach that comes from psychology, as opposed to the dominantly negative approach of computing science (remove all insecurities).

As an example, consider the difference between a proprietary and secret computer program and an open-source project. In the former, we need to trust the vendor with respect to the security of the program, and would rather not need to do so, which might be the case if the software can be proven to be secure. In the latter, a community will be formed around the program, in which a consensus may emerge about how secure the program is. Trust can then be based on this social process, and may actually be considered a good thing.

We will label these two conceptions of trust *bad trust* and *good trust,* respectively. We deliberately avoid the terms negative and positive in our distinction of trust, because these are used in the definitions of both freedom and security as indicators of how the concepts are defined (certain things *not* being there vs. certain things *being* there), not of their desirability. Bad and good instead indicate whether we should try to minimise or maximise the associated appearance of trust. Thus, we linked the two different interpretations of trust to two different conceptions of security. Bad trust is linked to a negative conception of safety and security, and good trust to a positive conception.

9.2.2 *Confidence and Trust*

A similar distinction was made by the German sociologist Niklas Luhmann. Luhmann (1979) provides an extensive model of trust, based on the view of systems theory. According to Luhmann, trust is a mechanism that helps us to reduce social

[1] Cf. Cunningham (2002 pp. 36–39). The notion was originally introduced by Berlin (1969 (1958)).

complexity.[2] Without reducing complexity, we cannot properly function in a complex social environment. Luhmann distinguishes several types of trust relations. First of all, he distinguishes between *familiarity* and *trust.* Familiarity reduces complexity by an orientation towards the past. Things that we see as familiar, because "it has always been like that", are accepted—we do engage in relations with those—and things that we see as unfamiliar are rejected—we do not engage in relations with those. For example, especially elderly people often refuse to use ATM's or ticket vending machines, precisely because they are not used to them.[3]

Trust, on the contrary, has an orientation towards the future: it involves expectations. We trust in something because we expect something. For example, we use ATM's because we expect these machines to provide us with money faster than a bank employee behind the counter.

In later work, Luhmann (1988) also draws a distinction between *trust* and *confidence.* Both confidence and trust involve the formation of expectations with respect to contingent events. But there is a difference. According to Luhmann, trust is always based on assessment of risks, and a decision whether or not to accept those. Confidence differs from trust in the sense that it does not presuppose a situation of risk. Confidence, instead, neglects the possibility of disappointment, not only because this case is rare, but also because there is not really a choice. Examples of confidence that Luhmann gives are expectations about politicians trying to avoid war, and of cars not suddenly breaking down and hitting you. In these cases, you cannot decide for yourself whether or not to take the risk.

When there *is* a choice, trust takes over the function of confidence. Here, the risky situation is evaluated, and a decision is made about whether or not to take the risk: "If you do not consider alternatives (…) you are in a situation of confidence. If you choose one action in preference to others (…), you define the situation as one of trust." (Luhmann 1988) If you choose to drive a car by evaluating the risks and accepting them, this is a form of trust.

Apparently, Luhmann ascribes the same negative characteristics to confidence that are ascribed to bad trust from a computing science perspective, in the sense that people do not have a choice. People *have to* have confidence in "trusted" parts of the system. Moreover, what Luhmann calls trust has the positive connotation of our good trust, in the sense that people can decide for themselves whether they want to trust something. Trust is then necessary for a system to be successful. We have to note, however, that Luhmann does not regard confidence as a bad thing in general; it is even necessary for society to function. Still, with respect to information systems, confidence means accepting a system without knowledge of risks involved, and computer scientists are generally not willing to do this.

---

[2] The function of trust as a means for reduction of complexity seems to be known in computing science. For example, Nikander and Karvonen (2001) mention this aspect. However, this paper does not refer to the work on trust by Luhmann.

[3] One may argue instead that the reason is not that they are not used to them, but rather the fact that it is harder for them to learn new things. Yet this is precisely one of the conditions that invites relying on familiarity rather than trust.

Thus, Luhmann distinguishes between two kinds of relations of self-assurance, based on whether people engage in these relations because they have to or because they want to. Luhmann calls these two relations: confidence and trust, respectively. These observations also cover the situation we described in computing science. This means that the distinction we made is not something that characterises social aspects of security in information systems only, but something that can be considered a general characteristic of trust relations.

Computing scientists generally try to replace confidence with trust, i.e. exchange unconscious dependence on a system for explicit evaluation of the risks, and minimising the parts in which we still have to have confidence.[4] Philosophers (and social scientists), instead, recognise the positive aspects of confidence, and may evaluate positively people having a relation of self-assurance with the system without exactly knowing its risks (i.e. confidence).

Starting from the distinction between confidence and trust, we also propose a distinction between reliability and trustworthiness. A system acquires *confidence* if it is *reliable,* and it acquires *trust* if it is *trustworthy*.[5] A reliable system is a system that people can use confidently without having to worry about the details. A trustworthy system is a system that people can assess the risks of and that they still want to use.

9.2.3 Trust in E-voting

Based on the analysis in the previous section, we will show how the distinction between reliability and trustworthiness influenced the electronic voting debate in the Netherlands.

Electronic voting systems *may* be seen as alternatives to paper voting systems. Whether this is indeed the case depends on the situation. If they are merely seen as improvements upon the paper system and they seem to behave correctly, the confidence in the paper system may easily be transferred to the electronic systems. If they are seen as alternatives, people suddenly get the option to *choose* a voting system. This invites active assessment of the risks of the different systems, as well as a decision based on the analysis of these risks. This means that *trust* now becomes the dominant form of self-assurance, as opposed to confidence. This has as a consequence that voting systems are required to be *trustworthy* rather than reliable only.

In the Netherlands, electronic voting machines were seen as an instrumental technology to do the same thing in a better way. The confidence that people had in the paper voting system was smoothly transferred to the electronic machines. Only

---

[4] This general approach is not without exceptions; cf. Nikander (2001).

[5] Reliability is used in the more limited sense of continuity of correct service in Avižienis et al. (2004). Our notion of reliability roughly corresponds to the "alternate definition of dependability" in their taxonomy, whereas trustworthiness corresponds to the "original definition of dependability".

after the offensive of the pressure group: *Wij Vertrouwen Stemcomputers Niet* (We Don't Trust Voting Computers) in 2006, did the two methods of voting come to be perceived as truly different. Drawing this distinction was a major achievement of the pressure group, and it prominently featured in their publications. One important achievement was the replacement in public discussions of the term "voting machine" by "voting computer". The main difference is that a computer is programmed to perform a certain task, and can therefore also be programmed to perform another. This contributed to the perception of e-voting being really different from paper voting.

Thusly, did the pressure group initiate a shift in perception from e-voting as an improvement to e-voting as an alternative. Due to this shift, electronic voting systems were now conceived as subject to a decision, and needed to be trustworthy (suitable for trust) rather than reliable (suitable for confidence) only. This meant that properties such as verifiability and secrecy had to be expressed in measurable terms, and needed to be compared between different voting systems.

In the Netherlands, the main thrust of ensuing discussions was driven by the compromising radiation emitted by electronic devices (tempest). Because this might endanger the secrecy of the ballot, the Netherlands abolished electronic voting. This is a risk that seems to be specific to the Dutch risk perception. In other countries, verifiability is more on the foreground of electronic voting politics.

Paper voting seems to have a natural advantage when it comes to trustworthiness, because it is easier to understand how the security mechanisms work. Still, electronic voting may be more *reliable,* because it eliminates human error in for example the counting of the ballots, and may thus contribute to confidence in the election procedures and the political results. For electronic voting, the *trust* relations are more complex, and necessarily involve expert judgement about the properties of the voting system. People will need to have confidence in the electronic devices based on their confidence in the experts, who in turn should have trust in the procedures based on their analysis and comparisons.

If such more complex trust relations are judged to be unacceptable for elections, for example because they might yield too much power to the experts (they can misuse the confidence they receive from the public), paper voting will be the only option. When they are judged to be acceptable, various improvements in the trustworthiness of electronic voting are possible. In terms of the software used in elections, trustworthiness with respect to verifiability may be increased by introducing the option to verify one's vote or even the total count. This ensures at least that voters have a role in verifying the result of the election, which may give more confidence than expert judgement only, even though the voters may not understand the details of the procedure. Several such mechanisms have been proposed in the literature. In the following, we investigate the primary differences between such mechanisms, and relate them to the problems they may solve with respect to the trustworthiness of electronic voting.

9.3 Verifiability

Traditionally, verification of electronic voting in the Netherlands meant that each type of machine was tested by the testing agency TNO. Additionally, a small number of machines were tested before each election. Interestingly, TNO had also been involved in the design of the machines, and even in the drafting of the legislation, making the independence of the testing questionable (Hermans and van Twist 2007).

This type of testing is mainly directed towards finding unintentional errors in the design of the machines. If a malicious programmer wants to insert manipulated program chips, this does not help much. Of course, requirements concerning the security of the machines against such attacks might have been included in the legislation, but security was hardly addressed there.

Moreover, verifiability of the *machines* is of a completely different category than verifiability of the *results*. When the demands changed from reliability to trustworthiness, it became apparent that manufacturers could no longer get away with verification of the machines only. Each election result would need to be verifiable. It is this type of verifiability that is the focus of the following analysis. We investigate the concept of verifiability vis-à-vis the scientific literature and the concrete developments in the Netherlands. We propose a distinction between various concepts of verifiability.

9.3.1 Voter-Verifiable Elections

Verifiability of electronic voting systems has attracted a great deal of attention in computing science literature. In the context of electronic voting machines (DRE's), much discussion has taken place—especially in the US—around the solution of a voter-verified paper audit trail (VVPAT) (Mercuri 2002). Typically, this includes a paper copy of each vote being kept as a backup trail for recovery or recount. This should increase trust in the proper operation of the black-box DRE machines. More than half of the states in the US have now passed legislation making a paper trail mandatory.

Some people argue that a VVPAT does not help much in improving security, because people will have a hard time checking their vote, due to the large number of races on which they have to vote in a single election in the US. It has been suggested to use an audio trail instead (Selker and Goler 2004). Also, an important question is what to do if the electronic trail and the paper trail differ. Which one prevails over the other? It could be argued that for small differences, the electronic trail will probably be the more reliable one, whereas for larger differences, the paper trail may be more trustworthy.

A VVPAT anchors the verifiability of electronic voting in organisational features that should ensure that the paper copies are indeed (statistically) checked for correspondence to the electronic result. Such a procedure aims at re-establishing the trust voters placed in the paper counting system. In Internet voting, a paper trail is not feasible, because "(t)he voter is not at the point of vote summarization to examine a receipt" (Saltman 2006, p. 211). For such applications, one needs to look into software solutions. For these purposes, various cryptographic receipts have been proposed, e.g. in Chaum (2004). Below, we will focus on these software-oriented approaches.

In the Netherlands, several experiments with online voting have been conducted in the last couple of years. In the European Elections 2004, Dutch citizens staying abroad were allowed to vote online. The system used, called KOA (Kiezen Op Afstand), was designed by Logica CMG for the Dutch Ministry of Domestic Affairs. Meanwhile, a second system was being developed by the "waterschap" (public water management authority) of Rijnland, in cooperation with the company Mullpon. This system was labelled RIES (Rijnland Internet Election System), and was used in the elections of the "waterschappen" Rijnland and Dommel in fall 2004 (Hubbers et al. 2005).

There are several interesting features offered by the systems experimented within the Netherlands. For example, the KOA system uses personalised (randomised) ballots, in order to prevent attacks by e.g. viruses residing on the voter's computer. Moreover, the counting software, written at the Radboud University Nijmegen, was specified and verified using formal methods (Hubbers et al. 2004). Unfortunately, the KOA system does not offer verifiability to the voters.

The RIES system does offer verifiability, and people seem to appreciate this.[6] However, the kind of verifiability that is offered by RIES seems to be quite different from the verifiability that is offered in more advanced cryptographic systems in the literature. In some sense, RIES seems to be *too* verifiable to provide resistance against coercion or vote buying.

Traditionally, two types of verifiability have been distinguished in research on electronic elections. When a system establishes *individual verifiability,* every voter can check if her vote has been properly counted. In *universal verifiability,* anyone can check that the calculated result is correct (Kim and Oh 2004; Malkhi et al. 2002). Typically, a bulletin board or some other electronic means is used to publish a document that represents the received votes. Voters can look up their own vote there, and people interested in the results can do correctness checks on the tally.

However, these types of verifiability have been implemented in very different ways. We think that at least one more conceptual distinction is necessary to categorise the different systems appropriately (Pieters 2006b). We will introduce this distinction via an analysis of the relation between verifiability and receipt-freeness.

[6] Much depends on the interface. Before RIES was actually used in an election, a trial session revealed that too difficult a verification procedure *decreases* trust in the system among voters. The user-friendliness of the verification procedure was improved after the trial.

9.3.2 *Verifiability and Receipt-Freeness*

One of the basic requirements of election systems is resistance against coercion and vote buying. Therefore, people should not be able to prove how they voted, even if they want to. This makes it impossible for someone who forces them to vote in a certain way, or someone who buys their vote, to check if they actually complied. This requirement is hard, if not impossible, to realise in an environment without public control, as opposed to the classical polling booth. People can watch over your shoulder if you are not guaranteed a private environment for voting, and thereby obtain proof of your vote (Pieters and Becker 2005).[7] Some scientists hold the view that this and other security problems make it advisable not to implement Internet voting at all (Jefferson et al. 2004).

There is empirical evidence, however, that vote buying may "survive the secret ballot" despite isolating the voter in a polling booth (Brusco et al. 2004). This means that buying *does* happen, even if individual votes are secret. Brusco et al. (2004) mention three possible explanations for the fact that voters comply to the buyer's wishes in spite of the secret ballot. These include the expectation of future benefits if enough people in a district vote for the desired party, feelings of moral obligation on the part of the voters, and the preference of immediate benefits over vague political promises. Similar effects may exist for coercion.

Thus, some may argue that the fact that people vote in a non-controlled environment does not need to be a fundamental problem compared to the current situation. In any case, the risks of vote buying and coercion are the same as those involved in postal ballots. Organisational and legal measures may be put in place to minimise the risks.

If we accept this argument, there is still a second problem involved. For it is one thing that people physically present at the act of voting can influence the voter, the possibility to prove *remotely* that you voted for a certain party is more problematic. This means that people could provide proof to a coercer or get money for their votes *after* they voted themselves. This is more convenient for attackers than buying or stealing access codes and casting all votes themselves. There is a trade-off between verifiability and resistance against coercion here. If a voter can check if her vote has been counted correctly, i.e. if the vote in the results corresponding to her own vote falls to the right party or candidate, then she can also show this check to a coercer or buyer as a proof. Thus, we generally do not want voters to be able to show a proof of their vote *after* the election is over. In the literature, this restricted property is often called receipt-freeness (Benaloh and Tuinstra 1994; Hirt and Sako 2000).[8]

---

[7] Some systems introduce "practice ballots", or similar measures, to prevent such attacks. However, these measures severely limit verifiability, because the tallier still needs to be able to distinguish real ballots from practice ballots, whereas the attacker should not be able to detect this via the means of verification offered to the voter. See e.g. http://zoo.cs.yale.edu/classes/cs490/03-04b/adam.wolf/Paper.pdf, consulted December 9, 2005.

[8] If a system is resistant against coercion even if the coercer can interact with the voter during voting, the term coercion-resistance is sometimes used instead of receipt-freeness (Juels et al. 2005). In order to avoid confusion, we consequently use the term receipt-freeness here.

Some systems, among which the RIES system, do indeed allow voters to check after the elections for which party or candidate their vote has been counted (Baiardi et al. 2004, 2005; Hubbers et al. 2005; Malkhi et al. 2002; Storer and Duncan 2004). These systems are therefore not receipt-free in the technical sense. Although the fact that people can see what they voted for after the elections may increase trust in the system, the lack of resistance against coercion and vote buying makes these systems debatable candidates in elections for which we cannot be sure that the chances of buying and coercion are low.

In many systems (Chaum 2004; Joaquim et al. 2003; Kim and Oh 2004), this is remedied by allowing a voter to check *that* her vote has been counted, but not *how*. The idea is that it is impossible, or at least computationally infeasible, for an attacker to make the system count a different vote for this voter in case the check turns out to be OK. Receipt-freeness can thus be provided by limiting the information that voters can retrieve about their vote after the election, while still assuring cryptographically that this is indeed a proof that the vote has been counted for the party or candidate that was chosen when voting.

Thus, the relation between individual verifiability and receipt-freeness gives rise to a distinction between two different types of individual verifiability. In the following section, we discuss the different options for verifiability in remote electronic elections based on this observation.

9.3.3 Variants of Verifiability

Following the analysis of the relation between individual verifiability and receipt-freeness, we observed a distinction between two kinds of individual verifiability. We will label these two types based on an analogy with the distinction between classical logic and constructive logic. In classical logic, one can prove an existential formula without actually showing an instance in the domain that satisfies this formula.[9] In constructive logic, one has to produce a witness in order to prove the existential formula. We argue that there is a similarity with verifiability in electronic voting here.[10]

When a voter can only verify *that* her vote has been counted, this amounts to showing that a certain vote exists in the results that can be attributed to this voter. However, the actual witness (i.e. the choice this voter made) cannot be recovered from the verification procedure. Here, the voter will believe that her vote was recorded correctly if the election authority can show something that proves the existence of a vote by this voter in the results, without re-examining the original vote.[11] Proving the existence of something without showing a witness can be done in classical logic. We will label this type of verifiability: *classical individual verifiability*.

[9] Equivalently, one shows that the negation of the formula does not hold for all instances.

[10] The analogy does not hold for computational issues around finding a witness. Still, we think that it is useful for understanding what the difference is between the two types of verifiability.

[11] Equivalently, one shows that it is not the case that one's vote has not been counted.

On the other hand, some systems allow voters to check afterwards *for which candidate* their vote has been counted. This means that the actual instance of a vote is shown as a proof to the voter. Here, the voter does not believe the election authority unless she can reproduce the original vote from the results. This corresponds to the proof of an existential formula in constructive logic. Therefore, we will label this type of verifiability *constructive individual verifiability.*

Definition 1 *Classical individual verifiability is the property of an election system that a voter can verify that her vote has been counted correctly based on a document representing the received votes,* without *being able to reconstruct her choice from that document.*[12]

Definition 2 *Constructive individual verifiability is the property of an election system that a voter can verify that her vote has been counted correctly by reconstructing her choice from a document representing the received votes.*

The first type of individual verifiability has become fairly standard in computing science discussions on voting systems. However, the second type has been used in practice as well, and we think these developments deserve some consideration from both a scientific and a political perspective.

For universal verifiability we can make a similar distinction. We take universal verifiability, to prevent confusion, to mean that any observer can verify that the *final tally* is correct, *given a document representing the received votes.* Thus, universal verifiability does not necessarily mean that anyone can check that all cast votes have been included in this document.

Definition 3 *Classical universal verifiability is the property of an election system that it can be shown that the tally is correct given a document representing the received votes, without all the data necessary to perform the calculation being publicly accessible.*

Definition 4 *Constructive universal verifiability is the property of an election system that all data necessary for calculating the result from a document representing the received votes are publicly accessible, and that a verifier can compute the tally from this set, independently of the election authorities.*

Systems in which votes are encrypted with public keys[13] of election authorities typically establish classical universal verifiability, e.g. via so-called zero-knowledge proofs by these authorities that show that they did their job correctly, or via homomorphic encryption schemes (Chaum 2004; Kim and Oh 2004; Neff 2001). This proves that there is a set of votes corresponding to the published document and to the tally, but the calculation of the tally from the document is not public.

---

[12] All types of proof discussed in this section may be relative to cryptographic assumptions.

[13] In public key cryptography, a secret message can be composed by encrypting it with the *public key* of the recipient, which is publicly known. The recipient can then recover the contents with her *private key*, which only she possesses.

Constructive universal verifiability is not possible in this case, unless the private keys are made public after the elections. However, this typically violates secrecy requirements; the encryption is usually *intended* to maintain secrecy of the individual votes.

Systems that only use public functions to calculate the result from the set of received votes typically do establish constructive universal verifiability (Hubbers et al. 2005; Malkhi et al. 2002; Storer and Duncan 2004). However, these systems need special measures to prevent the votes from being linked to individual voters. Because the received votes are used in public calculations of results, without any intermediate trusted computations that scramble them, the link between voter and vote should be destroyed in a non-trusted environment beforehand. In the UK, the situation is even more complicated due to the requirement that this link is recoverable in special cases (Storer and Duncan 2004).

Moreover, all the systems we included in our research that offered constructive universal verifiability, *also* offered constructive individual verifiability, and are therefore not receipt-free. For example, the RIES system used in the Netherlands (Hubbers et al. 2005) establishes both constructive individual verifiability and constructive universal verifiability. In technical terms, hash functions[14] are used to publish the links between all possible votes and the corresponding candidates before the elections. The original votes are only derivable from a secret (a cryptographic key) handed to the voter. The confidentiality of these secrets is achieved via organisational security measures, in the same way that identification codes for bank cards are handed out. A table of received votes is published after the elections. By computing hashes, individual voters can check for which party or candidate their vote was registered, and any observer can calculate the result from the list of received votes.

Thus, systems that allow constructive individual verifiability and constructive universal verifiability are beginning to be used in practice, in small-scale or low-risk elections. Meanwhile, many advanced cryptographic systems that establish classical individual verifiability and classical universal verifiability are being developed. We also saw that when the latter type of systems is adapted in order to offer constructive universal verifiability, constructive individual verifiability seems to emerge as a side-effect, and receipt-freeness is thereby sacrificed. But which combination of individual and universal verifiability is most desirable? And why do we care?

9.4 Verifiability and Trust

The dynamics of trust, discussed in the previous section, have shifted the expectations of electronic voting from reliability to trustworthiness. Verifiability may be implemented to provide such trustworthiness. However, technical measures are not

[14] A hash function produces a fingerprint (hash) of the input, such that it can be checked if a new input matches the original one by comparing the hashes. The original input value should not be recoverable from the hash.

by themselves sufficient to establish a relation of trust. The social and political framework has to be taken into account as well, both in terms of the context in which trust can be established and in terms of the social and political effects of technical choices.

9.4.1 The Politics of Voting Technology

In his famous study "Do artifacts have politics?", Winner (1980) showed that technological designs may have political implications. These may occur either intentionally or unintentionally. Winner's famous example of intentional political effects refers to the building of bridges in New York between 1920 and 1970 that were too low for public buses, and therefore for the lower income classes, to pass underneath. One can easily imagine similar things happening unintentionally as well. Since then, many cases of such influences have been investigated, and many theories about how they come about have been developed in philosophy of technology and science and technology studies (STS).

We may assume similar effects, be they unintentional, occurring in Internet voting technology. Internet voting will undoubtedly, depending on the way in which it is implemented, make certain things possible and others impossible, just as the New York bridges did. One can easily imagine that an Internet voting system will, depending on the types of verifiability that are offered, include different voters in different ways in the election procedure, and thereby alter the image of and trust in democracy.

In this sense, choosing a particular kind of verifiability in a particular experiment is not a choice that only influences this particular system. Instead, the type of verifiability offered and the surrounding practices in the elections may mediate the idea that people have of elections. For example, if the RIES system is successful in an experiment with elections for the local water management authorities, people may start to think that constructive individual verifiability is a good thing in general. People may also wonder why they cannot verify their choice in the same way in a later election that uses a different system.

Thus, we would like to stress that choosing a particular kind of verifiability in an experiment may have political repercussions, not only for the elections in which the system is being used, but also in terms of expectations raised about future elections. This may lead to changes in public trust not only in the elections, but also in the democratic system as a whole.

9.4.2 What Proof Do We Prefer?

How, then, can we decide which kind of verifiability we wish to implement or use? Because of the role of voting systems in people's experience of democracy, basing a decision on technical requirements only is not the way to go. We argue that the choice between different types of verifiability should be the outcome of a political discussion, rather than the unconscious influence of techno-social developments.

Technology, and especially a politically sensitive one such as electronic voting, occupies a place in people's lifeworlds, i.e. their daily experiences and actions (Ihde 1990). Based on such a phenomenological approach to technological innovation (Ihde 1990; Verbeek 2005) and the work on trust by Luhmann (1979, 1988), it appears that there are two basic ways of acquiring trust in large-scale technology such as electronic voting:

- connecting to experiences already familiar to people (focusing on familiarity of experience);
- connecting to a clear vision of a future good to be achieved, for which democratic support exists (focusing on expectations of action).

In the case of voting, a good example of the former strategy is the introduction of the Nedap voting machines in the Netherlands in the mid-nineties. Because the layout of the interface of the voting machines was very similar to the previously used paper ballots, one of the reasons that the system was so easily accepted may have been the familiarity of the interface. Now that people are already familiar with voting machines, the introduction of a Voter Verified Audit Trail can be considered an example of the latter strategy, since there is a strong public agreement on the beneficial properties of audit trails.

If we choose to implement verifiability features, we have to face the fact that people are generally *not* familiar with vote and result verification, and people will probably not be happy with their verifiability if the complete election system is turned upside down. So how can we maintain familiarity in Internet elections if people are not familiar with verification, but at the same time demand the possibility of verification of the results? The best we can do is preserve as many of the familiar features in current elections, while offering verification to make Internet elections acceptable. Two main demands, that are not only functional requirements, but also part of a ritual that establishes familiarity with elections, can be mentioned here:

- the demand for the secret ballot;[15]
- the demand for the public character of vote counting.[16]

How do these requirements relate to the various types of verifiability? In the case of individual verifiability, the demand for the secret ballot implies that constructive individual verifiability is not desirable. Thus, from the perspective of connecting to existing experiences, we should opt for classical individual verifiability. This does *not* mean that we argue for this type because of functional requirements, but rather from an "if it ain't broke, don't fix it" perspective. *Unless* there is democratic consensus about the desirability of constructive individual verifiability, either from the

[15] Cf. Dutch constitution Article 3.2 and Dutch election law ("Kieswet") Article J 15.

[16] Cf. Dutch election law ("Kieswet") Articles 1, 8 and 9.

point of view of enhancing trust or from the point of view that democracy functions better without the secret ballot (which is held for many representational bodies such as parliament and meetings such as party congresses), we had better stick to the demand for the secret ballot, and implement classical individual verifiability.

However, the existing schemes that offer classical individual verifiability, to the best of our knowledge, also offer classical universal verifiability. The limitation of the ability of result computation to dedicated parts of the system, with accompanied proofs of correctness, goes against the demand for the public character of vote counting. Typically, *any* encryption with a public key implies that the public character of vote counting is being set aside, unless the corresponding private key is made public afterwards, which is generally not the case. As much as ballot secrecy is an important part of the ritual of voting, so is the public character of vote counting. Therefore, we think that *constructive* universal verifiability, in which any party can perform an independent calculation of the result, is preferable, *unless* there is democratic consensus about arguments for the opposite point of view.

9.4.3 Beyond Electronic Voting

Verifiability is a way to increase trustworthiness, as opposed to reliability, of e-voting systems. Implementing verifiability features not only influences trust in the elections themselves; different variants of verifiability also have different trust assumptions on a smaller scale.

Constructive individual verifiability leads to high trustworthiness with respect to the validity of the results, but low trustworthiness with respect to the secrecy of the ballot. In this case, assuring that individual choices will be kept secret requires high confidence in voters: they should not succumb to the persuasion of selling their vote, or to coercion. In classical individual verifiability, there is no need to have such confidence in voters, since they will not be able to prove the contents of their vote. However, in this case, voters cannot “see” if their vote has been registered correctly; they can only see *that* it has been registered. Accepting the assurance that it must then also be correct requires confidence of the voter in the verification procedure as designed by mathematicians (cryptographers) and computing scientists. These scientists, in turn, must have analysed the procedures and have found them trustworthy. Similar trust assumptions are present in the two types of universal verifiability.

These relations between verifiability and trust can be generalised to other systems and properties (e.g. privacy). In general, verifiability can be necessary when some data processing is done by a third party on behalf of the party who is responsible for the results, or when there are other parties who have interest in correctness and security properties of the results. Constructive verifiability then means repeatability of the data processing by other parties, whereas classical verifiability means a (mathematical) proof obligation on the part of the calculator, without revealing the details of the calculation. In case of privacy, we have the data processor, the processing of which may need to be verified by either the data controller or the individual the data concerns. These correspond to the e-voting provider, the Electoral Commission and the voter in the election process.

As an example, we take the profiling of an individual by an organisation, on the basis of which a decision about the individual is made by the organisation. Profiling can be defined as "the process of 'discovering' correlations between data in databases that can be used to identify and represent a human or nonhuman subject (individual or group) and/or the application of profiles (sets of correlated data) to individuate and represent a subject or to identify a subject as a member of a group or category" (Hildebrandt 2008, p. 19). Hildebrandt distinguishes between *group profiling* and *personalised profiling*. In the former, correlations between people are derived from a dataset by constituting a group of similar people and identifying the (probable) characteristics of people belonging to this group. In the latter, individual preferences are recorded and analysed to personalise services.

Both individual and universal verifiability can be useful concepts in such a setting. The processing here concerns the calculation of a decision based on the information derived about an individual. For personalised profiling, this may be, for example, the decision whether or not to issue a credit card. Laws and regulations may apply that limit what the organisation is allowed to consider in this decision. The individual and other parties such as the government may demand the opportunity to verify that these rules were indeed adhered to. In case of classical individual verifiability, the organisation would have to prove that the calculations made concerning an individual—both in terms of creating the profile and in terms of applying it to make a decision—were made in compliance with the rules. In case of constructive individual verifiability, all the data that was used as input as well as the calculation procedure would need to be made available to individuals, such that they can repeat the calculation or ask an independent institution to do so. Which of the types of verifiability is most desirable should be discussed based on the required level of transparency as well as the sensitivity of the information involved.

Similar considerations apply to universal verifiability. Here, the calculations concern groups of persons rather than a single individual (group profiling instead of personalised profiling). Typically, group profiles will affect decisions about individuals that are members of the established groups, whether or not the attributes associated with the group apply to them. For example, if someone lives in a poor neighbourhood, this may affect decisions about issuing her a credit card. The acceptability of such a decision depends on a) the correctness of the calculations concerning the group and b) the acceptability of applying the group profile in this particular decision. In classical universal verifiability, the organisation would have to prove that statistical data concerning groups was calculated and applied in compliance with the rules. In constructive universal verifiability, all data used to calculate the statistics would have to be made available (possibly in anonymous form), such that stakeholders can validate the calculations by performing them themselves.

These concepts may be useful in discussions on the alignment of technical and legal aspects of profiling. Depending on the application area, different forms of verifiability may be prescribed. One can imagine that the heavier the consequence of a decision, the stronger the verifiability requirements. This requires classifications of both decisions and verifiability properties. Such verifiability requirements may also enable assurance that forms of profiling that are considered illegal—e.g. in relation to race or religion—are indeed absent from the decision-making process. In such cases, data processors would either need to prove that their processing of the data has certain properties, or allow independent parties to redo the calculations and confirm the fairness and correctness.

Similar arguments apply to any form of externalised data processing, such as cloud computing or outsourcing. The data controller inevitably has an interest in assessing whether the externalised calculations conform to certain desirable properties, i.e. establishing verifiability of the calculations. Investigating the implications of the present analysis for these fields is future work.

9.5 Conclusions

In controversies on electronic voting, like in 2006 in the Netherlands, different types of trust play a major role. In the Netherlands, e-voting was represented as a possibly disastrous alternative to paper voting, and the existing "blind" trust (confidence) had to give way to rational trust (trust). This is a process that computing scientists can contribute to: they aim at minimising blind trust in information systems, and replacing this by a provably correct behaviour. Although some computing scientists claim that there are no good solutions except for a print of each vote, many people work on advanced methods to provide verifiability in electronic elections.

We distinguished between two types of individual verifiability and two types of universal verifiability in electronic elections, based on scientific literature and concrete developments. We made this distinction based on an analogy with proofs in classical and constructive logic, and labelled the corresponding types of verifiability classical and constructive verifiability, respectively. This distinction is meaningful both for individual and universal verifiability, and we think that it is a useful tool for explicating the hidden assumptions behind implementations of verifiability in concrete systems.

We argued that choices for particular kinds of verifiability in experiments may have political implications, not only for a specific election in which a particular system is used, but also in terms of expectations of future elections. Therefore, it is wise to attempt to arrive at political consensus about desirable kinds of verifiability. We argued that even if verifiability is widely accepted as a good thing, we need to maintain familiarity with elections in order to make the whole system acceptable. The best we can do here is uphold the existing properties of vote secrecy and public counting. This can be done with a system that establishes classical individual verifiability and constructive universal verifiability, which, as far as we are aware, has not been invented yet.

We showed that the types of verifiability we distinguished can also be useful beyond electronic voting. In that case, they denote which information individuals or organisations may access about data that is stored or processed either concerning them or on behalf of them. This broader notion may for example be used when discussing the acceptability of different forms of profiling. In this sense, we will have learnt something from the controversy, even if the time of electronic voting were to have come to an end.

Acknowledgments The ideas described here were partly developed while the author was employed by Radboud University Nijmegen, and are based on earlier publications (Pieters 2006a, b). This work was supported by a Pionier grant from NWO, the Netherlands Organisation for Scientific Research.

References

Avižienis, A., J.C. Laprie, B. Randell, and C. Landwehr. 2004. Basic concepts and taxonomy of dependable and secure computing. *IEEE Transactions on Dependable and Secure Computing* 1 (1), 11–33.

Baiardi F., A. Falleni, R. Granchi, F. Martinelli, M. Petrocchi, and A. Vaccarelli. 2004. SEAS: A secure e-voting applet system. In *Software security: Theories and systems,* eds. K. Futatsugi, F. Mizoguchi, and N. Yonezaki, 318–329. LNCS, vol. 3233. Berlin: Springer.

Baiardi F., A. Falleni, R. Granchi, F. Martinelli, M. Petrocchi, and A. Vaccarelli. 2005. SEAS, a secure e-voting protocol: Design and implementation. *Computers & Security* 24, 642–652.

Benaloh, J.C., and D. Tuinstra. 1994. Receipt-free secret ballot elections (extended abstract). In *Proceedings 26th ACM symposium on the theory of computing (STOC),* eds. J.C. Benaloh and D. Tuinstra, 544–553. New York: ACM.

Berlin, I. 1969. *Four concepts of liberty*. Oxford: Oxford Univ. Press (1958).

Brusco, V., M. Nazareno, and S.C. Stokes. 2004. Vote buying in Argentina. *Latin American Research Review* 39 (2), 66–88.

Chaum, D. 2004. Secret-ballot receipts: True voter-verifiable elections. *IEEE Security & Privacy* 2 (1), 38–47.

Cunningham, F. 2002. *Theories of democracy: A critical introduction*. London: Routledge.

Evans, D., and N. Paul. 2004. Election security: Perception and reality. *IEEE Security & Privacy* 2 (1), 24–31 (January/February 2004).

Hermans, L.M.L.H.A., and M.J.W. van Twist. 2007. Stemmachines: Een verweesd dossier. Rapport van de Commissie Besluitvorming Stemmachines, April 2007. Also available online at http://www.minbzk.nl/contents/pages/86914/rapportstemmachineseenverweesddossier.pdf. Consulted April 19, 2007.

Hildebrandt, M. 2008. Defining profiling: A new type of knowledge? In *Profiling the European citizen: Cross-disciplinary perspectives,* eds. M. Hildebrandt and S. Gutwirth, 17–45. Berlin: Springer.

Hirt, M., and K. Sako. 2000. Efficient receipt-free voting based on homomorphic encryption. In *Advances in cryptology EUROCRYPT 2000,* ed. B. Preneel, 539–556. LNCS, vol. 1807. Berlin: Springer.

Hubbers, E., B. Jacobs, J. Kiniry, and M. Oostdijk. 2004. Counting votes with formal methods. In *Algebraic methodology and software technology (AMAST'04),* eds. C. Rattray, S. Maharaj, and C. Shankland, 241–257. LNCS, vol. 3116. Berlin: Springer.

Hubbers, E., B. Jacobs, and W. Pieters. 2005. RIES—Internet voting in action. In *Proceedings 29th annual international computer software and applications conference, COMPSAC'05,* ed. R. Bilof, 417–424. IEEE Computer Society, July 2005. ISBN 0-7695-2413-3.

Ihde, D. 1990. *Technology and the lifeworld.* Bloomington: Indiana Univ. Press.

Jefferson, D., A.D. Rubin, B. Simons, and D. Wagner. 2004. Analyzing internet voting security. *Communications of the ACM* 47 (10), 59–64.

Joaquim, R., A. Zúquete, and P. Ferreira. 2003. REVS: A robust electronic voting system. *IADIS International Journal of WWW/Internet* 1 (2), 47–63.

Juels, A., D. Catalano, and M. Jakobsson. 2005. Coercion-resistant electronic elections. In *Proceedings WPES'05*. Alexandria: ACM.

Kim, S., and H. Oh. 2004. A new universally verifiable and receipt-free electronic voting scheme using one-way unwappable channels. In *AWCC 2002,* eds. C.-H. Chi and K.-Y. Lam, 337–345. LNCS, vol. 3309. Berlin: Springer.

Luhmann, N. 1979. *Trust and power: Two works by Niklas Luhmann*. Chichester: Wiley.

Luhmann, N. 1988. Familiarity, confidence, trust: Problems and alternatives. In *Trust: Making and breaking of cooperative relations,* ed. D. Gambetta. Oxford: Basil Blackwell.

Malkhi, D., O. Margo, and E. Pavlov. 2002. E-voting without 'cryptography'. In *Financial cryptography'02,* 1–15. Berlin: Springer.

Mercuri, R.T. 2002. A better ballot box? *IEEE Spectrum* 39 (10), 26–50.

Neff, C.A. 2001. A verifiable secret shuffle and its application to e-voting. In *Proceedings of the 8th ACM conference on computer and communications security,* ed. P. Samarati, 116–125. New York: ACM.

Nikander, P. 2001. Users and trust in cyberspace (transcript of discussion). In *Security protocols: 8th international workshop, Cambridge, UK, April 3–5,* 2000, *revised papers,* eds. B. Christianson, B. Crispo, J.A. Malcolm, and M. Roe, 36–42. LNCS, vol. 2133. Berlin: Springer.

Nikander, P., and K. Karvonen. 2001. Users and trust in cyberspace. In *Security protocols: 8th international workshop, Cambridge, UK, April 3–5, 2000, revised papers,* eds. B. Christianson, B. Crispo, J.A. Malcolm, and M. Roe, 24–35. LNCS, vol. 2133. Berlin: Springer.

Pieters, W. 2006a. Acceptance of voting technology: Between confidence and trust. In *Trust management: 4th international conference (iTrust 2006), proceedings,* eds. K. Stølen, W.H. Winsborough, F. Martinelli, and F. Massacci, 283–297. LNCS, vol. 3986. Berlin: Springer.

Pieters, W. 2006b. What proof do we prefer? Variants of verifiability in voting. In *Workshop on e-Voting and e-Government in the UK,* eds. P. Ryan, S. Anderson, T. Storer, I. Duncan, and J. Bryans, 33–39. Edinburgh: e-Science Institute, Univ. of St. Andrews (February 27–28).

Pieters, W. 2008. La volonté machinale: Understanding the electronic voting controversy. PhD thesis, Radboud University Nijmegen, January 2008.

Pieters, W., and M. Becker. 2005. Ethics of e-voting: An essay on requirements and values in Internet elections. In *Ethics of new information technology: Proceedings sixth international conference on computer ethics: Philosophical enquiry (CEPE'05),* eds. P. Brey, F. Grodzinsky, and L. Introna, 307–318. Enschede: Center for Telematics and Information Technology.

Randell, B., and P.Y.A. Ryan. 2006. Voting technologies and trust. *IEEE Security & Privacy* 4 (5), 50–56.

Saltman, R.G. 2006. *The history and politics of voting technology*. New York: Palgrave Macmillan.

Selker, T., and J. Goler. 2004. Security vulnerabilities and problems with VVPT. Caltech/MIT Voting Technology Project, Working Paper 16, 2004. Also available online at http://www.vote.caltech.edu/media/documents/wps/vtp_wp16.pdf. Consulted February 10, 2006.

Storer, T., and I. Duncan. 2004. Practical remote electronic elections for the UK. In *Proceedings of the second annual conference on privacy, security and trust,* ed. S. Marsh., 41–45. Canada: National Research Council Canada.

Verbeek, P.P.C.C. 2005. *What things do: Philosophical reflections on technology, agency, and design*. Pennsylvania: Pennsylvania State Univ. Press.

Winner, L. 1980. Do artifacts have politics? *Daedalus* 109 (1), 121–136.

Chapter 10
Electronic Voting in Germany

Melanie Volkamer

10.1 Introduction

In the past, election reforms have taken place several times all over the world: In the ancient world, shards were used to write the candidate's name on it. Later, in the Middle Ages, elections were organized by public acclamation. In the Renaissance, polling bowls or polling stones were used and later voters wrote down their decisions in public electoral registers. By the end of the nineteenth century, many, especially industrial, countries started establishing more and more of today's election principles: The principle of a universal franchise (in this context the right to vote was extended to poor people as well as to women) as well as that of a direct and secret election were introduced. Later, the principles of free and equal suffrage were added. In Germany, all five principles are integrated in the law since 1949. More recently, several (industrial) countries all over the world have introduced further reforms: Postal voting (in Germany in 1956) and early voting have been introduced to strengthen the universal franchise as voters became more and more mobile. These reforms show that the election laws have been adjusting to changing society.

Therefore, it is not surprising, that—with the modernization and mechanization of our society—mechanical and later electronic voting machines were introduced to rush the counting and modernize the voting process. Similarly, it is not surprising, that with the rising impact of the Internet, people started implementing remote electronic voting (Internet Voting) to modernize and improve postal voting and provide more comfort to modern voters who are even more mobile and use the Internet for arbitrary purposes like shopping and banking.

This chapter provides an overview of the different electronic voting approaches applied in Germany (Sect. 10.2) and proposes existing regulations and requirement

M. Volkamer (✉)
Center for Advanced Security Research (CASED), Technische Universität Darmstadt, Darmstadt, Deutschland
e-mail: volkamer@cased.de

S. Gutwirth et al. (eds.), *Data Protection in a Profiled World*,
DOI 10.1007/978-90-481-8865-9_10,

catalogues (Sect. 10.3). Further, it presents the main activities of German activists (Sect. 10.4) and discusses the judgment of the Federal Constitutional Court (Sect. 10.5). The chapter concludes with a discussion of the future of electronic voting in Germany.

10.2 Approaches Applied in Germany

In Germany, there were and are different types of electronic voting systems in use: mechanical voting machines, electronic voting devices without (so called direct recording electronic voting computers) and with paper trail (so called paper-based electronic voting systems), and Internet voting systems. These approaches are introduced in this section.

10.2.1 Mechanical Voting Machines

Mechanical voting machines record votes by mechanical components. The most popular examples are lever machines patented by Thomas Alva Edison. Here, as with odometers, the number of votes for a particular candidate is incremented each time a voter casts a vote by moving the lever that corresponds with the particular candidate. In order to tally the votes, poll workers open up the back of the device and determine from the counting wheels how many votes were cast for each candidate. These mechanical voting machines are the precursor of direct recording electronic voting computers.

In Germany, mechanical voting machines were introduced in 1975, but are no longer in use. Figure 10.1 shows one of these machines as used in Germany.

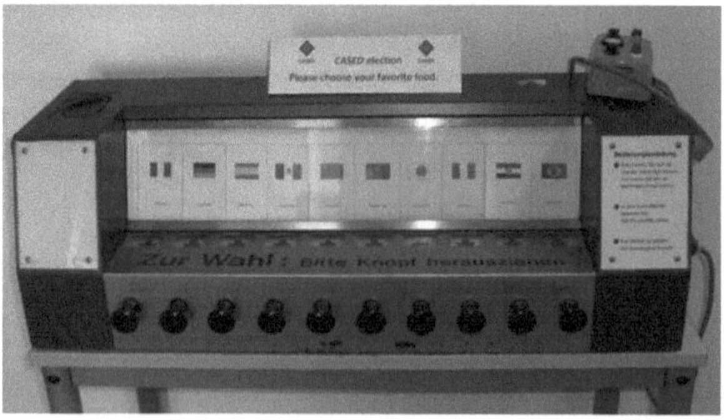

Fig. 10.1 German mechanical voting device

10.2.2 Direct Recording Electronic (DRE) Voting Computers

Direct recording electronic (DRE) voting computers are dedicated voting devices which can either be networked or used in a stand-alone mode. Stand-alone DRE voting computers can only transfer data by physically transporting the storage medium. DRE voting computers display the ballot on the device and mechanical or electro-optical buttons (like a touch screen) are used to cast a vote. A DRE voting computer processes electronic votes by means of a computer program that locally stores electronic votes in memory components. The tallying software can either be a part of the DRE voting computer or run on another device. Usually, after tallying is completed, a copy of the result is printed. In contrast to paper-based election systems, DRE voting computers do not provide the voter with a confirmation or physical record for (later) verification of the correct tallying of his vote. The voter needs to trust the computer is correctly entering his vote into the memory and, furthermore, that the tallying works correctly.

In Germany, only stand-alone DRE voting computers have been used and only those from the Dutch company called NEDAP (one of these devices is shown in Fig. 10.2). Their machines were evaluated by the Department of Metrological Information Technology in the National Metrology Institute and certified by the Federal Ministry of the Interior for arbitrary governmental elections on different levels.

The NEDAP voting devices were used in almost 2,000 voting districts for the federal election in 2005 which means that between 2 and 2.5 million voters used

Fig. 10.2 NEDAP voting computer. (http://www.spiegel.de/netzwelt/tech/0,1518,grossbild-599450-441637,00.html)

the machines for voting. The Chaos Computer Club provides on their web page an overview of polling stations where NEDAP voting devices were used.

10.2.3 Paper-Based Electronic Voting Systems

Paper-based electronic voting systems provide in contrast to DRE voting systems a paper audit. Thus it is possible to verify the election's integrity. In general, there are different possibilities to implement such systems: e.g. scanning-based approaches (which scan the vote cast on a paper ballot either during or after vote casting or in the tallying process) or verifiability-based on cryptographic approaches (which provide an encrypted paper audit to the voter which is used to later verify the correctness of the tallying). The paper-based electronic voting systems which were used—at least for shadow elections—in Germany are the Digital Voting Pen, the Bingo Voting System and the e-counting approach. These systems are proposed in the following subsections.

10.2.3.1 Digital Voting Pen

Due to changes in the election law of the Free and Hanseatic City of Hamburg, the vote tallying of the 2008 state parliament election were expected to become a very complicated and time consuming event. Thus, the parliament decided on using an electronic voting system and, specifically, the Digital Voting Pen. The decision was made not to use the NEDAP machines mainly because the pen solution can be implemented in a way that the vote casting procedure is very similar to the traditional one. The developed solution called Dot Vote (see Fig. 10.3) was evaluated according to a Common Criteria Protection Profile (Volkamer and Vogt 2006a), according to regulations for electronic voting machines (Wahlgvo 2006) (corresponding to the Federal Ordinance for Voting Machines (Bundeswahlgeräteverordnung 1999)), and according to the German Datenschutz-Gütesiegel (Unabhängigen Landeszentrum für Datenschutz 2002). A prototype version was used in 2005 for a shadow election. However, for the real election in 2008, it had been decided not to use the Digital Voting Pen system due to negative press and security reservations. As a consequence, the counting process took 4 days and the whole paper-based election cost 12 million Euros.

The Digital Voting Pen is slightly larger than common pens, because of an integrated camera besides the usual lead. It is currently used in other contexts, namely in hospitals, logistics, and banks. In voting applications, voter marks his choice on a paper ballot and this digital pen stores the corresponding positions (scanning is done based on a thin pattern on the paper ballot—the so called Anoto Pattern). At the end of the individual's vote casting, the voter drops the paper ballot into the ballot box as usual and, additionally, inserts the Digital Voting Pen into a docking station. The vote casting data is copied from the pen to an electronic ballot box and is erased from the pen. Thereafter, the pen is re-initialized for the next voter. For more information see (Volkamer and Vogt 2006a, b; Mergemeier et al. 2007).

Fig. 10.3 Digital voting pen from Dot Vote. (http://www.hamburg.de/image/103302/digitaler-stift-400×518.jpg)

10.2.3.2 Bingo Voting System

In contrast to the above-mentioned approach, the Bingo Voting System (see Fig. 10.4) provides a paper trail to the voter that he can take away with him in order to verify the correctness of the tallying after the election using a so called Bulletin Board—a particular web page. However, the provided voting scheme is coercion-free meaning the voter cannot use his paper trail to prove his vote nor can someone else use his paper trail to get any information on the voter's choice. This approach is based on a trustworthy random number generator (comparable to a bingo cage).

This approach is the only German electronic voting system providing voters with verifiability, that is, the voter can verify that his vote is stored and counted as intended. In addition, everyone is able to verify that all votes are correctly counted as recorded on a bulletin board (without breaking election secrecy). The authors of this scheme received the German Security Award in 2008. The system is implemented and was used for students' elections at the Technical University of Karlsruhe in 2008. For more information see (Bohli et al. 2007).

Fig. 10.4 Bingo voting. (http://www.kit.edu/fzk/groups/kit-presse/documents/presseinformationen/%7Eexport/ID_066790%7E1%7EWORD_KIT2/25933-1.jpg)

10.2.3.3 E-counting with Barcode Scanners

In Bavaria, local election systems are as complicated as the Hamburg ones. Thus, manual tallying would require several days, too. To speed the counting, they use e-counting with Barcode Scanners. Here, the votes are manually recorded and either continuously or at the end tallied by the e-counting software (e.g. from PC-Wahl or IWS-EM). To do so, a barcode system is used (see Fig. 10.5). Therefore, for each candidate a barcode is printed on the ballots. During tallying, the poll worker

Fig. 10.5 Barcode scanner. (http://www.sueddeutsche.de/computer/324/434072/text/)

scans the barcode next to the candidate who is marked on the ballot. The software displays the recorded vote on the screen. Note, in the case of a contested election the paper votes could be tallied manually. The applied software has not been evaluated.

10.2.4 Internet Voting Systems

In Germany, Internet voting has been under discussion since 1998. From a practical point of view, the systems were investigated by Prof. Dieter Otten. And since then, two systems have emerged and been developed: The vote remote system and the Polyas System. Both are proposed in this section.

10.2.4.1 Vote Remote System

In 2001, T-Systems started to develop an electronic voting system in the context of the W.I.E.N (Wählen in elektronischen Netzwerken, Voting in electronic networks) research project funded by the former German Federal Ministry of Economics and Labour. This project addressed the implementation of electronic voting at networked polling stations in non-parliamentary elections. Based on this project, the follow-up project 'vote remote' was initiated. Here T-Systems extended the W.I.E.N.-system to a remote electronic voting system, the so called vote remote system. Development of the voting protocol was supported by the Department of Metrological Information Technology in the National Metrology Institute, the research group of Prof. J. Buchmann from Technische Universität Darmstadt and the research group 'provet' from Prof. A. Roßnagel from Kassel University. For more information see (Langer and Schmidt 2009).

10.2.4.2 Polyas System

The Polyas system was developed by a German company called Micromata GmbH. It has a long-standing history: Already in 1996, the first election was carried out with the Polyas system. Here about 64,000 Finnish pupils had the possibility to vote electronically. Since then, the Polyas system has been continuously improved and more than 500,000 votes have been cast, 210,000 of which were in Germany. There is close cooperation between the company and the German society of computer scientists (GI). Since 2005, the GI has used the Polyas system in parallel to postal voting for their yearly elections. In addition, the Polyas system is also used for the elections of the board of the Initiative D21 since 2003, the elections of the German Research Foundation since 2007, as well as for THESIS e. V. and MPI in 2009. (For more information see (Reinhard and Jung 2007)).

10.3 Requirement Documents

A couple of documents defining requirements for e-voting systems have been developed in Germany. They address different types of electronic voting systems. There is the German Federal Ordinance for Voting Machines addressing stand-alone DRE voting computers, then the requirements of the Department of Metrological Information Technology in the National Metrology Institute addressing network DRE voting computers, the Protection Profile for the Digital Voting Pen, the ad hoc GI catalogue for Internet voting, and the Protection Profile defining basic requirements for Internet voting systems. These are shortly introduced in the following subsections.

10.3.1 German Federal Ordinance for Voting Machines

The very first version of the Federal Ordinance for Voting Machines (Bundeswahlgeräteverordnung 1999) was published in 1975. This ordinance holds for Bundestag election and for EU elections. While original regulations only addressed mechanical devices, the list of permitted electronic voting machines was extended in 1999 to include electronic and software based systems. The ordinance defines organizational, technical as well as certification requirements. According to the ordinance, the device needs to be evaluated by the Department of Metrological Information Technology in the National Metrology Institute and certified by the Federal Ministry of the Interior, while the certification has to be renewed for each election. This federal ordinance was adopted by a couple of states for state parliament and local elections.

10.3.2 Protection Profile for the Digital Voting Pen

In the context of the Digital Voting Pen for state parliament elections, the international Common Criteria evaluation standard (Common Criteria 2006) was applied for the first time to electronic voting. To do so, the city of Hamburg contracted the German Research Center of Artificial Intelligence to develop a corresponding Protection Profile (PP) (Volkamer and Vogt 2006a). This Protection Profile mainly addresses the software running on a PC to record the votes from the pen, initialize the pen and to compute the result but not the environment in which it is used and not the pattern on the ballot paper which is necessary for the pen to know the position on the paper. The PP successfully passed the evaluation by the accredited laboratory TÜV Informationstechnik GmbH and was certified by the German Federal Office for Information Security. The Protection Profile requires an evaluation of the Digital Voting Pen according to EAL3 (evaluation assurance level). The DotVote system was evaluated by Datenschutz cert GmbH and its compliance with the PP is certified by the German Federal Office for Information Security.

10.3.3 Online-Voting System Requirements for Non-parliamentary Elections

A catalogue of requirements for "Online-Voting Systems for Non-parliamentary Elections" (Hartmann et al. 2004) was developed by the Department of Metrological Information Technology in the National Metrology Institute within the project. "Development of Concepts for Testing and Certification of Online Voting Systems" funded by the former German Ministry of Economics and Labour. This project ran in parallel to the W.I.E.N. project which addressed networked polling stations. Correspondingly, (Hartmann et al. 2004) addresses this type of electronic voting systems, too. This catalogue is only a recommendation without corresponding mandatory regulation and has not yet been used to evaluate a system.

10.3.4 Catalogue of the German Society of Computer Scientists

The German society of computer scientists (GI) enabled the application of remote electronic voting in 2004. The GI established a group of security experts to accompany the introduction of this new voting channel. One of their tasks was to develop and enforce ad-hoc security requirements. These are summarized in the catalogue for "Internet-based elections in societies" (Gesellschaft für Informatik 2005). The provider of the GI's remote election system—Micromata—explains in a security functional document why and how the Polyas system meets these requirements.

10.3.5 GI/BSI/DFKI Protection Profile

In 2008, a second "Common Critiera Protection" for electronic voting was certified. This PP addresses remote electronic voting systems and describes a "Basic set of security requirements for Online Voting Products" (Volkamer and Vogt 2008). After having published (Gesellschaft für Informatik 2005), the GI established an expert group to develop such a "Common Criteria Protection Profile" based on the first catalogue (Gesellschaft für Informatik 2005). Participants in this expert group included employees from the German Federal Office for Security in Information Technology, from universities, ministries, and administrations, as well as systems developers and data protection authorities. Additionally, the German Federal Office for Security in Information Technology contracted the German Research Center of Artificial Intelligence to formally develop a corresponding Protection Profile in conjunction with the expert group. The PP was evaluated by SRC Security Research & consulting GmbH and is certified by the German Federal Office for Security in Information Technology. The Protection Profile requires that an evaluation according to EAL2 (evaluation assurance level) be augmented. Micromata has started to evaluate the Polyas system according to this Protection Profile.

10.4 Activists' Activities

The German campaigns against electronic voting (mainly for parliamentary elections) are spear headed by the "Chaos Computer Club" (CCC). They provide a lot of information on their web site including reports on election observations in polling stations with voting machines (e.g. elections in Cottbus and Brandenburg). There is also a close cooperation with Dutch activists from "Wij vertrouwen stemcomputers niet". Together, they were able to hack into a Dutch NEDAP machine (not during an election; they bought one machine). Supported by the CCC, a voter lodged a claim to object to the use of voting machines for the state parliamentary elections of Hesse. This claim was rejected by the court as such a claim is only possible after the election. Other claims have been submitted for the state parliament election of Rhineland-Palatinate 2006, for the mayor elections in Cottbus (2006) and Alsbach-Hähnlein (2007).

In October 2006, a petition at the German Bundestag was entered against the application of insecure and in-transparent voting computers for elections of the German Bundestag. Although 45,126 people signed the petition, the committee on petitions stated that the advantages brought on by the use of the computers prevailed over the claim.

Ulrich Wiesner and his father filed a protest against the German Bundestag elections in 2005 regarding the application of the voting computers at the scrutiny committee of the German Bundestag. This protest was rejected as "obviously causeless" (Deutsche Bundestag 2006). Thereafter, they filed a protest against the election at the Federal Constitutional Court. This protest was accepted and discussed in an open hearing in October 2008.

10.5 The Federal Constitutional Court Judgment

On March 3, 2009, the Second Senate of the Federal Constitutional Court ruled that the use of the NEDAP voting computers as well as the Federal Voting Machine Ordinance (Bundeswahlgeräteverordnung) is unconstitutional (Bundeswahlgeräteverordnung 2009). This judgment is based on the decision that the "essential steps of the voting and of the determination of the result can be examined by the citizen reliably and without any special knowledge of the subject" (Bundesverfassungsgerichts: Press 2009) (according to the public nature of the election). This includes that the voter himself understands without detailed knowledge of computer technology whether his cast vote is recorded in an unadulterated manner and is included in the same way in the result or a later recount. However, the "voting machines did not make an affective examination of the voting possible due to the fact that the votes were exclusively recorded electronically on a vote recording module" (Bundesverfassungsgerichts: Press 2009).

Furthermore, the Second Senate states that "the possibility for the citizens to examine the voting cannot be compensated by an official institution testing sample machines in the context of their engineering type licensing procedure, or the very voting machines which will be used in the elections before their being used, for their compliance with specific security requirements and for their technical integrity" (Bundesverfassungsgerichts: Press 2009).

The judgment does not prevent use of electronic voting machines in other types of elections. Thus, the Second Senate ruled that removal of § 35 of the Federal Electoral Act (Bundeswahlgesetz), which permits the use of voting machines, is not required because "it is, admittedly, constitutionally unobjectionable" but a corresponding ordinance has to ensure that only "voting machines are permitted and used which meet the constitutional requirements of the principle of the public nature of elections" (Bundesverfassungsgerichts: Press 2009). Moreover, they recognized that other constitutional interests can justify further exception.

However, the Second Senate ruled that the identified errors "do not lead to a repetition of the election in the constituencies affected" (Bundesverfassungsgerichts: Press 2009) as the protection of the continued existence of Parliament is more important.

10.6 Future of Electronic Voting in Germany

The judgment, on the one hand, clarifies (for the Bundestag election in 2009, no electronic voting machines will be used) but, on the other, leads to new research questions and opens venues of discussions. Open issues of discussions are whether the voter can use assistive technology to verify that his vote is correctly included in the election result and that the election result is calculated correctly. Should a paper trail be required, this requirement needs to be discussed as to whether paper ballots are only counted in case of a complain, whether paper ballots are counted in a statistically relevant number of randomly chosen polling stations, or whether all paper ballots are counted because paper ballots are the legal instruments. If a paper trail is not required, such absence of requirement must be defined in a discussion between lawyers and computer scientists on which technical strength and type of verifiability is required (compare to Volkamer et al. 2009). Open research questions are: Whether the judgment holds in the same strength for elections other than Bundestag elections and whether it holds for remote electronic voting in parallel to postal voting? Here, awareness-raising campaign on postal voting will play a major role. Furthermore, whether verifiability must also be provided for the election secrecy requirement is also up for discussion?

Thus, many issues are due for further discussion and clarification. However, given the numerous and complicated voting systems including large ballots currently in use in Germany that cause elections to become very expensive; given the time consuming and error prone nature of counting and re-counting procedures; given that poll workers are harder to find, researchers and developers will continue trying their best to find solutions to implementing constitutional electronic voting systems.

References

Arzt-Mergemeier, J., W. Beiss, and T. Steffens. 2007. The digital voting pen at the hamburg elections 2008: Electronic voting closest to conventional voting. In *E-Voting and identity: First international conference*, 88–98, VOTE-ID 2007. LNCS, vol. 4896. Berlin: Springer.

Bohli, J.-M., J. Müller-Quade, and S. Röhrich. 2007. Bingo voting: Secure and coercion-free voting using a trusted random number generator. In *E-Voting and identity: First international conference*, 111–124, VOTE-ID 2007. LNCS, vol. 4896. Berlin: Springer.

Bundesverfassungsgerichts. 2009. Zweiter Senat des Bundesverfassungsgerichts: Urteil in den Verfahren über die Wahlprüfungsbeschwerden. http://www.bundesverfassungsgericht.de/entscheidungen/cs20090303_2bvc000307.html.

Bundesverfassungsgerichts: Press. 2009. Zweiter Senat des Bundesverfassungsgerichts: Press Office: Federal Constitutional Court. http://www.bundesverfassungsgericht.de/pressemitteilungen/bvg09-019en.html.

Bundeswahlgeräteverordnung. 1999. Verordnung über den Einsatz von Wahlgeräten bei Wahlen zum Deutschen Bundestag und der Abgeordneten des Europäischen Parlaments aus der Bundesrepublik Deutschland (Bundeswahlgeräteverordnung), 1975. BGBl I 1975, 2459, Zuletzt geändert durch Art. 1 V v. 20. 4.1999 I 749.

Common Criteria. 2006. Common criteria for information technology security evaluation. Version 3.1. http://www.commoncriteriaportal.org/thecc.html.

Deutsche Bundestag. 2006. Wahlprüfungsausschuss des Deutsche Bundestag: Dritte Beschlussempfehlung des Wahlprüfungsausschusses zu 44 gegen die Gültigkeit der Wahl zum 16. Deutschen Bundestag eingegangenen Wahleinsprüchen; Drucksache 16/3600. http://dip21.bundestag.de/dip21/btd/16/036/1603600.pdf.

Gesellschaft für Informatik. 2005. Online-Wahlen Expertengruppe der Gesellschaft für Informatik. GI-Anforderungen an Internetbasierte Vereinswahlen. http://www.gi-ev.de/fileadmin/redaktion/Wahlen/GI-Anforderungen_Vereinswahlen.pdf.

Hartmann, V., N. Meissner, and D. Richter. 2004. Online voting systems for non-parliamentary elections: Catalogue of requirements. Laborbericht PTB-8.5-2004-1, Physikalisch-Technische Bundesanstalt Braunscheig und Berlin (Fachbereich Metrologische Informationstechnik). http://ib.ptb.de/8/85/LB8_5_2004_1AnfKat.pdf.

Langer, L., and A. Schmidt. 2009. Abschlussbericht zum Projekt voteremote: Online-Wahlen außerhalb von Wahllokalen (Teilvorhaben Sicherheitsanalyse); Förderkennzeichen 01 MS 06 002.

Reinhard, K., and W. Jung. 2007. Compliance of POLYAS with the BSI protection profile: Basic requirements for remote electronic voting systems. In *E-voting and identity: First international conference*, 62–75, VOTE-ID 2007. LNCS, vol. 4896. Berlin: Springer.

Unabhängigen Landeszentrum für Datenschutz. 2002. Unabhängigen Landeszentrum für Datenschutz Schleswig-Holstein: Seal of privacy for IT-products and privacy protection audit for public authorities. https://www.datenschutzzentrum.de/download/audsieen.pdf.

Volkamer, M., and R. Vogt. 2006a. Digitales Wahlstift-System. Common Criteria Protection Profile BSI-PP-0031. http://www.bsi.de/zertifiz/zert/reporte/PP0031b.pdf.

Volkamer, M., and R. Vogt. 2006b. New generation of voting machines in Germany The Hamburg way to verify correctness. In *Proceedings of the frontiers in electronic elections workshop—*

FEE'06. http://fee.iavoss.org/2006/papers/fee-2006-iavoss-New-Generation-of-Voting-Machines-in-Germany.pdf.

Volkamer, M., and R. Vogt. 2008. Basis set of security requirements for Online Voting Products. Commom Criteria Protection Profile BSI-CC-PP-0037. http://www.bsi.de/zertifiz/zert/reporte/pp0037b_engl.pdf.

Volkamer, M., G. Schryen, L. Langer, A. Schmidt, and J. Buchmann. 2009. Elektronische Wahlen Verifizierung vs. Zertifizierung. In proceedings of Informatik 2009, volume 154 of LNI, pages 1827–1836.

Wahlgvo. 2006. Richtlinien für den Einsatz des Digitalen Wahlstift-Systems bei Wahlen zur Hamburgischen Bürgerschaft und Wahlen zu den Bezirksversammlungen. http://www.hamburg.de/contentblob/260056/data/richtlinie.pdf.

Part III
Third Pillar Issues

Chapter 11
The New Council Decision Strengthening the Role of Eurojust: Does It also Strengthen Data Protection at Eurojust?

Diana Alonso Blas

11.1 Introduction

Eurojust, the European Union's judicial cooperation unit, was created by a Council Decision of 28 February 2002.[1] Eurojust has proved to be a successful initiative, improving judicial coordination and cooperation between national authorities in Europe and dealing with more than 1000 transnational cases on a yearly basis.[2]

However, Eurojust has stated at several occasions its feeling that its capacity to deal with casework is not being fully exploited.[3] Besides, after 5 years of existence, it was felt that it was time to assess the implementation of the Decision setting up Eurojust.[4] The Council, in its conclusions on the Eurojust Annual Report 2006, stressed the need for a mid-term assessment of the effectiveness and unexploited potential of Eurojust. "Comments" in the same line were made in the European

Diana Alonso Blas is the Data Protection Officer of Eurojust since November 2003. The opinions expressed in this article are however her personal ones and do not necessarily represent those of the organisation.

[1] Council Decision of 28 February 2002 setting up Eurojust with a view to reinforcing the fight against serious crime, *Official Journal* L63, (6 March 2002): 1.

[2] Eurojust dealt with 202 cases in 2002 and with 1193 in 2008. 723 cases had been registered until 30 June 2009.

[3] See statement of Michael Kennedy, president of the College of Eurojust, in the preamble to the annual report 2004, available at www.eurojust.europa.eu under Press&PR.

[4] See the preamble of Jose Luis Lopes da Mota, president of the College of Eurojust, to the annual report 2007.

D. Alonso Blas (✉)
Data Protection Officer, Eurojust, Maanweg 174, NL-2516 AB The Hague,
Tel: +31 70 412 5510
Fax: + 31 70 412 5515
e-mail: dalonsoblas@eurojust.europa.eu

S. Gutwirth et al. (eds.), *Data Protection in a Profiled World*,
DOI 10.1007/978-90-481-8865-9_11,

Commission Communication on the Future of Eurojust and the European Judicial Network (EJN) issued in 2007.[5]

It was in this spirit of self-evaluation that Eurojust, supported by the Portuguese Presidency of the Council of the European Union, organised a seminar in Lisbon in the autumn of 2007, on the 29 and 30 of October. This seminar, with the title "Eurojust—Navigating the Way Forward", aimed at identifying areas where action was necessary to better achieve Eurojust's objectives.[6]

This seminar identified three main areas where improvement was necessary or in any case desirable, based on the practical experiences gained by Eurojust during its first 5 years of operation, but also in the light of the lack of full implementation of the Eurojust Decision in national legislation:

1. Strengthen and increase the powers of National Members and the College;[7]
2. Improve and expand the exchange of information;
3. Clarify the relationship between Eurojust and the EJN.

The debates in Lisbon, expected by, among many others, the national authorities of all Member States, undoubtedly inspired the following discussion on possible legislative proposals to strengthen Eurojust and the EJN. In fact, before the end of the year 2007, fourteen Member States presented an initiative to amend the Eurojust Decision.[8] Following the efficient work of the Slovenian and French presidencies during 2008, the Council Decision on the strengthening of Eurojust and amending Decision 2002/187/JHA setting up Eurojust with a view to reinforcing the fight against serious crime was adopted by the Council of the 16 December 2008.[9]

This article aims at outlining and discussing the elements of the new Eurojust Decision which are relevant from the data protection viewpoint or which have consequences for the activities of the independent data protection supervisory authority to Eurojust, its Joint Supervisory Body (JSB).

---

[5] Communication from the Commission to the Council and the European Parliament of 23 October 2007 on the role of Eurojust and the European Judicial Network in the fight against organised crime and terrorism in the European Union, COM(2007) 644 final—Not published in the Official Journal.

[6] The outcome of the seminar can be found in the general report on the seminar, Council document 15542/07. The Eurojust annual report 2007 also contains a whole section on the Lisbon seminar.

[7] Eurojust can act through its College, composed of 27 National Members, one seconded from each member state in accordance with its legal system being a prosecutor, judge or police officer of equivalent competence, or through the individual National Members. National Members are subject to the national law as their status and are also paid by the Member States, not being EU officials but linked to their national authorities. The nature and extent of the judicial powers of the National Members is, as stated in Article 9 of the Eurojust Decision of 2002, defined by each Member State, leading in practice to serious differences of powers within the various Member States.

[8] The fourteen countries in question were Belgium, Czech Republic, Estonia, Spain, France, Italy, Luxembourg, Netherlands, Austria, Poland, Portugal, Slovenia, Slovakia and Sweden, see Council document DS 1092/07.

[9] Council Decision 2009/426/JHA of 16 December 2008, published on the *Official Journal* L138 (4 June 2009): 14.

11.2 Amendments with Data Protection Relevance

Amending the data protection regime of Eurojust was not one of the objectives of the revision of the Eurojust Decision. However, some of the changes introduced have an impact or relevance from the data protection viewpoint. In the following paragraphs attention will be paid to those new elements in the decision, grouped by topics.

11.2.1 Preservation of the Specificity of the Eurojust Data Protection Regime

The new Decision does not only not amend the data protection regime of Eurojust, it confirms explicitly that the existing provisions are not affected by the new Framework Decision on the protection of personal data processed in the framework of police and judicial cooperation in criminal matters,[10] which was finalised shortly before the adoption of the revised Eurojust Decision. This is clearly stated in Recital 13 of the preamble to the new Decision: *"The relevant set of data protection provisions of Decision 2002/187/JHA will not be affected by Framework Decision 2008/977/JHA and contains specific provisions on the protection of personal data regulating these matters in more detail because of the particular nature, functions and competences of Eurojust."*

Such statement is complemented by a the "mirror provision" in Recital 39 of the preamble of the Framework Decision: *"Several acts, adopted on the basis of Title VI of the Treaty on European Union, contain specific provisions on the protection of personal data exchanged or otherwise processed pursuant to those acts. In some cases these provisions constitute a complete and coherent set of rules covering all relevant aspects of data protection (principles of data quality, rules on data security, regulation of the rights and safeguards of data subjects, organisation of supervision and liability) and they regulate these matters in more detail than this Framework Decision. The relevant set of data protection provisions of those acts, in particular those governing the functioning of Europol, Eurojust, the Schengen Information System (SIS) and the Customs Information System (CIS), as well as those introducing direct access for the authorities of Member States to certain data systems of other Member States, should not be affected by this Framework Decision."*

This explicit and clear exclusion from the scope of application of the Framework Decision is of vital importance for Eurojust as, after having worked very hard in putting in place a robust tailor-made and highly protective data protection regime for the organisation, it would have been a disastrous result if Eurojust would have been bound by the low level and too general provisions of the Framework Deci-

[10] Council Framework Decision 2008/977/JHA of 27 November 2008, *Official Journal* 350 (30 December 2008): 60.

sion.[11] This instrument, generally considered by the data protection community as a "missed opportunity" respected, after various requests from the actors involved, the specific regimes of Eurojust, Europol and the Schengen and Customs Information Systems.

Recital 13 of the preamble to the new Eurojust Decision further clarifies the fact that the Framework Decision will be applicable to the processing by the Member States of the personal data transferred between the Member States and Eurojust.

11.2.2 Clear Definition of National Competences

The new Article 9(a) (and following) deals with the powers of the National Members of Eurojust conferred to them at national level. From the data protection viewpoint and, in the light of Article 2 of the Eurojust data protection rules,[12] which defines its scope of application by excluding from its scope of application the information transmitted to a National Member of Eurojust exclusively in the context of his/her judicial powers, such provisions is welcome.

The text of the new Decision makes now clear that the National Member is then acting as competent national authority in accordance with national law, making previous discussions as to which processing operations take place under the Eurojust umbrella and which ones, under the national law pointless.

11.2.3 Extension of the Categories of Personal Data Which Eurojust May Legally Process

Article 15 of the original Eurojust Decision contained a limitative list of personal data that Eurojust may process concerning three categories of people: persons subject of a criminal investigation, victims and witnesses. It is important to mention that the limitation concerned in this article is double: as to the categories of persons and as to the kind of data for each one of these categories, which are enumerated in a closed list in the various paragraphs of the article.

[11] See for further information on the discussions regarding the Framework Decision the opinions of 19 December 2005, 29 November 2006 and 27 April 2007 of the European Data Protection Supervisor on this instrument (the third opinion is published in the Official Journal C139 (23 June 2007): 1; the first Opinion can be found in the Official Journal C47 (25 February 2006): 27; the second Opinion is available on EDPS website: www.edps.europa.eu) as well as the article by Alonso Blas, D.2009. First pillar and third pillar: Need for a common approach on data protection? In *Reinventing data protection?* eds. S. Gutwirth et al., 225–237. Dordrecht: Springer.

[12] Rules of procedure on the processing and protection of personal data at Eurojust, adopted by the College of Eurojust unanimously in October 2004 and by the Council in Brussels in February 2005, *Official Journal* C68 (19 March 2005): 1. These rules are often referred to as the "Eurojust data protection rules".

In practice, difficulties arose in the application of this article due to the fact that the list of personal data initially contained in Article 15 was not in line with the fact that other legal texts, in particular the Council Decision of 20 September 2005 on the exchange of information and cooperation concerning terrorist offences[13] and the Council Framework Decision on the European Arrest Warrant (EAW),[14] both adopted after the Eurojust Decision, had foreseen the provision of data not included on this list to Eurojust.

In the context of the EAW Decision Eurojust is mentioned[15] as the instance to be informed if a Member State cannot observe the time limits provided in Article 17 of this decision. Eurojust might also play a role transmitting EAWs from one to another authority. In both contexts it has to be taken into account which kind of information is contained in the EAW form. This form, contained in the annex to the EAW Decision[16] mentions a number of items that were not included in Article 15 of the Eurojust Decision such as languages which the requested person understands, distinctive marks or description of the requested person, photo and fingerprints of the requested person if they are available and can be transmitted or a contact person or contact details of the person to be contacted in order to obtain such information or a DNA profile.

Recital 14 of the preamble to the new Decision summarises the main changes included in Article 15, which had in the past been criticised by the Joint Supervisory Body that considered that the former text was too limitative and therefore almost impossible to comply with. The JSB was of the opinion that this article should be amended to allow greater flexibility and to be aligned with the real processing needs of the organisation.

Basically, under the new Decision, Eurojust may now process personal data on one additional category of individuals: persons who have been convicted of an offence for which Eurojust is competent, which is a very important addition, especially in the field of terrorism. In addition to this, Eurojust may now process some additional categories of data such as telephone numbers, e-mail addresses, vehicle registration data, DNA profiles, photographs, fingerprints, traffic and location data related to persons who, under the national legislation of the Member State concerned, are the subject of a criminal investigation or prosecution or have been convicted. These new categories are crucial in order to allow Eurojust to legally receive the full information which could be transmitted under the EAW decision and the Council Decision on terrorism data. The new Decision has not touched upon the short closed list of data which Eurojust may legally process on victims and witnesses, which has remained unchanged.

---

[13] Council Decision 2005/671/JHA of 20 September 2005 on the exchange of information and cooperation concerning terrorist offences, *Official Journal* L253/22 (29 September 2005).

[14] Council framework decision of 13 June 2002 on the European arrest warrant and the surrender procedures between Member States (2002/584/JHA), *Official Journal* L190/1, (18 July 2002).

[15] Article 17.7 of the EAW Decision.

[16] The text of the EAW form in all languages can be found at: http://www.consilium.europa.eu/cms3_Applications/applications/PolJu/details.asp?lang=EN&cmsid=545&id=134.

The list of personal data which Eurojust may legally process contained in Article 15, remains a closed list, contrary to what the first draft proposal of the fourteen Member States had put forward. The maintenance of a closed list has been most probably caused by the opinions issued by the European Parliament[17] and the European Data Protection Supervisor,[18] which both pleaded against the opening of such list. In particular, the EDPS wrote on this opinion the following: *"The initiative proposes replacing the limited list of personal data that may be processed under Article 15(1) and (2) by similar lists, but with an open nature. (...) The modification changes the nature of the list with a negative effect for data protection and for legal certainty, without an adequate underlying reason.*

The EDPS does not understand why this modification is needed, in particular since the lists of data are already quite extensive. If a specific category of data is lacking it would be better to include this category in the Decision itself. The present initiative is a good opportunity to do so, as it is shown by the proposed addition of a category (l) to Article 15(1)."

Obviously, from a data protection viewpoint, the continued use of a closed list of personal data should be seen as an additional safeguard. However, from the practical viewpoint, the examples of the EAW and terrorism information decisions, which created a mismatch between what Eurojust was allowed to process and what, following these rules, was supposed to receive, shows that new legitimate needs might appear in the near future. As the situation is now, additional data may only be exceptionally processed under the conditions of paragraph 3 of Article 15, for a limited period of time, or, should these needs be more structural, an amendment of the Council Decision will again be required to update the list.

In any case, the amendments to Article 15 are most welcome and necessary and, as the automated Case Management System (CMS) of Eurojust is built to only allow the processing of the categories of data mentioned in the former text of Article 15, they will require the creation of new categories of persons and of new data types in the CMS.

11.2.4 Improvement of the Information Provision from Member States

During the Lisbon seminar in autumn 2007,[19] the necessity to improve the exchange of information with the Member States had been put into evidence. In particular, the need for systematic and structured transmissions of relevant information and the establishment of a secure information system were stressed. In line with the conclu-

[17] Opinion delivered on 2 September 2008 (Rapporteur Madame Weber).

[18] Opinion of the European Data Protection Supervisor of 25 April 2008 on the review of the Eurojust Decision.

[19] See the Eurojust annual report 2007 for a summary of the deliberations during the Lisbon seminar.

sions of this seminar, the new decision contains some provisions with the intention of increasing the information flow from the Member States to Eurojust.

Recital 17 of the preamble to the new Decision affirms that, *"with a view to increasing the operational effectiveness of Eurojust, transmission of information to Eurojust should be improved by providing clear and limited obligations for national authorities."*

The amendments included in Article 13 are crucial in the new decision as they comprise an obligation for the Member States to provide "at least" the information mentioned in paragraphs 5, 6 and 7 of this revised article. From the data protection viewpoint it is important to mention that the purpose for which this information is provided is different than that of the information Eurojust receives in order to provide immediate cooperation, coordination or support to the national authorities. The information supplied under this article will be, unless otherwise indicated,[20] not considered as a request for assistance; it is more information which might require Eurojust involvement at a later stage or which might allow Eurojust to detect existing links between ongoing investigations in various Member States thanks to the link capabilities of the Eurojust automated Case Management System (CMS).[21]

This article also mentions in its paragraph 4 the obligation for the Member States to provide terrorism-related information as regulated in the separate Council Decision of September 2005.[22]

It is important to note that, given the different purpose for which information is provided under Article 13.5, 6 and 7 and the fact that some specific rules regarding time-limits apply to this kind of information (as we will see when dealing with Article 21), it will be necessary to mark in the CMS the information received under these sections as well as it is presently done with the data received under the Decision on terrorism data and to rework the time-limits mechanism controls taking account of this, as the CMS generates automatically reminders to the data controllers when data are about the reach their time limits. Such notifications are also automatically sent to the Data Protection Officer.[23]

---

[20] Article 13.2 prescribes that *the transmission of information to Eurojust shall be interpreted as a request for the assistance of Eurojust in the case concerned only if so specified by a competent authority.*

[21] The CMS regularly checks for possibly identical entities. If, for instance, two persons with the same name, surname, date of birth and place of birth are detected, while belonging to different temporary work files, a possible link between cases is suggested. The working groups owning the entities will be notified and informed about the entities and the respective temporary work file. The notification will reveal no personal data. Working groups involved are free to decide which information they disclose to the other working group to confirm or deny the existence of a link. The confirmation or rejection of a link is stored in the system. In addition to connecting cases through a link discovery, the CMS also allows users to manually connect two cases.

[22] *Official Journal* L253/22 (29 September 2005).

[23] Working groups and the DPO are automatically notified about temporary work files that contain data that is about to expire. The data owner then takes a reasoned decision (to be recorded in the system) to retain, where needed, or delete the data.

11.2.5 CMS-Related Issues and Secure Communication with Member States

The original Eurojust Decision only referred to the processing of personal data in the temporary work files (case files) and in the index, which contains only a few items of information allowing the identification of the case, mentioning the countries involved, the type of crime and little more.[24] The Eurojust data protection rules[25] introduced in their Article 23 the concept of the automated Case Management System (CMS), including the temporary work files and the index. Chapter 3 of the data protection rules[26] regulates in detail various aspects of the processing of personal data in the CMS, which has become *the* crucial tool for the processing of personal data at Eurojust.

The CMS was designed taking full account of the data protection provisions in the Eurojust decision and in the rules on the processing and the protection of personal data. The design facilitates compliance with the legal base and prevents possible breaches of the data protection rules to a great extent. Only pre-defined data classes may be entered in the system preventing the insertion of non-allowed data. Compliance is also ensured in what regards notifications to the DPO, which are automatically generated by the system.

The new Eurojust decision raises a number of matters of relevance regarding the CMS. In some cases the new provisions only "import" articles from the Eurojust data protection rules into the Decision but in several cases new elements, some of them with important consequences, are brought into the text.

1. Recitals 11 and 12 of the preamble refer to the role of the new national coordination system[27] regarding the CMS stating the following:
   (a) The national coordination system should be connected to the CMS; such connection should take account of the national IT systems. This same idea is included in Article 12.6 of the decision which further specifies the need for access to the CMS to be in accordance with the new provisions added regarding the CMS, containing principles taken from the data protection rules (the new Articles 16, 16(a) and 16(b)), and Article 18 on authorised access to personal data. It is further underlined that the expenses of such connection should be covered by the EU budget;

[24] See Article 16 of the Eurojust Decision of 2002.

[25] *Official Journal* C68, (19 March 2005): 1.

[26] Articles 23–27.

[27] The concept of the national coordination system is introduced in the new Article 12 of the Decision. Its objective is ensure coordination of the work done by the national correspondents for Eurojust, the national correspondents for Eurojust for terrorism matters, the national correspondents and contact points of the EJN, the national members or contact points of the Network for Joint Investigation Teams and other networks such as the ones on genocide and war crimes created by other Council Decisions.

(b) Access at national level takes account of the decisive role of the National Member as controller of the temporary work files;
(c) The national coordination systems should ensure that the CMS receives the relevant national information[28] but it is up to the Member States to decide on the best channel for transmission of information.

2. As already mentioned under the previous section, the revised Article 13 implies the need to mark in the CMS the information received under this article, as it has been done so far with the terrorism data communicated under the specific Council Decision, and to rework the time-limits control mechanism taking this into account. It will also be necessary to ensure that all information provided under this article can be properly included in the CMS.
3. Article 14 includes the obligation for Eurojust, logical in the light of the revised Article 13, to inform the national authorities of the results of the processing of the information they provide Eurojust and in particular of any links with cases already stored in the CMS. In fact, it should be understood that the Member States will also benefit from the provision of data to Eurojust, as this will enable Eurojust to give useful feedback to them.
4. As mentioned before, the changes introduced in Article 15 will require the creation of new categories of persons and of new data types in the CMS.
5. Article 16 has been slightly modified to make clear, as it was stated already in Article 23 of the Eurojust data protection rules, that it is the CMS that contains the index and temporary work files as regulated in the Eurojust decision. This is now explicitly stated in the first two paragraphs of this article.
6. The new paragraph 2a of this article enables the possible connection of the CMS to the secure telecommunications connection referred to in Article 10 of the new EJN decision.[29]
7. Paragraph 2b adds a new category of data that may be included in the index, vehicle registration data, which will require to change the CMS in this respect.
8. Paragraph 4 of this article contains a very significant provision, confirming a point which the JSB had raised in their inspection reports: case-related data may only be processed using automated means in the CMS.
9. The new Article 16(a) basically "imports" some of the principles defined in the data protection rules into the Eurojust decision in order to ensure full consistency between both and introduces the new Article 13 "Information".
10. The new Article 16(b) brings into the Eurojust decision the system of authorisations of the National Members for the CMS, as regulated in Article 26 of the data protection rules,[30] regarding persons who are part of the national coordi-

---

[28] The same principle is also included in Article 12.5(a) of the Decision.

[29] A revised Council Decision on the European Judicial Network has been negotiated and adopted at the same time than the new Eurojust Decision: Council Decision 2008/976/JHA of 16 December 2008 on the European Judicial Network, *Official Journal* L348 (24 December 2008): 130. See for more details: http://www.ejn-crimjust.europa.eu/.

[30] Article 26.3 of the data protection rules reads as follows: *Each National Member of Eurojust shall document and inform the Data Protection Officer regarding the access policy he or she has*

nation system, but also introduces some additional specific rules which will require some changes in the CMS present system.
The principle remains the need to know and the power of each National Member to decide and authorise who has access to the data of its national desk and at which level, as defined in Article 26 of the data protection rules. The access is in any case linked to the data to which the national desk of its country has access and not to the whole CMS. The present system of authorisations signed by the National Members to allow access to the CMS to persons linked to their national desk would therefore also work for the persons of the national coordination system. However, the first paragraph introduces some complicating elements.
So far, all users of the CMS had access to the whole index as well as to the data accessible to the national desk under which they operate, without any viewing limitations.[31] The new Article 16(b) creates the possibility for National Members to deny access to members of the national coordinating system of other Member States to data they have introduced in the index (Article 16(b).1(a)) as well as to data included in a temporary work file of which they are owner but to which they have given some access to another national desk (Article 16(b).1(c)). This will mean in practice that it will have to be technically possible to limit access to users to some parts of the index and to some shared parts of temporary work files, what was not possible so far. These new technical possibilities will need to be studied when building the new profile for members of the national coordination system. It will also have to be decided how this "denial of access" will take place; ideally this should be done automatically in the CMS, allowing National Members to make this decision when they place data in the CMS or when they share it with other desks.
The last paragraph of Article 16(b).3 implies that the power of National Members to deny access to the index to one of their cases to members of the national coordination system of another Member States, will be limited when this would mean that this person could otherwise not have access to a temporary work file for which he/she has been authorised to have access by the National Member of his/her country.

11. Article 18 is amended just to include those linked to the national coordination systems as part of the group who can be authorised to have access to personal data processed by Eurojust in as far as they are authorised to have access to the CMS by their National Member and with the limitations included in Article 16(b).

---

authorised within his or her national desk regarding case-related files. In particular, National Members shall ensure that appropriate organisational arrangements are made and complied with and that proper use is made of the technical and organisational measures put at their disposal by Eurojust.

[31] Limitations could be included however by allowing only "read-only" access, but still to the whole set of data accessible to the desk.

12. Article 27(a) regulates in its paragraph 4 the connection to the CMS of liaison magistrates posted by Eurojust in third countries.[32] Given the fact that the article does not include any provisions as to the access regime of such individuals it has to be assumed that the procedure as defined in Article 26 of the data protection rules will also apply to them. If such liaison magistrates are posted by the College and do not represent a specific Member State, it can be assumed that the authorisation to the CMS should be done by the College and not by an individual National Member.[33]

11.2.6 Time Limits

11.2.6.1 Time Limits in the Eurojust Decision of 2002

The fact that case files are called "temporary work files" in the Eurojust Decision clearly expresses the fact that the legislator understood from the beginning that data should only be kept for as long as Eurojust needs it for the purpose of the tasks and mandate extremely granted to Eurojust. The Decision foresaw in its Article 21(1) the general principle that personal data shall be kept for only as long as necessary for the achievement of the objectives of Eurojust. This means that the need to retain the information should be considered at the moment of closing the case, when in principle the role of Eurojust has come to an end.

Next to the general principle, Article 21(2) provided in any case for the deletion of the data if:

1. the prosecution, to which they relate, is barred under the statute of limitations;
2. a judicial decision on the case has become final;
3. coordination of the case by Eurojust is no longer necessary.

If any one of these conditions is met, the data may not be retained, unless this is necessary 'in order to enable (Eurojust) to achieve its objectives'. This assessment has to be made by the National Member (controller) in the light of circumstances such as the relevance of the information for other related open cases or ongoing investigations in Member States or other circumstances that would make it necessary (not just useful or possibly handy) to retain the information.

Last, Article 21.3(a) underlined the need to monitor constantly the applicability of the circumstances enumerated under number 2 and provides in any case for a review every 3 years after the data were entered.

---

[32] Article 27(a) of the new Decision introduces the possibility for the College of Eurojust to post liaison magistrates to a third State, subject to an agreement as referred to in Article 26(a) with that third State, for the purpose of facilitating judicial cooperation with third States in the cases in which Eurojust is providing assistance in accordance with the Decision.

[33] See Article 26.4 of the data protection rules.

Regarding the "3 year review" it is relevant to mention the following:

- It applies only when the circumstances under 1 and 2 are not applicable. The need to retain the data must be assessed at the moment of closing the case, not only after 3 years;
- The 3 years apply from the moment the data are processed in the CMS, not from the moment of closing of the case;
- A review means that the controller has to take an active decision as to whether to delete the data (general rule) or to keep them when there are reasons for that linked to the achievement of the objectives of Eurojust.

11.2.6.2 Time Limits in the New Eurojust Decision

The new Decision introduces some changes in the system while respecting its general construction. Recital 15 of the preamble reflects the need for Eurojust to prolong the deadline for storage of personal data when there is a specific need to do so. It underlines however the fact that such extension can only take place regarding data where prosecution is barred in all Member States concerned when there is a specific need to provide assistance under this decision.

The revised Article 21 aims at allowing some more flexibility to Eurojust regarding time-limits but the text is, due to the compromise necessary to reach an agreement concerning this sensitive topic, very complicated and will undoubtedly raise questions regarding its implementation.

With regard to the previous drafting of Article 21, the following changes are introduced:

1. It introduces in its paragraph 2(a) new letter (aa) including a new date beyond which personal data may not be further processed by Eurojust: the date on which the person has been acquitted and the decision has become final. This date is an absolute one as the possibility to review the need to keep data after the dates mentioned in paragraph 2 have passed is only foreseen in paragraph 3(b) for all other circumstances included in paragraph 2 but not for this one. This means in practice that Eurojust will need to ensure that information regarding acquittals is provided timely by the Member States as processing of personal data beyond the date in which a decision of acquittal has become final is unlawful.
2. It creates a new regime for the so-called "Article 13 information", which is mentioned in two paragraphs. First, it is stated in letter (c) of paragraph 2 that the general principle of deletion of personal data after Eurojust and the Member States have mutually established that there is no further need of coordination by Eurojust does not apply when the information in question is covered by Article 13.6 or 7 or when it is covered by instruments regarding the provision of terrorism related data to Eurojust. Secondly, a new letter (d) has been added to paragraph 2 creating a general possibility to keep the same data (Article 13 data and terrorism-related) for a period of 3 years after its provision to Eurojust. This will require changes in the CMS to allow this information to be marked

accordingly and for this to be taken into account regarding time-limits reviews as automatic notifications are generated by the system warning users when there deadlines for review are getting closer.

3. Letter (b) of paragraph 3 regarding the possibility to exceptionally keep personal data beyond the dates mentioned in paragraph 2 has been amended to, as mentioned before, exclude this possibility for the acquittals but also to specify that, once prosecution has been barred under the statue of limitations in all Member States, data may only be kept if it is necessary for Eurojust to provide assistance in accordance with this decision. This addition requires therefore a very specific need to keep the data for a concrete assistance purpose, which should be understood as a specific "casework purpose" and not the more general purpose of the information provided under Article 13, which should be not considered as implying a request for assistance unless otherwise indicated.
4. Paragraph 5 of this article, embodying the obligation of Member States to provide Eurojust with information as to final judicial decisions relating to information supplied earlier to Eurojust is not new and has not been touched by the review. The importance of this obligation of the Member States being correctly and exhaustively complied with has become now crucial in the light of the amendments included in this article.

11.2.7 Relations with Third Parties

Recital 21 of the preamble to the new Decision mentions the need to strengthen the capacity of Eurojust to work with external parties, including third States, Europol, OLAF,[34] the Joint Situation Center and FRONTEX.[35]

The revised Articles 26 and 26(a) establish a more flexible and logical system of dealing with third parties making a difference between Community or Union related institutions, bodies and agencies,[36] which share a similar system of data protection and security rules based on European standards and are properly supervised by the EDPS or other independent bodies, and third parties and organisations, whose level

---

[34] The European Anti Fraud Office. See for more information: http://ec.europa.eu/anti_fraud/index_en.html.

[35] Frontex is an EU agency based in Warsaw, created as a specialised and independent body tasked to coordinate the operational cooperation between Member States in the field of border security. The activities of Frontex are intelligence driven. Frontex complements and provides particular added value to the national border management systems of the Member State. See for more information: http://www.frontex.europa.eu/.

[36] Eurojust has in place a cooperation agreement with Europol, signed on 9 June 2004, as well as a Practical Agreement on Arrangements for Cooperation with OLAF, the European Anti-Fraud Office, signed on 24 September 2008.

of data protection and system of supervision may vary and will need to be assessed on a case by case basis.[37]

Article 26, dealing now with the Community or Union related institutions, bodies and agencies creates, in line with the conclusions of the meetings of the Heads of EU third pillar agencies during the last 3 years, a more flexible regime allowing not only the conclusion of agreements but also of working arrangements and allowing, prior to the conclusion of such agreement or arrangement, to directly receive and use as well as transmit information to each other, including personal data, in so far as this is necessary for the performance of their tasks.

Regarding third states and organisations, the new Article 26(a) generally maintains the system of the present Article 27 with a few novelties:

1. Paragraph 3 underlines the need to carry out an assessment of the level of protection of a third party before concluding an agreement including provisions on exchange of personal data. The text refers now to *an assessment confirming the existence of an adequate level of data protection ensured by that entity.*
2. The new paragraph 4 adds the need to include provisions on the monitoring of the implementation of the agreement, including the implementation of the data protection rules.[38]

These two points, mentioned in paragraph 3 and 4 of Article 26, had been raised in the report of Madame Weber, rapporteur of the LIBE Committee of the European Parliament,[39] but in fact are already a cornerstone of the current practice of Eurojust regarding agreements with third parties so no changes are required in that regard. It is however positive that those elements of data protection are included in the text of the Decision.

---

[37] So far Eurojust has agreements in place with Norway (2005), Iceland (2005), the United States of America (2006), the Republic of Croatia (2007), Switzerland and the former Yugoslav Republic of Macedonia (both concluded in 2008). Eurojust has Memoranda of Understanding in place, not implying any exchange of personal data, with the European Judicial Training Network (2008) and IberRed (2009).

[38] The Model Agreement, used by Eurojust as a starting point of every negotiation, includes already two provisions of relevance in that respect:

Article 17: Regular consultations

The Parties shall consult each other regularly, and at least once a year, on the implementation of the provisions of this Agreement. In particular, regular exchanges of views shall take place with regard to the implementation and further developments in the field of data protection and data security. To that end the Data Protection Officer of Eurojust and the Data Protection Authority of (…) will report to each other at least once a year on the state of implementation of the data protection provisions of the Agreement.

Article 18: Oversight of implementation

The execution and implementation of this Agreement by the Parties shall be subject to oversight in accordance with their applicable law and procedures. The Parties shall utilise their respective administrative, judicial or supervisory bodies that will ensure an appropriate level of independence of the oversight process.

[39] Opinion delivered on 2 September 2008 (Rapporteur Madame Weber).

3. Article 26(a) introduces in its paragraphs 5 and 6(a) clearly distinct regime than what Article 26 foresees for "EU sister organisations". In the case of third parties, Eurojust may directly receive information from that party, including personal data, prior to the existence of an agreement if this is necessary for the legitimate performance of its tasks; however, Eurojust may only transmit information but not personal data to that party prior to the entry into force of an agreement. The circumstances under which Eurojust may transmit personal data to a third party are clearly mentioned in paragraph 5 of this article including both the conclusion of an agreement which is in force and allows for such transfer, and the need to transmit data in individual cases for the purposes of preventing or combating criminal offences for which Eurojust is competent.
   This new formulation makes very clear that the only possibility of transmitting personal data to a third party without an agreement is that regulated in the old Article 27.6 and now in Article 26(a).6: under exceptional circumstances and by the National Member acting in his/her national capacity with the aim of taking urgent measures to counter imminent serious danger threatening a person or public security. An addition guarantee from the data protection viewpoint exists due to the fact that such exceptional transfers, which so far have never taken place since the existence of Eurojust, need to be documented in the temporary work file of the case in the CMS and the Data Protection Officer has to be informed and shall verify if such transfers only take place in exceptional and urgent cases.[40]
4. Both Articles 26 and 26(a) foresee the obligation for Eurojust to inform the Council of any plans it has of entering into any negotiations and the possibility for the Council to draw any conclusions it sees fit. So far no obligation existed for Eurojust to inform the Council before entering into negotiations and, differently from the system of Europol, Eurojust only had to involve the Council at the moment of approval of an agreement. This new formulation is still rather flexible but the consequences of it will depend of course of the way in which the Council interprets the possibility "to draw conclusions if it sees fit". In theory the Council could use such possibility to strongly influence the choice and priorities of Eurojust or to make comments as to the level of data protection of the country or third country in question.
5. Article 27 in its new formulation contains in its first paragraph the text of the present Article 27.2. The second paragraph introduces the obligation for Eurojust to keep a record of transmission of data transferred under Articles 26 and 26(a). This is in itself new in the Eurojust decision but has always been a standard provision in all Eurojust agreements so it does not really imply a new obligation.[41]

[40] See in that regard Article 28.4 of the Eurojust data protection rules. *Official Journal* C68 (19 March 2005): 1.

[41] Article 8.5 of the Eurojust Model Agreement contains the following clause: *The Parties shall keep a record of the transmission and receipt of data communicated under this Agreement.*

11.2.8 EU Classified Information

The new Article 39(a) prescribes the application of Eurojust of the security principles and minimum standards set out in the Council security regulation[42] when dealing with EU classified information.

This provision will not have any major consequences for the organisation as in fact the Council security regulation was used by the Eurojust security committee as the model for Eurojust security rules, which were adopted by the College on 28 June 2007.[43]

11.3 Amendments with Relevance to the Joint Supervisory Body of Eurojust (JSB)

The compliance with Eurojust data protection regime is supervised internally by the Data Protection Officer, as regulated in Article 17 of the Eurojust Decision, but there is also an independent external supervisor, the Joint Supervisory Body. This body, composed of judges or members with an equal level of independence,[44] has a very important task *ensuring that the processing of personal data is carried out in accordance with this Decision* (the Eurojust Decision).[45]

So far, in accordance with the Decision, the JSB worked with a troika of three appointees, each of them becoming permanent members one year before his Member State assumes the presidency of the Council and remaining member for 18 months.[46] In the course of the discussion at the Council on the new Eurojust Decision, the JSB decided, under Slovenian presidency, to put forward on its own initiative a proposal to amend Article 23 regarding its composition explaining the motivation for such a change in an opinion of the 3 March 2008:[47] *"The Joint Supervisory Body appreciates the fact that the composition of this body by three members is a very workable construction facilitating its operation and quick decision making process and it is also a non burocratic and cost effective structure. It regrets however that the very frequent changes of members every six months and the short length of the participation in the troika of Eurojust for only eighteen months, makes it difficult to keep a high level of knowledge of the Eurojust complex legal and technical framework, its organisation and the state of play regarding the many developments at Eurojust*

[42] Regulation 2001/264/EC of 19 March 200, *Official Journal* L101 (11 April 2001): 1.

[43] College Decision 2007–2010 adopting the security rules of Eurojust.

[44] In practice a good part of the Member States have appointed Data Protection Commissioners, as people with a clear independent status. The combination of judges, with expertise in the judicial field, with data protection experts has shown to be fruitful and efficient in this body.

[45] See Article 23.1 of the Eurojust Decision.

[46] See Article 23.3 of the Eurojust Decision of 2002.

[47] Opinion of the Joint Supervisory Body of Eurojust on the opportunity to amend Article 23 of the Eurojust Decision regarding the composition of this body, of 3 March 2008.

having impact on the protection of personal data. It therefore considers that a more permanent structure would be beneficial, while keeping the reduced size and efficient operation of the body."

The new Eurojust Decision has fully taken over the written proposal of the JSB, establishing in the reviewed paragraph 3 of Article 23 an annual election at the plenary meeting of the JSB in which a new member is chosen between the appointees of the Member States for a period of 3 years.[48] The member in its third year will chair the troika. This new system should allow for more continuity and expertise in the JSB as members will have more time to be acquainted with the work of Eurojust and to build expertise in that regard. Further, given the fact that individuals have to present themselves as candidates and "campaign" to that purpose,[49] it will also entail that those persons are really motivated to be part of the JSB and ready to commit time and efforts to the work of the body.

In practical terms this change implied the need for the JSB to amend its rules of procedure of the 2 March 2004[50] to foresee all practical details linked to this new election system, to have these new rules approved unanimously in their first plenary meeting after the entry into force of the new Eurojust Decision[51] and to hold elections at the same meeting as otherwise it would take a whole year before the new rules can be applied. Indeed, on 23 June 2009, at its first plenary meeting after the entry into force of the new Eurojust Decision, the JSB approved its new rules of procedure[52] and held its first election replacing the whole troika at once by three new members.[53] Commencing in 2010, elections will be held every year to replace one member and the elected new member will be part of the JSB troika for 3 years. This new system is seen as a step forward both by the JSB and by Eurojust.

The new Decision also adds a new sentence in paragraph 10 of Article 23 allowing the possibility for the JSB secretariat to rely on the expertise of the data protection secretariat at the Council.[54] This paragraph, supported by the JSB in its letter

---

[48] The length of the appointment to the JSB has been modified accordingly in paragraph 1 of the article from the initial 18 months of participation to the troika to three years.

[49] In accordance with the last sentence of the new Article 23.3, *appointees wishing to be elected shall present their candidacy in writing to the Secretariat of the Joint Supervisory Body ten days before the meeting in which the election is to take place.*

[50] Act of the Joint Supervisory Body of 2 March 2004 laying down its rules of procedure, *Official Journal* C86 (6 April 2004): 1.

[51] The need to amend the rules of procedure of the JSB is implied in the new Recital 16 of the preamble which indicates that *the rules on the JSB should facilitate its functioning.*

[52] Not yet published at the time of writing this article.

[53] As a result of this first election, the new troika is composed as follows: Ms Lotty Prussen, appointee from Luxembourg, will be member of the JSB troika for one year and is chair during this one year mandate; Mr Hans Frennered, appointee from Sweden, will be member of the JSB troika for two years and will be chair during his second year of mandate and Mr Carlos Campos Lobo, appointee from Portugal, will be member of the JSB troika for three years and will be chair during his third year of mandate.

[54] The Secretariat established by Council Decision 2000/641/JHA of 17 October 2000 establishing a secretariat for the joint supervisory data protection bodies set up by the Convention on the establishment of the European Police Office (Europol Convention), the Convention on the Use of

to the Council of March 2004 as well as by the EDPS in its opinion,[55] constitutes a legal basis for the so-far only informal cooperation with this secretariat, which had proved to be very useful in the past for the inspections carried out by the JSB in 2005 and 2007. The introduction of this paragraph in the text will facilitate the practical arrangements around this cooperation, which was until now conditional on approval by various instances linked to this secretariat.

Finally, Article 27(a) includes in its paragraph 5 the supervision of the JSB of the activities of liaison magistrates posted by Eurojust in third countries and who shall be connected to the CMS. The provision of the supervision of the JSB in the text was strictly speaking not needed as, being part of Eurojust, the liaison magistrates posted by Eurojust in third countries automatically fall under the Eurojust rules including the data protection rules and, therefore, the DPO and JSB are competent. However, given the fact that such magistrates will in practice be posted abroad, it is always good to make this point completely clear in the text of the Decision itself.

11.4 Concluding Remarks

The new Eurojust decision consolidates the current data protection regime of Eurojust by maintaining its main principles but clarifying some matters and even bringing into the decision some of the provisions further developed through the data protection rules and the implementation of the CMS as well as some of the good practices already existing in the organisation. It also improves it by adding flexibility to some areas in which practical difficulties had been encountered in the past such as the limitations of Article 15, the time-limits and the exchanges of data with other EU bodies, while still preserving the existing high level of protection.

The revised decision has also reinforced the role of the JSB by taking on board its own proposals to further improve the stability and expertise of the supervisory body.

Information Technology for Customs Purposes and the Convention implementing the Schengen Agreement on the gradual abolition of checks at the common borders (Schengen Convention), *Official Journal* L271 (24 October 2000): 1.

[55] Opinion of the European Data Protection Supervisor of 25 April 2008 on the review of the Eurojust Decision.

Chapter 12
The Case of the 2008 German–US Agreement on Data Exchange: An Opportunity to Reshape Power Relations?

Rocco Bellanova

12.1 Introduction

Capture, storage, exchange and processing of personal and non-personal (contextual) data seem to have become ubiquitous, turning into one of the main practices of a "liquid" modernity (Ceyhan 2005).[1] Even if the adoption of measures based on data processing is not new in the public sector, the spread of data processing is deeply affecting the management of security, further blurring the borders between internal and external security and sharpening the focus on the preventive control of individuals' behaviour (Amoore 2008).

The legislative activism of institutions, governments and agencies in the United States and the European Union, calls for an analysis of power relations among relevant actors. In fact, apart from their potential value as security instruments and drivers of Europeanization and transatlantic cooperation, security practices based on data processing seem to specific actors offer an occasion to increase their powers. Both the transatlantic and the European levels could provide several interesting case studies, but a comprehensive analysis of the cluster of security measures is out of the scope of this study. However, it is possible to attempt a first analysis of power relations by focusing on a specific, but relevant, case, such as the international agreement concluded in 2008 between Germany and the United States on the exchange of personal data.[2] This case is particularly relevant for several reasons. It

This chapter includes parts of a previously published working paper: Bellanova, R. 2009. *Prüm: A model 'Prêt-à-Exporter'? The 2008 German–US agreement on data exchange*. CEPS Challenge Paper No. 13.

[1] For a definition of "liquid" modernity, cf. Bauman (2002, pp. v–xxii).

[2] Agreement between the Government of the Federal Republic of Germany and the Government of the United States of America On Enhancing Cooperation in Preventing and Combating Serious Crime, Washington, 11 March 2008. Hereinafter: Transatlantic Agreement or US–DE agreement.

R. Bellanova (✉)
Facultés universitaires Saint-Louis/CReSPo, Vrije Universiteit Brussel/LSTS,
Brussel, Belgium
e-mail: rocco.bellanova@vub.ac.be

S. Gutwirth et al. (eds.), *Data Protection in a Profiled World*,
DOI 10.1007/978-90-481-8865-9_12,

is the first case in which a security measure initially developed within the European context is "exported" to the US. Furthermore, in the months following the conclusion of the US–Germany agreement, other EU Member States signed similar agreements, creating a "ping-pong" effect of extra-territorialization. Finally, given its geographical scope and a wording based on intra-European and EU existing legal instruments, it provides researchers with the possibility to analyse how measures are set up and promoted in different fields, how they change and with which potential impacts in terms of power shifts and protection of fundamental rights.

The research assumes as hypothesis that the setting up of security measures is readable as a "plateau", a transversal field in which actors' ability to shape new configurations of actors and fields is a key asset to enhance their powers.[3] The most successful actors are those who can easily create new fields, move across the existing ones as well as generate multiple initiatives and different alliances in order to retain a reference position in several fields.

12.2 Towards a "Prüm Model"?

On 11 March 2008, the Government of the Federal Republic of Germany and the Government of the United States of America have signed an international *Agreement on Enhancing Cooperation in Preventing and Combating Serious Crime.*

This agreement provides for wide personal data exchanges, and in particular fingerprints, DNA and sensitive data. As stated in the preamble,[4] the agreement follows the example of the Treaty of Prüm[5] and thus seems to reinforce the idea of the success and diffusion of what could be called a "Prüm model". In fact, since

---

[3] This hypothesis is partially inspired by the reflection of Beck (2002) on the reinforcement of Interior Ministries' powers through international cooperation among them. It is also based on the notion of "champ" of Bourdieu (1992, pp. 66–83) and the "two-level game" theory of Putnam (1988). Notwithstanding the fact that the notion of "plateau" as expressed in this paper presents several differences with Deleuze and Guattari's concept, there is also a common point in the conception of a "plateau" as a sort of transversal field, including, overlapping and linking several different fields: "(w)e define 'plateau' as any multiplicity which can be bonded to others through superficial subterranean roots, in a way to form and expand a rhizome" (Deleuze and Guattari 1980; p. 33). Finally, the definition of power relations has to be understood with the words of Foucault: "(a) power relationship (…) can only be articulated on the basis of two elements that are indispensable if it is really to be a power relationship: that 'the other' (the one over whom power is exercised) is recognised and maintained to the very end as a subject who acts; and that, faced with a relationship of power, a whole field of responses, reactions, results, and possible inventions may open up" (Foucault 2003, pp. 137–138).

[4] Paragraph 4.

[5] Treaty between the Kingdom of Belgium, the Federal Republic of Germany, the Kingdom of Spain, the French Republic, the Grand Duchy of Luxembourg, the Kingdom of the Netherlands and the Republic of Austria on the stepping up of cross-border cooperation, particularly in combating terrorism, cross-border crime and illegal migration, May 2005. Hereinafter: Prüm Treaty, Convention, Treaty.

the conclusion of the Treaty on May 2005 (Council 2005), some governments have promoted the Prüm Convention as an EU-wide tool to be formally proposed and adopted within the EU framework. Finally, quite at the same moment in which parts of the Convention are formally adopted under EU law,[6] the Prüm Treaty is being again promoted as model, this time within the transatlantic framework. In the meantime, and even if part of the provisions were already on course for adoption at the European level, several Member States have declared their interest in joining the "Prüm club", and some finally entered it.[7] The reasons of this quite astonishing success seem to reside especially in the pro-active role of the German Government—and a strong continuity between two governments and two interior ministers of different political orientations—as well as in the appeal of its provisions. Moreover, the Prüm Treaty, and its EU transposition, has become, since its very beginning, a major issue not only in the debate on police cooperation and data exchange (EDPS 2006, 2007), but also in Europeanization and its values and rules (Apap and Vasiliu 2006; Balzacq 2006a, b).

In order to outline the features of the "Prüm model", the rest of the paper provides for a comparative analysis of the context of construction, the main actors involved, the content of the measures, the divergences among specific provisions and the layers of resistance.

12.3 Context: Transitional Periods?

All the "Prüm based" instruments have been discussed and concluded in a mixed context, made of institutional thrusts and discussions toward integration and political statements as well as speeches on the so-called variable geometry approach (cf. Dehousse et al. 2004; Dehousse and Sifflet 2006). The Treaty was signed merely 2 days before the French referendum on the European Constitution, and the German Initiative (General Secretariat of the Council 2007b) was presented at the same time as the negotiations on the Lisbon Treaty. Both initiatives have been presented as an occasion to intensify European cooperation, and even if this concept was challenged by numerous critics, it was frequently used, and accepted by policy-makers, at European and national level.

At the time of the conclusion of the negotiations of the US–Germany Agreement, Europe seems to be living through another transitional process: the adoption of the Lisbon Treaty and its process of ratification. Besides the purely "internal" European

[6] Council Decision 2008/615/JHA of 23 June 2008 on the stepping up of cross-border cooperation, particularly in combating terrorism and cross-border crime, *Official Journal* L210/1, 6.8.2008.

[7] Italy has been the first non-Prüm country to sign a declaration of intent to join the group (Repubblica Italiana 2006). It was followed by three other countries before the end of 2006: Slovenia, Portugal and Finland. During the first months of 2007, at least three additional Member States asked to join: Hungary, Bulgaria and Romania. Among them, Hungary and Finland had already signed the agreement by the end of 2007. Data about the process of signature and ratification have still to be researched.

aspects of transition, it is relevant to the context of transatlantic relations between the US and EU Member States and institutions. In the previous years, measures concerning data access progressively moved up on the transatlantic agenda. Security and visa issues are among the main topics of discussion both at international level, with the US pursuing an active policy of further data access and bilateral diplomacy, as well as at internal level, with a potential clash on the defence of Member States and the Commission's prerogatives and powers. All transatlantic agreements have raised fierce struggles in the field of European institutions, as demonstrated by the PNR and SWIFT dossiers,[8] both on content and form. Finally, in 2008 the legitimacy of the European Commission as the leading actor in transatlantic relations is stressed between the ongoing activities of the High Level Contact Group (Council 2008) paving the way to a possible transatlantic data protection agreement (De Hert and Bellanova 2008) and Eastern EU Member States negotiating bilateral agreements in order to enter into the US Visa Waiver Program (DHS 2008a, b). Such a picture seems to confirm the idea that the Germany–US agreement has entered the arena of transatlantic and European fields at a very delicate moment of transition. Therefore, in line with what had already happened at the conclusion of the Prüm Treaty, the Transatlantic Agreement and its promoters immediately proceeded to disseminating it. Seven months later, the text of the US–Germany agreement was codified as a "standard agreement" between the US and non-VWP EU Member States.[9]

Both the first extra-territorialization of (parts of) the Prüm Treaty into the EU frame, and the subsequent "ping-pong" transatlantic extra-territorialization appear to confirm the idea that the first feature of the "Prüm model" is its ability to present itself as a quick and effective solution of international cooperation as well as a "prêt-à-exporter" model. The idea of transposing the Prüm Treaty within the EU framework was already spelled out in the preamble and in the first article of the Convention.[10] It is now also echoed by the preamble of the Transatlantic Agreement (4th paragraph). Both governments state their expectation that the agreement will be considered a model for similar future agreements (5th paragraph). Besides such statements, the European and transatlantic contexts themselves offer this

[8] Agreement between the European Union and the United States of America on the processing and transfer of Passenger Name Record (PNR) data by air carriers to the United States Department of Homeland Security (DHS) (2007 PNR Agreement), *Official Journal* L 204, 4.8.2007. For SWIFT, cf. Council (2007b).

[9] At the writing of this paper, at least six other Eastern EU Member States signed a similar agreement: Hungary, Estonia, Lithuania, Latvia, Czech Republic and Slovakia.

[10] The 4th paragraph of the Prüm Preamble states: "(s)eeking to have the provisions of this Convention brought within the legal framework of the European Union", and then, Article 1(4) further defines the guidelines of the process of transposition: "(w)ithin three years at most following entry into force of this Convention, on the basis of an assessment of experience of its implementation, an initiative shall be submitted, in consultation with or on a proposal from the European Commission, in compliance with the provisions of the Treaty on European Union and the Treaty establishing the European Community, with the aim of incorporating the provisions of this Convention into the legal framework of the European Union".

Transatlantic Agreement the occasion to set forth the basic model. The active US diplomatic policy favouring bilateral agreements (DHS 2008a, b) on data access measures as well as the strong interest of Eastern Member States in taking part to the Visa Waiver Program provides a fertile ground for reproduction of the model. Furthermore, the previous adoption of a Prüm system at EU level could compel several Member States toward the adoption of similar agreements at transatlantic level. Obviously, such a political, juridical and diplomatic choice would have consequences on the conception and shape of transatlantic security and data protection relations as well as on the concept of Europeanization itself. Given the proliferation of agreements and the lack of a common framework, this could pave the way to "piece-meal" legislation built around pivot governments and agencies, rather than centrally coordinated (cf. De Hert and De Shutter 2008).

12.4 Contents and Core Provisions. Which Core? Which Provisions?

The Prüm Treaty covers a wide range of fields. It promotes data exchange of DNA, fingerprints and vehicle registration data (Articles 2–12). It organises the supply of data for security management during major events (Articles 14–15), as well as the transmission of data for anti-terrorism purposes (Article 16). It reinforces police cooperation in the field, allowing for intervention of foreign agents within national borders (Articles 24–32) and the use of so-called air-marshals (Articles 17–19). Finally, it deals with immigration issues on repatriations and control of fake documents (Articles 20–23). The Treaty also provides for an *ad hoc* data protection framework based on existing legal instruments (Articles 33–41). Such wide range of provisions was partially narrowed down in the wording of the first two Council Decisions aimed at incorporating the Treaty within the UE framework (General Secretariat of the Council 2007a, b). In particular, sensitive issues such as cooperation concerning illegal immigration and air marshals were withdrawn from the proposed text. The scope of the Treaty was even further reduced between February and July 2007 by Council discussions, bringing to the exclusion of Article 25: "Measures in event of imminent danger". Since December 2006, some documents,[11] as well as officials, started to refer to the transposition of the "core parts" of Prüm. *Ex post*, the "core parts" could be defined as the provisions coinciding with the

[11] Joint Declaration of The Kingdom of Belgium, The Federal Republic of Germany, The Kingdom of Spain, The French Republic, The Italian Republic, The Grand Duchy of Luxembourg, The Kingdom of the Netherlands, The Republic of Austria, The Portuguese Republic, The Republic of Slovenia, The Republic of Finland, on the occasion of the Meeting of Ministers on 5 December 2006 in Brussels, within the framework of the Treaty between the Kingdom of Belgium, the Federal Republic of Germany, the Kingdom of Spain, the French Republic, the Grand Duchy of Luxembourg, the Kingdom of the Netherlands and the Republic of Austria on the increased cross-border cooperation, particularly in combating terrorism, cross-border crime and illegal migration (Treaty of Prüm), Brussels, (5 December 2006).

text of the Council Decision (Council 2007a; Guild 2007). This covers the articles related to all types of data exchanges, data protection and police cooperation. Data exchange provisions were generally considered the most important, and the most controversial part. However, it could be difficult to argue that other provisions were not originally felt as part of the "core", or at least as important for specific Member States and agencies. The contentious debates over the inclusion of "Measures in the event of imminent dangers" seem to demonstrate this idea, as well as the tendency of Member States to sign the Prüm Treaty even if already in the adoption stage at the EU level (Bellanova 2008).

Compared to the Council Decision, the Transatlantic Agreement seems to go one step further in the process of lightening the text: the agreement focuses entirely on establishing a system of data exchange. Therefore, the Agreement drawn from the very "core" of Prüm and its specific added value: the "hit/no hit" system of DNA and fingerprint data sharing (Chap. 2 of the Council Decision). One could say that, with two significant exceptions that will be discussed below, all the data sharing provisions have been deeply inspired, or directly "cut & pasted" from the 2005 Prüm text.

The focus on data sharing could show the significant relevance acquired by such practices and forms of cooperation. It also suggests the tendency of the "Prüm model" to shape its own "core" in order to contain possible debates with strong actors, such as Member States with a veto power over the adoption at EU level, or to attract new actors and enter new fields as in the case of transatlantic relations. Besides, the potential negative aspects of losing some "core" provisions of the 2005 agreement seem contained by the dissemination of the model in different fields. Certain core-differences could even strengthen the appeal of the model by attracting new actors to previous, and more complete, agreements. In fact, the contemporary and cross-cutting presence of three different legal instruments with different memberships, permit to some actors to retain a certain power over multiple and parallel fields.

12.5 Memberships and Actors

This last point offers the occasion to point out the main actors involved in the Prüm model. The negotiations of the Prüm Treaty developed during 2003–2005, and involved a limited number of Member States. Seven countries finally signed the Convention: Germany, Austria, Belgium, Netherlands, Luxembourg, France and Spain. However, the last two had only a limited say, because they joined the core group merely some weeks before the signature. Such initial membership pushed some critics, and later on many supporters, to refer to Prüm as Schengen III (Balzacq et al. 2006). According to interviews conducted during the preparation of a previous study (Bellanova 2008), within Member States, the main actors were the Ministries of Interior and Justice, often supported by Foreign Affairs. With the exception of these ministries, very few actors had the possibility to intervene officially in the discussions. Data Protection Authorities were quite marginalised, with the partial exception of the German and French authorities (German Federal Commissioner for Data Protection 2005; HoL 2006b). The European Commission was even working on a parallel initiative covering the principle of availability (Commission 2005). Only 2 years later, at the moment of the presentation of the German Initiative in February 2007, did the European Parliament become formally involved. However, since its signature in May 2005, Prüm started to attract growing attention, as well as critics, from quite all the potential stakeholders: EU institutions, European and National Data Protection Authorities (AEPD 2005; CNIL 2006; EDPS 2006, 2007), national Parliaments (Deutscher Bundestag 2006) and civil society (Balzacq et al. 2006). Notwithstanding this strong interest, only few actors had the possibility to retain some power over the entry into force of the Treaty or its transposition. For example, the legal structure of decision-making under the third pillar weakened the power position of the European Parliament (EP 2007) leaving all the powers of control to national parliaments (Guild and Geyer 2008).[12] However, this concentration of policy-making in the hands of executive branches, and the little room left for parliamentary debates had raised criticism on negotiations, so accused to be held behind "closed doors" (HoL 2006a).

All along this process, the German government, and in particular the Ministries of Interior and Justice, seems to have maintained a pivotal, and crucial, position. It was able to capitalize on the interest of other governments and institutions, and showed a strong capacity to present both initiatives as the best and only way to further integration. The conclusion of the Transatlantic Agreement seems to reinforce the idea of the role and astute ability of the German Government to promote the "Prüm model". One could assume also that German ministries were the actors that possessed the best capacity, and maybe the stronger motivation, to move on and across different fields and different channels. This ability reinforced a power position in all fields. For example, one should consider the fact that other Member States are concluding similar agreements on DNA and fingerprints data exchange, implementing the same German system of data exchange. Building a parallel system could prove both expensive and redundant, especially if all potential partners have already accepted and developed a common one. The analysis of membership and actors could bring forth the definition of another feature of the "Prüm model": it is not just an instrument of governance, but a semi-open configuration of relations among actors and fields, originally built in order to leave some actors with a decisive capacity on how and whether to open the structure, or resist to external pressures.

---

[12] Legislative initiatives under Title VI of the Treaty of the European Union (TEU), "Provisions on Police and Judicial Cooperation in Criminal Matters", have to undergo a process of decision making that leaves to the European Parliament a mere power of consultation. In fact, the adoption of instruments such as framework decisions (Article 34(2)(b) TEU), Council decisions (Article 34(2)(c)) and conventions (Article 34(2)(d)) imply only the consultation of the European Parliament (Article 39(1)). For an insightful analysis of the modifications to such a scenario under the Lisbon Treaty, cf. Carrera and Geyer (2008).

12.6 Divergences Among Provisions of Prüm Instruments

Before presenting and discussing the resistance opposed to the conclusion of the Transatlantic Agreement, and thus to this segment of the process of extra-territorialization, it is important to conclude the tentative outline of the "Prüm model" by comparing some key provisions of the three Prüm instruments. Such a comparison aims at offering an assessment of new power increases according to the text of the Transatlantic Agreement.

As already stated, the preamble of the Agreement underlines the direct influence of the Prüm Treaty.[13] However, a first close comparison already reveals some meaningful differences. In particular, at least four other discrepancies deserve to be mentioned.[14]

The first two discrepancies highlight the fact that in the last re-definition of the core provisions, the powers of data exchange were strongly increased.

Article 10 of the agreement concerns the "Supply of personal and other data in order to prevent terrorist offenses". It echoes Article 16 of both the Prüm Treaty and the Council Decision, and strongly extends its scope. The supply of personal data remains allowed even on spontaneous basis, but the number and quality of personal data that could be sent have increased. To the list of categories of data provided in Article 16(2)—surnames, first names, date and place of birth, description of the circumstances giving rise to the belief of terrorism involvement—the following data were added: former names, other names, aliases, alternative spelling of names, sex, current and former nationalities, passport number, numbers from other identity documents, and fingerprinting data. Finally, paragraph 6 also partially integrates and extends the scope of the wording of Article 13 of the Prüm Convention: "Supply of non personal data". "Non personal, terrorism related data" supply is no more limited only to major events security management.[15]

Article 12 of the agreement covers the "Transmission of Special Categories of Personal Data". This article is completely new, and explicitly admits the possibility, under suitable safeguards that seem still to be defined, of providing sensitive data. Even if paragraph 1 limits the supply of such data "only if they are particularly relevant to the purposes of (this) Agreement", it also establishes a very comprehensive list of categories of data: "personal data revealing racial or ethnic origin, politi-

[13] The 4th paragraph of the Preamble states: "Following the example of the Treaty of Prüm".

[14] Surely, a deeper analysis is needed to detect and assess others discrepancies. For example, apart the lack of provisions on vehicle registration, data that is obviously linked by geographical evidence, another issue warranting deeper analysis concerns the differences and the future implementation of DNA-related provisions (Articles 7–9). At present, Article 24 on "Entry into force", explicitly excludes the exchange of DNA data lest the implementing agreement(s) has entered into force. Given the extreme sensitiveness of such data, a true assessment of such provisions can be done only on the basis of implementing measures. Here, it should be noted that no automated comparison of DNA and no collection of cellular material and supply of DNA profiles (Articles 4 and 7) is provided for in the text of the Transatlantic Agreement.

[15] Article 10(6) US–DE agreement.

cal opinions or religious or other beliefs, trade union membership or (concerning) health and sexual life".

The other two discrepancies focus on the other aspect of the core provisions of the "Prüm model": data protection.

Articles 11–18 of the agreement provide the frame for data protection. In that case, the Prüm Treaty and the Council Decision texts were a secondary source of inspiration. While the Prüm Treaty data protection framework strongly relies on security and on the very architecture of the system,[16] it also provides a juridical set of references and safeguards, both within national and international law (Articles 34 and 40). In comparison, the new Transatlantic Agreement focuses even more on a (future) technical-security approach with the risk of marginalising juridical guarantees. This could be linked to different juridical and institutional approaches to data protection on the two sides of Atlantic (Council 2008) and should require further and deeper analysis. However, it is already possible to point out at least two discrepancies, two elements absent in the new text.

Article 40 of the Prüm Treaty, literally translated into Article 31 of the Council Decision, defines the data subjects' right to information and damages. Of such rights, only the part on data subject access right was maintained in the transatlantic text. The second part of Article 40(1), providing for the possibility to lodge a complaint to "an independent court or a tribunal" is not present. Furthermore, the rights of access of the first paragraph of Article 17, are strongly limited by a series of exception listed in paragraph 2.[17]

The second divergence is the absence of reference to the role of data protection authorities. In fact, reading Article 15(1) one could wonder if such lack of reference is not intended as a shift of control powers over to government agencies. For example, Article 15 provisions establish "a record of the transmission and receipt of data communicated to the other party". In particular, this record shall serve not only to ensure effective monitoring of data protection and data security, as was the case in the texts of the Prüm Treaty and the Council Decision, but also to "enable the Parties to effectively make use of the rights granted to them according to Articles 14 and 18". Articles 14 and 18 rights, "Correction, blockage and deletion of data" and "Information" are state agencies rights, and not explicitly independent authorities' rights.

It is worth remembering that these divergences could be due to the specific nature of US legislation (De Hert and Bellanova 2008, pp. 13–20). Nevertheless, the apparent shift in the powers of control and supervision as well as a reduced set of data subjects' rights highlight once again the difficulties of reaching agreements on data access and exchange with the US in the absence of a European and transatlantic

---

[16] Prüm Treaty, Chap. 7, in particular Articles 37–39 as well as the provisions on the automated search system for DNA and fingerprints in Chap. 2.

[17] Article 17(2) states: "Such information may be denied in accordance with the respective laws of the Parties, including if providing this information may jeopardize: (a) the purposes of the processing; (b) investigations or prosecutions conducted by the competent authorities in the United States or by the competent authorities in Germany; or (c) the rights and freedoms of third parties".

framework of data protection covering data used for security purposes. Therefore, the decision of continuing the process of extra-territorialization seems strongly motivated by the will of reinforcing state and law enforcements agencies' capacities.

12.7 Resistance to the "Prüm Model"?

On the basis of a first round of interviews, published documents and press releases, it is already possible to identify a primary layer of resistance to the ratification and entry into force of the Transatlantic Agreement. At the writing of this study, German actors animate the main fields of resistance: several political parties, some trade unions, the federal data protection authority and an association of German civil rights and privacy activists. Such a picture is clearly not exhaustive for three main reasons: documentation is still poor and generally not translated, and direct interviews require a longer period of research; the research is German-focused, because a first overview of US sources has brought few if any results and finally, other layers of resistance, in particular legal constraints, could arise later.

As was the case at the moment of the conclusion of the Prüm Treaty, and later at the first adoption of the Council Decision, the main line of potential resistance lays with national parliaments. In particular, the German Bundestang is called to discuss and ratify the Transatlantic Agreement. The US Senate and Congress seem not to be called into question by the legal form of the agreement, in fact no modification to present legislation is required.

According to an interview with the legislative assistant of the Free Democratic Party (FDP) speaker for Policy of the Interior,[18] all the Parties composing the opposition in the Parliament have voiced criticism on the government initiative. In particular, the FDP and the Green Party have, separately, lodged a Motion to the government. The Motion of the FDP focuses on seven shortcomings of the Transatlantic Agreement and asks the government to intervene on six points (Deutscher Bundestag 2008). Shortcomings mainly refer to the lowering of data protection guarantees when compared to the Prüm Treaty; to the fact that such lower guarantees are probably due to the difficulties in finding a good solution when dealing with the US legal framework of data protection; to the practice of closed doors negotiations, and to the lack (or even denial) of information to the Parliament. In fact, according to the same interview, even if Parliament has no explicit right to be associated to international negotiations, it nevertheless has a right to be correctly informed. The government infringed this right when, previously asked about negotiations with the US on data sharing, it denied any activity. Among the points raised, the most important ones are proposals of amendments to the text, with the scope

[18] Interview with Mrs. Maja Pfister, Legislative Assistant to Mrs. Gisela Piltz (MP), Speaker for Policy of the Interior in the Parliamentary Group of the FDP in the Deutsche Bundestag, 29 October 2008.

of improving data protection, limiting exchange of sensitive data, specifying the purpose of the agreement and keeping Parliament informed.

Notwithstanding the resistance of opposition Parties, the present government parliamentary support will outnumber any opposition. According to the previously quoted interview, a possibility of opposing strong numerical resistance to the agreement could make headway if trade unions continue their critical posture towards the agreements and lobby on Social-Democrats (SPD) members of the parliament. At present, SPD is part of the coalition government, but is highly sensitive to pressures from trade unions. As stated before, Article 12 of the Transatlantic Agreement leaves the possibility of transmission of sensitive data, including trade unions' membership. Media and trade unions' discussions on this article could become a driver for pressure on SPD members.

Even if no official report has yet been released by the German Federal Data Protection Authority, the same day of the signature of the Agreement, its President underlined, in a published press-release (BFDI 2008), the insufficient level of data protection of the agreement: "data protection remains far below the level which is common standard when transferring data within Europe (…) an independent data protection control is missing, and rules on purpose limitation are insufficient". The way in which exchange of sensitive data is conceived is also lamented. An interview with the Data Protection and Freedom of Information Commissioner of Berlin, Alexander Dix, has highlighted the same concerns, adding criticisms of the "illusion" of exchange legal data protection with technological data security, the tendency towards a maximization of data exchange and the principal problem of decision-making behind closed doors.[19]

Finally, the last actor resisting the Transatlantic Agreement is the Arbeitskreis Vorratsdatenspeicherung (Working Group on Data Retention), an association of German civil rights and privacy activists. They were the first, on September 2008, to publish the German version of the Transatlantic Agreement, and started a civil society campaign on this issue.[20] Their criticism focuses on the lowering of data protection and the shortcomings of the US data and human rights protection system.[21] They also identify several faults on "basically all of the preconditions set out by the German Constitutional Court for interferences with (…) basic rights".[22] They ask Parliament to not ratify the agreement and, in case ratification does occur, they plan on challenging it before the Federal Constitutional Court.[23] This last case is particularly relevant in the study of resistance to security measures based on data access and their extra-territorialization. Despite an apparent silence on the other side of the Atlantic in this specific case, generally, US NGOs are very active in promoting

[19] Interview with Alexander Dix, Berliner Beauftragter für Datenschutz und Informationsfreiheit, 29 October 2008.

[20] Cf. http://www.vorratsdatenspeicherung.de/content/view/253/1/lang,de/.

[21] Cf. http://www.vorratsdatenspeicherung.de/content/view/253/1/lang,en/.

[22] *Ibid.*

[23] Interview with Mr. Patrick Breyer, jurist and member of the Arbeitskreis Vorratsdatenspeicherung, 3 November 2009.

resistance to such security measures, using communication and legal instruments (Bennett 2008). By contrast, Arbeitskreis Vorratsdatenspeicherung's activities are one of the few European examples.

According to this first overview of resistance, it is important to note that several issues raised by "resistant actors" are not dissimilar to those already raised at the moment of the transposition of parts of the Prüm Treaty within the EU legal framework. They both focus on the content (data protection, scope and aim of the instrument) and on the decision-making process ("behind closed door" practice). Moreover, different actors share similar criticisms, even if they propose different solutions, ranging from the re-negotiation of the agreement to the non-ratification. The main novelty of this resistance is the diffusion of the layer of resistance, due to the entry of new actors, such as NGOs, and to a critical posture of other actors, such as trade unions. Every actor has specific powers and limitations, as highlighted before in the case of parliamentary opposition. However, as interviews seem to confirm, flows of communication and expertise among them could play a role in linking their different fields.

12.8 Final Considerations

The success of the "Prüm model" confirms the initial hypothesis that security measures based on data processing are an opportunity for specific actors to acquire stronger powers in several fields. Moreover, the case study highlights parallelism and overlap with variable geometry governance. Both can contribute to catalyse pending European and transatlantic issues. Notwithstanding strong political and juridical appeal, such re-configurations of power relations may ultimately create distortions detrimental to the values and the forms of European integration: lowering of citizens' privacy and data protection rights, limited and scattered supervision of executive powers by independent authorities and parliaments, "ping-pong" multilateralism as a short cut for the diffusion of norms and policies.

This overview has also underlined that the "Prüm model" is not a fixed structure or package of provisions. While some provisions remain the same, the "core" is partially re-shaped every time it generates a new legal instrument, by subtraction of contested parts or enlargement of others. However, nothing is completely lost for the actors that are able to move on the different fields and levels—international, European and transatlantic. On the contrary, this could reinforce their position in every field because they can move across them. Finally, it is worth underlining that the "Prüm model" still remains a highly symbolical–political form of cooperation rather than an implemented measure. In fact, despite its proliferation in several frameworks, its implementation is still not complete even among the "founding members".

Drawing from those provisional conclusions, it is possible to advance some considerations. Firstly, the proliferation of similar measures calls for an in-depth analysis of the main changes in terms of content, contexts and relations among the stakeholders. Even if the measures proposed are very similar to those already accepted (or already legitimised), every change, even if apparently minor, is not without consequences, and risks triggering a different *status quo* in the related fields of fundamental rights, Europeanization and transatlantic relations. Cases in point are the worrisome lowering of individual rights, and the relative increase in terms of surveillance, both deserving further attention.

Secondly, the proliferation of security measures aiming at widening the number of data to be processed clashes with both the idea of data minimization (focusing on the quality, pertinence and necessity of data access and process) and of simplification (clear rules on procedures and easily recognisable rights). Those criteria could contribute to avoid perilous shifts in power relations among actors, by channelling the activities of the controllers (in this case, states' security agencies and probably immigration services) and empowering individuals. This followed by a more open decision-making process combined with sound assessments of what is needed and what is at disposal could prove a step forward. Finally, given the linkage between security measures and other key issues such as visas, other political priorities play in favour of a rapid adoption of similar agreements within different national settings. This contributes to disseminate a model that, *de facto*, undermines resistance and possible amendments in other countries. How to avoid this sort of "self-fulfilling process" and the relative marginalisation of layers of resistance, is a great challenge for civil society, concerned individuals and researchers. Apart from the possible changes to the decision-making structure of the EU, probably the "plateau" model of Prüm should be reverse-engineered, participated and re-appropriated by concerned actors.

References

Primary sources

Agreement between the European Union. 2007. Agreement between the European Union and the United States of America on the processing and transfer of Passenger Name Record (PNR) data by air carriers to the United States Department of Homeland Security (DHS) (2007 PNR Agreement). *Official Jouranl* L204 (4.8.2007).

Agreement between the Government of the Federal Republic. 2008. Agreement between the Government of the Federal Republic of Germany and the Government of the United States of America on enhancing cooperation in preventing and combating serious crime. Washington (11 March 2008).

Agencia Española de Protección de Datos—AEPD. 2005. *Informe del Gabinete Juridico, N. ref. 37530/2005.* Madrid.

Bundesbeauftragte für den Datenschutz und die Informationsfreiheit—BFDI. 2008. Peter Schaar: Insufficient data protection in the agreement on data exchange with the USA. Bonn.

Commission of the European Communities—Commission. 2005. Proposal for a council framework decision on the exchange of information under the principle of availability, COM(2005) 490 final. Brussels.

Commission Nationale Informatique et Libertés—CNIL. 2006. *Note de Synthèse: Traité de Prüm & annexe technique et administrative pour sa mise en application.* Paris.

Council Decision. 2008. Council Decision 2008/615/JHA of 23 June 2008 on the stepping up of cross-border cooperation, particularly in combating terrorism and cross-border crime. *Official Journal* L210/1 (6.8.2008).

Council of the European Union—Council. 2005. *Prüm convention. doc.10900/05 CRIMORG 65 ENFOPOL 85.* Brussels.

Council of the European Union—Council. 2007a. Draft council decision 2007/.../JHA of ... on the stepping up of cross-border cooperation, particularly in combating terrorism and cross-border crime, doc.6566/1/07 REV1 CRIMORG 33 ENFOPOL 18. Brussels.

Council of the European Union—Council. 2007b. Processing of EU originated Personal Data by United States Treasury Department for Counter Terrorism Purposes—"SWIFT", doc.10741/2/07 REV 2 JAI 319 ECOFIN 270. Brussels.

Council of the European Union—Council. 2008. EU US Summit, 12 June 2008—final report by the EU–US High Level Contact Group on information sharing and privacy and personal data protection, doc.9831/08, JAI 275 DATAPROTECT 31 USA 26. Brussels.

Department of Homeland Security—DHS. 2008a. Memorandum of understanding between the ministry of the interior of the Czech Republic and the Department of Homeland Security of the United States of America regarding the United States Visa Waiver Program and related Enhanced Security Measures. Prague.

Department of Homeland Security—DHS. 2008b. Agreement between the Government of the Republic of Hungary and the Government of the United States of America for the Exchange of Screening Information concerning Known or Suspected Terrorists. Budapest.

Deutscher Bundestag. 2006. *Kleine Anfrage (...)Prümer Vertrag und die europäische Integration, Drucksache 16/3871.*

Deutscher Bundestag. 2008. *Antrag der Abgeordneten Gisela Piltz, Christian Ahrendt, Ernst Burgbacher, (...) und der Fraktion der FDP, Abkommen zwischen der Bundesrepublik Deutschland und den Vereinigten Staaten von Amerika über die Vertiefung der Zusammenarbeit bei der Verhinderung und Bekämpfung schwerwiegender Kriminalität neu verhandeln.* Berlin.

European Data Protection Supervisor—EDPS. 2006. Opinion of the European Data Protection Supervisor on the Proposal for a Council Framework Decision on the exchange of information under the principle of availability (COM (2005) 490 final). Brussels.

European Data Protection Supervisor—EDPS. 2007. Opinion of the European data protection supervisor on the initiative of the Kingdom of Belgium, the Republic of Bulgaria, the Federal Republic of Germany, (...) and the Kingdom of Sweden, with a view to adopting a Council Decision on the stepping up of cross-border cooperation, particularly in combating terrorism and cross-border crime. Brussels.

European Parliament—EP. 2007. Committee on Civil Liberties, Justice and Home Affairs (2007), Report on the initiative by the Kingdom of Belgium, the Republic of Bulgaria, the Federal Republic of Germany, (...) and the Kingdom of Sweden on the stepping up of cross-border cooperation, particularly in combating terrorism and cross-border crime, doc. A6-0207/2007. Brussels.

General Secretariat of the Council. 2007a. Draft Council Decision 2007/.../JHA of ... on improving cooperation on request, working document. Brussels.

General Secretariat of the Council. 2007b. Draft Council Decision 2007/.../JHA of ... on the stepping up of cross-border cooperation..., working document. Brussels.

German Federal Commissioner for Data Protection. 2005. *Annual Report 2003/2004 of the Federal Commissioner for Data Protection.* Bonn.

House of Lords—HoL. 2006a. *Behind closed doors: The meeting of the G6 Interior Ministers at Heiligendamm.* London.

House of Lords—HoL. 2006b. *Corrected Oral Evidence given by: Dr. Wolfgang von Pommer Esche, Head of Unit, Police Intelligence Service, Federal Data Protection Office, Inquiry into the development of the second generation Schengen Information System.* London.

Joint Declaration of The Kingdom of Belgium. 2006. Joint Declaration of The Kingdom of Belgium, The Federal Republic of Germany, The Kingdom of Spain, (...) on the occasion of the

Meeting of Ministers on 5th December 2006 in Brussels, within the framework of the Treaty between the Kingdom of Belgium, the Federal Republic of Germany, the Kingdom of Spain, the French Republic, the Grand Duchy of Luxembourg, the Kingdom of the Netherlands and the Republic of Austria on the stepping up of cross-border cooperation, particularly in combating terrorism, cross-border crime and illegal migration (Treaty of Prüm). Brussels (5 December 2006).

Secondary sources

Amoore, L. 2008. Governing by identity. In *Playing the identity card. Surveillance, security and identification in global perspective*, eds. C.J. Bennett and D. Lyon, 21–36. New York: Routledge.

Apap, J., and E. Vasiliu. 2006. *'Variable geometry': A solution for closer co-operation in criminal matters in an enlarged EU? The implications of the Prüm treaty in relation to EU developments.* Brussels: DG Internal Policies of the Union, Policy Department C: Citizens' Rights and Constitutional Affairs, European Parliament.

Balzacq, T. 2006a. *The treaty of Prüm and the principle of loyalty (Art.10 TEC).* Brussels: DG Internal Policies of the Union, Policy Department C: Citizens' Rights and Constitutional Affairs, European Parliament.

Balzacq, T. 2006b. *From a Prüm of 7 to a Prüm of 8+: What are the implications?* Brussels: DG Internal Policies of the Union, Policy Department C: Citizens' Rights and Constitutional Affairs, European Parliament.

Balzacq, T. et al. 2006. *Security and the two-level game: The treaty of Prüm, the EU and the management of threats.* Brussels: Centre for European Policy Studies.

Bauman, Z. 2002. *Modernità liquida.* Roma-Bari: Laterza.

Beck, U. 2002. The terrorist threat, world risk society revisited. *Theory, Culture & Society* 19 (4): 39–55.

Bellanova, R. 2008. The 'Prüm process': The way forward for police cooperation and data exchange? In *Security vs. justice? Police and judicial cooperation in the European Union*, eds. E. Guild and F. Geyer, 203–221. Aldershot: Ashgate.

Bennett, C.J. 2008. *The privacy advocates: Resisting the spread of surveillance.* Cambridge: MIT Press.

Bourdieu, P. 1992. *Risposte: Per una antropologia riflessiva.* Torino: Bollati Boringhieri.

Carrera, S., and F. Geyer. 2008. The reform treaty and justice and home affairs: Implications for the common area of freedom, security and justice. In *Security vs. justice? Police and judicial cooperation in the European Union*, eds. E. Guild and F. Geyer, 289–307. Aldershot: Ashgate.

Ceyhan, A. 2005. La biométrie: une technologie pour gérer les incertitudes de la modernité contemporaine. *Les Cahiers de la sécurité* 56: 61–89. 1er trimestre.

De Hert, P., and R. Bellanova. 2008. *Data protection from a transatlantic perspective: The EU and US move towards an International Data Protection Agreement?* Brussels: DG Internal Policies of the Union, Policy Department C: Citizens' Rights and Constitutional Affairs, European Parliament.

De Hert, P., and De B. Schutter. 2008. International transfers of data in the field of JHA: The lessons of Europol, PNR and swift. In *Justice, liberty, security, new challenges for EU external relations*, eds. B. Martenczuk and Van S. Thiel, 303–339.Brussels: Brussels Univ. Press.

Dehousse, F. et al. 2004. *Integrating Europe, multiple speeds: One direction?* Brussels: EPC.

Dehousse, F., and D. Sifflet. 2006. *Les nouvelles perspectives de la coopération de Schengen: le Traité de Prüm.* Brussels: IRRI-KIIB.

Deleuze, G., and F. Guattari. 1980. *Mille plateaux, Capitalisme et schizophrénie 2.* Paris: Les Éditions de Minuit.

Foucault, M. 2003. The subject and power. In *The essential Foucault, selections from essential works of Foucault, 1954–1984*, eds. P. Rabinow and N. Rose, 126–144. New York: The New Press.

Guild, E. 2007. *Merging security from the two level game: Inserting the treaty of Prüm into EU law?* Brussels: Centre for European Policy Studies.

Guild, E., and F. Geyer. 2008. Introduction: The search for EU criminal law: Where is it headed? In *Security vs. justice? Police and judicial cooperation in the European Union*, eds. E. Guild and F. Geyer, 1–12. Aldershot: Ashgate.
Putnam, R.D. 1988. Diplomacy and domestic politics: The logic of two-level games. *International Organization* 42 (3): 427–460.

Chapter 13
DNA Data Exchange: Germany Flexed Its Muscle

Sylvia Kierkegaard

13.1 Introduction

Criminals do not respect borders. The enlargement of the European Union and the abolition of the borders between Member States have led to security challenges. In the context of improving security, recent initiatives have focused on the exchange of law enforcement information with effect in 2008 under the "availability" principle.

The principle of availability is defined in the 2004 Hague Program for strengthening freedom, security and justice in the European Union of November 2004 as the possibility whereby "a law enforcement officer in one Member State of the Union who needs information in order to carry out his duties can obtain it from another Member State and that the law enforcement authorities in the Member State that holds this information will make it available for the declared purpose, taking account of the needs of investigations pending in that Member State." (Council Decision 2008/615/JHA) Under this principle, full use should be made of new technology and there should be reciprocal access to national databases, while stipulating that new centralized European databases should be created only on the basis of studies that have shown their added value.

On October 12, 2005, the European Commission adopted a proposal for a Framework Decision on exchange of information under the principle of availability. The aim of this proposal is to make certain types of relevant existing law enforcement information available in one Member State also available to authorities with equivalent competences of other Member States or Europol. With this proposal, the Commission answers the request of the European Council in the Hague Programme of November 2004, and the JHA Council of 13 July 2005, requesting to present legislation for implementation of the availability principle in October 2005.

This principle of availability was also introduced in the Prüm Treaty. The core element of the treaty is the creation of a network of national databases to promote the exchange of information between law enforcement authorities. In particular, re-

S. Kierkegaard (✉)
International Association of IT Lawyers, Denmark
sylvia.kierkegaard@iaitl.org

S. Gutwirth et al. (eds.), *Data Protection in a Profiled World*,
DOI 10.1007/978-90-481-8865-9_13,

ciprocal access is given to Contracting States' national databases, containing DNA profiles, fingerprints and vehicle registration data. The use of biometrics and DNA registration has been touted as an efficient means of preventing and solving crime. Decade-long cases have been solved through registration and joint mobilization of police and judicial resources.

Although this initiative started as a multilateral agreement, a small group of influential countries led by Germany successfully contrived other EU countries into integrating the provisions of the agreement into the legislative framework of the European Union under the Third Pillar. The Treaty has been incorporated into a Council Decision binding on all EU Member States. While the treaty represents a progress in the field of cooperation against crime, its implications are far reaching. It raises privacy and data protection issues that will affect all EU citizens, primarily because of the absence of common legally binding data protection standards. There currently exists no standard EU policy for the collection and retention of the sorts of data referred to in the Decision (Prüm). The objective of this chapter is to discuss the political and legal ramifications of this legislation. This study will also discuss the UK legislation on DNA collection and retention, as well as the recent ECHR judgement on the Marper case, which ruled that the UK government and police indefinite retention of innocent people's tissue samples, DNA profiles and fingerprints is illegal.

13.2 Background

The Prüm Treaty is an agreement amongst seven Member States—Germany, Austria, Spain, France, Belgium, the Netherlands and Luxembourg (other States later joined, namely Finland, Italy, Portugal etc.) outside the EU framework and aimed at improving co-operation in fighting terrorism and serious cross-border crime. It was signed on May 27, 2005 in Prüm, a small town in the West German Land of Rhenania Palatinate. The Treaty is often referred as the Schengen III because the same original intergovernmental grouping of powerful countries that signed the Schengen agreement (Belgium, Netherlands, Luxembourg, France and Germany) initiated the Prüm Convention. Although it bears the mark of the Schengen integration process, it is not a part of the Schengen Treaty.

Balzacq (2006) noted that not only have all of the signatory states participated both in the 1985 Schengen Agreement and the 1990 Schengen Implementing Agreement, but they also played a central role in intergovernmental cooperation in fields of central interest and importance to the EU. He also noted that the signatories were participants in the 1997 decision in the context of the intergovernmental conference that led to the Amsterdam Treaty and to the insertion of the Schengen acquis into the EC/EU treaties.

The objective of the contracting states is to create a network of national databases where signatories can gain automated access to each other's national databases containing DNA analysis files and dactyloscopic (fingerprint) files in what is called a hit/no hit system. Police could also launch a query into the data system of a contracting partner to find out whether it contains data concerning a specific profile, and are automatically informed of the result within a matter of minutes. The Prüm Treaty provides that reference data will not contain any information directly identifying a person although, in some cases, Member States will also share suspects' personal data. They can also request case-related specific personal data from the Member State administering the file and, where necessary, request further information through the mutual assistance procedures, including those adopted pursuant to Framework Decision 2006/960/JHA on simplifying the exchange of information and intelligence between law enforcement authorities of the Member States of the European Union (OJ L386, 29.12.2006, p. 89).

From the onset, the ultimate objective of the framers under the German Presidency is to incorporate the wording of the Prüm Treaty into EU legislation. The initial push for stronger EU-wide security legislation came from Germany, which co-authored the original Prüm Treaty. Article 1 (4) of the Prüm Treaty states:

> Within three years at most following entry into force of this Convention, on the basis of an assessment of experience of its implementation, an initiative shall be submitted, in consultation with or on a proposal from the European Commission, in compliance with the provisions of the Treaty on European Union and the Treaty establishing the European Community, with the aim of incorporating the provisions of this Convention into the legal framework of the European Union.

On 15 January 2007, using its EU Council Presidency, Germany submitted a proposal to make the Treaty applicable to all Member States. The German Presidency put the proposal forward without any explanatory memorandum, or impact assessment, or estimate of the cost to Member States, nor allowed time for proper consultation with Member States and the European Parliament. The intention clearly was to ensure that the essential elements of the Treaty would be transferred into a new EU law without change since the Treaty by then had been signed by seven (7) Member States. Four days later, the Council Secretariat published a Working Paper containing a first draft of a Council Decision incorporating the Convention into EU law. It was *fait accompli.*

On 15 February 2007, the Council agreed to integrate those parts of the Treaty relating to information exchange and police cooperation into the EU legal framework. The draft Council Decision was sent to the European Parliament (EP) on February 28. Although the latter does not have a co-decision power in Third Pillar matters, Article 39 of the Treaty on European Union requires the Council to consult Parliament, and to give it a minimum of 3 months to deliver its opinion. The German Presidency requested the EP to deliver its opinion on or before the 7th of June.

On April 4, 2007, the European Data Protection Supervisor (EDPS) (2007a) Peter Hustinx issued an opinion *ex officio*, since no request for advice had been sent to the EDPS (2007/C169/02). Hustinx questioned its legal basis since the Treaty was conceived and initiated outside of EU institutional bodies by a limited number of individual Member States and was to be incorporated into EU law within 2 years of its signing. He also expressed his concerns as to the impact of the Treaty on liberty since the long awaited general framework on data protection is not yet in place and negotiations are leading to a limited scope of application with minimal harmonization. He was concerned that in view of the absence of a general framework guaranteeing that data protection is embedded in this large scale exchange, a high rate of false matches in DNA and fingerprint comparisons could affect both the rights of the citizens and the efficiency of law enforcement authorities. At the EU level, current legislation protecting privacy and personal data protection has little, if any, application at the Third Pillar level. The Data Protection Commissioner recommended that a general framework for data protection in the Third Pillar first be passed before implementing the Treaty into a Council Decision.

On April 24, 2007, the EP Committee on Civil Liberties, Justice and Home Affairs headed by Rapporteur Fausto Correia issued its committee report. The members of the Parliament Committee supported the idea of applying the Prüm treaty to all Member States, but called on the Council to amend the text accordingly (Draft European Parliament Legislative Resolution of April 2, 2008). As the initiative relates to the purpose of approximation of laws and regulations of the Member States, the Committee recommended that the appropriate instrument be a Framework Decision under Article 34(2) (b) of the EU Treaty, rather than a decision pursuant to Article 34(2) (c). The crucial difference, as far as the European Parliament is concerned, is that, whereas Parliament is consulted on the decision or framework decision itself pursuant to Article 39(1) of the EU Treaty, Article 34(2) (c) empowers the Council to subsequently adopt implementing measures by a qualified majority without consulting Parliament.

The Committee Report also suggested several amendments aimed at raising the level of protection of personal data, particularly in the specific case of DNA data, and at establishing that the future framework decision on the protection of personal data will have to apply to these provisions. In particular, the amendment sought to ensure full compliance with citizens' fundamental rights for respect of their private life and communications and for the protection of their personal data as enshrined in Articles 7 and 8 of the Charter of Fundamental Rights of the European Union. It also recommended that monitoring measures be established. Furthermore, the Members of the European Parliament (MEPs) introduced an amendment to ensure that data collected under this draft Decision will not be transferred or made available to a third country or to any international organisation. A number of amendments were suggested to ensure that the supplying of data not be made automatically but only when necessary and proportionate and, based on particular circumstances that give reasons to believe that criminal offences will be committed in the absence of the potentially available data. The rapporteur introduced and negotiated amendments aimed at transforming the decision into a framework decision (on the advice of the EP's Committee on Legal Affairs), at strengthening operational cooperation (possibility of pursuit across borders and police cooperation on request).

On 9 May 2007, the European Union Committee of the House of Lords (UK) published a report examining the proposals to incorporate the Prüm Treaty into EU law (House of Lords 2007) and criticised the German EU Presidency for its failure to allow any opportunity for full consideration of the initiative by all Member States. However, the British government ignored the reservations raised by the House of Lords and signed the parallel binding decision that replicates Prüm.

On June 7, 2007, the European Parliament issued its opinion and expressed regrets as to the obligation imposed on the Parliament by the Council to express its opinion as a matter of urgency. This had been without adequate and appropriate time for Parliamentary review and in the absence of both a comprehensive impact assessment and an evaluation of the application of the Prüm Treaty to date. There was also a lack of an adequate framework decision for the protection of personal data in police and judicial cooperation that was considered necessary before any legislation could be adopted under the Third Pillar (European Parliament legislative resolution 7 June 2007).

At the European Council of Ministers of Justice and Home Affairs (JHA Council) in Luxembourg on 12 June, the EU Home Affairs Ministers agreed to transfer substantial parts of the Treaty into the EU's legal framework, i.e. into *Council Decision on the stepping up of cross-border cooperation, particularly in combating terrorism and cross-border crime* (also referred to as the Prüm Decision), which is binding on the Member States. In forcing it through, the German Presidency opted to ignore the views of the European Parliament and the concerns of the EU data protection supervisor. The Council Decision on the stepping up of cross-border cooperation, particularly in combating terrorism and cross-border crime was identical to the Prüm Treaty, except that it omitted the right for police forces in "hot pursuit" of suspects to cross borders, and cooperation around such issues as air marshals and immigration.

The Prüm Treaty is a Third Pillar instrument devoted to police and judicial cooperation in criminal matters, under Title VI of the EU Treaty. The concept of "Pillars" is generally used in connection with the Treaty on the European Union. Three Pillars form the basic structure of the European Union, namely:

- the Community Pillar, including the three Communities: the European Community, the European Atomic Energy Community (Euratom) and the former European Coal and Steel Community (ECSC) (First Pillar);
- the Pillar devoted to common foreign and security policy, which comes under Title V of the EU Treaty (Second Pillar);
- the Pillar devoted to police and judicial cooperation in criminal matters, which comes under Title VI of the EU Treaty (Third Pillar).

The Three Pillars operate on the basis of different decision-making procedures: the Community procedure for the First Pillar and the intergovernmental procedure for the Second and Third Pillars. In the case of the First Pillar, only the Commission can submit proposals to the Council and Parliament, and a qualified majority is sufficient for adoption of a Council act. In the case of the Second and Third Pillars, the right of initiative is shared between the Commission and the Member States, and unanimity in the Council is generally necessary. With this Council decision, the Prüm Treaty (or a version of it) became part of the *aquis communitaire*, moving from the Third Pillar to the first and, therefore, from a mere form of cooperation into Community methodology.

13.3 Substantive Law

The Council Decision 2008/616/JHA on the stepping up of cross-border cooperation, particularly in combating terrorism and cross-border crime (Prüm Decision) is based on the essential parts of the Prüm Treaty with the exception of the provision relating to cross-border police intervention in the event of imminent danger and affirms the principle of availability- the concept that information that is available to one law enforcement authority in the EU should be made available to others. The Decision contains rules in the following areas:

- Conditions and procedure for automated transfer of DNA profiles, dactyloscopic data and certain national vehicle registration data.
- Conditions for the supply of data in connection with major events with a cross-border dimension;
- Conditions for the supply of information in order to prevent terrorist offences, and; Conditions and procedure for stepping up cross-border police cooperation through various measures.

Chapter 3 contains rules on the conditions and procedure for the automated transfer of DNA profiles. Member States are required to open and keep national DNA analysis files for the investigation of criminal offences. Member States are also required to ensure the availability of reference data from their national DNA analysis files to other Member States. The DNA reference data that exchangeable are composed of a DNA profile and non DNA specific data.

Reference data shall include only DNA profiles established from the non-coding part of DNA and a reference. Reference data must not contain any data from which the data subject can be directly identified. DNA databanks normally register a profile not under the name of a person. A "DNA profile" means a letter or a number code representing a set of identification characteristics of the non-coding part of an analysed human DNA sample, i.e. the particular chemical form at the various DNA locations (loci). A non-DNA specific data comprises an identification code or number allowing, in case of a match, the parties to retrieve personal data and/or other information in their databases, a party code to indicate the national origin of the DNA profile, and a code to indicate the type of DNA profile as declared by the parties.

For the investigation of criminal offences, Member States shall allow other Member States' national contact points access to the reference data in their DNA analysis files, with the power to conduct automated searches by comparing DNA profiles. Should an automated search show that the supplied DNA profile matches DNA profiles entered in the receiving Member State's searched file, the national contact point of the searching Member State will receive in an automated way the reference data for which a match has been found. The DNA profile data provided by each Member State have to be prepared in compliance with a common data protection standard, such that requesting countries can receive an answer indicating mainly a Hit or No Hit, devoid of any personal information. Should there be a match, additional information can then be requested, such as the identity of the person concerned, pursuant to the existing national legal and administrative regulations of the respective Member State's sites.

Chapter 4 contains provisions regulating the exchange of dactyloscopic data, defined as fingerprint images, images of fingerprint latents, and palm prints. For the prevention and investigation of criminal offences, Member States shall allow other Member States' national contact points access to the reference data in the automated fingerprint identification systems established for that purpose, with the power to conduct automated searches by comparing dactyloscopic data. Should the procedure show a match between the dactyloscopic data, additional information can be requested through the national contact point. Reference data shall only include dactyloscopic data and a reference number. Reference data shall not contain any data from which the data subject can be directly identified. Reference data though not attributed to any individual ("unidentified dactyloscopic data") must be recognizable as such.

Chapter 5 deals with the rights of the Member States to access the vehicle databases and to be given priority, especially in combating serious crimes.

Member States may also conduct joint patrols and other joint operations, in which designated officers or other officials from other Member States participate in operations within a Member State's territory (Chap. 5). Chapter 7 contains general provisions on data protection. Each Member State is required to guarantee a level of protection of personal data in its national law at least equal to that resulting from the Council of Europe Convention for the Protection of Individuals with regard to Automatic Processing of Personal Data of 28 January 1981.

13.4 German Hegemony & Democratic Deficit

The Legislative process within the EU has its own set of problems. The proposed Decision was decried by numerous sectors as "undemocratic". The Council Decision bypassed the democratic process based on a treaty signed by only seven nations, and passed in the EU's Council of Ministers with little debate. Because it is an initiative of a Member State rather than a Commission proposal, there is no obligation to include an explanatory memorandum, a regulatory impact assessment or a cost estimate, and none are included.

All Community acts must be founded upon a legal basis as laid down in the Treaty (or in another legal act which they are intended to implement). The legal basis defines the Community's competence *ratione materiae* and specifies how that competence is to be exercised, namely the legislative instrument(s) that may be used and the decision-making procedure. The Council ignored the European Parliament's recommendation that the draft legislation must be a Framework Decision under Article 34(2) (b) of the EU Treaty, rather than a Decision pursuant to Article 34(2) (c).

The Parliament Committee on Legal Affairs stressed from settled case-law of the Court of Justice (Case C-300/89, *Commission v. Council* (1991) ECR I-287, para. 10, and Case C-42/97, *European Parliament v. Council* (1999) ECR I-869, para. 36) it is clear that the choice of legal basis is not at the discretion of the Community legislator, but must be determined by objective factors that can be subject to judicial review, such as the aim and content of the measure in question. In Case C-105/03 *Pupino*, the Court of Justice made it clear in its judgment of 16 June 2005 that "the wording of Article 34(2) (b) EU is very closely inspired by that of the third paragraph of Article 249 EC". Article 34(2) (b) EU confers a binding character on framework decisions in the sense that they 'bind' the Member States 'as to the result to be achieved, but shall leave to the national authorities the choice of form and methods'. Consequently, a framework decision is the equivalent to a First-Pillar directive, but without direct effect. (Parliamentary Report 2007)

The Committee also stressed that since "decisions" within the meaning of Article 34(2) (c) expressly exclude any approximation of national laws and regulations, it goes without saying that if the initiative under consideration involves any such approximation, it (the initiative) should take the form of a framework decision pursuant to Article 34(2) (b) instead.

> Article 34
> 2. The Council shall take measures and promote cooperation, using the appropriate form and procedures as set out in this title, contributing to the pursuit of the objectives of the Union. To that end, acting unanimously on the initiative of any Member State or of the Commission, the Council may:
> b) adopt framework decisions for the purpose of approximation of the laws and regulations of the Member States. Framework decisions shall be binding upon the Member States as to the result to be achieved but shall leave to the national authorities the choice of form and methods. They shall not entail direct effect;
> c) adopt decisions for any other purpose consistent with the objectives of this title, excluding any approximation of the laws and regulations of the Member States. These decisions shall be binding and shall not entail direct effect; the Council, acting by a qualified majority, shall adopt measures necessary to implement those decisions at the level of the Union;

The choice for basing the Prüm rules on a "decision" and not a "framework decision" is made possible by resorting to "decisions" by qualified majority (Article 34(2) (c) EU Treaty); for "framework decisions", this option does not exist. In this way, qualified majority voting could be introduced into matters of the Third Pillar.

The substantive provisions of the Decision were not merely based on the main provisions of the Prüm Treaty, but replicated word for word. The Council Decision initiative takes existing mechanisms—procedures for access rights to automated DNA files, automated dactyloscopic identification systems and vehicle registration data—and, in certain circumstances, subject to specified conditions, affords them cross-border effect, which, as is abundantly clear from an analysis of the text, requires approximation of the relevant national rules. Moreover, in the text there is a substantial chapter on data protection that can also be regarded as an approximation of national laws and regulations. Thus, the Committee on Legal Affairs further stressed that the initiative for a Council Decision on the stepping up of cross-border cooperation, particularly in combating terrorism and cross-border crime, should take the form of a framework decision and be based on Article 34(2) (b) of the EU Treaty and not the form of a decision based on Article 34(2) (c).

Nevertheless, the Council ignored the democratic control of the European Parliament and further weakened the Parliament already suffering for its failure to exist as a natural conduit connecting citizens to the European Union.

The UK House of Lords European Union Committee also assailed the undemocratic process that forced the Prüm Treaty upon other Member States. The UK House of Lords European Union Committee published the report Prüm: an effective weapon against terrorism and crime? (18th Report, Session 2006–2007, HL Paper 90) examining the proposals to incorporate the Prüm Treaty into EU law and criticising the German EU Presidency for its failure to allow any opportunity for full consideration of the initiative by all Member States. The Committee criticised that the Council Decision was an initiative of a handful of Member States. The Council Decision extended the application of the Treaty of Prüm, concluded between seven Member States, to the whole EU without allowing for any major revision. As such, the other Member States that were not involved from the beginning of the negotiation have had no chance to shape the choice of rules. Their only choice is to "take-it or leave-it."

The European Data Protection Supervisor also criticised the legislative shortcuts taken by the German Presidency through the EU's complex procedures. The UK House of Lords commented: "The EDPS has said that the parties to the Prüm Treaty have 'evaded the substantive and procedural requirements of enhanced cooperation' and that it is arguable that 'the Prüm Convention breaches the law of the European Union'". (House of Lords 2007, p. 31)

It must be pointed out that an initiative of this significance was adopted on a multi-lateral intergovernmental basis, with a hard core of countries negotiating and signing up to an initiative and leaving the door open for other countries to join later, rather than developing this process through EU channels. This was a way for Germany and its cohorts to push the Treaty through the back door and avoid substantive debate and possible public protest.

EU Commissioner Franco Fratinni threw his weight behind the German initiative. Speaking before the Parliament's Civil Liberties Committee, he declared:

> You either accept Prüm (Treaty) or we (the European Commission) have to make a proposal for enhanced cooperation. (Eurofacts 2007)

In spite of the Commissioner's threat, the fact remains that the German Presidency bypassed the Commission as representative of the community's interest. Had the Decision been a Commission initiative, it would contain an explanatory memorandum and assessment of cost for consideration. (The haste of the German presidency to force its initiative on EU citizens caused it to fail to produce the necessary impact assessment and explanatory memorandum). British officials also expressed several reservations about the plan, in spite of the assurances of the German Interior Minister Wolfgang Schäuble that it had cost Berlin only €930,000, or $1.2 million, to create the database. (Dempsey 2007) The amount is not reassuring given the fact that no actual cost estimates, even for internal purposes, were ever been made by the Member States. The UK Government estimated that the total startup cost for the United Kingdom would be in the region of £31 million pounds for the exchange of fingerprint, DNA and vehicle registration data. (House of Lords p. 24)

The cost is not the real issue. The fundamental point is that community policies, that affect the rights of EU citizens, must be transparent, open to scrutiny and accountable to citizens and their representatives.

13.5 Innocent 'Lambs for Slaughter'

There is no standard EU policy for the collection and retention of the sorts of data to which the Decision (Prüm) pertains. MEP Philip Bradbourn, Conservative Spokesman on Justice and Home Affairs, commented (Conservatives 2007):

> This Treaty fundamentally goes against the rules of data protection and civil liberties that we have come to expect in Europe. This "one size fits all" approach is clearly inapplicable for countries with very different legal traditions and even senior police in the UK have called for this Treaty to be scrapped, proposing that voluntary bilateral agreements between Member States should be the way forward in security co-operation.

The British have legitimate reasons to worry. The most developed database in Europe (and in the world) is the DNA database in the United Kingdom. Set up in 1995 by the Forensic Science Service (FSS), the national DNA Database (NDNAD) of England and Wales is the largest in the world. It contains over 4.5 million profiles. The NDNAD dwarfs other genetic databases in countries with similar populations (such as Germany) and those with significantly larger populations (such as the US). It is the largest database of its kind worldwide in both relative and absolute terms (Application Nos. 30562/04 30566/04 in the European Court of Human Rights 2007). Laws currently allow samples to be taken from anyone suspected of, charged with, reported for or convicted of a recordable offence. At present, DNA samples (intimate or non-intimate can be obtained from:

- Anyone arrested/detained for a recordable offence
- Volunteers (with irrevocable consent)

The NDNAD is unique in that it retains biological information and DNA profiles of individuals on a permanent basis, relating to individuals who have never been may have never been charged or convicted of an offence. No other country has adopted this system. The situation is different in other countries. For instance, in Germany profiles are only held for those who have been convicted of serious offences. Some countries permit the insertion of profiles from all convicted offenders (Austria), but, more frequently, the type of offence (usually serious offences, such as in Belgium, France and Germany) or length of sentence (Holland) is considered. France does not allow the police to take samples without the consent of the targeted person; in other countries, a court order is needed in order to obtain samples (for example, Holland, Luxembourg and Malta). Other countries, Italy, Portugal and Greece, do not have specific laws yet. DNA profiles of convicted offenders are stored for up to 40 years after the conviction in countries Germany, for instance, or for 10 years after the death of the convicted person in Finland. In general, profiles of suspects acquitted or not prosecuted are removed from the database. (Scaffardi 2008)

England and Wales also have the largest fingerprint database (NAFIS) in the world, in relative terms. They are unusual because the law allows them to retain fingerprint information even after acquittal or the removal of charges against a suspect. In most other countries, it is routine for those prints to be destroyed if the individual is not subsequently convicted of a crime. Thus, the current system of safeguards, given the privacy implications of the information contained in samples and profiles, is inadequate in the UK. The purpose of retaining an individual's DNA profile is to treat them as a suspect for future crime.

The implication for innocent people is worrying. According to David Davis, the Shadow Home Secretary,

> The government's track record with IT and database projects is woeful. Take the Home Office. The criminal records bureau wrongly labelled 2,700 innocent people as having criminal records. The sex offenders' register lost more than 300 serious criminals. And the convictions of 27,000 criminals—including murderers, rapists and paedophiles—were left off the police national computer. Finally, the DNA database combines the worst of all worlds: 100,000 innocent children who should never have been on it, 26,000 police-collected samples left off it and half a million entries misrecorded. (Application Nos. 30562/04 30566/04 in the European Court of Human Rights 2007)

The misgivings come down to the citizen's mistrust of the government and the people's fears of an Orwellian future. It has just been made public that there are some 550,000 false misspelt or incorrect names on the existing (UK) database. So, there are fears that the bumbling government cannot be entrusted to keep the data secure. (Woolf 2007) There are also legitimate worries that government could use the DNA records to track down innocent movements, come up with unknown uses and applications for the DNA, or even sell the DNA profiles to insurance companies at some future date.

While DNA assists in solving crimes, the fact remains that 661,433 profiles added in 2007, but crimes detected only rose by 839. (Bloxham 2008; Genewatch 2006) For example, Britain provided some 5,000 DNA profiles to Dutch authorities in a special programme. The profiles brought up two matches of suspected criminals and helped in three other investigations related to murder, robbery and rape.

Since the British government has given its assent to the Prüm Decision, the NDNAD will be open to further cross border access. Other Member States will have access to samples and profiles of innocent persons who have been profiled in the databases. The Decision unfortunately fails to specify the categories of persons that will be included in the databases. Different Member States have different reasons for collecting DNA or different criteria for retaining people's DNA and dactyloscopic files. Many fear that officials of a country holding DNA data for serious crimes only will inevitably start with the presumption that DNA data are held in the

United Kingdom for the same purpose, and perhaps put at risk those whose DNA is held because they have committed only a minor crime, or perhaps no crime at all.

In probably one of the most important human rights cases of all time (*S and M. Marper v. UK*), two British men asked the European Court of Human Rights on February 27, 2008 to have their DNA removed from the national database. Mr. Michael Marper was arrested in 2001 when his former partner accused him of harassment. The charges were dropped, but the police refused to destroy his DNA profile. The other case involves a 19-year-old man, referred to as "S", arrested in the same year when he was only 11, but later acquitted of all charges in court. For 6 years, the two men have fought their respective case all the way to the House of Lords which upheld the government's DNA data retention policy. The two men then complained to the ECHR, who had to rule whether the current system of retaining innocent Britons DNA permanently on the database breaches the rights to privacy.

The ECHR ruled that the retention of the men's DNA "failed to strike a fair balance between the competing public and private interests," and that the UK government "had overstepped any acceptable margin of appreciation in this regard". The court also ruled "the retention in question constituted a disproportionate interference with the applicants' right to respect for private life and could not be regarded as necessary in a democratic society".

Despite the European judges' ruling that the system is illegal, the British government figures showed that more than 300,000 profiles were added between 5 December 2008 and 8 July 2009, equivalent to more than 40,000 a month (Telegraph 2009).

The German Presidency's enthusiasm for the results achieved by matching DNA profiles held in the German database with those held in Austria ignores other problems likely to arise when the same exercise is carried out among 27 Member States. The DNA bases are also characterized by high error rates, due to either fault rates intrinsic to the technologies used or to the lack of police database updates, inter alia in accordance with judicial outcomes of the recorded cases. Sharing such files among 27 countries would certainly increase not only massive surveillance, but also the risk of flaws endangering innocents (Davis 2007).

The absence of a harmonised approach to the collection and retention of data means, for instance, that there will continue to be differences between the criteria on which Member States collect DNA and fingerprints, and the length of time they are allowed to retain these data under their national law. (eGov Monitor 2007) The sensitive personal data of innocent people should not be shared around Europe.

13.6 Data Protection

The Prüm Decision is mainly concerned with the exchange of data and not with collection, storing, domestic processing and supply of personal data. Thus, the collection and retention of data are subject to differing national rules. Although the

Council of the European Union passed a Resolution of 9th June 1996 on the exchange of DNA analysis urging the Member States to set a fix standard criteria for national DNA Database in 2001, there is no standard EU policy for the collection and retention of the sorts of data that the Prüm provisions contains.

This situation inevitably raises data protection issues. As such, the European Data Protection Supervisor should be entitled to have a say in the classes of information that are to be exchanged, the procedures for exchanging them and the safeguards that will apply. However, the Council did not bother to seek the opinion of the European Data Protection Supervisor, even though under Article 41 of Regulation (EC) No 45/2001, the European Data Protection Supervisor is responsible for advising on this initiative since it falls within his competencies.

The European Data Protection Supervisor issued a detailed opinion on the Prüm Decision (2007b). Although he is not opposed to the idea of cooperation between Member States in fighting terrorism, he proposed some amendments to strengthen data protection and privacy. While it is his opinion that the draft Council Decision offers in substance an appropriate protection, he nevertheless opposed it as it would rely on local and possibly inconsistent data protection laws. There is presently no general rule on data protection in the Third Pillar. The current Data Protection Directive is only binding in the First Pillar.

Although the Council Decision refers to the Council of Europe Convention for the Protection of Individuals with regard to Automatic Processing of Personal Data of 28 January 1981 and its Additional Protocol of 8 November 2001, it is not precise. The Council of Europe Convention 108 states that the purpose for the supply of information must be respected and that the data subject has the right to know the information about him and can claim and receive damages for inaccurate information. The subject of police investigation in a particular case had a right to know the information held, not just a right to know if they ask, a right to be told it had been collected even if it was not used.

The European Data Protection Supervisor emphasized that the Prüm Decision should build on a general framework of data protection in the Third Pillar, and should not be adopted before the adoption of a framework on data protection guaranteeing an appropriate level of data protection.

The harmonization of data protection laws under the Third Pillar would harmonise national laws. A legal framework for data protection is a *condicio sine qua non* for the exchange of personal data by law enforcement authorities, as is required by Article 30 (1) (b) of the EU Treaty, and recognised in several EU policy documents (Opinion of the Data Protection Supervisor 2007).

The Data Protection Supervisor further stated:

> The initiative relies on the presupposition that matching DNA profiles is the key instrument in police cooperation. For this reason, all Member States have to establish DNA databases for the purposes of criminal justice. Taking into account the costs of these databases and the risks from the perspective of data protection, a thorough ex ante assessment is needed of the effectiveness of this instrument. (Ibid)

The Framework Decision on the protection of personal data processed in the framework of police and judicial cooperation in criminal matters was passed and adopted by the Council and published in the Official Journal on 30 December 2008. It is the first general data protection instrument in the EU Third Pillar. However, the Framework Decision in respect of the data protection provisions governing the automated transfer between Member States of DNA profiles, dactyloscopic data and national vehicle registration data pursuant to the Council Decision 2008/615/JHA of 23 June 2008 is excluded from the Framework Decision.

The Prüm Decision is not covered under the Oviedo Convention, which guarantees against discrimination regarding any biomedical research involving intervention on the person. The (Protocol) Convention states, "any form of discrimination against a person based on genetic heritage is prohibited" (Article 11).

The Justice Committee of the UK House of Commons just issued on 3 January 2008 a report on public data protection since the Chancellor announced to Parliament in November 2007 that HMRC had lost confidential records affecting 25 million UK citizens. The report expresses Parliament's apprehension about the risks associated with big databases containing personal data that are open to large numbers of licensed users, as well as with the obligation to share the data under the Prüm Decision. The House of Commons Justice report (2008) stated:

> Linked to issues of adequacy of data protection in the UK is the matter of data exchange and protection at EU level in the context of greater interoperability of Government databases, which the UK Government and those of other EU member states aspire to. The EU Framework Decisions incorporating the Prüm Treaty into EU law and establishing the 'principle of availability' of Government-held information between EU member state authorities will have a direct impact on the protection of data of UK citizens held by the UK Government. If data held by the Government is available for inspection outside the jurisdiction, then the importance of restricting the amount of data held, as well as proper policing of who had access to it, takes on even greater importance.

The report also recommends that personal data should be held only where there are proper safeguards for the protection of the respective data, which, in the Justice Committee's opinion will become ever more difficult as data can be easily shared within the country as well as between countries.

13.7 Conclusion

It is important that law enforcement authorities in the European Union have the tools available to obtain information held by other EU countries as quickly as possible to help with the investigation and prevention of crime. While there is indeed a legitimate reason to exploit the full potential of databases to combat terrorism and combat serious crimes, it should not be used as a rationale for adopting such measures behind hidden doors and bereft of a national debate. What is appalling is the way a few Member States led by the German Presidency made agreements, with limited or inadequate protections for their own citizens, and then forced it on other Member States.

While it is normal for Germany to use the Presidency to promote legislative proposals, it should not be a reason for cutting short full consideration of the Member States, sidelining the European Data Protection Supervisor's opinion and ignoring the views of the European Parliament.

The most appalling aspect of this process is the lack of democratic control and protection of data privacy. The German presidency—with not even a pang of conscience—felt free to increase its investigative and police hegemony over the other Member States. This is the kind of lapse that wills nations' collapse. *It is just sheer tastelessness. It is just sheer greediness. It is pure arrogance.*

The attempt to subvert legitimate resistance in other countries, through striking a special agreement with some of the Member States, is being described in the German press as a novelty in the European integration process. It is being voiced, that this is opening the possibility of enforcing numerous legal norms, in spite of their far reaching consequences, without ratification by the entire EU (European Achievement 2007).

This is a dangerous precedent. *Privacy has become subservient to security.*

Acknowledgments An earlier extended version of this article was published in Computer Law and Security Report, Vol. 24, Issue 3, 2008, Pages 243–252.

References

Application Nos. 30562/04 30566/04 in the European Court of Human Rights. 2007. Application Nos. 30562/04 30566/04 in the European Court of Human Rights (March 15, 2007). http://www.poptel.org.uk/statewatch/news/2007/nov/echr-marper-submissions-15-03-07-final.pdf. Retrieved 27 Jan 2008.

Bloxham, Andy. May 2008. DNA bank solves one crime per 800 profiles. *Telegraph.* http://www.telegraph.co.uk/news/uknews/1929849/DNA-bank-solves-one-crime-per-800-profiles.html.

Conservatives. June 7, 2007. EU Constitution moves in by the back door. *Conservatives.* http://www.conservatives.com/tile.do?def=wales.news.story.page&obj_id=137043. Retrieved 27 Jan 2008.

Council Decision. 2008. Council Decision 2008/615/JHA. Also available online at http://eur-lex.europa.eu/LexUriServ/LexUriServ.do?uri=OJ:L:2008:210:0001:0011:EN:PDF.

Davis, D. 2007. Beware the state's ID card sharks (Dec. 30, 2007). *Sunday Times Online.* http://www.timesonline.co.uk/tol/comment/columnists/guest_contributors/article3108069.ece. Retrieved 27 Jan 2008.

Dempsey, J. June 15, 2007. Germany seeks to modernize policing across EU. *International Herald Tribune.* http://www.iht.com/articles/2007/01/15/news/germany.php. Retrieved 26 Jan 2007.

Draft European Parliament Legislative Resolution. 2008. *Draft European parliament legislative resolution: Report* 2, April 2008. Also available online at http://www.europarl.europa.eu/sides/getDoc.do?language=EN&reference=A6-0099/2008.

eGov Monitor. 2007. Home affairs ministers back initiative to create a pan-European network of police databases for more effective crime control. *eGov Monitor.* (January 18, 2007). http://www.egovmonitor.com/node/9093. Retrieved 27 Jan 2008.

European Achievement. 2007. *German-Foreign-Policy.com*; 1/17/2007. Also available online in its entirety at http://ftrsupplemental.blogspot.com/2007/01/european-achievement.html.

European Parliament legislative resolution. 2007. European Parliament legislative resolution on the initiative by the Kingdom of Belgium, the Republic of Bulgaria, the Federal Republic of Germany, the Kingdom of Spain, the French Republic, the Grand Duchy of Luxembourg, the Kingdom of the Netherlands, the Republic of Austria, the Republic of Slovenia, the Slovak Republic, the Italian Republic, the Republic of Finland, the Portuguese Republic, Romania and the Kingdom of Sweden on the stepping up of cross-border cooperation, particularly in combating terrorism and cross-border crime (6566/2007—C6-0079/2007—2007/0804(CNS)) (June 7, 2007). http://www.europarl.europa.eu/sides/getDoc.do?type=TA&language=EN&reference=P6-TA-2007-0228. Retrieved 27 Jan 2008.

Eurofacts. 9 February 2007. Slimmed down treaty: The greatest threat to UK. *Eurofacts.* http://www.junepress.com/PDF/Vol%2012%20No%20%209%20-%209th%20February%202007.pdf. Retrieved 27 Jan 2008.GeneWatch. 2006. Would 114 murderers have walked away if innocent people's records were removed from the National DNA Database? *GeneWatch.* http://www.genewatch.org/uploads/f03c6d66a9b354535738483c1c3d49e4/brown.pdf.

House of Commons Justice report. 2008. House of commons. http://www.publications.parliament.uk/pa/cm200708/cmselect/cmjust/154/15402.htm. Retrieved 28 Jan 2008.

House of Lords. 9 May 2007. Prüm: An effective weapon against terrorism and crime? *Statewatch.* http://www.statewatch.org/news/2007/may/eu-hol-prum-report.pdf. Retrieved 27 June 2008.

Parliamentary Report. 2007. Parliamentary Report on the initiative by the Kingdom of Belgium, the Republic of Bulgaria, the Federal Republic of Germany, the Kingdom of Spain, the French Republic, the Grand Duchy of Luxembourg, the Kingdom of the Netherlands, the Republic of Austria, the Republic of Slovenia, the Slovak Republic, the Italian Republic, the Republic of Finland, the Portuguese Republic, Romania and the Kingdom of Sweden on the stepping up of cross-border cooperation, particularly in combating terrorism and cross-border crime. (6566/2007—C6-0079/2007—2007/0804(CNS)) (May 24, 2007). http://www.europarl.europa.eu/sides/getDoc.do?type=REPORT&mode=XML&reference=A6-2007-0207&language=EN#_part2_def1_part2_def1. Retrieved 27 Jan 2008.

Scaffardi, Lucia. 2008. Legal protection and management of genetic databases: Challenges of the European process of harmonisation. Jean Monnet Working Paper 19/08. European Union.

Telegraph. 14 July 2009. DNA database expanding by 40,000 profiles a month. *Telegraph.* http://www.telegraph.co.uk/news/newstopics/politics/lawandorder/5827457/DNA-database-expanding-by-40000-profiles-a-month.htmlchaos.

The European Data Protection Supervisor. 2007a. Opinion of the European Data Protection Supervisor on the Initiative of the Kingdom of Belgium, the Republic of Bulgaria, the Federal Republic of Germany, the Kingdom of Spain, the French Republic, the Grand Duchy of Luxembourg, the Kingdom of the Netherlands, the Republic of Austria, the Republic of Slovenia, the Slovak Republic, the Italian Republic, the Republic of Finland, the Portuguese Republic, Romania and the Kingdom of Sweden, with a view to adopting a Council Decision on the stepping up of cross-border cooperation, particularly in combating terrorism and cross-border crime (2007/C 169/02). Also available online at http://www.edps.europa.eu/EDPSWEB/webdav/site/mySite/shared/Documents/Consultation/Opinions/2007/07-04-04_crossborder_cooperation_EN.pdf.

The European Data Protection Supervisor. 2007b. Opinion of the European Data Protection Supervisor on the Initiative of the Kingdom of Belgium, the Republic of Bulgaria, the Federal Republic of Germany, the Kingdom of Spain, the French Republic, the Grand Duchy of Luxembourg, the Kingdom of the Netherlands, the Republic of Austria, the Republic of Slovenia, the Slovak Republic, the Italian Republic, the Republic of Finland, the Portuguese Republic, Romania and the Kingdom of Sweden, with a view to adopting a Council Decision on the stepping up of cross-border cooperation, particularly in combating terrorism and cross-border crime, Council of the European Union, Brussels, 20 April 2007, 8656/07. Also available online at http://www.edps.europa.eu/EDPSWEB/webdav/shared/Documents/Consultation/Opinions/2007/07-04-04_crossborder_cooperation_EN.pdf

Woolf, M. 2007. DNA database with 500,000 false or misspelt entries. *The Independent.* http://www.independent.co.uk/news/uk/politics/dna-database-chaos-with-500000-false-or-misspelt-entries-463055.html. Retrieved 3 Sept 2009.

Part IV
Technology Assessment Views

Chapter 14
Information Privacy in Europe from a TA Perspective

Walter Peissl

14.1 Introduction

Information and communication technologies are spreading everywhere and are applied increasingly in almost every area of daily life. This leads to a dramatic rise in the potential for privacy infringements. At present we use PC, Internet, PDAs, mobile phones, credit and debit cards and other devices in our electronic environment. In the near future we will be faced with the "Internet of things" (ITU 2005; Commission of the *European* Communities 2009), almost any object around us will be equipped with electronic capabilities, enabling them to store data and to contact a wider network. Thus, those objects not only will be able to observe the environment and the individuals within, but there is an opportunity for control also. This vision is often described as ubiquitous or pervasive computing. The technological basis for this "Internet of things"—RFID technology—is already out there.

Beyond these technological developments there are political trends towards enhancing societal security by way of increased surveillance.[1] Business also appreciates the most comprehensive data gathering possible of their customers. Monitoring the entire delivery system as well as the consumers' behaviour helps to optimize logistics and the product range, resulting in reduced costs and increased profits. Both "the war against terror" and the search for perfect marketing strategies seem to be diminishing fundamental rights.

But the discussion on privacy is not only about "rights"; it's also about the philosophy of autonomy and freedom and, hence, about basic pillars of liberal democracy (Rössler 2001; Pauer-Studer 2003). Following (Rössler 2001, p. 25) privacy

[1] For a brief discussion of different approaches towards "security", the historical development and recent EU-policy in this field see: (Raguse et al. 2008). Further reading: (Daase et al. 2002; ÖAW 2005; Study Group on Europe's Security Capabilities 2004; Hayes 2006; Eriksson and Giacomello 2007; von Bredow 2005; Council of Europe 2003).

W. Peissl (✉)
Institute of Technology Assessment, Austrian Academy of Sciences, Vienna, Austria
e-mail: wpeissl@oeaw.ac.at

S. Gutwirth et al. (eds.), *Data Protection in a Profiled World*,
DOI 10.1007/978-90-481-8865-9_14, © Springer Science+Business Media B.V. 2010

may be defined as the possibility to control the access of others to oneself. It can be split into three dimensions: first, the dimension of private decisions and actions ("dezisionale Privatheit"), which means that the individual has control over his/her own decisions and is (relatively) free of heteronomy. The second dimension is called local privacy ("lokale Privatheit"), which means that the individual has control over rooms and spaces such as the own residence. Information privacy ("informationelle Privatheit"), the third dimension, deals with the knowledge and control of information about oneself. Beyond this "privacy paradigm" (Bennett and Raab 2003) we can see a tendency towards a "surveillance society" (Wood et al. 2006) that imposes other threats to individuals, such as categorisation and social sorting (Lyon 2003).

The actual EPTA project on "ICT and privacy in Europe" dealt mainly with information privacy and some aspects of surveillance. The most important means to ensure information privacy are policy instruments on data protection. They evolved from a long discussion starting in the 1960s and 1970s of the twentieth century (Bennett 2003). Today, a broad range of policy instruments have been established, which include trans-national policy instruments such as the Convention for the Protection of Individuals with regard to Automatic Processing of Personal Data (Convention 108) (Council of Europe (CoE) 1981), the OECD Guidelines on the Protection of Privacy and Transborder Flows of Personal Data (OECD 1980) or the European Union's Directive on the protection of individuals with regard to the processing of personal data and on the free movement of such data (European Parliament and Council 1995). The European directive was a strong impetus for establishing laws on data protection and other legal instruments on a national basis. Meanwhile, all EU member states have implemented the directive through national law (Commission of the European Communities 2007). Apart from this strong legal framework there is a set of self-regulatory and technological instruments (Bennett and Raab 2003).

The project aimed at answering the question how technology assessment could contribute to preserving the fundamental right to privacy or—if necessary—which adaptations to the existing regulation might be necessary. To answer this question, six European technology assessment institutions established the first common European Parliamentary Technology Assessment (EPTA) project. The "ICT and Privacy in Europe" project analysed 28 TA reports submitted by these institutions. Since many of them use different approaches and methodologies, the basic material for the study was rather heterogeneous. Furthermore, attitudes towards privacy differ depending on the national, cultural and political context. In spite of this heterogeneity it was possible to define a common framework of "trade-offs" and to derive policy options.

14.2 About EPTA

European Parliamentary Technology Assessment is a network of institutions that advise their respective national or regional parliaments on the possible social, economic and environmental impact of new sciences and technologies. Technology Assessment (TA) is an interdisciplinary endeavour to provide impartial and high quality accounts and reports on developments in issues such as bioethics and biotechnology, public health, environment and energy, ICTs, and R&D policy. The concept emerged from a discussion on the democratic control of scientific and technological innovation. Over the 1970s, the US Congress's Office of Technology Assessment (OTA) pioneered its implementation but discontinued it in the mid-1990s.

Today, TA bodies flourish in Europe mainly. They are institutionalized in many different ways and use a broad variety of methodological approaches (Vig and Paschen 2000). Some of them are more scientifically oriented and apply a broad array of methods derived from the social sciences, including desktop research, document and literature analysis as well as expert interviews. Other EPTA-members are more engaged in discursive methods and participatory approaches such as focus groups, lay people involvement in different forms and stakeholder events (Peissl 1999).[2]

EPTA aims to advance the establishment of technology assessment as an integral part of policy consulting in parliamentary decision-making processes in Europe, and to strengthen the links between TA units in Europe. (EPTA 2008). At present, EPTA has its members in Catalonia (Spain), Denmark, Finland, Flanders (Belgium), France, Germany, Greece, Italy, the Netherlands, Norway, Switzerland, the United Kingdom and the European Parliament. Associated members are from Austria, Belgium, Sweden and the Council of Europe.[3]

14.3 ICT and Privacy in Europe: The First Common EPTA Project

Many EPTA members conducted TA-studies on ICT and their societal consequences in their respective home countries. In most of these studies, privacy and data protection proved to be one of the main concerns in the social and political analysis. The idea of the first common EPTA project was to bundle the knowledge generated in the national studies and to look for common grounds.

Apart from the privacy-oriented aim to derive policy options from an analysis of existing TA-projects, the second objective of the project was to figure out whether or not it would be possible to take advantage of the diversity of the underlying projects and approaches[4] and so to create added value for both national and European policy and decision makers by applying a problem-oriented approach.

[2] For a theoretical analysis of participatory TA in Europe and a comprehensive overview of participatory methods used in Technology Assessment see (Joss and Bellucci 2002; Stef Steyaert and Hervé Lisoir 2005).

[3] For further information on EPTA and especially on the TA projects undertaken by its members, please refer to the EPTA website at http://www.eptanetwork.org/EPTA/.

[4] Methods used in the underlying projects were: desktop research, expert interviews, citizens' panels, consensus conferences, desktop research, expert panels/work groups and focus group studies (Klüver 2006, p. 103ff).

In summer 2004, six institutions[5] decided to set up a 2-year analytical project (Peissl 2005). At the time, EPTA was a rather lightweight network of institutions for information and knowledge transfer only. This project was the first attempt to become operational as a network. Some of the members already had common working experience in several EU-funded projects on the theory and methodology of Technology Assessment.

In addition to the above objective, the project was also meant to increase EPTA's visibility at European level as well as to strengthen internal relations. It provided an opportunity for the participants to learn from each other and create added value for both the TA community and decision makers.

A total of 28 projects from six partners were analysed. A particular challenge was finding a way, how to deal with the heterogeneity of the basic material. Partners used different approaches and methods—from classical methods in the social sciences to the more discourse-oriented methods for lay people and stakeholder participation.

Not only the methodological orientation but also the institutional settings differed. Some EPTA members are part of their respective Parliament; others are independent but work for Parliament, while some are academic institutions at a distance from political bodies.

An additional influencing parameter emerged from the cultural and political diversity of the project members' home countries and the attitudes towards privacy in the respective national contexts.

14.3.1 Methodology of the Project

From a methodological point of view the main challenge was to find a common analytical framework for the different project reports. In a first step all projects were presented and described according to a common scheme. It consisted of a short description of the project and its outcome as well as bibliographic information and links to the longer official project descriptions or other related sites. These project descriptions provided the common knowledge base for the analysis.

The whole set of project descriptions was reviewed, clustered and analysed. The aim was to find similarities and differences as well as key aspects the projects had in common. It turned out that thinking in "trade-offs" that affect attitudes and behaviour with regard to safeguarding the citizens' privacy could be a valuable tool. Five trade-offs were used as starting points for the discussion. However, it emerged that most of the trade-offs or underlying dilemmas can be overcome by organisational, legal or technical measures. These measures contributed to the policy options in the end of the report.

The most prominent trade-off seems to be that between privacy and security. It is often perceived that widespread surveillance only can achieve higher security, and

[5] Teknologirådet (Denmark), Teknologirådet (Norway), the UK Parliamentary Office of Science and Technology (POST), ViwTA from Flanders, TA-SWISS and ITA from Austria.

that there must be a trade-off between privacy and security therefore. The report addressed and challenged this perception.

The second trade-off is between privacy and access. In order to be able to fully take part in economic and social life in modern societies it is of increasing importance to gain access to ICTs and services. By deploying them users leave information traces and often give away personal data. The question is how we can ensure access to important ICT systems and services in a secure and privacy-friendly way.

There is another trade-off between privacy and societal interaction. The use of social networks changes the way social interactions are organised; it opens new possibilities but also bears threats to privacy. The challenge is to design systems that allow for a way of using the system in a "privacy aware" way. Another necessary endeavour is to render the users aware of the importance of privacy.

Convenience is important for individual users. In order to be flexible and mobile many use mobile phones, which are devices that generate a lot of personal data. In order to get easy access to certain websites we accept cookies. These technologies gather personal data and many people are willing to trade in their privacy for increased convenience. Again the challenge is to overcome an apparent zero-sum game thinking and to find solutions in technical, organisational and legal terms, which can increase both, convenience and privacy.

Finally, economic benefit may be seen as counteracting privacy. ICTs are used in business processes in order to increase efficiency or to create new economic opportunities. Personal data in this respect may well be seen as a source of economic benefit. Optimising logistics and the range of goods provided may increase profits, but it often does so for the price of reducing the users' privacy. Possible strategies to overcome this dilemma may be seen in higher user awareness and self-regulation schemes like privacy seals.

The analysis of the trade-offs followed a common scheme, too. In a first step, the "issue at stake" was discussed. Subsequently, three different subchapters described "technological, social and economic and political and legislative developments". Each of them ended with concluding remarks. They served as a basis for the final conclusions and policy options derived from the analysis of the different trade-offs.

14.3.2 Outcome

The project findings were presented in a final report (Klüver 2006). It featured a description of the technological trends that might affect privacy, such as the digitalisation of telecommunication systems, mobile services, the Internet, pervasive computing and privacy enhancing technologies (Cas 2006), followed by a discussion of the legal situation in Europe (Peissl 2006). Seven chapters dealt with the above trade-offs, and two with areas of application of ICTs where privacy infringements can be anticipated and where European policy is promotive: e-Health and e-government. The report also provides a short overview of the projects described, a section on the methods used in the primary projects and, as the main result, seven challenges for future policy in the field. For each challenge policy options are presented on how to deal with the challenges at national or European level.

The challenges and policy options were derived from the discussion of the trade-offs. In a final international expert workshop, group discussion results were contrasted with the opinions of external experts. The final results were presented to the public in a policy workshop in Brussels.

14.3.3 Some Findings

As more and more areas of daily life are supported by ICTs the users leave an increasing amount of electronic traces. It is almost impossible for individuals to oversee the amount of personal data generated, stored and analysed. And because systems do not forget, these data remain for a very long time. Hence, today's behaviour may have unintended and unexpected implications for an individual's future. The authors consider it necessary to devise erasing routines for older data, e.g. built-in expiry dates.

Another phenomenon is the discrepancy between short-term gains and possible long-term effects. The drive for rationalisation and efficiency entails increased ICT use, data storage and procession. Short-term gains in terms of cost reduction or higher turnover can be realised more or less immediately. The long-term costs of privacy impairment cannot be assessed directly; neither can the social costs of widespread surveillance be easily calculated. In the end, the latter may lead to mainstreaming peoples' behaviour and, subsequently, to a loss of momentum in social change (Peissl 2003). This results in an underestimation of the value of privacy and consequently to a low awareness among the public and on the political agenda.

There is a great divide in knowledge about possible usage and economic value of personal data between the individual users and professional parties setting up complex IT systems. Because of the complexity of new systems, the asymmetry of knowledge and the need for privacy, the government should take responsibility to strengthen the "privacy culture" by encouraging privacy enhancing system design. This could be done by promoting privacy seals or by giving privacy-oriented or even certified products and services a competitive advantage in public procurement processes.

The development of ICT is an irreversible phenomenon in many ways. This means that the poorly designed ICT products of today could affect privacy in 10 or 20 years time. For this reason a precautionary approach has to be applied. This, however, does not mean that the development of ICT has to be halted; rather, it implies the necessity of finding a balance. Such a sound balance must be built upon a precautionary approach as exercised by users, developers as well as policy-makers, in order to reduce the risk of privacy infringement to a minimum. One step towards adopting the precautionary principle may be to create awareness and to trigger a broad social dialogue on the impacts of the widespread use of ICT or of pervasive computing.

14.3.4 The Challenges: and How to Deal with Them

This final section presents a short overview of the challenges to privacy, and the policy options that could be considered in response to these challenges.

In the wake of the attacks on 9/11 in New York, privacy has been considered an obstacle to security. Although recent studies (Raguse et al. 2008) show that privacy and security are not strictly linked as in a zero-sum game the *most prominent challenge is still to provide security without infringing privacy.*

The real benefit of surveillance systems for security is not always indubitable. Therefore, surveillance systems should only be implemented if likely to be effective, not easily circumvented and if they can be shown to create a real security benefit. In addition, these systems should undergo periodic evaluation.

The *second challenge arises from ongoing e-government initiatives*, which render citizens more transparent to the authorities. Policy options addressing the privacy infringing potential of e-government systems include measures to empower citizens to provide genuinely informed consent. The exchange of data between various administrative agencies in e-government should strictly follow the principle of being purpose bound and should only be carried out after a formal request for the disclosure of personal data has been issued. In order to provide more transparency for the citizens, they should have easy access to their own records and even to the log files containing information on who has created, seen, changed, forwarded, or received information regarding the respective citizen.

Challenge three is a consequence of the enforcement of privacy legislation being too weak. This is due to the fact that many data protection authorities lack sufficient resources. Both the mandate and the resources available to data protection authorities should be increased to enable them to fulfil their tasks. Sanctions and penalties for the misuse of personal data should be high enough to discourage individuals and institutions from ignoring privacy rules.

The fourth challenge relates to systems development neglecting privacy. Accordingly, policy should encourage, where possible, data minimisation and privacy enhancing system designs. Making privacy impact assessment mandatory could help. Especially in the public sector, privacy impact assessments should become a prerequisite for procurements. Furthermore, there is a need for more international privacy standards. Such standards are a prerequisite for developing privacy-compliant IT systems. National standard bodies, ISO, trade associations, relevant European and national ministries and data protection authorities should take part in the development of pertinent standards. Another way to strengthen privacy-oriented systems design is to encourage research in the field and to make privacy part of the funding criteria for ICT research.

The fifth challenge is that private bodies still underestimate privacy. There is little understanding among private enterprises that respecting privacy may enhance consumer trust, produce consumer loyalty and may well be an asset leading to a competitive advantage in global trade. In order to promote trust in privacy-friendly IT systems the report suggested the policy option that data protection authorities should issue a privacy label. Meanwhile, the European Privacy Seal[6] has been created and already been granted to a number of products or services.

Challenge six is to create privacy policies based on research. Effective regulation is based on knowledge. Few of the possible medium and long-term effects of data collection and analysis are already apparent. To meet this challenge it will be necessary to explore the trends in technological development and its legislative implications. In particular, there is a need to encourage research on the social consequences of increased data retention. Overall, this should contribute to a better understanding of the consequences of widespread surveillance. Based on this and supported by a broad public discourse on the issue a need for adapting the existing regulation could arise.[7]

New technological developments will pose new challenges for privacy. Pervasive computing is the vision of networked processors, communicating with each other to perform defined tasks. In order to function, such pervasive systems will require the collection of huge amounts of data on their environment. Hence *challenge seven* arises from the expectation that *future pervasive systems will multiply the challenges to privacy.* A regulatory approach for dealing with such future challenges is the development of "Systems data protection" (ULD 2006). This includes all techno-organisational measures that support informational self-determination and adopt principles of privacy enhancing systems design at an early stage. The Canadian approach of "Privacy by Design" (Cavoukian 2009) builds on a similar method but is more market-oriented. It may nevertheless be supported by regulations that demand to check for privacy relevant features of the technology to be developed on several occasions throughout the IT system design process. In order to provide users a possibility to observe what is happening, it seems necessary to make pervasive systems visible, to ensure that log-on and switch-off remain possible alternatives, and—as a necessary further step—to create IT-free zones for retreat.

References

Bennett, C.J. 2003. Information privacy and "Datenschutz": Global assumptions and international governance. In *Privacy: Ein Grundrecht mit Ablaufdatum? Interdisziplinäre Beiträge zur Grundrechtsdebatte*, ed. W. Peissl, 61–81. Wien: Verlag der Österreichische Akademie der Wissenschaften.

Bennett, C.J., and C.D. Raab. 2003. *The governance of privacy.* Aldershot: Ashgate.

von Bredow, W. 2005. The Barcelona report on a Human Security Doctrine for Europe, overview and some critical remarks. *Berlin Symposium on Human Security and EU-Canada Relations Canadian Universities' Centre Berlin.* March 3, Berlin.

Cas, J. 2006. Technologies that affect privacy. In *ICT and privacy in Europe: A report on different aspects of privacy based on studies made by EPTA members in 7 European countries*, eds. L.

[6] https://www.european-privacy-seal.eu/.

[7] Web 2.0 applications and their consequences for future generations are one example, and are now being dealt with at national and international level.

Klüver, W. Peissl, T. Tennøe, D. Bütschi, J. Cas, R. Deboelpaep, C. Hafskjold et al. 19–24. EPTA. Copenhagen/Oslo/Vienna. http://epub.oeaw.ac.at/ita/ita-projektberichte/e2-2a44.pdf.
Cavoukian, A. 2009. *Privacy by design ... take the challenge.* Toronto: Information and Privacy Commisioner of Ontario, Canada. http://www.privacybydesign.ca/pbdbook/PrivacybyDesign-Book.pdf.
Commission of the European Communities. 2007. COM(2007) 87 final. Communication from the Commission to the European Parliament and the Council on the follow-up of the Work Programme for better implementation of the Data Protection Directive. http://ec.europa.eu/justice_home/fsj/privacy/docs/lawreport/com_2007_87_f_en.pdf. Accessed 7 September 2009.
Commission of the European Communities. 2009. COM(2009) 278 final. Communication from the Commission to the European Parliament and the Council, the European Economic and Social Committee and the Committee of the Regions: Internet of Things: —An action plan for Europe; Last update: Brussels, 18.6.2009. http://ec.europa.eu/information_society/policy/rfid/documents/commiot2009.pdf. Accessed 7 September 2009.
Council of Europe (CoE). 1981. Convention for the protection of individuals with regard to automatic processing of personal data (Convention 108), Strasbourg, 28.I.1981. http://conventions.coe.int/Treaty/EN/Treaties/Html/108.htm.
Council of Europe (CoE). 2003. Convention for the protection of human rights and fundamental freedoms as amended by Protocol No. 11 with Protocol Nos. 1, 4, 6, 7, 12 and 13. http://www.echr.coe.int/ECHR/EN/Header/Basic±Texts/Basic±Texts/The±European±Convention±on±Human±Rights±and±its±Protocols/.
Daase, C., S. Feske, and I. Peters, eds. 2002. *Internationale Risikopolitik: Der Umgang mit neuen Gefahren in den internationalen Beziehungen.* Baden-Baden: Nomos Verlag.
David, Murakami Wood, ed. 2006. *A Report on the surveillance society*, by Ball, K., D. Lyon, C. Norris, and C. Raab, commissioned by: Information Commissioner. September 2006, London. www.ico.gov.uk/.../surveillance_society_full_report_2006.pdf.
EPTA (European Parliamenty Technology Assessment). 2008. About EPTA. http://www.eptanetwork.org/EPTA/about.php. Accessed 19 May 2009.
Eriksson, J., and G. Giacomello, eds. 2007. *International relations and security in the digital age.* Routlegde Advances in International Relations and Global Politics. Oxford: Routledge.
European Parliament and Council. 1995. Directive 95/46/EC of the European Parliament and of the Council of 24 October 1995 on the protection of individuals with regard to the processing of personal data and on the free movement of such data. http://europa.eu.int/smartapi/cgi/sga_doc?smartapi!celexapi!prod!CELEXnumdoc&lg=EN&numdoc=31995L0046&model=guichett.
Hayes, B. 2006. *Arming big brother: The EU's security research programme.* No. TNI Briefing series 2006/1. Amsterdam: Transnational Institute.
ITU. 2005. IITU internet reports 2005: The internet of things: Executive summary. www.itu.int/dms_pub/itu-s/opb/pol/S-POL-IR.IT-2005-SUM-PDF-E.pdf. Accessed 07 September 2009.
Joss, S., and S. Bellucci, eds. 2002. *Participatory technology assessment. European perspectives*, edited by CSD. London: Centre for the Study of Democracy (Centre for the Study of Democracy and Swiss Centre for Technology Assessment).
Klüver, L., W. Peissl, T. Tennøe, D. Bütschi, J. Cas, R. Deboelpaep, C. Hafskjold, et al. 2006. *ICT and privacy in Europe: A report on different aspects of privacy based on studies made by EPTA members in 7 European countries*, 16 October 2006. EPTA. Copenhagen/Oslo/Vienna. http://epub.oeaw.ac.at/ita/ita-projektberichte/e2-2a44.pdf.
Lyon, D., ed. 2003. *Surveillance as social sorting. Privacy, risk and digital discrimination.* London: Routledge.
ÖAW. 2005. *Sicherheitsforschung, Begriffsfassung und Vorgangsweise für Österreich.* Vienna: ÖAW.
OECD. 1980. *Guidelines on the protection of privacy and transborder flows of personal data.* OECD, 23 September 1980. http://www.oecd.org/document/20/0,2340,en_2649_33703_15589524_1_1_1_37409,00.html.

Pauer-Studer, H. 2003. Privatheit: ein ambivalenter aber unverzichtbarer Wert. In *Privacy: ein Grundrecht mit Ablaufdatum? Interdisziplinäre Beiträge zur Grundrechtsdebatte*, ed. W. Peissl, 9–22. Wien: Verlag der Österreichische Akademie der Wissenschaften.

Peissl, W. 1999. Parlamentarische Technikfolgen-Abschätzung in Europa. In *Handbuch der Technikfolgen-Abschätzung*, eds. S. Bröchler et al., 469–478, 2nd ed. Berlin: Edition Sigma.

Peissl, W. 2003. Surveillance and security: A dodgy relationship. *Journal of Contingencies and Crisis Management* 11 (1 March 2003): 19–24.

Peissl, W. 2005. ICT and privacy: Das erste gemeinsame EPTA-Projekt, *Technikfolgen-Abschätzung: Theorie und Praxis* 14 (2): 88–91.

Peissl, W. 2006. Legislation: Current situation and recent developments. In *ICT and privacy in Europe: A report on different aspects of privacy based on studies made by EPTA members in 7 European countries*, eds. L. Klüver, W. Peissl, T. Tennøe, D. Bütschi, J. Cas, R. Deboelpaep, C. Hafskjold et al., 26–31. EPTA. Copenhagen/Oslo/Vienna. http://epub.oeaw.ac.at/ita/ita-projektberichte/e2-2a44.pdf.

Raguse, M., M. Meints, O. Langfeldt, and P. Walter. 2008. *PRISE D6.2: Criteria for privacy enhancing security technologies.* Commissioned by: European Commission PASR. Vienna: Institute of Technology Assessment Austrian Academy of Sciences. http://prise.oeaw.ac.at/docs/PRISE_D_6.2_Criteria_for_privacy_enhancing_security_technologies.pdf.

Rössler, B. 2001. *Der Wert des Privaten.* Frankfurt am Main: Suhrkamp (Philosophie an der Universität von Amsterdam).

Stef, Steyaert, and Hervé, Lisoir, eds. 2005. *Participatory Methods Toolkit: A practitioner's manual.* Brussels: King Baudouin Foundation and the Flemish Institute for Science and Technology Assessment (viWTA). http://www.viwta.be/files/30890_ToolkitENGdef.pdf.

Study Group on Europe's Security Capabilities. 2004. *A human security doctrine for Europe the barcelona report of the study group on Europe's security capabilities presented to EU High representative for common foreign and security policy Javier Solana*, 15 September 2004. Barcelona: Study group on Europe's security capabilities. http://www.lse.ac.uk/Depts/global/Publications/HumanSecurityDoctrine.pdf.

ULD. 2006. *Systemdatenschutz.* ULD.https://www.datenschutzzentrum.de/systemdatenschutz/index.htm. Accessed 7 September 2009.

Vig, N.J., and H. Paschen, eds. 2000. *Parliaments and technology.* Albany, USA: State Univ. New York Press.

Chapter 15
Privacy and Security: A Brief Synopsis of the Results of the European TA-Project PRISE

Johann Čas

15.1 Introduction

Technical progress in information and communication technologies and the increasing pervasiveness of these technologies in everyday life taken alone are already sufficient for an immense increase in the amount of generated personal data. New sensor technologies and biometric identification make it possible to collect personal data without the active contribution or even notice of the persons concerned. Permanently increasing storage capacities and processing capabilities offer the opportunity to store this data for virtually unlimited periods, to link the created data bases with each other and to analyse them with ever more efficient algorithms. Consequently, the fundamental right of respect for privacy is under increasing pressure; economic interests, the promise of improved private and public services and security concerns encourage excessive use of these increasing technical capabilities.

The tragic terrorist events of September 2001 and subsequent terrorist attacks in Europe considerably increased the political interest in issues of public security and induced the development of new security concepts and strategies. Frequently they attributed a clearly higher value to security aspects than to fundamental and human rights. In recent years Europe has seen the development of new security technologies and the implementation of measures that are assumed to increase the security of the citizens, but which at the same time subject the citizens to ever-increasing surveillance, implying serious intrusions into their privacy. The protection of privacy is a human right, which is manifested on the one hand in several international declarations, conventions and national constitutions, and on the other, in European law, primarily in the Data Protection Directive and its implementation in the national laws of the member states. Privacy protects citizens from governmental arbitrariness and constitutes an elementary precondition for personal freedom and for the sustainability of democratic societies. The protection from permanent surveillance is not

J. Čas (✉)
Institute of Technology Assessment,
Austrian Academy of Sciences, Strohgasse 45/3rd floor, A-1030 Vienna, Austria
e-mail: jcas@oeaw.ac.at

S. Gutwirth et al. (eds.), *Data Protection in a Profiled World*,
DOI 10.1007/978-90-481-8865-9_15, © Springer Science+Business Media B.V. 2010

only a prerequisite for personal self-fulfilment but also for societal and economic development, the capability to innovate and to maintain economic competitiveness. Investments in the protection of privacy are therefore also investments in the future of democratic societies (Čas 2004).

15.2 Background and Objectives of PRISE

PRISE[1] was conducted within the framework of PASR[2], financially supported by the European Commission. The PASR-programme was launched to assist the European Commission in the preparation and design of the "Security Research" theme within the Seventh Framework Programme of the European Union. PRISE was the only project within this programme exclusively dedicated to the protection of human rights, in particular to the protection of privacy. The project ran for about two and a half years and was concluded in the summer of 2008. The PRISE consortium[3] was coordinated by the author of this contribution.

The primary objective of the PRISE project was to develop criteria and guidelines for security technologies and measures in line with human rights in general and with the protection of privacy in particular. The starting point of the project was the premise that security technologies, which respect and enhance privacy, will allow the development and implementation of accepted and acceptable security solutions. The integration of the protection of privacy into the design of security technologies should allow for more security in the future without loss of privacy and, last but not least, constitute a competitive advantage for European security industries.

The criteria for privacy enhancing security technologies, developed by PRISE, are primarily aimed at supporting the proposal writers of security research projects and the evaluators of such proposals to achieve and assess compliance with human rights. In this way the objective of data protection compliant and privacy enhancing security technologies should become the focal point during the conception phase of a project. However, in order to achieve security solutions in line with human rights, it is inevitable that consequential uses of these technologies must also comply with privacy protection principles. The aim was therefore to formulate the guidelines and criteria in such a way that they can also be utilized for and applied to the later implementation and use of security technologies.

---

[1] The full title of the PRISE project is "Privacy enhancing shaping of security research and technology—A participatory approach to develop acceptable and accepted principles for European Security Industries and Policies".

[2] PASR stands for "Preparatory Action on the enhancement of the European industrial potential in the field of Security research".

[3] Apart from the Institute of Technology Assessment of the Austrian Academy of Sciences as coordinator further project partners were the Danish Board of Technology, the Norwegian Board of Technology and the Independent Centre for Data Protection Schleswig-Holstein. The participatory technology assessment activities in Spain and in Hungary were conducted by the subcontractors Consejo Superior de Investigaciones Científicas, Unit of Comparative Policy and Politics, Madrid and the Medián Opinion and Market Research Institute, Budapest.

15.3 Project Methods

Whereas the knowledge base was primarily developed with the help of traditional methods like desktop research and expert interviews, the development of the criteria and guidelines themselves was based on an innovative mix of methods, with participatory approaches playing a central role. The main elements of the knowledge base embrace the identification and analysis of relevant security technologies—whereas in this case relevance was related to potential or actual intrusions into privacy—and the identification of technical, organisational and legal options for the privacy enhancing design, implementation and use of security technologies. A further important element of the knowledge base related work was the development of scenarios which demonstrate possible uses and impacts of different security technologies in a way that they are also accessible to non-experts.

The inclusion of users and stakeholders was one of the central participatory elements of PRISE. In two user and stakeholder workshops preliminary project results were presented to and discussed with representatives of the security industry, security research, data protection authorities, human rights organisations and users of security technologies. These workshops served several objectives. On the one hand, they aimed to guarantee that all points of view would be taken into account and that early feedback on preliminary conclusions would be heard. On the other hand, an important objective was also to initiate and support communication and interaction among the different stakeholder groups and in this way at the same time to start the dissemination of the PRISE results at an early stage.

The second central participatory method applied was a series of so-called "Interview Meetings", a methodology developed by the Danish Board of Technology for the involvement of citizens in technology assessment projects. In the framework of the PRISE project this method was applied simultaneously in several countries for the first time. This method cannot produce statistically significant statements for the population of the concerned country; it is however very well suited to gain qualitative and quantitative data about the predominant opinions, attitudes and lines of argument existing for a specific theme in the population at large. Apart from the countries of origin of the participating PRISE project partners—Austria, Denmark, Germany and Norway—interview meetings were additionally conducted in Spain and Hungary in order also to integrate the perspectives from both southern and eastern European nations. In each of these countries a group of about 30 persons was invited; this group was selected at random, but had to fulfil certain demographic criteria. The participants were provided with information in advance on the theme of the discussion in the form of the above mentioned scenarios. They also included brief descriptions of the security technologies used in the different scenes of the scenarios. The interview meetings, lasting about 3–4 hours, were opened with expert presentations, which also offered the opportunity to clarify any open technical questions or misunderstandings. In the next phase the participants were asked to fill in a comprehensive questionnaire. Subsequently the citizens were divided into several smaller groups and asked to discuss the questions contained in the questionnaire with each other and to give reasoned answers. These discussions were recorded, anonymised, transcribed and subsequently analysed.

15.4 Results of the Interview Meetings

A summary of the results of all six interview meetings can be found in the PRISE Synthesis Report—Interview Meetings on Security Technology and Privacy (Jacobi and Holst 2008). Some central conclusions, which were shared by a vast majority of participants in all countries, are:

The threat of terrorism does not justify violations of privacy by security technologies. This was a dominant attitude in all countries, regardless of whether the country concerned has been suffering from internal or external terror attacks in recent years—as in Spain—or not.

Technologies, which intrude the intimate region of the body, are not accepted by a vast majority. Terra Hertz Scanners, also known as so called "naked machines", which allow the naked body to be looked at through clothing to detect hidden objects are a prime example of such technologies.

A further big concern was related to the potential abuse of security technologies. Citizens demanded strict measures to avoid any kind of abuse. At the same time they did not believe, that abuse can be circumvented entirely.

Important factors which could increase acceptance of security technologies were for example the proportionality of the measures carried out or mandatory court orders for their concrete application. Proportionality here relates to the relation between the assumed security gains and the gravity of the intrusion into privacy as well as the existence of a concrete suspicion. Measures which violate privacy are considered acceptable only if they are based on solid suspicion; in this case—and if investigations are also accompanied by court orders—deep intrusions into privacy are regarded as acceptable. A general demand was that measures, which reduce privacy, should only be taken if no alternatives are available which will not restrict fundamental rights.

15.5 Criteria for Privacy Enhancing Security Technologies

The criteria developed in the PRISE project (Raguse et al. 2008) are related to three different areas of evaluation: the first one concerns the core area of privacy, which shall not be violated under any circumstances, the second one examines compliance with the fundamental principles of data protection and the third one deals with trade-offs and questions of proportionality which depend on the specific context of the security technology under discussion.

Security technologies frequently conflict with one or more of these criteria. Therefore the PRISE project also developed possible precautions and measures to minimise or eliminate these violations of privacy. The proposed measures again relate to three different areas: the first one concerns technical measures, primarily the proposed deployment of PETs (privacy enhancing technologies); the second concerns regulative and legal precautions which usually belong to the policy area of responsibility, and the third discusses organisational measures, which apply to both, the development as well as the later implementation and use of these technologies. Another important objective of PRISE was to support the integration of these aspects into the design phase of current research projects, furthermore PRISE aimed to assist proposal evaluation and review processes in such a way as to make it easier for evaluators to judge whether in fact all necessary precautions have been taken to avoid conflicts with data protection and privacy.

The core area of privacy relates to human dignity, the integrity of the human body and to non-interference with the personal conduct of life. Although restrictions on privacy must of course be allowed for reasons of security, these restrictions must never eliminate privacy totally and they must be in accordance with the principle of proportionality. The area of data protection compliance concerns questions of legitimacy, fulfilment of purpose, proportionality, transparency as well as the quality and security of the collected and processed data. The third area, the contextual trade-offs, involves and questions—amongst other issues—the efficiency of the proposed technology or measure: does it really result in demonstrable security gains and, for this purpose, are restrictions of privacy really inescapable? In this context it must also be taken into consideration that the protection of privacy itself is an inevitable component of individual security.

15.6 Next Steps and Continuative Recommendations

In order to maintain privacy protection in a security focused world, a series of further measures and steps will be necessary, apart from applying the PRISE results to R&D projects in the security area. The following recommendations from the PRISE team and the PRISE scientific advisory board were regarded as particularly important and summarised in a PRISE Statement Paper (PRISE 2008):

An untouchable core area of privacy should be defined. It will almost always be possible to find individual examples which also appear to justify deep intrusions in privacy. It is therefore necessary to define in advance a limit which must not be violated in any case—analogous to the prohibition of torture.

There is no linear relation between privacy and security. Whereas in some cases more surveillance can increase security, the contrary also exists. The protection of privacy is a core element of protection from state arbitrariness and abuse of power. The relation between privacy and security is therefore not a zero-sum game.

The minimisation of the processing of personally identifiable data is a core principle of data protection. Access to and linking of huge databases in order to analyse the behaviour of the whole population without specific suspicion—just in order to identify potentially suspicious behaviour—violates the constitutional right of presumption of innocence and the principle of proportionality. Privacy enhancing security technologies must therefore aim at the minimisation of data collection and ensure that access is only permitted in the case of concrete suspicion.

The protection of privacy is the joint responsibility of all persons and stakeholders taking part in the design, implementation and use of security technologies. Whereas the industry can develop and produce privacy conforming and enhancing security technologies, for subsequent compliant use all involved parties must take responsibility.

The design of security technologies should aim at avoiding intrusions of privacy. Current practice often ignores the protection of privacy in the R&D phase or offers the protection of privacy only as an additional feature, supplementing the core functions if specially asked and paid for. Compliance with and enhancement of the protection of privacy should, however, become a mandatory non-functional requirement of security technologies.

Last but not least, criteria for privacy enhancing security technologies must be continuously further developed and reassessed. On the one hand, this is necessary to keep pace with the permanently increasing technical possibilities and the resulting potential violations of privacy; on the other hand, it will not always be possible to evaluate the efficiency of security technologies nor the resulting violations of privacy in advance with sufficient accuracy. Precautions therefore must be taken and revisions to legislation foreseen as well as the withdrawal of implemented security measures in the event of negative evaluations.

References

Čas, J. 2004. Privacy in pervasive computing environments: A contradiction in terms? *IEEE Technology and Society Magazine* 24 (1): 24–33.

Jacobi, A., and M. Holst. 2008. *PRISE synthesis report: Interview meetings on security technology and privacy*, Nr. D 5.8. http://www.prise.oeaw.ac.at/docs/PRISE_D_5.8_Synthesis_report.pdf.

PRISE. 2008. *PRISE concluding conference statement Paper*, Nr. D 7.6. http://www.prise.oeaw.ac.at/docs/PRISE_Statement_Paper.pdf.

Raguse, M., M. Meints, O. Langfeldt, and W. Peissl. 2008. *PRISE—Criteria for privacy enhancing security technologies*, Nr. D 6.2. http://prise.oeaw.ac.at/docs/PRISE_D_6.2_Criteria_for_privacy_enhancing_security_technologies.pdf.

Part V
Legal Practitioner's Views

Chapter 16
The Role of Private Lawyers in the Data Protection World

Christopher Kuner

While much attention has been given to the role of data protection authorities (DPAs), other governmental authorities involved in data protection (such as the European Commission), and company privacy officers (CPOs), the role of data protection lawyers in law firms seems by comparison to be unappreciated. However, private lawyers do in fact play a crucial role in the data protection world.

16.1 The Roles of Data Protection Lawyers

Law firm lawyers may assume a variety of roles in the data protection world, which can be summarized as follows:[1]

16.1.1 Legal Practice

The data protection lawyer's primary activity is naturally to represent clients and give advice on questions of data protection law. This may range from providing ad hoc opinions on brief questions of the law, to managing large and complex compliance projects. As is the case in any form of law practice, in such situations the lawyer is obligated both to serve the interests of his client, and at the same time to help the client realize its plans within the limits of the law. Clients typically turn to data protection lawyers with questions such as the following:

- A multinational company wishes to centralize the processing of its employee data in a single database outside of Europe. What steps must the company take to

[1] This article is written from the point of view of a data protection lawyer in Europe who represents multinational companies, and so is concerned mainly with European issues. However, much of the discussion is applicable to data protection and privacy lawyers in other regions as well.

C. Kuner (✉)
Hunton & Williams, Brussels, Belgium
e-mail: ckuner@hunton.com

S. Gutwirth et al. (eds.), *Data Protection in a Profiled World,*
DOI 10.1007/978-90-481-8865-9_16,

ensure that the transfer of data from Europe, and its subsequent access by various company entities located around the world, is in compliance with the law?
- The company is investigating a new project involving the profiling of customers that access its web sites. Is such profiling permissible, and if so, under what conditions?
- The company is presented with a lawful subpoena from a US court ordering that certain personal data stored in Europe be sent to the court for use in litigation. May the company comply with the subpoena?
- The company has lawfully transferred personal data to its headquarters outside the EU. The headquarters now seeks to engage a third party to perform routine maintenance on the database. What steps must the company take to ensure that this complies with EU law?
- The lawyer receives a telephone call from the client, explaining that it has just discovered that criminals have hacked into its online customer database and stolen much of the data. What steps must the company take to comply with the law, aid its customers whose data have been stolen, and mitigate its risk?

These projects typically require the data protection lawyer to perform tasks such as the following:

- develop an overall strategy for complying with data protection requirements;
- draft necessary documentation, in particular Internet and employee privacy policies, access procedures, and complaint procedures;
- prepare regulatory filings, including notification of data processing to the DPAs;
- represent clients before DPAs with regard to any complaints or concerns;
- evaluate the various mechanisms for the transfer of personal data outside the EU (for example the EU-approved standard contractual clauses, the safe harbor system for data transfers to the US, and binding corporate rules), and advise the client on the one(s) that are appropriate for its particular circumstances;
- counsel the client on employee data protection issues; and
- assist the client in developing procedures to deal with data security breaches.

The lawyer often has to act as an interface for the client, both with the client's own staff, and with the data protection authorities. One of the lawyer's most important tasks is to work with the client's employees (which can include personnel in areas such as marketing, information technology, human resources, etc.) to understand the facts of the particular data processing scenario at issue, to interpret the business and technical details of the project and develop a legal analysis based on the requirements of data protection law, and then to draft a roadmap or set of steps for the client to take in order to ensure that its data processing complies with the law.

Working with data protection authorities has also become a significant part of law practice. Contact with DPAs can occur not only when the lawyer represents the client in a formal proceeding before the authority, but also when the client needs to obtain information about how the DPA would view a particular issue. The lawyer can often do so more effectively than the client can, since he[2] can inquire with the DPA on a "no name" basis and without revealing the identity of the client.

---

[2] Or she! The data protection bar includes numerous women lawyers.

The data protection lawyer increasingly must work with colleagues in other disciplines in order to meet the client's needs (thus, for example, issues involving the processing of employee data frequently require consultation with an employment lawyer). There are also an increasing number of situations in which obligations under data protection law conflict with other legal obligations (for example, seeking to process IP addresses to combat violations of intellectual property rights, or gaining access to employee e-mails to ensure compliance with anti-corruption requirements), which may similarly require consultation with colleagues specializing in areas such as intellectual property law or international litigation.

16.1.2 Speaking, Writing, and Other Pro Bono Activities

In order to keep his knowledge current and to satisfy his interest in data protection law, the private lawyer may also be involved in a variety of other activities, such as participating in the work of business associations; writing books and articles; giving comments to DPAs and regulatory authorities on policy documents; and teaching and giving speeches. These activities are crucial to keep him aware of the latest developments and ensure that he is in touch with the thinking of companies and regulators. A good data protection lawyer will be involved in such activities not only out of his own business interest, but out of genuine interest in the topic.

For example, private sector lawyers (including the author) took a leading role in proposing and negotiating the European Commission Decision 2004/915/EC of 27 December 2004 regarding approval of a set of standard contractual clauses for international data transfers.[3] This work was completed over several years without remuneration, and represented a huge investment of time (and thus of money, since most lawyers bill by the hour) for the lawyers involved. Such projects can benefit all sides, since they result in tools that companies can use in their daily business, allow regulators a chance to better understand the business issues that companies face, and provide valuable experience for lawyers.

16.2 The Challenges of Practicing Data Protection Law

Practicing data protection law as a private lawyer holds a number of challenges, but also many rewards. Until fairly recently, data protection law was viewed by many companies and regulators from a largely regional or national perspective, so that the private lawyer involved in this area tended to give advice only on his or her local law. However, the advent of the Internet and electronic commerce and globalization of the world economy have brought about a corresponding increase in demand

[3] Commission Decision (EC) 2004/915 of 27 December 2004 amending Decision (EC) 2001/497 as regards the introduction of an alternative set of standard contractual clauses for the transfer of personal data to third countries, *Official Journal* L385/74 (2004).

for lawyers who can give advice on data protection across borders, or even across regions. This has meant that the market for data protection lawyers has expanded greatly, and this area has become a legal specialty unto itself.[4]

These changes have also generated challenges. The data protection lawyer is now expected to be familiar with the law of many more jurisdictions than in the past, and also to stay current on recent developments, which can take a great deal of time and effort. In addition, companies and clients are under greater economic pressure than ever before, and often approach the lawyer with highly complex legal issues needing clarification within a short time frame. The private lawyer must therefore be able to craft his legal advice to fit the client's needs; sometimes, this may require a detailed legal opinion, but in many cases the time and resources necessary to prepare an in-depth opinion may be lacking, and the client's needs may best be met by a brief or high-level response to the question at hand. As many data protection questions nowadays arise with regard to the use of information technologies (such as RFID technologies, biometrics, or video surveillance), it is also of considerable benefit if the lawyer is familiar with recent developments in electronic commerce, the Internet, and computer technologies.

The rewards of data protection law practice are also clear. While data protection has existed as a discrete legal topic in Europe for over thirty years, it has undergone a dramatic transformation within the last five years or so, as electronic commerce has become ubiquitous and the resulting data protection issues recurrent. In particular, data protection law has moved from being a niche area of local interest to one of broad interest to companies in almost every sector. This gives the data protection lawyer the opportunity to work on many cutting-edge issues and participate in the development of the law. The necessity of often having to give quick advice without a full knowledge of the facts can be quite stressful, but also enables the lawyer to experience the sort of stress his clients are under, and helps develop the lawyer's ability to sift through the salient facts in a case and to give advice crafted to the client's needs. Data protection is a fast-moving and dynamic area of the law, and is therefore an interesting and rewarding area to practice that offers particular opportunities for young lawyers.

16.3 Outlook for Data Protection Law Practice

As electronic commerce has developed and the resulting data protection issues have become ever more important, the amount of legal work for data protection lawyers has greatly increased, and ever more attention is being given to this area. At

[4] For example, in the last few years the US periodical Computerworld has conducted a survey of "the best privacy advisers", see http://www.computerworld.com/action/article.do?command=viewArticleBasic&articleId=9122519. And the UK-based company Chambers and Partners, which publishes directories of lawyers, publishes rankings of leading data protection law firms and lawyers at the global (http://www.chambersandpartners.com/Editorial.aspx?ssid=30699), UK (http://www.chambersandpartners.com/Editorial.aspx?ssid=29845), and US (http://www.chambersandpartners.com/Editorial.aspx?ssid=29083) levels.

the same time, insufficient attention is often given to the skills and abilities that data protection lawyers can bring to the discussion and resolution of difficult legal and political questions of data protection law. In the last few years, data protection authorities have become much more open about discussing difficult issues with company privacy officers, recognizing rightfully that buy-in from CPOs is crucial in order to ensure respect for the law and hence legal compliance. However, DPAs may not realize that, precisely because they work for a number of clients, data protection lawyers can exercise considerable influence on the development of practices in a particular sector or geographic region. Data protection authorities and company privacy officers also have their own membership organizations which can exercise considerable influence on policy debates, whereas there is no corresponding organization of data protection lawyers.

Data protection lawyers are often the forgotten participants in policy debates, because they have many clients and do not represent a specific organization. In particular, DPAs and government entities may consult with CPOs about upcoming legislation or regulatory developments, while neglecting to obtain input from data protection lawyers, and CPOs may believe that they are best placed to provide input on such developments. In this regard, both regulators and CPOs often forget that private data protection lawyers may have a greater breadth of experience than other participants in the data protection world, since they have to deal with legal issues covering numerous sectors and projects. Indeed, in order to survive economically, the private lawyer needs to cover a wide range of data protection topics, whereas the CPO, for example, only deals with topics occurring within his particular company. Because companies often turn to their outside counsel with particularly complex or novel issues, private lawyers can also have excellent insight into the cutting-edge issues of data protection law.

Moreover, the private lawyer must navigate the shoals of satisfying his client's needs on the one hand, and developing strategies to help the client comply with the law on the other hand. This requires highly-developed skills of identifying potential data protection issues and dealing with them in a way which is both pragmatic and yet legally-compliant. Furthermore, the private lawyer will likely have to deal with legal issues in a wide variety of geographic locations, whereas most DPAs are confined to issues within their own country or region. The data protection lawyer also acts as the first line of examination for complex questions of data protection law before they reach the data protection authorities, and accordingly as the interface between the client and the DPAs with regard to compliance issues. These factors all indicate the level and breadth of expertise that a successful data protection lawyer must have, which can be valuable resources for companies and regulators alike.

16.4 Conclusions

The practice of data protection law has undergone a fundamental change in the last few years. Just as happened in the past in other legal specialties like environmental law, data protection law has evolved from a narrow niche area to one of broad relevance. In line with this development, the private lawyer must become ever more adept at dealing with difficult legal issues, tight deadlines, and projects that span a variety of geographic regions. At the same time, there has been less general awareness of the valuable experience which data protection lawyers can bring to policy questions. In part, this is because data protection lawyers have not organized themselves as have CPOs and DPAs, and because the breadth of experience of data protection lawyers has been underestimated. Private data protection lawyers should thus become more active and vocal in participating in important data protection debates, and CPOs and DPAs should recognize the breadth and depth of skills which data protection lawyers have in dealing with complex legal and policy issues.

Chapter 17
Transfer and Monitoring: Two Key Words in the Current Data Protection Private Practice: A Legal Practitioner's View[1]

Tanguy Van Overstraeten, Sylvie Rousseau and Guillaume Couneson

17.1 Introduction

A growing number of legal practitioners are showing strong interest and becoming increasingly busy in data protection matters, encompassing all aspects of information governance. The authors have been asked by the editors of this book to review issues they are facing in their daily practice regarding this area of law and the way they are tackling them. This article provides the authors' insights around two key words: transfer and monitoring.

Many data protection issues indeed boil down to either (in)validation of cross-border data transfers or the legality of data monitoring:

- The globalisation of the economy makes it crucial that large corporations be able to share and transfer data all over the world. Technologies increasingly facilitate this but what about the law? How to reconcile the legal environment, which is largely set out locally (each country adopting its own rules even when transposing a directive, as is the case in the European Economic Area), with transnational activities and technologies? Are the binding corporate rules (BCRs) an effective answer?
- On the monitoring front, many companies are genuinely willing to ensure that their employees make legal and appropriate use of the technology at their (professional) disposal. How can employers' monitoring of such use be compatible with their employees' legitimate right to privacy? Likewise, with the increasing threat of terrorist attacks, governments are developing ever more intrusive

Tanguy Van Overstraeten (tvanover@linklaters.com) is a member of the Brussels Bar. He is a partner of Linklaters LLP where he heads the privacy practice on a global basis and the technology, media & telecommunications (TMT) practice in Belgium.

Sylvie Rousseau (sylvie.rousseau@linklaters.com) and Guillaume Couneson (guillaume.couneson@linklaters.com) are members of the Brussels Bar. They both work in the technology, media & telecommunications (TMT) practice in Belgium, respectively as managing associate and associate.

[1] This article was completed on 15 June 2009 and does not take into account developments since that date.

DOI 10.1007/978-90-481-8865-9_17, © Springer Science+Business Media B.V. 2010

techniques to neutralise their perpetrators. How to tackle the dilemma between rules enabling these intrusions in one country and rules protecting privacy in another?

This article does not provide an exhaustive and academic review of the applicable rules but rather highlights some issues the authors have faced in their recent practice and analyses the proposed work-around.

17.2 International Data Flows: The Issue of Transfer

Let us first consider the classic issue of the increasing international transfer of personal data in the framework of the current globalisation. In practice, this may take many forms, from a centralised HR database (e.g. in the context of a bonus scheme or to process information generated from a whistle blowing hotline) to complex off-shoring or cloud computing. More generally, the Internet enables users to access—and therefore triggers the transfer of—applications and data from any computer anywhere in the world. This real ubiquity raises the difficult issue of international data transfers.

As a reminder, the principle is that personal data may only be transferred outside the European Economic Area (i.e. the EU Member States plus Iceland, Liechtenstein and Norway) if the data is adequately protected in the country of reception.

It is the European Commission that determines whether the level of protection that a particular country grants to personal data is adequate. So far, only a few countries have been found to offer such an adequate level (the so-called white-listed countries): Argentina, Canada (under certain conditions), Guernsey, Jersey, the Isle of Man and Switzerland. Other countries are or should soon be under review with a view to taking them into consideration for addition to the white list if their laws are ultimately deemed adequate. These include Israel, some Latin American countries and Morocco which has recently adopted new legislation to protect personal data. Practitioners are also looking forward to the inclusion of a number of other countries which are key players in the market, such as Australia, Hong Kong, Japan or Russia.

The current system for assessing third countries is burdensome and time-consuming and some have advocated a system of black-listed countries rather than the current scheme which automatically excludes countries outside the EEA and requires their assessment, which means in fact a test of equivalence of their local system with Directive 95/46/EC on the protection of individuals with regard to the processing of personal data and on the free movement of such data (the "**Data Protection Directive**").[2]

---

[2] For a detailed review of the current system, see C. Kuner, Chap, 16—Developing an adequate legal framework for international data transfers, in *Reinventing data protection?*, eds. S. Gutwirth et al. Dordrecht: Springer, 2009.

When data is sent to a third country not yet recognised, companies must rely on other transfer mechanisms set forth in their national legislation.

In our practice, three compliance mechanisms are most often used by companies to ground their international data transfers: unambiguous consent, the conclusion of the standard contractual clauses and, more recently, the adoption of binding corporate rules.

17.2.1 Unambiguous Consent: A Subsidiary Solution?

One of the available exceptions to the prohibition of transfer under Article 26(1) of the Data Protection Directive which can be relied upon to enable data transfer to a country not offering an adequate level is the "unambiguous consent". Such consent must be given by the person whose personal data is to be transferred. It must be clear, specific, freely given and informed.

In the virtual world of Internet, a key issue is to ensure that the consent may be evidenced and enforced. As a result, increasingly sophisticated mechanisms to collect consent have been designed. These include, for example, pop-ups with an option to consent or not requesting users to indicate their preference by ticking the box of their choice before they may continue browsing on the website.

In the employment context (e.g. in the framework of a centralised HR database or a whistle blowing scheme), one of the key issues is the freedom of consent. The Article 29 Working Party[3] has released a document in which it considers that employees would not be able to provide a freely given consent due to their subordination link with their employer.[4]

In practice however, certain companies still rely on employees' consent as a valid derogation to the prohibition of transfer depending on the specific circumstances. This may be the case, for example, when the transfer issue is submitted to the works council or when the transfer is made to the benefit of the employees, e.g. in the context of an employees' incentive plan globally centralised by the parent or the listed company of the group or in case of employees' e-learning requiring data transfer for access purposes.

In general however, the consent-based exception is not viewed favourably by the Article 29 Working Party which considers that *"consent is unlikely to provide*

[3] The advisory body composed of representatives of the national data protection authorities and the European Commission.

[4] According to the Article 29 Working Party, *"reliance on consent should be confined to cases where the worker has a genuine free choice and is subsequently able to withdraw the consent without detriment"*, see Opinion 8/2001 on the processing of personal data in the employment context, WP 48, (13 September 2001), 3, available at http://ec.europa.eu/justice_home/fsj/privacy/docs/wpdocs/2001/wp48en.pdf.

an adequate long-term framework for data controllers in cases of repeated or even structural transfers for the processing in question".[5]

This position is controversial, however, as the unambiguous consent is listed together with all other exemptions in Article 26(1) of the Data Protection Directive with no indication of priority of any exemption over the others.

17.2.2 Standard Contractual Clauses: A Solution to be Further Harmonised

The data transfer solution that is probably the most commonly relied upon by businesses is the use of the so-called standard contractual clauses. The European Commission approved three sets of these clauses enabling the transfer of data to an entity located in a third country not offering an adequate level of protection. Two sets of clauses cover the relationship between data controllers and one covers the relationship between a data controller as exporter of the data and a data processor.

In practice, the use of these clauses raises a number of issues that are primarily due to the fact that they have not been drafted for global businesses transferring data all around the world but rather for much easier situations involving two parties only. This means that their implementation often requires amendments to allow their use in a global context.

Both the Article 29 Working Party and the European Commission recognise such practice, and support the use of standard contractual clauses in a multi-party context. In that respect, the Article 29 Working Party commented that[6]: *"companies are making broad use of these instruments in a very positive and encouraging way* (e.g., ***the standard contractual clauses with many parties to the contract***)*"* (over emphasized). In its Staff Working Document of 20 January 2006, the European Commission added: *"the Commission services see no objection to the subscription of standard contractual clauses by several data exporters and/or importers as long as it is made very clear that the information must be provided with the same level of clarity and specificity that is currently foreseen in Appendix 1 for a single data exporter and a single data importer".*[7]

---

[5] Working document on a common interpretation of Article 26(1) of Directive 95/46/EC of 24 October 1995, WP 114, (25 November 2005), 11, available at http://ec.europa.eu/justice_home/fsj/privacy/docs/wpdocs/ 2005/wp114_en.pdf.

[6] Working document on transfers of personal data to third countries: Applying Article 26(2) of the EU data protection directive to binding corporate rules for international data transfers, WP 74, (3 June 2003), 7, available at http://ec.europa.eu/justice_home/fsj/privacy/docs/wpdocs/2003/wp74_en.pdf.

[7] Commission Staff Working Document (SEC (2006) 95) on the implementation of the Commission decisions on standard contractual clauses for the transfer of personal data to third countries (2001/497/EC and 2002/16/EC).

The second issue faced in practice when applying standard contractual clauses relates to the procedural requirements which still vary considerably from one Member State to the other.

Some Member States require data controllers to file the clauses (sometimes merely for statistical purposes), while others still require approval of these clauses and the underlying transfer.

In addition, the level of detail required in the schedules of the standard contractual clauses also vary significantly among Member States. Some regulators require only a general overview of the types of data transferred, whereas others require very detailed information about these data flows.

More harmonisation on these points will be crucial in the future to ensure a smooth and efficient use of the standard contractual clauses as an effective solution for data transfers.

Another growing concern in the application of the standard contractual clauses relates to the lack of an appropriate mechanism to enable subsequent data processing. This issue is particularly acute in relation to offshoring, when a customer contracts with a service provider who in turn subcontracts part of its contractual obligations to a third party. If one assumes that both service providers act as data processor, the current set of standard clauses relating to the export of data to a processor is not suitable as it does not address the subsequent transfer to another processor. With the increasing development of IT offshoring, the absence of an appropriate mechanism considerably weakens the benefit of the standard contractual clauses. It is expected that this significant loophole will be addressed in the long-awaited new set of controller to processor standard clauses which should include provisions enabling sub-processing.[8]

17.2.3 Binding Corporate Rules: The Way Forward

An alternative to other derogations allowing for international data transfers are the so-called Binding Corporate Rules (BCRs). They are a way for multinational organisations to transfer personal data outside the EEA within their group of companies. Such solution requires the approval by the data protection regulators in the EU countries in which the group is processing personal data.

BCRs are in principle more flexible than the standard contractual clauses although, in order to facilitate the mutual recognition of BCRs throughout Member States, a standard application form has been designed for companies wishing to submit BCRs for authorisation in an EU country. This form has been worked out by

[8] See Opinion 3/2009 on the Draft Commission Decision on standard contractual clauses for the transfer of personal data to processors established in third countries, under Directive 95/46/EC (data controller to data processor), WP 161, (5 March 2009), available at http://ec.europa.eu/justice_home/fsj/privacy/docs /wpdocs/2009/wp161_en.pdf.

the Article 29 Working Party,[9] together with specific elements to be complied with by applicants.[10]

Although burdensome, as it entails a thorough review of all internal procedures dealing with personal data processing, BCRs undoubtedly offer some key advantages. First, they are an excellent tool for a multinational company to demonstrate and ensure data privacy accountability. They also deliver real benefits for individuals, as specific procedures have to be put in place within the companies concerned, while allowing them to carry out global data flows.

So far however, it has proven difficult to obtain regulators' approval of BCRs. At the time of writing this article, only a handful of companies have had their BCRs approved by their relevant lead national regulator (primarily in France, Germany, the Netherlands and the UK) and there are still serious obstacles for mutual recognition by the regulators in some other Member States.

The European Commission and the Article 29 Working Party are conscious of these hurdles and are working towards simplifying the current process and agreeing on a coordinated approval process.

As part of these efforts, a number of national regulators have formed a "club" to set forth in concrete terms a mutual recognition procedure whereby the positive opinion on BCRs by a lead regulator should be automatically accepted by the other regulators as a sufficient basis for granting their own national authorisation. At present, 13 EEA regulators have joined this club, and their number is expected to grow.[11] The future expansion of BCRs as a solution to trans-border data flow will demonstrate whether this promising development is effective.

Although some significant steps have been taken to favour BCRs, improvements are still required to enable them to fully take off as one of the most appropriate solutions for multinational businesses. Such improvements include (1) ensuring that all data protection regulators are in a position to recognise BCRs, which may require a change in their national laws,[12] (2) ensuring more transparency regarding national procedures and requirements (including access to precedents), (3) extending mutual recognition to all regulators in the 30 EEA Member States and (4) not making BCRs subject to overly onerous national procedural requirements.

---

[9] Recommendation 1/2007 on the standard application for approval of binding corporate rules for the transfer of personal data, WP 133, (10 January 2007), available at http://ec.europa.eu/justice_home/fsj/privacy/docs/wpdocs/ 2007/wp133_en.doc.

[10] "Working Document Setting up a Table with the Elements and Principles to be Found in Binding Corporate Rules, WP 153", (24 June 2008), available at http://ec.europa.eu/justice_home/fsj/privacy/docs/wpdocs/2008/wp153_en.pdf.

[11] The countries are: Cyprus, France, Germany, Iceland, Ireland, Italy, Latvia, Liechtenstein, Luxembourg, the Netherlands, Norway, Spain, and the United Kingdom. See http://ec.europa.eu/justice_home/fsj/privacy/news/docs/pr_10_12_08_en.pdf.

[12] In Belgium for example, it is being seriously considered to leave out the burdensome legal requirement for a Royal Decree to validate a transfer to a third country not offering an adequate level of protection as per Article 22 of the Law of 8 December 1992 on privacy protection in relation to the processing of personal data.

17.2.4 No One Size Fits-All Solution to the Data Transfer

Each data transfer mechanism carries its own set of advantages and disadvantages:

- Consent is increasingly disfavoured in the employment context and can be withheld or revoked at any time.
- Standard contractual clauses entail joint and several liability, third party beneficiary rights and in certain countries require the regulator's approval.
- Binding Corporate Rules are still too burdensome and time-consuming; they are not yet feasible in all Member States.

The European and local regulators should foster further simplification in the area of international data transfers by innovative and streamlined mechanisms, as should be the case with the upcoming revised controller to processor standard contractual clauses.

Companies need to weigh those mechanisms to determine which approach works best for them, taking into account their factual situation (countries of destination,[13] number of countries relevant to the transfer, number of entities involved and their interdependence, etc).

Unfortunately, the existing solutions are still in need of adaptation to an increasingly global environment. The overall scheme of notifying data transfers to regulators and, where required, obtaining their approval prior to a transfer is bureaucratic and burdensome and does not necessarily provide increased protection to data subjects.

Regulators should work on reducing the time and efforts required to obtain data transfer clearance and approval to ensure that companies established and operating in Europe do not face competitive disadvantages in today's global information society. Centralised filings or approvals covering data transfers at EU level should be seriously considered in that respect.

17.3 Big Brother Is Watching You: the Issue of Monitoring

In today's society, monitoring covers an increasing variety of situations. It can include for example surveillance of employees as regards their use of e-mails and Internet on the workplace, security monitoring by closed-circuit television (CCTV) e.g. in a bank or in the street in front of an automated teller machine, monitoring of the behaviour of customers on the Internet to design advertising more targeted to

[13] Another crucial solution for transfer is the adhesion to the safe harbour, but this mechanism is only available to companies exporting data to the USA.

their interests or the interception of communications by the authorities in the framework of their fight against terrorism.[14]

Every business and every authority may now take advantage of a number of technologies developed for monitoring. The underlying purpose of monitoring may be perfectly valid and legitimate—for example, to ensure the security of the public, it is nevertheless subject to legal limitations.

In what follows, we emphasise the complexity of the matter and identify the hurdles that may be faced in practice, looking at monitoring from three angles: monitoring by private companies, by public authorities but also by individuals.

17.3.1 Monitoring by Private Companies

The key driver pushing companies to engage in monitoring activities is to ensure a certain level of control. Regarding employees, this can consist of controls over their productivity (time recording, monitoring of Internet usage) but also control for their own security (safety on the work floor, identification of visitors) and the security of the company (monitoring of activities on the company's Intranet, downloads and uploads of software).

As regards their customers, companies may be interested in their behaviour in terms of purchases (quantity and type of purchased products/services) but also in the reasons motivating such behaviour. Straightforward examples include the well-known customer loyalty cards that are used to collect customers' data for marketing purposes. As with monitoring of employees, the purpose is to gain a better understanding and "control" over the customers in order to improve the company's profits.

17.3.1.1 Monitoring of Employees

The monitoring of employees in the workplace is characterised by a complex set of rules, which are often misapplied or even somewhat disregarded in practice. This is especially true in Belgium where legal practitioners are faced by a number of rules that are difficult to combine.

Although employers are entitled to control their workers' activities under employment law (Law of 3 July 1978), this right of control is indeed subject to privacy and personal data protection[15] as well as the protection of electronic communications.[16]

---

[14] For a detailed analysis of the Belgian regulation on CCTV monitoring, see P. De Hert, and M. Loncke. 2005. Camera surveillance and workplace privacy in Belgium. In *Reasonable expectations of privacy?*, eds. S. Nouwt et al., 167–209. The Hague: ITeR.

[15] The Law of 8 December 1992 on Privacy Protection with regard to the Processing of Personal Data, as modified by the Law of 11 December 1998 ("**DPA**").

[16] Article 124 of the Law of 13 June 2005 relating to Electronic Communications ("**Article 124**") and, to a more limited extent, Article 314bis of the Belgian Criminal Code ("**Article 314bis**").

In addition, a Collective Bargaining Agreement has been adopted to provide further guidance regarding employer's rights and obligations relating to monitoring.[17]

In this article, we do not analyse these rules in detail but rather highlight the difficulties raised by this combination of rules.

It should be pointed out that most companies in Belgium allow their personnel to make use of their electronic communication equipment (fixed and mobile phone, Internet access, e-mail) for private matters. This approach complies with the jurisprudence of the European Court of Human Rights.[18]

Although this element reinforces the need for employers to comply with the applicable rules when they monitor how their personnel make use of their electronic communication means, the fact whether or not their employees are using equipment for private matters is not decisive as most of these rules apply to any data regardless of whether they have a private or confidential nature.

Applied to the monitoring of personnel (e.g. regarding its usage of Internet or e-mails), the DPA requires a verification of a number of key factors:

- The existence of a legal ground: the consent of employees may be considered but raises the issue of freedom which has been discussed above (Sect. 17.2.1). Alternatively, many businesses rely on their legitimate interest to justify the monitoring, but this interest may not be outweighed by the fundamental rights of the employees, a balance which is often difficult to measure in practice but should depend on the extent of the monitoring and also the compliance with the other rules (including CBA No. 81).
- The employees subject to the monitoring must be adequately informed about the processing of their data, including the purpose of the control and their right of access and correction. In practice, this is often done via the works council and the information included in the works regulations.
- Obviously, the monitoring must comply with the quality and proportionality principles of the DPA (adequacy and relevance of data, etc).
- Technical and organisational security measures must be in place to ensure the confidentiality of the data which is processed as part of the monitoring.
- As often the case for multinationals, the data that is subject to the monitoring is transferred or rendered accessible by the headquarters. If located outside the

---

[17] Collective Bargaining Agreement No. 81 of 26 April 2002 on the Protection of Employees' Privacy with regard to the Monitoring of Electronic Communications Data in Network (**"CBA No. 81"**).

[18] See *Niemitz v. Germany*, 251/B, para. 29 (ECHR, 23 November 1992): *"respect for private life must also comprise to a certain degree the right to establish and develop relationships with other human beings. There appears, furthermore, to be no reason of principle why this understanding of the notion of private life should be taken to exclude activities of a professional or business nature since it is, after all, in the course of their working lives that the majority of people have a significant, if not the greatest, opportunity of developing relationships with the outside world. This view is supported by the fact that, as was rightly pointed out by the Commission, it is not always possible to distinguish clearly which of an individual's activities form part of his professional or business life and which do not".*

EEA in a country not offering an adequate level of protection, the issue must be carefully assessed in line with the above (Sect. 17.2).

- The employer must also notify the data protection authority, the Belgian Privacy Commission, of the processing of data carried out in the framework of the monitoring.

Compliance with the DPA is not the end of the story. The employer must also deal with Article 124,[19] which prohibits in very broad terms the access by third parties to electronic communications except with the consent of all persons concerned. Like the DPA, Article 124 is criminally sanctioned.

Article 314bis[20] contains a prohibition similar to that of Article 124, but its scope of application requires in principle an interception (such as voice tapping). Although also criminally sanctioned, this article is therefore applicable only during transmission and is thus less relevant in the case of monitoring at the workplace.[21]

Last but not least, the employer must also pay consideration to CBA No. 81, which defines for which purposes and under which modalities monitoring of electronic communications of employees, including their use of e-mails and of Internet, is allowed.

CBA No. 81 enables employers to monitor certain activities of their employees for four specific purposes: (1) prevention of slander and indecent acts, (2) protection of the economic, commercial and financial interests of the employer, (3) protection of its network and (4) compliance with the policies put in place by the employer. The employer is required to inform accordingly the workers' representatives (again, this is usually done via the works council) and each worker individually.

The main principle contained in CBA No. 81 is that, initially, only aggregate data may be processed, in other words, data not linked to a particular worker (such

---

[19] Article 124 prohibits, unless all persons directly or indirectly involved in the communication have agreed thereto, (1) to intentionally acquire knowledge of information of any nature whatsoever transmitted by electronic communication means that is not intended to be received personally by such person, (2) to intentionally identify persons concerned by the transmission of said information or contents, (3) to intentionally acquire knowledge of electronic communication data relating to another person and (4) to modify, delete, disclose, store or use in any manner whatsoever information, identification or data, obtained intentionally or not. Article 124 applies to all types of electronic communications both during and after transmission. This article is subject to few exceptions, such as when the law allows the performance of these acts (e.g. to assist in a legal prosecution).

[20] Article 314bis protects the confidentiality of private (tele)communications by prohibiting third parties (1) from intentionally taping, taking cognizance of or recording private (tele)communications during their transmission or request someone to do so, by using whatever tool, without the consent of all participants or (2) from knowingly holding or divulging illegally taped or illegally recorded private (tele)communications.

[21] In addition, this article does not apply in a few cases, such as (1) when all persons concerned (e.g. the senders and recipients of the e-mails intercepted) have given their consent to the prohibited acts or (2) when the law allows the performance of these acts (e.g. to assist in a legal prosecution).

as transmission volume and traffic), and it is only in specific cases that data may be individualised.[22]

The second principle relates to proportionality. It requires that the means used to control should be adequate and proportionate to the legitimate purposes of the monitoring. This prohibits the general and systematic control and individualisation of communications data.

Finally, although CBA No. 81 admits that the employer may examine the contents of electronic communications data if their professional nature is not contested by the employee, this position is questionable in consideration of the prohibition contained in Article 124 to intentionally access communications data relating to a third party, except when the consent of all persons involved in the communication is obtained. The key issue in that respect is that these persons not only include the employees themselves but also all their correspondents (senders or recipients of e-mails originating from or received by these employees).

Given the above rules, organising legitimate and valid monitoring is a challenge for employers. Some specific recommendations should be followed. Although they may not necessarily be sufficient to meet all legal requirements, they should significantly alleviate the risks of the employers.

The first step is to ensure satisfactory transparency. This includes a review and discussion of the contemplated monitoring technologies with the works council. These discussions should be implemented in the form of policies that could usefully be included in the company's works regulations. Consideration should also be given to the feasibility of including an appropriate wording mirroring the policies in the employment agreements (via an addendum). In addition, to address the issue of consent required under Article 124, it is advisable to include an automatic disclaimer in all outgoing e-mails of the company that includes satisfactory wording informing recipients of these e-mails that messages sent to and from the company may be monitored for defined purposes. Although this solution is certainly not waterproof and to our knowledge has not been recognised by the case law, over time it could lead to a tacit consent of all third party recipients of e-mails regularly dealing with the company's personnel.

17.3.1.2 Monitoring of Customers

Under Belgian law, the key piece of legislation limiting the monitoring by private companies of their customers is again the DPA.

---

22 The CBA No. 81 makes a distinction on the basis of the purposes of monitoring. The employer may directly individualise data when the control has revealed an abnormal behaviour falling under the above three first purposes (1)–(3) while direct individualisation is not allowed when the exclusive purpose of monitoring is to ensure respect of the policies set out by the employer as per the last purpose (4). In the latter case, the employer must warn all workers when a violation of these policies has been detected and inform them that individualization of the data will be performed should such violation re-occur.

First, the DPA requires that personal data only be processed on the basis of a limited list of legitimate grounds, several of which could be relied upon to legitimate some form of monitoring, in particular the consent of the data subject, the necessity of the processing for the performance of a contract (e.g. in case of outsourcing of call centre services) and the legitimate interests of the data controller.

However, such grounds may not legitimise just any form of monitoring. Personal data must also be processed fairly and lawfully, for specified, explicit and legitimate purposes and not further processed in a way incompatible with those purposes.

In compliance with the duty of information, the validity of the monitoring of customers is only ensured to the extent that the customers are made aware of such monitoring and its specific purposes. Further processing purposes which the customers would not be aware of (including the sale of the information to third parties) is not allowed.

This issue of awareness is indeed the second key element set forth in the DPA. It is part of the rights granted to the data subjects whose personal data is under processing. In addition to the above right of information, data subjects are granted a right of access and rectification (in certain specific cases, this may include a right of deletion). It is therefore clear that any surprise effect or secret monitoring of customers should be excluded.[23]

The third boundary is the obligation for data controllers to notify any processing of personal data to the data protection authority, the Privacy Commission in Belgium, before any such operation is carried out. The notification is published in a register which is accessible online[24] and may thus be consulted by any customer willing to verify which types of personal data are processed by a private company.[25]

These boundaries have been further strengthened by the Belgian Privacy Commission and the Article 29 Working Party through their opinions and recommendations. For example, the Commission recently issued a note on direct marketing activities (which are often the aim of customer monitoring).[26] The note sets out strict guidelines for data controllers wishing to process personal data for such purposes. The Article 29 Working Party recently considered that IP addresses (often used for monitoring of online activities of customers) should be regarded as personal data[27] and therefore subject to all the above obligations.

---

[23] This is equally true for monitoring through the use of CCTV for which the Law of 21 March 2007 regulating the installation and utilisation of CCTV mirrors the principles of the DPA.

[24] At www.privacycommission.be.

[25] It must be underlined that this is largely wishful thinking in practice given that the information available online is often insufficient to enable data subjects to actually understand whether, how and why their data are processed by a data controller.

[26] See the advice on direct marketing and the protection of personal data available on the Commission's website in French at http://www.privacycommission.be/fr/static/pdf/direct-marketing/20080805-nota-direct-marketing-fr.pdf and in Dutch at http://www.privacycommission.be/fr/static/pdf/direct-marketing/20080805-nota-direct-marketing-nl.pdf.

[27] Opinion 4/2007 on the concept of personal data, WP 136, (18 June 2007), available at http://ec.europa.eu/justice_home/fsj/privacy/docs/wpdocs/2007/wp136_en.pdf.

One of the most striking illustrations of monitoring of customers by private companies has recently come from the United Kingdom: the US company Phorm teamed up with a number of UK Internet service providers (ISPs) to implement behavioural targeting software which would effectively allow companies to provide Internet users with targeted advertising on the basis of their online behaviour.[28] It emerged last year that a telecommunications operator had been testing this technology without informing its customers about the trials. This resulted in an in-depth review being launched regarding this technology.[29]

In Belgium, there have also been a number of documented cases of monitoring of customers by businesses, including a pub owner who filmed his customers and printed a list of those that caused problems.[30] Similar cases involving the publishing of pictures of shoplifters and other criminal acts caught on camera have also been encountered by the Belgian Privacy Commission.[31]

None of the above examples has so far resulted in court actions. This should not come as a surprise since private companies usually quickly adapt their ways when challenged by the Commission or their customers, as they do not want to risk alienating the latter.

This contrasts with the situation of employees, who are obviously in a weaker position towards their employer.

17.3.2 Monitoring by Public Authorities

As with private companies, the States also started to adopt new information technologies to monitor their citizens (both individuals and private companies).

This development has taken a new turn since the terrorist attacks of 11 September 2001, which brought the USA to implement legislation granting new investigatory powers to law enforcement agencies, including new monitoring tools.[32]

As mentioned above, the monitoring in question is aimed at achieving a higher degree of security and safety in the light of the rise of terrorist attacks. Monitoring may serve both crime prevention and crime investigation purposes.

Monitoring of citizens by the States is also subject to a number of rules, the main rules in Belgium being Article 8 of the European Convention of Human Rights[33]

---

[28] The software, called Webwise, works by categorising user interests and matching them with advertisers who wish to target that type of users. For more details, see http://www.phorm.com.

[29] For the history of the case and background information, see http://news.bbc.co.uk/1/hi/technology/7283333.stm.

[30] "Schendingen van de privacywet", *Het Nieuwsblad*, 4 February 2009.

[31] *Ibid.*

[32] The key piece of legislation is the famous USA Patriot Act of 24 October 2001.

[33] According to which *"Everyone has the right to respect for his private and family life, his home and his correspondence"* and *"There shall be no interference by a public authority with the exercise of this right except such as is in accordance with the law and is necessary in a democratic*

and its mirror in Article 22 of the Belgian Constitution.[34] Although the right to privacy is a fundamental right and is in principle enforceable by any citizen to the State, it is not an absolute right.[35] Article 8 explicitly lists a number of purposes for which the right to privacy can be set aside by the State, mostly in the area of public safety and the investigation and prosecution of crimes.

In application of the above principles, the Belgian Criminal Procedural Code (CPC) contains a number of specific provisions regulating investigatory measures in the context of judicial proceedings. Such measures include the registration and localisation of telephone conversations,[36] identification of subscribers,[37] tapping of electronic communications,[38] collecting bank data,[39] searches of IT systems and seizure of data.[40]

In principle, the DPA rules equally apply to monitoring by the State where it is aimed at individuals (legal entities being excluded from the scope of the DPA). Indeed, although the DPA excludes most police, judicial and intelligence activities from its scope,[41] in its other administrative dealings with citizens, the State must comply with the same rules as those outlined above for private companies.

A number of recent cases illustrate the boundaries of monitoring of individuals by the State as set out above. The Court of Cassation considered in 2007 that the trailing and observing of an individual by the intelligence services constituted an interference of the State in an individual's private life but that such interference for purposes of national security and the fight against terrorism may be legitimate under Article 8 of the European Convention of Human Rights.[42] The same court held a similar reasoning with respect to wiretapping.[43]

The Belgian Constitutional Court considered in 2005 that the State could not publish online the names of sports people that had been caught using performance-

---

society in the interests of national security, public safety or the economic well-being of the country, for the prevention of disorder or crime, for the protection of health or morals, or for the protection of the rights and freedoms of others".

[34] For a detailed analysis of the relationship between the Belgian Constitution and the fundamental rights (including the privacy) of citizens online, see E. Kindt, E. Lievens, E. Kosta, T. Leys, and P. De Hert. 2008. Constitutional rights and new technologies in Belgium. In *Constitutional rights and new technologies: A comparative study*, eds. R. Leenes, B.-J. Koops, and P. De Hert, 11–56. The Hague: T. M. C. Asser Press.

[35] See Article 8.2 European Convention of Human Rights above and Article 22 § 1 of the Belgian Constitution.

[36] Article 88bis, § 1 CPC.

[37] Article 46bis CPC.

[38] Article 90ter CPC.

[39] Article 46quater CPC.

[40] Article 36, 39bis, 88ter and 89 CPC.

[41] See the exclusions contained in Article 3 of the DPA, in particular in § 4, § 5 and § 6.

[42] Court of Cassation, RG P.07.0333.F, 27 June 2007 (E. A. E. M., B. K., e.a.), http://www.cass.be (24 July 2007); *T. Strafr.* 2008, liv. 4, 271, note F. Schuermans.

[43] Court of Cassation, RG P.07.0864.F (10 October 2007) (V.A., E./La Poste, M.F., A.L., L.P.), http://www.cass.be (8 November 2007).

enhancing products as this would infringe their fundamental right of privacy as set forth in the Belgian Constitution.[44]

Finally, the judgement of the European Court of Human Rights regarding compulsory registration in a DNA database of all persons sentenced to a prison term of more than 4 years in the Netherlands is also remarkable. Although the Court recognised that such use of DNA material constitutes an interference of the State in these persons' private lives, it considered that such a database was legitimate given its limitations to persons that have committed serious offences. It also considered the goal pursued by this database, i.e. the investigation and prosecution of crimes but also the refutation of suspicions allowing proof of innocence.[45]

17.3.3 Monitoring by Individuals

Finally, and although it may prima facie look less relevant, one should not forget the monitoring possibilities of individuals. Much like private companies, individuals have increasingly access to technology allowing them to monitor others. Such monitoring can take place where an individual carries out a business activity (in which case the limitations set out above for private companies should apply mutatis mutandis) or within his own family circle.

However, monitoring may go further than the above situations. A recent case in Belgium illustrates this somewhat unexpected development. It involved the placing online by a Dutch citizen of the names and addresses of convicted paedophiles in Belgium, in full contradiction with the rules set forth in the DPA and the criminal law principles. The website was eventually blocked by Belgian Internet service providers upon request of the judicial authorities.[46]

17.4 Conclusion

The complexity of the rules governing monitoring derives from the combination of a variety of rules with relatively few court precedents to help their interpretation. In our globalised world, the issue is even more acute due to conflicting rules from one country or one region to the other.

---

[44] Constitutional Court No. 16/2005 (19 January 2005), http://www.const-court.be (31 January 2005); *Arr. C.A.* 2005, liv. 1, 207; *Computer. (Pays-Bas)* 2005, liv. 3, 136 and http://www.computerrecht.nl (22 June 2005), note J. Dumortier; *NjW* 2005, liv. 98, 127, note E. Brems; *R.D.T.I.* 2005, liv. 22, 129, note R. Marchetti; *R.W.* 2005–06, liv. 11, 418 and http://www.rwe.be (15 November 2005).

[45] European Court of Human Rights No. 29514/05, 7 December 2006 (Van der Velden/Netherlands) http://www.echr.coe.int (5 July 2007); *NJB* (Pays-Bas) 2007 (obs.), liv. 9, 504 and http://www.njb.nl (5 July 2007); *T. Strafr.* 2007 (obs. F. Olcer, P. De Hert), liv. 2, 135.

[46] "On ne fait pas ce qu'on veut avec les données privées", *La Libre Belgique*, 23 April 2009.

The difficulties that SWIFT had to face in recent years perfectly illustrate this problem.

Following the terrorist attacks on 11 September 2001, the US Treasury ordered SWIFT to disclose the information contained in the financial messages transported on behalf of its customers. The matter hit the press a few years later, placing SWIFT before a dilemma between complying with the subpoena received from a sovereign State, that was legally enforceable, and complying with the European data protection rules to which SWIFT is also subject as a private company established in Belgium.[47]

SWIFT found itself caught between a rock and a hard place. After an investigation of almost 2 years, the Belgian Privacy Commission acknowledged that SWIFT had committed no serious or repeated violation of data protection laws. It found indeed that SWIFT's disclosures were made in response to binding orders of a competent authority and that SWIFT had obtained satisfactory assurances from that authority regarding the conditions of disclosure, with a high degree of protection to the individuals concerned.[48]

In an increasingly computerised and interconnected world, such complex questions arising out of monitoring activities are only likely to increase. Legislators and regulators will have to find pragmatic responses in consideration of endless technological developments and the evolution of cultures. Legal practitioners should play a proactive role in that respect, anticipating tomorrow's issues and contributing to resolve them with a view to avoiding costly and unnecessary disputes and challenges. They should seek to answer their clients' needs and enable them to carry on their business with the lowest hurdles possible, making compliance with privacy and data protection their marketing brand towards their personnel and their customers.

---

[47] See the WP 29's Opinion No 10/2006 on the processing of personal data by the Society for Worldwide Interbank Financial Telecommunication (SWIFT), available online on the WP 29's website at http://ec.europa.eu/justice_home/fsj/privacy/docs/wpdocs/2006/wp128_en.pdf.

[48] *Decision of 9 December 2008 on the control and recommendation procedures initiated regarding the SWIFT scrl company*, available on the Commission's website in French at http://www.privacycommission.be/fr/static/pdf/cbpl-documents/swift—projet-de-d-cision-modifications-09-12-200.pdf and in Dutch at http://www.privacycommission.be/nl/static/pdf/cbpl-documents/swift—nl-final-09.pdf.

Part VI
Technologist's Views

Chapter 18
Architecture Is Politics: Security and Privacy Issues in Transport and Beyond

Bart Jacobs

18.1 Architectural Issues

Mitchell Kapor is one of the founders and the first chairman of the Electronic Freedom Foundation (EFF), an international non-profit organisation that aims to defend civil rights in the digital age. Kapor has coined the phrase "Archtitecture is politics", see also Lessig (2001). It does not refer to architecture as the design and structure of buildings or bridges, but of ICT systems. In a broad sense ICT-architecture involves the structural organisation of hardware, applications, processes and information flow, and also its organisational consequences, for instance within enterprises or within society at large.

Why is this form of architecture so much a political issue—and not chiefly a technical one? An (expanded) illustration may help to explain the matter.

Many countries are nowadays in the process of replacing traditional analog electricity meters in people's homes by digital (electronic) meters, also known as smart meters. The traditional meters are typically hardware based, and have a physical counter that moves forward due to a metallic disc that turns with a speed proportional to the electricity consumption. This process takes place within a sealed container, so that tampering is not so easy and can be detected. It is in general fairly reliable. Such domestic meters may last for decades.

From the (information) architectural perspective the main point is that the usage data are stored decentrally, in one's own home. The reading of the meters must also be done locally, either by the customer or by a representative of the electricity provider. This is of course cumbersome.

Hence, one of the main reasons for the introduction of digital meters is to optimise this process of meter reading. These digital meters can be read from a distance,

B. Jacobs (✉)
Division Institute for Computing and Information Sciences,
Radboud University Nijmegen, 6525 Nijmegen,
The Netherlands
URL: www.cs.ru.nl/B.Jacobs

S. Gutwirth et al. (eds.), *Data Protection in a Profiled World*,
DOI 10.1007/978-90-481-8865-9_18, © Springer Science+Business Media B.V. 2010

by the electricity provider. What happens[1] is that the digital meters report the electricity consumption every 15 minutes to the provider, for instance via a dedicated GSM connection or via a special signal on the power line. The electricity provider thus stores very detailed usage information about domestic electricity consumption via such remote meter reading. We are moving from a decentralised (information) architecture to a centralised one!

Within this centralised set-up electricity providers offer their clients the option to view their own electricity consumption patterns via a personalised webpage. An important argument in favour of the introduction of such smart meters is an ecological one: energy conservation. The idea is that if customers are more aware of their actual consumption, they will become more careful and buy for instance more energy-efficient appliances.

Remarkably, these two arguments—remote meter reading and energy conservation—have nothing to do with the architectural change, from decentralised to centralised storage of usage data. Remote reading can also happen within a decentralised architecture: consumption data are stored locally within the smart reader, and only passed once every three months (say) to the electricity provider. Also, if it is beneficial for energy preservation that I get direct access to my electricity consumption, why should my usage data make such a detour, and first go to the electricity company, after which I can see them again via the web? One can also put USB connectors on smart meters so that people can read their data locally, via some open standard. Then I can decide for instance to connect my meter to a big screen in my hallway that shows consumption levels and starts flashing if my consumption is above a certain threshold.

Moreover, a detailed picture of my electricity consumption gives information about my way of life: what time I get up or go to bed (per day), whether or not I have visitors, when I'm on vacation etc. Especially this last point shows once again that privacy protection is important for one's own personal security. If people at the electricity company can see when I'm on holidays, burglars may become interested to get access to this data, for instance via bribery or blackmail, or even infiltration. Why am I exposed to such security risks and privacy violation with the introduction of smart meters?

Information is power. This is a basic law in politics, in marketing, and in many other sectors (like the military). The more electricity companies know about their customers, the better they can influence and steer their behaviour.

Is this far-fetched? Based on one's long-term detailed electricity consumption, the electricity provider can observe certain (statistical) patterns, like when the fridge switches itself on and how much electricity it uses. The provider can even observe if such a fridge becomes old (less efficient) and could be replaced. This information can be used for targeted (fridge) advertisements. Consumers may view this positively as a form of service or negatively as a form of intrusion. Also, one can of course be skeptical how much of a service this really is: the electricity company

[1] At least in the Netherlands; the situation in other countries may vary, but the differences are not essential at this stage.

will probably have a contract with a specific fridge supplier and provide information selectively. These scenario's are not imaginary but exist within the electricity supply community.

The (information) architecture determines how information flows within a particular IT-system: who can see what about whom. Since knowledge about others gives a stronger position and thus more power, IT-architecture is a highly political matter. After all, centralised informational control supports centralised societal control. Therefore, such architectural power issues are best discussed and decided upon within political fora, such as parliaments. Unfortunately the level of awareness of the sensitivity of these matters is fairly limited. In practice these issues are decided in different places, such as enterprise board rooms, or within ministries, via civil servants, consultants and lobbyists. Those in control tend not to opt for architectures that reduce their power. But who defends the interests of individual citizens, and tries to protect their autonomy?

An architectural issue that comes up time and again is centralisation versus decentralisation (see also later in this paper). The architecture that often first comes to mind is a centralised one. It is the obvious one. Traditional privacy-enhancing technologies (PETs) focus on this approach. They use relatively low-level cryptography and rely to a large extent on organisational measures. Over the last years we are seeing that data-leakage and privacy incidents are becoming structural.[2] The centralised approach concentrates power and its protection model does not work well.

The decentralised approach, with in-context data storage under direct control and influence of individuals, is typically not so well-developed. It often requires more high-tech crypto, such as zero-knowledge proofs or secure multi-party computation. Also, identities are less prominent, since they can often be replaced by (anonymous) attributes, so that the possibilities of tracing individuals and identity theft are reduced.

Whether our ICT infrastructures will be organised in a centralised or in a decentralised manner will have a deep impact on the organisation of our society and in particular on the division of (political) power. It is a sign of the level of appreciation of individual autonomy (see also Jacobs 2009).

18.2 What Went Wrong: Smart Cards in Public Transport

This section will sketch the story of the bumpy introduction of a national smart card—called *OV-chipkaart*, or *OV-chip*, for short—in public transport in the Netherlands. It will focus on the architecture and privacy issues involved.

Almost a decade ago planning started in the Netherlands for the nation-wide introduction of a smart card based e-ticketing system for all forms of public transport:

[2] See for instance http://datalossdb.org/for an overview.

bus, train, metro, etc. Organisationally this is a non-trivial matter, because there are so many public transport companies, public authorities (at various levels, local, regional, national) and stakeholders involved. Various motivations for such a card exist: fair division of revenues and/or subsidies and improvement of service via detailed travel logs, public safety via restricted access (via electronic gates), fraud reduction, cost reduction (fewer inspectors needed), convenience for travelers, behavioural targeting and direct marketing via personal travel profiles, and simply the desire to look modern and high-tech.

Technically the matter became a nightmare. The RFID chip that was selected for the *OV-chip* was the Mifare Classic, because it was cheap and "field-proven" technology. It is indeed the most widely used RFID chip, of which around one billion copies have been sold worldwide, with around 200 million still in use, largely for access control (buildings and premises) and public transport (about 150 cities worldwide, including London, Boston and Beijing). The design of the Mifare Classic is from the early nineties. Its security depends on a proprietary authentication protocol and stream cipher using keys of only 48 bits long. In the beginning of 2008 it became clear that the card was broken (Nohl and Plötz 2007; Nohl et al. 2008; de Koning Gans et al. 2008; Garcia et al. 2008, 2009) and that its content (esp. its balance) can be accessed and changed within a matter of seconds. Hence the chip is not a data-vault, as it should be.

After a phase of denying, dismissing and trivialising these findings the main players started accepting them and began working on a replacement plan towards a new card. In the meantime the actual roll-out went ahead. The expectation (and hope) of the public transport companies is that fraud can be detected quickly in the back-office, leading to black-listing of fraudulent cards. These fraud detection mechanisms run overnight on the transactions of the previous day. Hence they are not perfect. For instance, buying a €5 prepaid card and manipulating its balance to let's say €100 enables you to travel anywhere (first class!) for a day. The card will be black-listed the next day, but by then you are ready to manipulate another card. The intention is to start migrating to a new card as soon as fraud levels reach a certain (unknown) threshold.

Apart from these technical difficulties, the *OV-chip* is a privacy disaster, at various levels.

1. Each Mifare Classic chip has a unique identity in the form of a UID. It is an identification number of 32 bits that is used in the so-called anti-collision phase when a card and a reader start to set up a conversation. The numbers' main purpose is to tell different cards apart.
   Hence the card tells this unique number immediately, in unencrypted form, every time it enters the electromagnetic field of an arbitrary card reader. It can be used to recognise and trace people. Soon, almost everyone in the Netherlands will be carrying such an *OV-chipkaart* and will thus be electronically recognisable via the UID of the card. Parties not affiliated with the *OV-chipkaart* may use these UIDs for whatever they like. Shopkeepers may start using this UID: "hey, hello, long-time-no-see; maybe it is time you buy new underwear!?" Since card read-

ers can be bought for around €10 everyone can set up its own card detection and tracing, for benevolent or malevolent (e.g. terrorist) purposes.
More modern smart cards, such as used in the Dutch e-passport, use a random UID. This is good enough for anti-collision, but prevents tracing.

2. As said, the cryptographic protection mechanism of the Mifare Classic is faulty and the contents of the card can be accessed with relative ease—certainly when the technique becomes available for script kiddies. Hence someone sitting next to you in the bus or in a cafe can in principle read the contents of your card. It contains the logs of your last ten trips so that it is publicly visible (in principle) where you have been (ah, …, the red-light district!). If the card is personalised, it also contains your date of birth, but not your name or address.
In principle someone who is reading your card in this manner can also surreptiously change the data on the card. In this way your balance or validity date or date of birth can be changed, without you noticing. Of course you can also do this yourself. The card is an open wallet, that does not protect the money you store on it.
European data protection acts generally put the obligation on data processors to appropriately protect privacy-sensitive data in their custody. It can be argued in this case that Mifare Classic based travel cards are not in accordance with the law. They have not been challenged in court so far.
3. Each entry or exit into the public transport system, in a bus or at a train station, generates an entry in the back-office of the travel companies,[3] involving among others the identity of the entry/exit point (often connected to a fixed location), time-of-day, and identity and balance of the card. This yields a huge database of travel transactions that can often be linked to specific clients, for personalised cards. Hence individual travel patterns can be determined easily. The travel companies have left no doubt that they are quite eager to do so and to use these data for behavioural targeting and direct marketing: if I often travel to Rotterdam I will get advertisement for certain shops or hotels in Rotterdam; and if I travel first class I will get advertisement for different shops and hotels. Travel companies have been fighting for years with the Dutch data protection officer over this matter, and have finally managed to reach a half-baked compromise with an opt-in for such direct marketing and an opt-out for more aggregated profiling for optimised travel advice—in order to stimulate the use of public transport.[4]
The former East-German *Stasi* would have been jealous of such a database. It will not take long before police and intelligence services start exploiting its potential. One may expect "public transport taps", analogous to phone taps, data retention obligations[5] and datamining. Reportedly, this is already happening with London's Oyster card.

[3] Which, for simplicity, are treated here as one organisation.

[4] It seems to be a new trend to use ecology, instead of terrorism, as argument to undermine privacy.

[5] Which are quite unnecessary actually, because the travel companies show no inclination whatsoever to delete any transaction data; the tax office even requires that these data are stored for seven (!) years.

4. Traditionally, when you enter a bus or a train you only have to show, when asked, that you possess an appropriate "attribute" (ticket) that permits you to travel in this way. Such an attribute is typically not personalised. With chip card based systems access to the public transport has suddenly changed from attribute-based to identity-based. The chip card tells its identity to the card reader upon entry (and exit). Is it really necessary to tell who you are when you enter a bus (and to keep this information for many years)? Do we want such a society?
   There are modern, more advanced cryptographic protocols (see e.g. Brands 2000; Verheul 2001) that allow anonymous, attribute-based access control. However, they require non-trivial computational resources and advanced, very fast smart cards. Getting them to work in practice is a topic of ongoing (applied) research.
5. Anonymous, prepaid cards do exist, but they are a sad joke. As soon as you charge them with your bank card, your anonymity is gone. They are even sold via the internet! They clearly show that privacy is the last thing the designers of the *OV-chip* system cared about—in sharp contrast with the principle of privacy by design (Le Métayer 2009).

With a migration to a new card the points (1) and (2) will hopefully be tackled, via a random UID and proper cryptographic protection of the card contents. The centralised, card-identity based architecture will however remain. Changing this architecture as well involves moving to attribute-based access control, which is not foreseen for the near future.

As described, the *OV-chip* smart card based e-ticketing system involves a centralised architecture giving the travel companies unprecedented access to individual travel behaviour. This aspect is not emphasised, to understate things, in the advertisements of the these companies (or of the government). There is little transparency. Politicians and the general public are only slowly (and partly) becoming aware of these architectural matters. Reactions vary, from complete indifference to strong indignation. Independent regulators, such as the Dutch Data Protection Authority (CBP) or the Dutch Central Bank (DNB), are reluctant to take decisive action. The stakes are high; the invested economical and political interests and the prestige at risk are high.

What is the role of academics when such technically and societally controversial infrastructure is introduced? The Digital Security Group of the Radboud University Nijmegen had to deal with this question because of its research into Mifare Classic chipcards (de Koning Gans 2008; Garcia et al. 2008, 2009). It has decided to speak openly about the security vulnerabilities, which in the end involved standing up to legal intimidation and defending its right to publish freely in court, see Cho (2008) for a brief account. The group decided to draw a line and stay away from political activism, but not to stay away from academic *engagement*, in the sense of speaking openly about the issues and giving a number of demonstrations, for instance during an expert session in national parliament where an *OV-chipkaart* of a volunteer member of parliament was cracked on the spot and read-out in public, and in raising the balance of a card of a journalist with one cent in order to see if this would be detected in the back-office.[6] In the end it is of course up to others to decide how to evaluate the warnings and to make their risk analysis. The underlying motivation was to make clear that the *OV-chip* system should not set the information security standard for large scale future (public) ICT-projects. It is probably too early to evaluate the developments but it seems that this approach may have had indirect influence on other projects but has had little direct impact on the actual roll-out of the *OV-chipkaart*.[7] In The Netherlands politicians and industrials have become aware of the fact that large ICT-projects can be made or broken by security issues. This applies for instance to electronic patient dossiers, electricity meters (see the previous chapter), or road pricing—which is the next topic. At the same time the European Commission is now calling for explicit privacy and security assessments before roll-out of RFID-based systems (European Commission 2009).

18.3 What Can Still Go Right: Road Pricing

There is another major ongoing ICT-project in the transport sector in the Netherlands, namely road pricing (also called electronic traffic pricing). It is however still in the design phase, with prototypes being developed. The idea is to equip every car registered in the Netherlands with a special box containing GPS and GSM functionality for determining its detailed whereabouts and for communication with the central back-office of the traffic pricing authority. The aim is to replace the existing flat road tax by a fair, usage-dependent road charge that allows congestion reduction—by making busy road segments expensive—and environmental impact reduction—by making charges depend on vehicle characteristics. The choice for time, location and vehicle category dependent kilometre tariffs makes this approach ambitious and new in the world. For each individual vehicle detailed time and location information must be collected and processed without endangering privacy. The correct amounts have to be calculated reliably with the help of a digital tariff and/or road map.

The main architectural choice in road pricing is, as before between a centralised and a decentralised system.

- In a centralised architecture the on board box is simple and all intelligence resides with the pricing authority. The box frequently sends, say every minute, its location data to the authority. At the end of each period, say each quarter year, the authority calculates the total fee due.

[6] The responsible company *Translink* claimed (afterwards) it had noticed the event as a mismatch of balances but had decided not to respond because one cent did not look like serious fraud. Hence the journalist could travel for a couple of days with the adapted card, until the manipulation was made public. Not everyone was amused. A similarly manipulated (Oyster) card was used earlier in London to demonstrate that free rides are possible.

[7] It did result in some additional delays, and in the development of a migration plan.

This architecture is simple and rather naive. Privacy violation is the main disadvantage: it means that the authorities have detailed travel information about every vehicle. This is unacceptable to many. An additional disadvantage is the vulnerability of this approach. The central database of location data will be an attractive target for many individuals or organisations with unfriendly intentions, like terrorists or blackmailers. The system administrators who control this database may not always behave according to the rules, voluntarily or unvoluntarily.

In this approach one needs to have confidence that the box in each car registers and transfers all actual road use correctly. This may be enforced by "spot checks" along the road, where vehicles are photographed on specific (but random) locations and times. These observations can then be compared with the transferred registrations. A fine can be imposed in case of discrepancy.

- In the decentralised architecture the on board box contains enough intelligence to calculate the fee itself, requiring additional local computing resources. The box must securely store data, contain tariff & road maps, and carry out tariff calculations. Additionally, in such a decentralised approach the road-side checks must involve two-way communication in order to be able to check that the last few registrations and associated fee calculations have been performed correctly. Such checks require requests and responses by the vehicle, and thus an additional communication channel.

This decentralised approach apparently also has disadvantages, mainly related to the required local complexity, making it more vulnerable. It does however leave privacy-sensitive location information in the hands of individuals, who may access it via direct (USB or Wifi) connection with their box—and plot it for instance on their own PC (for fun) or use it for reimbursement.

A privacy-friendly and fraud-resistant alternative is sketched in de Jorge and Jacobs (2009)[8] where the on board box regularly—for instance, once per day—sends hashes of its time-stamped location data to the pricing authority, in order to commit itself to certain trajectories without revealing any actual information. After a random photo spot-check the driver (or actually, the box) is asked to send in the pre-image of the submitted hash in order to show correctness of the submission. Fee submission can also be organised in such a way that checks can be performed "locally", so that the privacy violation associated with checks is limited. Further details can be found in de Jorge and Jacobs (2009).

The underlying point is that privacy-friendly architectures are often available, but may require a bit more thinking (and work). It is a political issue whether or not we, as a society, wish to use them (see also Le Métayer 2009).

[8] See Jacobs and de Jonge (2009) for a more accessible account.

18.4 Privacy and Trust for Business

This section addresses the question: is there any honest business in privacy protection? An actual proof of commercial viability can only be given in practice, but a scenario will be sketched, taking economic incentives (instead of regulation) as a starting point.

The first observation is that (commercial) services are quickly becoming both (a) electronic, and (b) personalised. It is especially in this personalisation that future business opportunities are expected, with targeted, on demand delivery, based on personal preferences. Hence it is important for businesses to become *trusted*, so that customers allow these businesses to know them better and to deliver specifically what they really want.

So how to obtain trust? Keeping users ignorant about business processes and information flows seems, certainly in the long run, not to be the right strategy. Hence transparency is needed. Standardly one uses *a priori* mechanisms such as certificates, or *a posteriori* mechanisms based on reputation to obtain trust. Here we propose an approach based on three points:

- build your infrastructure (architecture) so that a privacy freak would be happy;
- allow customers to switch various transparent options on or off, for additional services;
- do not ever try to make any money out the privacy freaks, who typically have every possible additional option switched off.

Such mode of operation may be covered by some sort of privacy seal (see e.g. EuroPriSe).

The role of the privacy freak in this model is to generate trust. Given enough trust, you, as a business, may hope that a large majority of your customers will actually switch on additional services, enabling you to do (more) business. If you ever dare to act against what you promised towards a privacy freak, this will have detrimental effect on the level of trust and thus on your reputation as a business. Hence these freaks form a necessary foundation for your business, which will not directly generate revenue, but only indirectly via the customers with enough trust and willingness to obtain services via your infrastructure.

Here is a more concrete version. In many countries postal services want to become "trusted parties". One way of starting such a service is starting a web portal offering "throw-away connectivity". This can be done for (mobile) phones or email addresses,[9] but here we shall describe ordinary, physical addresses.

Many people shop online, but online shops have a bad reputation in handling customer data. They frequently leak credit card details or other sensitive customer data. Hence my trusted (postal) web portal could offer to act as a (transparent) intermediary when I purchase an item online. After making my selection on a (redirected) webpage, the portal could handle the payment on my behalf—so that my

---

[9] Like at spamgourmet.com.

details remain hidden and cannot be abused by the shop owner—and provide the shop with a throw-away address in the form of one-time barcode that is printed and put on the box containing the item that I purchased. The box is put in the mail by the shop owner and ends up in one of the distribution centers of the postal company. There, the barcode can be read and be replaced by my actual physical (home) address, so that the box can be delivered to me.[10]

Personally, I would be strongly interested in such a service, even if it involves registration with one particular (trusted) company that can see everything that I do. Even more if such a company has a privacy seal and offers various options with respect to the level of logging that they carry out, either at a central level or at a decentralised level with logs (and personal preferences) stored under my own control, but signed by the portal for authenticity/integrity. Maybe I do want some limited level of logging for dispute resolution (for certain purchases only). Maybe the portal even has switches for (temporary!) advertisements for specific goods, whenever I need them (like a new car, or fridge). Long term trust requires the portal to really stick to its policy of not sending me anything else or bothering me with things I didn't ask for.

Such a portal can develop into a more general identity provider (or broker), using mechanisms such as OpenId. Who makes the first move, and wants to transparently use modern technology for personalised use without hidden control and manipulation agendas?

Acknowledgements Thanks to Wouter Teepe for his critical reading of an earlier version.

References

Brands, S. 2000. *Rethinking public key infrastructures and digital certificates: Building in privacy*. Cambridge: MIT Press. Also available online at www.credentica.com.

Cho, A. 2008. University hackers test the right to expose security concerns. *Nature* 322 (5906): 1322–1323. Also available online at http://www.sciencemag.org/cgi/reprint/322/5906/1322.pdf.

European Commission. 2009. Commission recommendation on the implementation of privacy and data protection principles in applications supported by radio-frequency identification. 12 may 2009. C(2009)3200 final.

Garcia, F., G. de Koning Gans, R. Muijrers, P. van Rossum, R. Verdult, R. Wichers Schreur, and B. Jacobs. 2008. Dismantling MIFARE classic. In *Computer security—ESORICS 2008*, eds. S. Jajodia and J. Lopez, 97–114. Lecture Notes Computer Science, vol. 5283. Berlin: Springer.

Garcia, F., P. van Rossum, R. Verdult, and R. Wichers Schreur. 2009 Wirelessly pickpocketing a mifare classic card. In *30th IEEE symposium on security and privacy (S&P 2009)*, 3–15. Oakland: IEEE.

Jacobs, B. 2009. Keeping our surveillance society non-totalitarian. *Amsterdam Law Forum* 1 (4): 19–34. Also available online at http://ojs.ubvu.vu.nl/alf/article/view/91/156.

[10] Such an address-blinding service is not something only postal services can do; anyone can do it by acting as distribution center oneself. However, this may involve double postal charges.

Jacobs, B., and W. de Jonge. 2009. Safety in numbers: Road pricing beyond 'thin' and 'fat'. *Thinking Highways* 4 (3): 84–87 (Sept./Oct. 2009).

de Jonge de, and B. Jacobs. 2009. Privacy-friendly electronic traffic pricing via commits. In *Formal aspects in security and trust*, eds. P. Degano, J. Guttman, and F. Martinelli, 143–161. Lecture Notes Computer Science, vol. 5491. Berlin: Springer.

de Koning Gans, G., J.-H. Hoepman, and F. Garcia. 2008. A practical attack on the MIFARE classic. In *8th smart card research and advanced application conference (CARDIS 2008)*, eds. G. Grimaud and F.-X. Standaert, 267–282. Lecture Notes Computer Science, vol. 5189. Berlin: Springer.

Le Métayer, D. 2010. Privacy by design: A matter of choice. This volume.

Lessig L. 2001. *The future of ideas*. Vintage. Knopf Doubleday Publishing.

Nohl, K., D. Evans, Starbug, and H. Plötz. 2008. Reverse-engineering a cryptographic RFID tag. In *17th USENIX security symposium*, 185–94. San Jose, CA. USENIX Association, see http://www.informatik.uni-trier.de/~ley/db/conf/uss/index.html

Nohl, K., and H. Plötz. 2007. Mifare, little security, despite obscurity, Dec. 2007. *Presentation on the 24th Congress of the Chaos Computer Club*. Berlin. see http://events.ccc.de/congress/2007.

Verheul, E. 2001. Self-blindable credential certificates from the Weil pairing. In *Advances in cryptology—ASIACRYPT 2001*, ed. C. Boyd, 533–550. Lecture Notes Computer Science, vol. 2248. Berlin: Springer.

Chapter 19
PETs in the Surveillance Society: A Critical Review of the Potentials and Limitations of the Privacy as Confidentiality Paradigm

Seda Gürses and Bettina Berendt

19.1 Introduction

> My concern has been and will continue to be directed solely at striking a balance between democracy and technology, between the advantages of computerization and the potential safeguards that are inherent in it and the right of every citizen to the protection of his right of privacy. (Gallagher 1967)

These are the words of Representative Cornelius Gallagher who through a series of hearings in 1966 had brought the problem of computerization and its threats to privacy to public consciousness. Interestingly, today many of the arguments that Gallagher gave in his hearings still prevail. At the time, Gallagher was responding to plans to introduce a National Data Center that would collect information about every U.S. citizen, and his hearings articulated important challenges to the then nascent scientific discipline of computer science. Shortly after these hearings Gallagher was a keynote speaker at the American Federation of Information Processing Societies' 1967 Spring Joint Computer Conference in New Jersey, USA[1], and consequently his words were echoed in the Communications of the ACM (Titus 1967).

Given that special historical constellation, we can state that 1967 was the year in which privacy as a research topic was introduced to the then young field of computer science.[2] At the conference a session on privacy problems was introduced, and a total of five papers were presented on the topic of privacy.[3] Privacy was never

[1] The series of conferences commenced in 1961 and were dissolved in 1990 (IEEE Computer Society Press Room 2007).

[2] Although in the presented papers articulations of privacy and security solutions have parallels to the much longer standing tradition of cryptography and security research, we in this paper start our account of computer science privacy research with the explicit introduction of the term "privacy" at the Spring Joint Computer Conference.

[3] Three of the authors were from the RAND Corporation (Ware 1967a; Petersen and Turn1967), one from M.I.T (Glaser 1967) and one from a company named Allen-Babcock Computing (Babcock 1967).

S. Gürses (✉)
ESAT/COSIC, IBBT and Department of Computer Science, K.U. Leuven, Heverlee, Belgium
e-mail: seda@esat.kuleuven.be

S. Gutwirth et al. (eds.), *Data Protection in a Profiled World,*
DOI 10.1007/978-90-481-8865-9_19, © Springer Science+Business Media B.V. 2010

defined in these papers but assumed to be confidentiality of data, the breach of privacy then meaning the leakage of data to unauthorized principals in military and non-military systems. Although Representative Gallagher defined privacy as the right to freedom of action, speech, belief or conscience and listed potential risks of information collection to these (Gallagher 1967), the transposition of the concept to research in computer science was limited to data confidentiality and secrecy of communications.

Privacy enhancing technologies (PETs) that guarantee some type of data confidentiality and hence user privacy have been an important research topic ever since.[4] The data that is kept confidential using PETs may be stored data, communicated data, or the conditions of a given communication—most often limited to the anonymity of the sender and/or receiver of the communication. This research has resulted in the development of various systems that have important functions for guaranteeing anonymous speech, encrypted communications and unlinkable electronic activities in a networked world.[5]

The objective of this paper is to show that data confidentiality and anonymous communications, two important properties of privacy enhancing technologies that represent what we call the *privacy as confidentiality* paradigm, are indispensable but are short of being the privacy solutions they claim to be given current day circumstances. We argue that this is the case because so far computer scientists' conception of privacy through data or communication confidentiality has been mostly techno-centric and consequently displaces end-user perspectives.

By techno-centric we mean a perspective which is mainly interested in understanding how technology leverages human action, taking a largely functional or instrumental approach that tends to assume unproblematically that technology is largely exogenous, homogenous, predictable, and stable, performing as intended and designed across time and place (Orlikowski 2007). This perspective tends to put technology in the center, blend out cultural and historical influences, and produce technologically deterministic claims.

For some critical perspectives on current day conditions and how these escape techno-centric narrations of PETs, we survey perspectives from an emerging field called surveillance studies. We later shortly evaluate the consequences of these perspectives for computer scientists and designers of systems. In this evaluation we point to the human-centric assumptions of the surveillance studies perspectives. Human-centricity focuses on how humans make sense of and interact with technology in various circumstances. The technology is understood to be different depending on meanings humans attribute to it and through the different ways people interact

[4] In the last 10 years privacy has become one of the central concerns of Pervasive Computing, in Europe often researched under the title Ambient Intelligence. The journal IEEE Security and Privacy, for example, was a side effect of these research fields, giving recent privacy research a visible publication (Cybenko 2003).

[5] Later, other sub-fields in computer science have proposed other types of PETs that often rely on the contractual negotiation of personal data revelation. A review of such PETs can be found in (Wang and Kobsa 2006) but are not the focus of this paper since they are not based on the same assumptions that "privacy as confidentiality" is dependent on.

with it. This approach takes cultural and historical contexts into consideration, but has a tendency to minimize the role of technology itself (Orlikowski 2007).

As suggested in Orlikowski (2007), in this paper we study how materiality i.e., in our case technology, and the social are constitutively entangled. This means that PETs and social privacy practices in a surveillance world cannot be seen as ontologically distinct matters but constitute each other: social practices in a surveillance world are constituted by existing surveillance practices, digital information systems and by PETs, whereas the latter are the product of humans and their social practices. Hence, we review both techno- and human-centric views on PETs, and propose ways forward that make use of their constitutive entanglement.

Our main contribution with this paper is a critical interdisciplinary review of PETs that explores their potentials and limitations in a world of rapidly developing technology, ubiquitous surveillance, as well as changing perceptions, legislation and practices of privacy. Comparable critiques of PETs have been written in the past (Phillips 2004; Stalder 2002; Tavani and Moor 2001). We have included the first two of these perspectives in the later sections. In addition to reviewing critiques, the contributions of this paper are valuable for the following: First, confidentiality as *the* way to preserve privacy is a recurring theme in privacy debates generally and in computer science specifically. Therefore, a review whether this holds given changing social conditions is important. Second, we have some additional arguments in the section on "the information perspective" which can provide interesting challenges to privacy research in computer science. Further and most important of all, our argument is not that anonymity and confidentiality tools should be done away with. On the contrary, we believe that they need to be re-contextualized in the surveillance world in order to adapt the assumptions and claims of PETs to changing user requirements.

The paper is organized as follows. In Sect. 19.2 we give an overview of computer science research on privacy as data confidentiality and anonymity. Here we also list some of the assumptions common to this type of research. Next, in Sect. 19.3 we give accounts of different perspectives on surveillance society and their implications for the privacy as confidentiality paradigm in general and for the use of PETs specifically. In Sect. 19.4 we introduce an information perspective on surveillance. We then return to the assumptions made by both, the PETs community and the surveillance studies authors, in Sect. 19.5. In the conclusion we argue for a multi-paradigm approach for privacy research in computer science and articulate some challenges to future data protection.

19.2 Privacy as Data Confidentiality and Anonymity

19.2.1 Personal Data as the Focus of PETs

In those initial papers on privacy presented at the 1967 Spring Joint Computer Conference (Glaser 1967; Babcock 1967; Petersen and Turn 1967; Ware 1967a, b), the researchers noticed the importance of sensitive data, but what actually counted as "private" sensitive data was difficult to define. The authors distinguished between military and non-military systems, with the latter meaning industrial or non-military governmental agencies. Their objective was to devise systems such that they could avoid intentional or accidental disclosure of sensitive confidential data belonging to other users (Ware 1967a). In defining how to classify private information, a pragmatic approach was to ask how the military classification of document confidentiality i.e. confidential, highly-confidential, top secret, could somehow be mapped onto sensitive personal data. It was also discussed whether such a mapping was unrealistic when a central authority and the necessary discipline were lacking in non-governmental/private computer networks (Ware 1967b).

In all the papers, confidentiality, a concept that played an important role in military thinking, was chosen as the main paradigm for privacy research. The authors were aware that military concepts could not be applied to society at large, hence all the papers tried to distinguish security (military) from privacy (non-military), yet they had few other frameworks to take as a reference.

Ever since, there has been much progress in "non-military" contexts defining what should count as *informational privacy* (Gutwirth 2002; Nissenbaum 2004; Solove 2006) and how sensitive data can be defined. Various data protection legislations have defined the category "personal data" as subject to privacy protection. An example is the EU Directive that states: *Personal data* are "any information relating to an identified or identifiable natural person (…); an identifiable person is one who can be identified, directly or indirectly, in particular by reference to an identification number or to one or more factors specific to his physical, physiological, mental, economic, cultural or social identity" (EU Directive 95/46/EC (1995), Article 2 (a)).

Important for our purpose is the emphasis on identity, which is assumed to be unique and fixable for one natural person, to which data traces can be linked to. In line with this emphasis, U.S. terminology talks about *personally identifiable* data. This emphasis on identity is coupled with a relative under-specification of content that counts as personally identifiable data. The standard types of personally identifiable data are profile data describing individuals, including name, address, health status, etc.

It is probably in line with this focus on identity and identifiability that, in comparison to the contributions at the 1967 Spring Joint Computer Conference, from the 1980s onwards PETs focusing on the unlinkability of identity from generated digital data gained in popularity. In addition to the legal definitions, in computer science identifiability included inferring the individual to whom data belongs to with certainty but also probabilistically. The construct of probabilistic identification has contributed to the expansion of what could count as personal data.[6]

[6] The consequences of probabilistic identification as legal evidence have been picked up by Braman (2006), but they are beyond the scope of this paper.

19.2.2 Anonymity as a Privacy Enhancing Mechanism

Once data about a person exists in a digital form, it is very difficult to provide that person with any guarantees on the control of that data. This lack of control has contributed to personal data leakages and undesirable secondary use of personal data on the Internet,[7] often leading to privacy breaches. Much of the personal data collected using current day technologies represent activities of individuals assumed to be private or shared by a few prior to their digitization. Not digitizing these activities and avoiding the exchange of such digitized data would avoid further parties acquiring knowledge of these activities. However, this would substantially limit many of the technologies we use daily, and it is often undesirable for reasons we will account for in later sections.

A weaker form of preserving privacy is then to keep personal data confidential, from a greater public. This would require the use of cryptography and secure systems: the prior has so far proven difficult for users, while the latter is extremely difficult to accomplish in networked systems.

Yet another form of privacy can be achieved through what is called anonymity. Anonymity keeps the identity of the persons in information systems confidential, but it is not primarily concerned with how public the traces eventually become. This is also reflected in data protection legislation which by definition cannot and does not protect anonymous data (Guarda and Zannone 2009). Anonymity is achieved by unlinking the identity of the person from the traces that his/her digital activities leave behind in information systems.

In technical terms, anonymity can be based on different models. In communications, anonymity is achieved when an individual is not identifiable within a limited set of users, called the anonymity set (Pfitzmann and Hansen 2008). An individual carries out a transaction anonymously if she cannot be distinguished by an observer from others. The observer, often also called the adversary, may obtain some additional information (Diaz 2005). This means that the observer captures probabilistic information about the likelihood of different subjects having carried out a given transaction. The observing party may be the service provider or some other party with observation capabilities or with the ability to actively manipulate messages. Depending on the observer's capabilities, different models can be constructed with varying degrees of anonymity for the given anonymity set. Exactly what degree of anonymity is sufficient in a given context is dependent on legal and social consequences of a data breach and is an open question (Diaz 2005).

The capabilities of anonymizers are not only limited by the size of the anonymity set and the powers of the observer, but also by the content of the communication. If the communication content includes personally identifiable information,

[7] The focus of this paper is on privacy concerns raised and privacy enhancing technologies used on the Internet. We are aware that breaches also occur with devices that are off-line and on networks other than the Internet. Further, mobile technology has opened up a whole new set of questions about the feasibility of privacy enhancement with respect to location data. Whether the same assumptions and analyses hold for these problems is beyond the scope of this paper.

then the communication partners can re-identify the source person. Worse, if the communication content is unencrypted, then intermediary observers may also re-identify persons (or institutions), as was shown by Dan Egerstad.[8] A last dimension of weaknesses depends on the persistence of communication, meaning after observing multiple rounds of communication, the degree of anonymity may decrease and (probabilistic) re-identification become possible.

In databases, the conditions for establishing anonymity sets are somewhat different. The end of the 1990s saw the development of a new research field called privacy preserving data mining (PPDM). Initially focusing on databases of so-called "anonymized" personal data, early results showed that simple de-identification is not enough for anonymization. In her seminal work, Sweeney (Sweeney 2002) showed that she could re-identify 85% of the persons in anonymized hospital reports using publicly available non-personal attributes i.e. gender, age and zip code. Sweeney proposed methods to achieve k-anonymity in databases: A database listing information about individuals offers k-anonymity protection if the information contained for each person cannot be distinguished from k-1 individuals whose information also appears in the database. Later work in the field proved k-anonymity itself is not enough to anonymize data sets (Kifer and Gehrke 2006; Li and Li 2007; Rebollo-Monedero et al. 2008; Domingo-Ferrer and Torra 2008).

The results of PPDM research have shown that what counts as personal data can be broad. The attacks based on communication content have shown that anonymization without encryption can actually produce false perceptions of security, causing the revelation of data meant to be confidential. These results demand that the definition of personal data be expanded and hence privacy as confidentiality be reconsidered. The results also invoke important research questions about the usability and practicability of PETs and PPDM methods. We will come back to some of these issues later.

For now, let us look at some of the assumptions that PETs make when defining confidentiality and anonymity as building blocks of privacy.

19.2.3 Anonymity and Confidentiality in the Internet: Assumptions of PETs

There are some basic assumptions of the privacy as confidentiality paradigm that inform the logic of PETs. These assumptions are often not made explicit in research papers on privacy technologies. They vary between technical and socio-technical assumptions. These can be summed up as follows:

---

[8] In 2007 Dan Egerstad set up a number of TOR exit nodes (a popular anonymizer, http://www.torproject.org) and sniffed over 100 passwords from traffic flowing through his nodes. The list included embassies and government institutions (Paul 2007).

1. *There is no trust on the Internet:* Users of the Internet cannot be provided with guarantees with respect to the following: that a communication has been established with the correct party, the communication has securely reached that other party, there was no eavesdropping during the communication, and the communication partner will not reveal the communication content to further parties.
2. *Users are individually responsible for minimizing the collection and dissemination of their personal data:* By suggesting that through the use of PETs privacy can be enhanced or protected, an implicit claim is that personal data on the Internet originates from the users themselves and they should therefore protect it individually. This is especially the case because, see Assumption 1, there is no trust on the Internet.
3. *If they know your data, then they know you:* When discussing the effects of data collection in privacy discourses, knowing data about individuals gets mixed up with knowing those individuals. Knowing a user or individual here refers to knowing some or all of the following: intentions, causalities, and reached objectives.[9]
4. *Collection and processing of personal data, if used against individuals, will have a chilling effect:* The personally identifiable data distributed on the Internet may be used against individuals in unwanted and unclaimed ways. Massive collection and misuse of personal data in repressive, discriminatory, or simply undesirable ways may have a chilling effect. Hence keeping personal data confidential is a secure way to avoid such chilling effects.
5. *Technical solutions should be used to protect privacy instead of relying solely on legal measures:* Data may leak legally or illegally since it is difficult to control data and (1) there is no trust on the Internet. In order to avoid such leakage of data despite legal protection, technical solutions like anonymity and confidentiality should be preferred.

We argue that all these assumptions, although coherent and strong in their arguments, are techno-centric. In order to show in which ways this is the case, we will look at some of the findings of surveillance studies authors with respect to life in the surveillance society. When appropriate, we will list critiques of PETs based on the privacy as confidentiality paradigm.

[9] There are numerous court cases in which digital data are used as evidence in ways which claim much more than the data seems at face value to represent. For example, a court in the U.S.A. accepted pictures from a social network site of a young woman enjoying a party a number of weeks after a car accident with casualties. The picture was used as proof that she lacked remorse (Wagstaff 2007).

19.3 Surveillance Society and Its Effects on PETs

In the following, we would like to give a short overview of some of the voices that we identify as the surveillance studies[10] perspectives. Each of the perspectives investigates surveillance spaces and their effects on our lives and on our understanding of privacy. We would like to use these perspectives to reconsider the assumptions around PETs that we listed above. We sum up the different perspectives in the daily, marketing, political, performative and information perspectives. We will shortly account for each of these perspectives and their critique of PETs.

19.3.1 The Daily Perspective on Surveillance

A typical critique of users is that they do not care for their privacy. Even though different types of PETs are available to them, and in different studies users express their concerns for the privacy of their data, when they do make use of systems, these concerns evaporate and PETs are rarely utilized (Berendt et al. 2005). This low adoption of PETs is often attributed to the usability problems that are associated with PETs (Whitten and Tygar 1999), while in other cases, the users have been accused of being insensitive to the abuse of their data, naive, or simply ignorant of the risks that they are taking (Gross and Acquisti 2005).

In a short article, Felix Stalder argues otherwise (Stalder 2002). He states that our societies are increasingly organized as networks underpinned by digital information and communication technologies. He claims:

> In a network, however, the characteristics of each node are determined primarily by its connections, rather than its intrinsic properties, Hence isolation is an undesirable option.

Stalder problematizes PETs that make use of anonymity or even unlinkable pseudonyms for daily encounters.[11] Widespread use of anonymity and unlinkable pseudonymity tools burden the individuals, more so than offering them tools of protection. Instead, Stalder argues that the burden to protect their privacy should be taken off the individual's shoulders and accountability should be asked of database holders.

---

[10] Surveillance studies is a cross-disciplinary initiative to understand the rapidly increasing ways in which personal details are collected, stored, transmitted, checked, and used as means of influencing and managing people and populations (Lyon 2002). Surveillance is seen as one of the defining features that define and constitute modernity. In that sense, surveillance is seen as an ambiguous tool that may be feared for its power but also appreciated for its potential to protect and enhance life chances. Departing from paranoid perspectives on surveillance, the objective of these studies is to critically understand the implications of current day surveillance on power relations, security and social justice.

[11] Unlinkable pseudonyms refer to systems in which users identify themselves with different pseudonyms for different sets of transactions. For an observer it should not be possible to identify whether two pseudonyms are coming from the same user. If implemented in an infrastructure with a trusted third party distributing the pseudonyms, then these can be revoked, ideally only under certain (legally defined) conditions.

19.3.2 The Marketing Perspective on Surveillance

One of the main concerns with the collection of personal data is that of categorization. A typical example of discriminatory categorization is the use of geodemographic systems, which have been critiqued in previous studies (Curry and Phillips 2003; Graham 2005). Using categorization, marketers and companies can decide on desirable and non-desirable customers, excluding parts of the population.

Anonymity offers little protection against these systems. The classification of individuals with respect to marketing categories (or for that matter governmental surveillance categories for crime suspects) is not necessarily based on the unique identity of persons but rather on attributes that they carry. In that sense, these systems continue to work even if the individuals using the systems are anonymized. The fact that data protection regulation does not apply to anonymized data also worsens the situation. A newcomer to marketing systems does not have to be identified uniquely, it is enough if their behavior can be matched given a set of categories.

Exactly this critique is picked up and taken a step further by Zwick and Dholakia (Zwick and Dholakia 2003). They state that the control of the consumer to determine his digital identity is minimal, because:

> Implicit in the conceptualization of all of these tactics is the assumption that the consumer self is ontologically distinct from its representation in the electronic market-space. Yet, from a poststructuralist perspective, the subject cannot be conceived in this way. Because the consumer is constituted by language and the language governing the electronic market space is constituted by databases. The consumer (as a meaningful cultural representation, not as a body) does not exist outside this constitutive field of discursive power. Hence, the consumer's digital identity is his or her real identity because marketing is targeted toward the consumer profile rather than the real person.

Hence, very much like Stalder the authors propose that a struggle for consumer identity needs to be fought at the level of the database. The authors claim that PETs offer "customers" only a false perception of autonomy. The consumer categories cannot be manipulated. As an alternative, the authors argue that the consumer must be given direct access to customer databases in order to ensure that he or she regains a viable voice in the act of his or her constitution as a customer. The customer has to be enabled in (co)authoring their own identity.

19.3.3 The Political Perspective on Surveillance

Within the privacy as confidentiality approach, there is an assumption that the protection of those issues, activities, opinions deemed to be private and the private sphere are ultimately a good thing. David Phillips produces a critique of this normative approach based on feminist and queer theory. He says that:

> Some feminist scholars have argued that it is this creation of a private, domestic sphere apart from the public realm, that is the privacy problem. Certain populations and issues are relegated to this private sphere, particularly women and issues of sexuality. The public/private distinction then serves as a tool of social silencing and repression. From this perspec-

> tive, the most important privacy issues are not those of freedom from intrusion into the domestic realm, but instead of the social construction of the public/private divide itself.

Privacy is not uniformly available and uniformly valued. The need for privacy can change depending on context, as in the case of abuse or violence in the private sphere. For those who have little public power, the apparent invasion of privacy can sometimes seem welcome (McGrath 2004). It is important to recognize that through new technologies and their ability to make things visible and invisible, we are forced to re-consider what should remain public and private. This needs to be a social and democratic process and not one defined solely by experts. As expected, in a good number of cases, the suggestions for making issues private are not and will not be devoid of other political messages that may or may not be related to technology. Hence, instead of inscribing into systems absolute values of what should remain private, it is advisable to build technologies that enable individuals or communities to safely push the boundaries between the public and the private.

19.3.4 The Performative Perspective on Surveillance

Mcgrath picks up on the theories of the poststructuralist Mark Poster, who states that "we are already surrounded by our data bodies in surveillance space." He gives examples of artists' works and everyday surveillance uses that highlight the discontinuities of the surveillance narrative. It follows from the examples that these data bodies are neither simple representations of ourselves, nor straight falsifications, but hybrid versions of ourselves susceptible to our interventions. McGrath is aware that this multiplicity of selves will be distorted and exploited by the consumer-corporate system. But, he concludes, the real danger lies in disengaging with the surveillance space.

McGrath in his book "Loving Big Brother" very much appreciates the wit and passion of such daily performative interventions. His analysis of surveillance space avoids a value judgement about the morality or desirability of surveillance technology per se. He adds that his objective is:

> (to) examine ways in which new understandings of surveillance, and particularly spatial understandings, can help us live creatively and productively in post-private society. However, it has also been clear throughout [this book] that the predominant ideologies of surveillance need to be actively and complexly challenged and deconstructed if this is to be achieved.

As a strategy, McGrath demands a shift from anti-surveillance to counter-surveillance. He points to the impossibility of controlling surveillance space itself, i.e. once surveillance space exists, it can be used in many unexpected ways by unexpected parties. In that, he accepts that there can be no trust on the Internet but derives different conclusions. Although the use of cameras at demonstrations against police brutality (Lewis 2009) or even the case of Rodney King in the USA (BBC 2002) are valuable examples of reversing the gaze, McGrath focuses on counter-surveillance that goes beyond the reversal strategy. Instead, he proposes counter-surveillance that opens a space for all sorts of reversals in relation to how the gaze and its imagery may be experienced.

McGrath argues that proliferation of surveillance will produce discontinuities in experience of surveillance and produce excess. The more the surveillance proliferates, and the more surveillances start competing, McGrath argues the more we will see a battle over meaning. If we accept that surveillance space is in suspense: meaning the way we take up surveillance, the way we are affected, and the way we respond are in suspense, then radical possibilities for counter-surveillance pop up. He also argues that the focus of these counter-surveillance strategies should be on deconstructing and subverting the tyranny of meaning given to surveillance material.

According to these arguments, recent forms of practiced surveillance like reality shows e.g., Big Brother, and even most articulations of web based social networks can be seen as a realization of the fact that we live in a surveillance saturated society, and participation in these programs and environments are actually ways in which we are exploring what to do about it. In that sense, McGrath encourages members of our society to enter surveillance space, to experience its effects and to challenge any narratives that are limited to those of control and authority or try to monopolize what data means and how it can be used.

19.4 The Information Perspective on Surveillance

In addition to the surveillance studies authors, who argue mostly along the lines of language, performance and social concerns, there are information or data centric conditions that also have an effect on the assumptions that PETs are based on. These conditions get amplified given the main properties of digital systems to easily duplicate and distribute information.

In most surveillance systems, data receives meaning because of its relationality. A single piece of data about a single person says very little unless there is a set of data to compare it to, a framework to give it some meaning. In the age of statistical systems, the collection of data sets is what makes it possible to make inferences on populations and to evolve undesirable categorizations. This is also what Phillips defines as surveillance:

> Surveillance is the creation and managing of social knowledge about population groups. This kind of privacy can easily be violated if individual observations are collated and used for statistical classification, which applied to individuals makes statements about their (non)compliance with norms, their belonging to groups with given properties and valuations, etc.

In that sense any data, by its potential to be aggregated, has many data subjects, or better said always carries the potential of pointing to a data population. Individual decision making on personal data always affects all correlated subjects (Rouvroy

2009). Individualized concealment of data or unlinking of identities from traces provides little or no protection against breaches based on statistical inferences or discriminatory categorization of all correlated data subjects. Any individual can be categorized, as long as enough information has been revealed by others and aggregated in databases.

The argument also holds the other way around, it is impossible to guarantee semantic confidentiality in statistical databases. This means that, it cannot be guaranteed that access to a statistical database would not enable the observer to learn anything about an individual that could not be learned without access (Dwork 2006). Hence, not only is categorization a problem, but also analysis of statistical databases could reveal information about individuals that may have undesirable effects on them.

Following the same logic, a set of studies on possible inferences from the aggregation of data from multiple sources have shown similar results. The presence of different explicit pieces of information on a person means that there is even more—implicit—information about them. With the help of a mashup that visualizes the homes (including addresses) of people interested in "subversive" books, (Owad 2006) demonstrated the simplicity of combining existing information to infer people's identity. The technique is known as attribute matching, which was shown by Sweeney (2003) to be an easy way of circumventing simple anonymization schemes. In social networks, recent studies have shown that attributes revealed by friends in a profile's vicinity may be used to infer confidential attributes (Zheleva and Getoor 2009; Becker and Chen 2009).

Further, much information is revealed about individuals by virtue of their associations with others. By now, we all carry digital devices that accumulate data about our environments, as well as providing information about us to those environments. We disseminate this information on the social web or simply among our little ecology of devices. We talk loudly on our cell phones about ourselves and others, reveal pictures of family, friends or visited locations, archive years' worth of emails on multiple backup devices from hundreds of persons, map out our social networks, which reveals information about all those in the network. In each of these cases it is evident that it is not only individuals that reveal information about themselves, but we all participate in multiple kinds of horizontal and vertical information broadcasts and surveillances. We collectively produce data: we produce collaborative documents on wikis, take part in online discussions and mailing lists, comment on each other's pictures etc. All of this data is relational and makes sense in its collectivity. It also works the other way: in the networked world that Stalder describes, much information is collected about us and is linked in order to give us access to systems.

Hence, looking at information as snippets of individual contributions to digital systems misses the actual value and problems of that data in its collectivity and relationality. It does not recognize the publics we create and share, one of the greatest promises of the Internet. Data protection follows the same logic by expanding protection only to "personal" data. Individualizing participation in the surveillance society makes it difficult to develop collective counter-surveillance strategies, and limits our engagements with surveillance systems to individual protections of our actions.

The depiction of information privacy and data protection analogous to individual property rights actually exacerbates the problem of a contested public sphere. Although the rise of the social web can be celebrated as a long expected gift or cooking-pot economy, not only its privatization through large companies, but also the privacy debates contribute to articulations against seeing information on the web as a public good.[12] The logic of privacy and private ownership has created the false perception that data in its singularity is of utmost value and is controllable. Privacy through confidentiality and anonymity follow this logic and can be detrimental to collective critical engagement in surveillance systems.

19.5 Revisiting the Assumptions

Both the proponents of PETs and the surveillance studies authors base their work on certain assumptions. These assumptions are useful, but at the same time can be both techno- or human-centric. In the following, we review some of these assumptions and consider where PETs may run short of their promise to protect privacy. We then critically review some of the surveillance perspectives to re-position PETs and other technological tools in a surveillance society.

Personal data is an undefined category that is widening ever since PPDM has introduced the concept of quasi identifiers. This means that practically all data are always potentially linkable to an individual and hence are personal data. And in the logic of privacy as confidentiality, any data may reveal something about the individual, and hence needs to be kept private. In the different surveillance perspectives, the authors discuss how this is inconvenient, undesirable, and sometimes impossible. Let us return to the assumptions of PETs using the prior critiques:

That there is no trust on the Internet (Assumption 1) is a technical fact. Especially the underlying design of the Internet makes it very difficult to give guarantees of the security of communication. The problem here is that the absence of technical measures to make certain guarantees gets conflated with social definitions of trust. Further, the protection offered through the confidentiality of personal data emanating from individuals is limited (Assumption 2). Anonymously collected data does not protect against surveillance systems and the reflexes of their controllers to manage and sort populations.

Next, surveillance data is often a placeholder. It points to something that has happened or that has been, it often loses a sense of sender and receiver. Data loses the intentions behind its creation and starts to float in digital systems as data bodies. We need to dismantle the power of such data to stand for some "reality" or "truth"

[12] It is therefore no surprise that in the latest uproar against the new Terms of Use of Facebook, users have argued for a radical deletion of their profile to include the deletion of all their contributions to other profiles and all their correspondences to other people. The protection of individual privacy in such instances is valued over the integrity of the discussions forums, mailboxes of friends, posted photographs etc.

(Assumption 3). When accountability is of concern, other technical mechanisms should be put into place that guarantee the necessary proof that certain data validly stands for something. We should be careful about claiming that surveillance data is a truthful representation of "reality" in order to strengthen arguments for privacy as confidentiality.

It is also true that collection and processing of data, if used against individuals, can have a chilling effect (Assumption 4), but there could also be other effects. There are multiple occurrences in which people have publicized data in order to protect themselves against the breach of their privacy.[13] In a surveillance world confidentiality and anonymity can actually make somebody suspect or devoid of protection, whereas counter-surveillance strategies can prove to be disruptive or even protective.

Last, given the number of surveillance measures that have been installed and the amount of information collected about each person by their friends and organizations they are affiliated with, it is unrealistic to expect that technical measures can be applied realistically to actually keep many of daily interactions confidential (Assumption 5).

In the surveillance perspectives sketched above, solutions are often delegated to the social: in the form of accountability, performativity and liability. Although these demands are correct and important, we would like to explore the potential constitutive role that PETs play or can play in the surveillance society. Hence, we revisit PETs from each of the surveillance perspectives that we have summarized above in order to explore both their limitations as well as their potentials.

We agree that putting the responsibility of re-establishing privacy should not solely lie with individuals. It is paradoxical to suggest that the solution to potential undesirable instances of control should lie in users having to control their actions and data all the time. Therefore visions of large scale anonymous or pseudonymous systems where users constantly hide their attributes and connections (Chaum 1985) and have to re-establish other forms of relatedness through digital reputation (Dingledine et al. 2002) are inconvenient and undesirable in a networked world.

Nevertheless, searching for ways to minimize the collection of data and disabling the users' options to exercise some control over revealing their personal data if they want to is just as undesirable. We would hence argue that the accountability that Stalder demands of data processing systems should also include services for anonymous and/or pseudonymous users, and should adhere to data minimality. The networked society should continue to offer access to those who do not want to be so engrained in the existing networks i.e., not being very well networked should not lead to individuals being excluded from services. Therefore, PETs that

[13] Anne Roth started a blog in which she documented their everyday activities after her partner was declared a terrorist in Germany in 2007 and they found out that their family had been subject to police surveillance for over a year (http://annalist.noblogs.org/). Similarly, New Jersey artist Hasan Elahi started documenting every minute of his life on the Internet after he was detained by the FBI at an airport (http://trackingtransience.net/). Both of these persons made the assumption that keeping their lives public protects their freedoms when their data is used against them.

enhance privacy through anonymity and confidentiality—or where better suitable unlinkable pseudonyms—should be integrated into all systems. Nevertheless, their mere existence should not be enough to relieve data controllers and processors of their responsibilities and accountabilities. This should also have a legal effect: we should reconsider whether it is desirable, and, if so, how anonymized data can also be legally protected? This protection should be viable for both the use of anonymous data for transparency tools as well as the protection of anonymous data from abuse.

We very much agree with the critique of Zwick and Dholakia with respect to the constitutive force of these marketing databases. PETs, and more specifically anonymizers, since they currently do not hide user behavior, do not protect against the behavioral categorizations and resulting discriminations enabled through marketing databases. Further, if we accept that categories of desirable and undesirable customers are constituted by the owners of those databases, then even hiding behavioral data may not protect against such constitutive forces. Hence, suggesting PETs can protect the privacy of individuals against aggressive marketing databases goes beyond burdening individuals, but actually produces a false perception of autonomy, and maybe even an illusion of control: if my data is important to me, then I can protect it, if I want to give away my data for a utility, I can do so. Such utility arguments are not an option in existing databases with categorization powers.

Further, Zwick and Dholakia's proposal for customer agency is limited to the engagement of the "customer" with the database. Their suggestions are to allow individuals to correct their profiles, which may go as far as deleting oneself from the marketing databases. But in a networked world, as Stalder argues, deletion will often not be an option. Never mind the technical problem of guaranteeing that all traces of data are deleted. In that sense, although their critique of PETs is substantial, by resurrecting a notion that they call "sense of autonomy" based on access and control of individual database entries, the authors re-install a false sense of autonomy.

Instead, agency with respect to databases may be found in making visible the established relationality of data. Phillips states that the only thing that remains private in current surveillance systems are the methods through which these discriminatory classifications are created and used. By that he refers to the databases and algorithms used for data mining in those databases. It is through engagement with surveillance methods that it is possible to actually determine possible discriminations as well as desirable effects. Also, it is then possible to understand what becomes known to a specific public e.g., governments or marketers, through the aggregation of individual revelations of information. Such transparency practices could also demystify the effects of data collection and processing. Ideally, we can then actually collectively as societies or communities discuss if and how desirable the newly created private or public spaces are.

Significant is also the role PETs can play in the negotiation of the public and private spheres. Tools such as anonymizers and anonymous publication services may allow users to challenge boundaries between private and public. Anonymous speech has always been an important tool in democracies and an extremely helpful tool in repressive regimes. Nevertheless, the ultimate goal is not to limit the articulation of such opinions to anonymized spaces, but to make it possible to state such opinions in public and to safely hold public discourse on issues that are repressed. In that sense, PETs are not normative tools for how we should ultimately communicate whether we want to have privacy, but can play an indispensable role in negotiating the public and private divide.

For McGrath engagement with surveillance is key rather than re-establishing private and public assembly absolutes within a relativistic culture. Instead, he suggests that: ownership of imagery and data selves; freedom of image and data circulation; the multiplicity and discontinuities of data experience; and, the emotional instability of security systems should be the focus of our attention. Therefore, in a first impression we can conclude that PETs can rather be categorized as anti-surveillance strategies. But, given their recent popularity to circumvent repressive governments i.e. as a way to reach Internet sites that have been blocked by governments, there may be more value in those tools than visible at first sight.

Last, methods for inferring implicit knowledge are trendy, powerful and at the same time controversial. For example, although inferencing attributes through social networks may return mathematically accurate results, the assumptions such inferences are based on are socially questionable. In Wills and Reeves (2009), for example, the authors problematize some of the heuristics used to probabilistically infer information from the attributes of a profile's network vicinity. They argue that the heuristics are comparable to notions like "birds of a feather flock together", "judge a man by the company he keeps", or "guilty by association". Inferences should be made visible and be open to public discussion. Certain types of inferences are important to show the limitations of anonymization. Recent work on text analysis to re-identify individuals based on their writing can significantly limit the protection offered by PETs. Nevertheless, inferences often function based on assumptions that fix user identities and the way both individuals and collectives interact. A critical understanding and use of inferences is only possible if they are made explicit and public, and if their utility is critically scrutinized.

19.6 Conclusion

We have argued in the last section that despite the problems with the assumptions underlying PETs, and despite the legitimate critiques articulated in the surveillance perspectives, PETs can and should be part of privacy research. The more we engage in surveillance space, the more we will find diverse uses for PETs. However, it was one of our objectives in writing this paper to give legitimacy to multiple approaches to "privacy design" in computer science. We are especially interested in those approaches that do not work solely with the privacy as confidentiality paradigm and are able to see techno-centric and human-centric perspectives as constitutive others.

We believe that a broader vision of privacy and a deeper understanding of surveillance could help both users and computer scientists to develop systems that support multiple kinds of privacies and data protection practices. For all of this, it is clear that an interdisciplinary approach is imminent.

In the past years, other approaches to privacy in computer science have started flourishing. Two of these can be shortly listed as follows:

- *privacy as control:* A wider notion of privacy, appearing in many legal codifications, defines the term not only as a matter of concealment of personal information, but also as the ability to control what happens with it. This idea is expressed in Westin's (Westin 1970) definition of (data) privacy: the right of the individual to decide what information about himself should be communicated to others and under what circumstances, and in the term "informational self-determination" first used in a German constitutional ruling relating to personal information collected during the 1983 census (Bundesverfassungsgericht 1983). Some examples of research in this area are accounted for under the title of identity management systems and trust based systems with (sticky) privacy policies. These approaches often rely on and make use of data protection legislation as well as technical mechanisms. This approach is hence valuable for improving accountability of information systems, a point emphasized in the different surveillance studies perspectives. These mechanisms also are based on the building blocks offered by the techniques developed in the privacy as confidentiality paradigm, but are not limited to it.
- *privacy as practice:* It can help users immensely to know what data exists about them, to understand how it travels, and to comprehend ways of improving privacy practices in the future. Privacy as practice demands the possibility to intervene in the flows of existing data and the re-negotiating of boundaries with respect to collected data. These two activities rest on, but also extend the idea of privacy as informational self-determination in that they demand transparency with respect to aggregated data sets and the analysis methods and decisions applied to them. In this sense, these approaches define privacy not only as a right, but also as a public good (Hildebrandt 2008). There is little but valuable research done on systems that support user's strategic revelation and concealment based on what is already known. Palen and Dourish argue that "privacy management in everyday life involves combinations of social and technical arrangements that reflect, reproduce and engender social expectations, guide the interpretability of action, and evolve as both technologies and social practices change" (Palen and Dourish 2003). Following the same line of thought, Lederer et al. (2004) suggest improving privacy sensitivity in systems through feedback that improves users' understanding of the privacy implications of their system use. They add that this can then be coupled with control mechanisms that allow users to conduct socially meaningful actions through them. Concretely, the authors suggest the use of mechanisms like the identityMirror (Liu et al. 2006). A similar approach is suggested in the concept of privacy mirrors (Nguyen and Mynatt 2002). Hansen

(2008) suggests combining such features with identity management mechanisms that implement privacy as control.

In order to make any privacy related guarantees, regardless of the approaches taken, the system developers will have to secure the underlying systems. Hence, the three approaches: privacy as confidentiality, control, and practice are not only complementary to each other, but also depend on the security of the underlying infrastructures.

Last but not least, there is a need to consider other approaches to surveillance data than just personal data. We have explained, in Sect. 19.4, the importance of the relationality of information. If we accept that data are relational, then we have to reconsider what it means to think about data protection. For legal frameworks this is the challenge of developing mechanisms to address privacy concerns with respect to data that is co-created by many, that has multiple data subjects, or that is controlled by many without "legalizing" minuscule daily interactions. For computer scientists, it requires thinking of collaborative tools, anywhere from new forms of access control to methods for negotiating the visibility, availability and integrity of data owned and shared by many.

In this paper, we have shown some of the problems that arise with the privacy as confidentiality approach in a surveillance society. We have done this by studying how PETs based on data confidentiality and anonymity function, what technocentric assumptions they rely on, and how these assumptions can be shaken by our surveillance realities. We have used surveillance perspectives to review the assumptions underlying PETs. We then returned to the surveillance perspectives to step out of some of their human-centric assumptions. In doing that we explored the potentials and limitations of PETs in a surveillance society. Last, we sketched two other approaches to privacy in computer science and pointed out the importance of understanding the relationality of data in statistical systems and our networked world. We believe it is through the combination of all three approaches: privacy as confidentiality, privacy as control and privacy as practice, that we can both: recognize user's abilities, wit and frustrations in navigating the surveillance world; and, develop critical and creative designs with respect to privacy.

Acknowledgements This work was supported in part by the Concerted Research Action (GOA) Ambiorics 2005/11 of the Flemish Government, by the IAP Programme P6/26 BCRYPT of the Belgian State (Belgian Science Policy), and by the European Community's Seventh Framework Programme (FP7/2007–2013) under grant agreement n 216287 (TAS³—Trusted Architecture for Securely Shared Services).[14] The authors also wish to thank Carmela Troncoso, Claudia Diaz, Nathalie Trussart, Andreas Pfitzmann, Brendan van Alsenoy, Sarah Bracke, Manu Luksch and Aaron K. Martin for their valuable and critical comments.

[14] The information in this document is provided "as is", and no guarantee or warranty is given that the information is fit for any particular purpose. The above referenced consortium members shall have no liability for damages of any kind including without limitation direct, special, indirect, or consequential damages that may result from the use of these materials subject to any liability which is mandatory due to applicable law.

References

Babcock, J.D. 1967. A brief description of privacy measures in the rush time-sharing system. In *AFIPS '67 (Spring): Proceedings of the April 18–20, 1967, spring joint computer conference,* 301–302. New York: ACM.

BBC. 2002. Flashback: Rodney king and the LA riots. *BBC.* Online, July 10, 2002.

Becker, Justin, and Hao Chen. 2009. Measuring privacy risk in online social networks. In *Web 2.0 security symposium.* Oakland.

Berendt, Bettina, Oliver Günther, and Sarah Spiekermann. 2005. Privacy in e-commerce: stated preferences vs. actual behavior. *Communications of the ACM* 48: 101–106.

Braman, Sandra. 2006. Tactical memory: The politics of openness in the construction of memory. *First Monday* 11 (7). http://firstmonday.org/htbin/cgiwrap/bin/ojs/index.php/fm/article/view/1363/1282

Bundesverfassungsgericht. 1983. BVerfGE 65, 1 – Volkszahlung. Urteil des Ersten Senats vom 15. Dczember 1983 auf die mündliche Verhandlung vom 18. und 19. Oktober 1983—1 BvR 209, 269, 362, 420, 440, 484/83 in den Verfahren über die Verfassungsbeschwerden.

Chaum, David. 1985. Security without identification: Transaction systems to make big brother obsolete. *Communications of the ACM* 28: 1030–1044.

Curry, Michael R., and David Phillips. 2003. Surveillance as social sorting: Privacy, risk, and automated discrimination. In *Privacy and the phenetic urge: Geodemographics and the changing spatiality of local practice,* ed. David Lyon. London: Routledge.

Cybenko, George. 2003. A critical need, an ambitious mission, a new magazine. *IEEE Security and Privacy* 1 (1): 5–9.

Diaz, Claudia. 2005. Anonymity and privacy in electronic services. PhD thesis, Katholieke Universiteit Leuven.

Dingledine, Roger, Nick Mathewson, and Paul Syverson. 2002. Reputation in privacy enhancing technologies. In *CFP '02: Proceedings of the 12th annual conference on Computers, freedom and privacy,* 1–6. New York: ACM.

Domingo-Ferrer, J., and V. Torra. 2008. A critique of *k*-anonymity and some of its enhancements. In *Third international conference on availability, reliability and security, 2008. ARES 08,* 990–993. Washington, DC: IEEE Computer Society.

Dwork, Cynthia. 2006. Differential privacy. In *ICALP,* vol. 2, 1–12. Berlin: Springer.

EU. 1995. Directive 95/46/ec of the European parliament and of the council of 24 October 1995 on the protection of individuals with regard to the processing of personal data and on the free movement of such data. *Official Journal of the European Communities,* 31. (November 1995).

Gallagher, Cornelius E. 1967. The computer and the invasion of privacy. In *SIGCPR '67: Proceedings of the fifth SIGCPR conference on Computer personnel research,* 108–114. New York: ACM.

Glaser, Edward L. 1967. A brief description of privacy measures in the multics operating system. In *AFIPS '67 (Spring): Proceedings of the April 18–20, 1967, spring joint computer conference,* 303–304. New York: ACM.

Graham, Stephen. 2005. Software-sorted geographies. *Progress in Human Geography* 29 (5): 562–580.

Gross, Ralph, and Alessandro Acquisti. 2005. Information revelation and privacy in online social networks. In *WPES '05: Proceedings of the 2005 ACM workshop on Privacy in the electronic society,* 71–80. New York: ACM.

Guarda, Paolo, and Nicola Zannone. 2009. Towards the development of privacy-aware systems. *Information and Software Technology* 51 (2): 337–350.

Gutwirth, Serge. 2002. *Privacy and the information age.* Lanham: Rowman and Littlefield Publishers.

Hansen, Marit. 2008. Linkage control: Integrating the essence of privacy protection into identity management. *eChallenges.*

Hildebrandt, Mireille. 2008. Profiling and the identity of the European citizen. In *Profiling the European citizen: Cross disciplinary perspectives,* eds. Mireille Hildebrandt and Serge Gutwirth. Dordrecht: Springer.

IEEE Computer Society Press Room. 2007. Computer society history committee names top 60 events (1946–2006). *IEEE Website.*

Kifer, Daniel, and Johannes Gehrke. 2006. l-diversity: Privacy beyond *k*-anonymity. In *IEEE 22nd International Conference on Data Engineering (ICDE'07).* New York: ACM.

Lederer, Scott, Jason I. Hong, Anind K. Dey, and James A. Landay. 2004. Personal privacy through understanding and personal privacy through understanding and action: Five pitfalls for designers. *Personal Ubiquitous Computing* 8: 440–454.

Lewis, Paul. 2009. Video reveals G20 police assault on man who died. *The Guardian,* April 7, 2009.

Li, Ninghui, and Tiancheng Li. 2007. t-closeness: Privacy beyond *k*-anonymity and—diversity. In *IEEE 23rd International Conference on Data Engineering (ICDE'07).* IEEE Computer Society Press: Los Alamitos, CA

Liu, Hugo Liu, Pattie Maes, and Glorianna Davenport. 2006. Unraveling the taste fabric of social networks. *International Journal on Semantic Web and Information Systems* 2 (1): 42–71.

Lyon, David. 2002. Editorial. Surveillance Studies: Understanding visibility, mobility and the phenetic fix. *Surveillance and Society* 1 (1): 1–7.

McGrath, John. 2004. *Loving big brother: Performance, privacy and surveillance space.* London: Routledge.

Nguyen, David H., Elizabeth D. Mynatt. 2002. *Privacy mirrors: Understanding and shaping socio-technical ubiquitous computing. Technical Report.* Georgia Institute of Technology.

Nissenbaum, Helen. 2004. Privacy as contextual integrity. *Washington Law Review* 79 (1): 101–139.

Orlikowski, Wanda J. 2007. Sociomaterial practices: Exploring technology at work. *Organization Studies* 28: 1435–1448.

Owad, T. 2006. Data mining 101: Funding subversives with amazon wishlists. http://www.applefritter.com/bannedbooks

Palen, Leysia, and Paul Dourish. 2003. Unpacking "privacy" for a networked world. In *CHI '03: Proceedings of the SIGCHI conference on human factors in computing systems,* 129–136. New York: ACM.

Paul, Ryan. 2007. Security expert used tor to collect government e-mail passwords. *Ars Technica,* September 2007.

Petersen, H.E., and R. Turn. 1967. System implications of information privacy. In *AFIPS '67 (Spring): Proceedings of the April 18–20, 1967, spring joint computer conference,* 291–300. New York: ACM.

Pfitzmann, Andreas, and Marit Hansen. 2008. *Anonymity, unobservability, and pseudonymity: A consolidated proposal for terminology. Technical report.* Technical University, Dresden.

Phillips, David J. 2004. Privacy policy and PETs. *New Media and Society* 6 (6): 691–706.

Rebollo-Monederom, David, Jordi Fornfie, and Josep Domingo-Ferrer. 2008. From t-closeness to pram and noise addition via information theory. In *PSD '08: Proceedings of the UNESCO Chair in data privacy international conference on Privacy in Statistical Databases.* Berlin: Springer.

Rouvroy, Antoinette. 2009. Technology, virtuality and utopia. In *Reading panel on autonomic computing, human identity and legal subjectivity: Legal philosophers meet philosophers of technology, CPDP 2009.* Heidelberg: Springer

Solove, Daniel J. 2006. A taxonomy of privacy. *University of Pennsylvania Law Review* 154 (3): 477 (January 2006).

Stalder, Felix. 2002. The failure of privacy enhancing technologies (PETs) and the voiding of privacy. *Sociological Research Online* 7 (2). http://www.socresonline.org.uk/7/2/stalder.html

Sweeney, Latanya. 2002. *k*-anonymity: A model for protecting privacy. *International Journal on Uncertainty, Fuzziness and Knowledge-based Systems* 10 (5): 557–570.

Sweeney, Latanya. 2003. Achieving *k*-anonymity privacy protection using generalization and suppression. *International Journal of Uncertainty* 10 (5): 571–588.
Tavani, Herman T., and James H. Moor. 2001. Privacy protection, control of information, and privacy-enhancing technologies. *SIGCAS Computer Society* 31 (1): 6–11.
Titus, James P. 1967. Security and privacy. *Communications of the ACM* 10 (6): 379–381.
Wagstafi, Evan. 2007. Court case decision reveals dangers of networking sites. *Daily Nexus News,* February 2007.
Wang, Yang, and Alfred Kobsa. 2006. Privacy enhancing technologies. In *Handbook of research on social and organizational liabilities in information security,* eds. M. Gupta and R. Sharman. Hershey, PA: IGI Global.
Ware, Willis H. 1967a. Security and privacy in computer systems. In *AFIPS '67 (Spring): Proceedings of the April 18–20, 1967, spring joint computer conference,* 279–282. New York: ACM.
Ware, Willis H. 1967b. Security and privacy: Similarities and difierences. In *AFIPS '67 (Spring): Proceedings of the April 18–20, 1967, spring joint computer conference,* 287–290. New York: ACM.
Westin, A.F. 1970. *Privacy and freedom.* Atheneum: Bodley Head Ltd.
Whitten, Alma, and J.D. Tygar. 1999. Why johnny can't encrypt: A usability evaluation of pgp 5.0. In *SSYM'99: Proceedings of the 8th conference on USENIX security symposium.* Berkeley: USENIX Association.
Wills, David, and Stuart Reeves. 2009. Facebook as a political weapon: Information in social networks. *British Politics* 4 (2): 265–81.
Zheleva, E., and L. Getoor. 2009. To join or not to join: the illusion of privacy in social networks with mixed public and private user profiles. *WWW 2009.*
Zwick, Detlev, and Nikhilesh Dholakia. 2003. Whose identity is it anyway? Comsumer representation in the age of database marketing. *Journal of MacroMarketing.* 24 (1): 31–43.

Chapter 20
Privacy by Design: A Matter of Choice

Daniel Le Métayer

20.1 Introduction

Privacy by design is often praised by lawyers as an essential step towards better privacy protection: in a world where privacy is more and more jeopardized by new information and communication technologies (ICT), the growing view is that part of the remedy should come from the technologies themselves (Poullet 2006, 2009; Cavoukian 2008; Rouvroy 2008). On the technological front, privacy enhancing technologies (PETs) have been an active research topic in computer science during the last decades (Rezgui et al. 2003; Deswarte and Aguilar Melchor 2006) and a variety of techniques have been proposed (including anonymizers, identity management systems, privacy proxies, encryption mechanisms, filters, etc.). One must admit however that the take-up of most of these techniques by consumers is still rather limited (Bygrave 2002; Goldberg 2003; Tynan 2007). The goal of this chapter is to review this gap between a toolset of available technologies and the still unrealized promises of privacy by design. We first revisit the definition of privacy by design and highlight the differences with privacy enhancing and security tools in Sect. 20.2. In Sect. 20.3, we review the current situation and argue that the first obstacle to privacy by design is not technological but political. In Sect. 20.4, we suggest a range of actions to get out of the current vicious cycle and enter into a virtuous cycle for a wider adoption of privacy by design.

20.2 What Do We Mean by Privacy by Design?

The general philosophy of privacy by design is that privacy should not be treated as an afterthought but rather as a first-class requirement in the design of IT systems: in other words, designers should have privacy in mind from the start when they define

D. Le Métayer (✉)
Grenoble Rhône-Alpes Research Center, INRIA (Institut National de Recherche en Informatique et Automatique), 655 avenue de l'Europe, 38000 Montbonnot, France
e-mail: daniel.le-metayer@inrialpes.fr

S. Gutwirth et al. (eds.), *Data Protection in a Profiled World*,
DOI 10.1007/978-90-481-8865-9_20,

the features and architecture of a system. To be more concrete, let us start with some examples of what we mean by "privacy by design":

- The first example is the architecture of an electronic healthcare record system which has been designed with the objective to address the privacy concerns of the patients (Anciaux et al. 2008). The key feature of the architecture is the combination of a central server and personal secure tokens. Personal tokens, which typically take the form of USB tokens, embed a database system, a local web server and a certificate for authentication by the central server. Patients can decide on the status of their data and, depending on their level of sensitivity, choose to record them exclusively on their personal token or to have them replicated (whether encrypted or not) on the central server. Replication on the central server is useful to enhance durability and to allow designated professionals to get access to the data. Health professional are also equipped with secure tokens and can access the personal data of the patients only with the cryptographic key installed on their token.
- Another example of privacy by design is the architecture for "localisation based services" put forward in the context of the PRIME[1] project (Kosta et al. 2008). In addition to the mobile operator and the service operator, this architecture introduces a third party, the "intermediary". This intermediate actor makes it possible to manage the information flow in order to implement the data minimisation principle. For example, the service provider knows the specific data related to the service but does not have access to location data nor to the address of the customer. Pseudonyms and cryptographic techniques are used to prevent information leaks, especially with respect to the intermediary, while ensuring the consistency of transactions.
- A third example of privacy by design is the architecture proposed in the PRIAM[2] project to enhance privacy protection in the context of ambient intelligence (Le Métayer 2009). One of the main challenges in this context is the effective implementation of the "explicit and informed consent" of the data subject. The PRIAM architecture is based on the notion of "privacy agents". Privacy agents are software components which are installed on a portable device which is assumed to reside around (or on) the subject. Privacy agents are in charge of the management of the personal data of the subject according to his wishes. These wishes are expressed in a restricted natural language dedicated to the definition of privacy policies. A formal specification of the agents is provided to ensure that their behaviour is defined without ambiguity. This specification can then be used to check to correctness of the implementation of the agents.
- Another interesting illustration of privacy by design is a novel architecture for an electronic traffic pricing system developed in the Netherlands (De Jonge and Jacobs 2008). This architecture makes it possible to reconcile privacy (in the sense that the central authority does not know the trajectories of the vehicles) with a good level of security (for the computation of fees). A sketch of this project

[1] PRIME: Privacy and Identity Management for Europe.

[2] PRIAM: Privacy and ambient intelligence.

and comparison with less privacy friendly options are presented in another paper in this volume (Jacobs 2009).

Further examples of privacy by design could be mentioned but our purpose is not to present a comprehensive survey here. More generally, it is possible to identify a number of core principles which are widely accepted and can form a basis for privacy by design. For example the Organization for Economic Co-operation and Development has put forward the following principles (OECD 1980):

- The collection limitation principle: lawful collection of data with the "knowledge or consent" of the data subject.
- The purpose specification and use limitation principles: specification of the purposes and use limited to those purposes.
- The data quality principle: accuracy of the data, relevance for the purpose and minimality.
- The security principle: implementation of reasonable security safeguards to avoid "unauthorised access, destruction, use, modification or disclosure of data".
- The openness and individual participation principles: right to obtain information about the personal data collected, "to challenge" the data and, if the challenge is successful, to have the data "erased, rectified, completed or amended".
- The accountability principle: data controllers should be accountable for complying with these principles.

These principles have inspired a number of privacy legislations. They are also very much in line with the European Directive 95/46/EC on the protection of individuals with regard to the processing of personal data and on the free movement of such data. The latter however puts more emphasis on the explicit consent of the subject.

The first point we want to make at this stage is that privacy by design is different from the use of privacy enhancing tools[3] or security tools:[4] privacy by design has to do with the general requirements of a system and definition of its architecture (Kalloniatis et al. 2008). As such, privacy by design is a matter of choice: multiple options are generally available to achieve a given set of functionalities, some of them being privacy friendly, others less. In a second stage, appropriate privacy enhancing and security tools have to be identified to implement the architecture (Bygrave 2002).[5] But, in the same way as the use of cryptography is by no means a guarantee of security, the use of privacy enhancing or security tools is not in itself a guarantee of privacy: the most important issue is to have a clear view of the overall system, the actors involved, their levels of trust or authority, their interactions, what they need

[3] Anonymizers, identity management systems, privacy proxies, filters, etc. The interested reader can find a list of privacy tools published by EPIC (Electronic Privacy Information Center) at http://epic.org/privacy/tools.html.

[4] Cryptographic tools, key management systems, erasers, etc.

[5] "An individual PET tends to have a narrow field of application (e.g., encryption of email or blocking of cookies) such that a consumer who is seriously interested in safeguarding his/her privacy interests across many contexts has to learn and acquire multiple PETs from multiple organizations."

to know and the information flows between them, in order to ensure that the choice of tools is consistent with the privacy requirements. To conclude this section, let us recall the definitions proposed in (ISTPA 2002) to highlight the differences between security and privacy:

- Security is the establishment and maintenance of measures to protect a system.
- Privacy is the proper handling and use of personal information throughout its life cycle, consistent with data protection principles and the preferences of the subject.

Even though these definitions refer more precisely to IT security and a form of IT privacy (focusing on the use of personal information) which should itself be generalized (as stated below, the border between personal and non personal data will more and more tend to blur), it clearly shows that, even if security is a prerequisite for its implementation, the scope of privacy is much broader and strongly tied to the notion of subject. The fact that privacy cannot be reduced to PETs and security tools is further explored in (Gürses 2009) in this volume. We come back to the consequences of these differences in the next section.

20.3 A Matter of Choice

A second comment on the examples of Sect. 20.2 is that privacy by design is not an inaccessible dream. Even though it is necessary to encourage the development of new privacy enhancing technologies, most of these examples can be implemented in the current state of the art. Unfortunately, one can observe that most of the IT systems which are on the market today are far away from the privacy by design principles. One could even say that the most current situations fall into the following categories:

- *Non-privacy by design* when the design of the system deliberately infringes privacy rights. This is the case, for example, for on-line reservation systems requiring more information than needed or offering very limited services in case of refusal by the user to disclose his personal data. Other examples include digital rights management (DRM) systems tracking the behaviour of customers or systems offering by default the less protective configurations.
- *Non-privacy by non-design* when privacy issues were just ignored during the design of the system. Such systems may typically miss "opt-in" or "opt-out" functionalities, or keep data without any time limitation.
- *Non-privacy by bad design* when privacy was considered from the outset but the design still does not provide sufficient guarantees. Design errors can be purely technical or come from a lack of knowledge or understanding of privacy regulations.

Several lessons can be drawn from these observations. As far as the first two categories are concerned, they fall outside the scope of technology: privacy by design is possible but largely ignored, if not flouted, in practice. These situations reflect the choices of the actors in power: as stated in (Jacobs 2009), they show that "architecture is politics". The first challenge to be met to ensure the development of privacy by design is thus political. We come back to this issue in the next section and suggest several lines of action to try to improve the situation. The third category however has to do with technology. As a matter of fact, one must admit that privacy is an extremely complex issue which raises specific technical challenges. We believe that one of the features of privacy which makes its implementation especially challenging is that fact that it is both a very general and a very subjective notion:

- Privacy is a very general notion in the sense that it is recognized in most parts of the world (even if in different ways and to different extents). It is even considered as a fundamental right in Europe and A. Rouvroy and Y. Poullet go even further, referring to privacy as a "fundamental fundamental" right (Rouvroy and Poullet 2009) to emphasize the fact that it is a prerequisite for the exercise of other fundamental rights. Another key issue supporting this view is that privacy protects not only individual life but also social life (Rouvroy 2008).
- But privacy is also a very subjective notion, with evolves over time and depends very much on the cultural and technological context. Even within a given country at a given time, the perceptions of privacy and the necessity to protect it vary a lot among individuals.

Reconciling generality and particularity is a challenge both for law and computer science:

- As far as law is concerned, one of the key issues is: where to draw the line between the protection of the weakest and the right to individual freedom? Looking at privacy as a fundamental right would lead to giving priority to the protection of the subject (possibly, in extreme cases, against his own will) while following the "user empowerment" philosophy would lead to giving the highest priority to the subject's freedom.
- The impact for computer science is the need to design systems offering a high level of parameterization or customization without encouraging individuals to make choices that they do not understand or to go systematically for the less protective options. The challenge is thus to provide to users ways to express their wishes, which in the case of privacy may involve many subtleties, without ambiguity and have them implemented by the system.

We believe that these unique features of privacy make it even more challenging than traditional security where at least the requirements can be understood in a rather standard way and applied systematically. Technically speaking, the difference shows in particular in what is called the "sticky policy" paradigm which requires that the privacy policy defined by the subject remains attached to the personal data when it is collected or transferred to third parties and must always be fulfilled by controllers who have collected the data.[6]

[6] Standard security policies do not include provisions for "importing" rules associated with data coming from outside the system.

20.4 From a Vicious Cycle to a Virtuous Cycle

As stated in Sect. 20.3, the first obstacle to the development of privacy by design is political. By political, one generally refers to a situation resulting from a collective choice, whether explicit or not, whether democratic or not, and, as such, reflecting a given balance of powers and interests. We can identify at least four categories of actors concerned by privacy issues: individuals, lawyers, computer scientists and industry. Not too surprisingly, these categories correspond to the sources of norms identifies by several authors (Lessig 1999; Dommering and Asscher 2006): society, law, technology and market. From the point of view of individuals, one may observe that their current range of options is often rather limited; this range more or less boils down to a dual choice: either refuse the service to avoid the privacy loss or accept the service and the associated loss of privacy.[7] One could argue that, for certain services, individuals still have the choice to install and use privacy enhancing tools such as anonymizers but one must admit that, even if these tools are indeed available, their installation and use are usually not straightforward. In addition, some of them incur performance penalties which make them less appealing than one would hope. Last but not least, it is not easy for a non-expert (and even, one must say, for experts, at least without a substantial investment) to understand precisely the extra guarantees provided by these tools. The first report on the implementation of the Data Protection Directive 95/46/EC (European Commission 2003) even mentions the fact that "some systems presenting themselves as PETs are not even privacy-compliant". For all these reasons the use of privacy enhancing tools is not so much widespread as of today. Not too surprisingly, if we now look at the problem from the economical point of view, one must acknowledge the fact that the "privacy market" is not very broad yet: companies building their business model on privacy are still too scarce. At this stage one could say that we are facing a standard chicken and egg problem: are there too few users because the offer is too narrow or are there few companies because the demand for privacy protection is not strong enough (Grossklags and Acquisti 2009)? To fully grasp the problem, it is necessary to consider also the legal point of view: very little is done today in most countries to create incentives for the development of privacy by design. Authors such as (Bygrave 2002) have already pointed out the contrast between the legal protection generously granted to digital rights management tools and the current lack of legal support for privacy tools. This contrast obviously reflects the "differences in the respective lobbying strengths of privacy advocates on the one hand and copyright-holders on the other" (Bygrave 2002). Even if this extreme solution is not adopted one may wonder why, if privacy is really considered as a fundamental right in our societies, legal measures could not be taken to balance a situation which is currently very unfavourable to the development of privacy by design. In the rest of this sec-

[7] Typically by providing more personal information than strictly required for the service, or disclosing data without any simple way to exercise legal rights such as access or rectification.

tion we identify some lines of (respectively legal and technical) actions to try to get out of the current vicious cycle and enter into a more virtuous cycle.

20.4.1 Lawyers and Legislators

- The development of new information technologies and their ever increasing penetration of all aspects of our everyday life raise so many issues that the very principles underlying privacy need to be revisited (Hildebrandt and Gutwirth 2008; Rouvroy 2008; Rouvroy and Poullet 2009). One of the key challenges in this respect, with strong practical consequences, is to understand where the red line should be drawn. In other words, what should be left to the appraisal of individuals (following the "user empowerment" philosophy) and what should be regulated by law? If privacy is really taken as a fundamental right and a condition for the integrity and autonomy of the individuals, its protection must be an imperative. Following this line of reasoning, one may argue that selling one's personal data, or relinquishing one's privacy in exchange for practical benefits, should be prevented in the same way as selling organs in most European and American countries. But new information technologies such as pervasive computing or the Internet tend to increase the exchange of quantities of pieces of data which may individually look insignificant but can become more important later on, possibly associated with other data or in contexts which were not foreseen initially. In other words, the status of "personal data" is not always clear and may change over time. Also, it is already the case today that business sectors such as retailing provide benefits (e.g. reduced prices, preferential services, etc.) in exchange for the collection of personal data (e.g. through loyalty cards). Similarly, many of the services available on the Web today would no longer be provided for free if advertisement companies were not allowed to collect and analyze personal data. We are thus in a situation where some form of privacy protection must be absolutely guaranteed by law but this protection cannot be absolute. The practical question is thus: where should the red line be drawn?
- When the first question is addressed there comes the issue of effectiveness: in other words, how could the law provide strong enough incentives to favour the development of privacy by design and the emergence of a larger market for privacy enhancing tools? In this respect, we believe that one of the instruments which has not been used strongly enough is certification.[8] Drawing a parallel with security, the Common Criteria for Information Technologies Security Evaluation,[9] or "Common Criteria" (CC 2006) form now a well established standard for IT security certification. Common Criteria certificates can be required either by law, by trade associations or through call for tenders for sensitive products

[8] This option is also mentioned by the European Commission in its first report on the implementation of the Data Protection Directive 95/46/EC (European Commission 2003).

[9] http://www.commoncriteriaportal.org/.

such as secured devices for electronic signatures, banking cards or identity cards. Even when not mandatory, they represent significant competitive advantages for certain software providers and product manufacturers. The Common Criteria catalogues include some privacy requirements but they are far from sufficient for a true privacy certification. The work done in the EuroPriSe project[10] (Bock 2008) is an important contribution to the definition of specific criteria for privacy certification and this effort should be pursued, both at the technical level (to refine the evaluation criteria) and in terms of promotion (to give rise to a privacy certification business in the same way as we have a security certification business today). Obviously this effort needs to be supported by the legislator, for example by requiring certificates in call for tenders or for certain categories of IT products or by creating an infrastructure for the official approval of privacy seals or certificates. The impact of such certification scheme would be both on consumers and on industry: consumers would be able to rely on independent evaluation schemes, and would thus get more motivation to opt for privacy preserving solutions, even when they are not required by law; industry would be more inclined to invest in this new market because privacy certificates would become a more visible differentiator.

- Another important instrument in the hands of the legislator is the information of the consumers. Indeed, proper information is the first condition for the validity of the consent of the subjects. It can also have an impact on the behavior of users of IT systems who are not necessarily conscious of the potential consequences of their actions[11] and of the availability of privacy enhancing tools. Increasing general awareness about privacy is thus of prime importance: national data protection authorities such as the CNIL have already done a lot in this respect but they need more support to further extend this line of action. Another facet of the information is the notification of the victims (and, in some cases, of the public in general) in case of a privacy breach. Beyond the legitimate right of information of the subjects, such requirement would provide a further incentive for companies to treat data more carefully. This notification is already required by law in a number of countries (and a majority of states in the USA) and should be introduced in the new version of the European Directive 2002/58/EC on ePrivacy in the electronic communications sector. However, there is no reason to restrict this duty to electronic communication services (WP29 2006, 2009): online retailers, banks, health services, search engine providers and all other information society services should be subject to the same obligation. In addition, for such provision to be really effective, clear criteria must be defined to identify the cases where the breach has to be notified (depending on the possible harm for subjects) and national regulatory authorities must have the possibility to impose financial sanctions in case of failure to report a breach (WP29 2009).

[10] https://www.european-privacy-seal.eu/.

[11] A striking and worrying example is the dramatic increase of complaints received by data protection authorities concerning young job seekers suffering from discriminations linked to their past activities on social networks.

20.4.2 Computer Scientists

- As mentioned above, the first obvious requirement for privacy tools is user-friendliness because these tools are supposed to be usable by all users of information technologies (which will very soon mean everyone). But user-friendliness is not just a matter of user interfaces: as suggested above, privacy is a complex issue in itself and different users may have very different expectations: they should be able to express these expectations without ambiguity and have them enforced by the system crest (Karat et al. 2005; Le Métayer 2009).
- Another observation concerning existing technologies is that computer scientists have focused very much on obscurity tools so far (anonymization, encryption, etc.), building on previous work on computer security. We believe that, as privacy is concerned, transparency tools are as important as obscurity tools: in a society where information flows will continue to increase and the border between personal and non-personal data will be more and more difficult to establish *a priori* (before disclosure), it will become more and more important to provide to subjects some kind of visibility and guarantees about the use of their data during (all) their life cycle. The first functionalities which should be provided by the controllers have to do with the legal rights of the subject: access right, correction right, deletion right, etc. The technical means provided to exercise these rights should facilitate as much as possible the actions of the subjects without introducing new vulnerabilities in the system. Since, once collected, the data remain under the control of the collector, complementary measures need to be provided to ensure accountability. Enough information should be recorded for the controller to provide evidence that he has complied with his legal obligations. Again, since this requirement necessarily leads to recording more information, such features should be devised with great care to avoid the introduction of security vulnerabilities.
- As mentioned before, the scope of privacy by design extends beyond the use of privacy enhancing tools. In the current state of the art, privacy by design can be defined in terms of general principles (OECD 1980; Langheinrich 2001) as suggested in Sect. 20.2. The next stage consists of proposing a methodology for privacy by design, defining more precisely the issues to be considered, the design steps, the actors involved and assessment criteria. A step in this direction is described in (ISTPA 2002) which uses a set of practices necessary to support privacy principles (the "fair information practices") and defines a group of "privacy services" (such as audit, control, enforcement, negotiation, validation, access, etc.) to be parameterized and integrated into a privacy framework. In the same spirit, (Agrawal et al. 2002) provides guidelines for the design of databases complying with general privacy principles ("hippocratic databases"). Methodological issues are tightly linked with evaluation issues: needless to say, even if privacy is not reducible to IT security, much inspiration can be taken from the work done in this area, both with respect to methodology and evaluation (CC 2006).

20.4.3 A Virtuous Cycle

As mentioned above, the first condition for individuals to be in a position to make a real choice is the existence of privacy preserving solutions. This existence cannot be imposed by law but law can provide more incentives to support it. The measures identified above are examples of such incentives and others can certainly be put forward. Privacy seals could very well be required for certain categories of systems, at least systems manipulating sensitive data, which would be an even stronger encouragement for providers of privacy technologies. In certain countries, security certificates are required to put credit cards on the market: why would it be impossible to apply the same level of standard for the protection of sensitive data if we really value privacy as much as we profess. If the incentives are strong enough, the range of privacy solutions will be larger, standards will emerge, tools will be granted privacy seals by independent authorities and it will be possible for users to compare them and make a true choice. As stated in (Jacobs 2009), trust would play a crucial role and represent a valuable differentiator in this new business. Last but not least, for users to really exert their possibility to make a choice, they must be aware of their rights, of the risks they may face when disclosing their data and the limitations imposed by law on the collection and treatment of personal data. Increasing the public awareness is a prerequisite for entering into this virtuous cycle. National data protection authorities have already made a lot of efforts to inform European citizens, but the observed behavior of IT users and the opinion polls clearly show that much more needs to be done.[12] This is essentially a matter of funding, and thus again a matter of political choice.[13]

Acknowledgements This work has been partially funded by ANR (Agence Nationale de la Recherche) under the grant ANR-07-SESU-005 (project FLUOR).

References

Agrawal, R., J. Kiernan, R. Srikant, and Y. Xu. 2002. Hippocratic databases. In *Proceedings of the 28th international conference on very large data bases (VLDB 2002),* eds. P.A. Bernstein, Y.E. Ioannidis, R. Ramakrishnan, and D. Papadias, 143–154. Hong Kong: VLDB Endowment.

Anciaux, N., M. Benzine, L. Bouganim, K. Jacquemin, P. Pucheral, and S. Yin. 2008. Restoring the patient control over her medical history. In *Proceedings of the 21st IEEE international symposium on computer-based medical systems*, eds. N. Anciaux, M. Benzine, L. Bouganim, K. Jacquemin, P. Pucheral, and S. Yin, 132–137. Washington, DC: IEEE Computer Society.

Bock, K. 2008. An approach to strengthen user confidence through privacy certification. *Datenschutz and Datensicherheit—DuD* 32 (9): 610–614.

[12] A review of relevant opinion polls can be found on the EPIC web site at http://epic.org/privacy/survey/#polls.

[13] As shown in (Grossklags and Acquisti 2009), "privacy legislation and privacy self-regulation are not interchangeable means to balancing the informational needs and goals of different entities".

Bygrave, L.A. 2002. Privacy-enhancing technologies: Caught between a rock and the hard place. *Privacy Law and Policy Reporter* 9: 135–137.
Cavoukian, A. 2008. Privacy and radical pragmatism: Change the paradigm. *White Paper.* Information and Privacy Commissioner of Ontario, Canada.
CC. 2006. The common criteria for information technologies security evaluation, CC V3.1, Part 1: Introduction and general model. CCMB-2006-09-001.
Deswarte, Y., C. Aguilar Melchor. 2006. Current and future *privacy* enhancing technologies for the *internet. Annales des télécommunications* 61 (3–4): 399–417.
Directive 95/46/EC. 1995. Directive 95/46/EC of the European Parliament and of the Council of the 24 October 1995 on the protection of individuals with regard to the processing of personal data and on the free movement of such data. *Official Journal* L281(23/11/1995): 31–50.
Dommering, E., and L. Asscher, eds. 2006. Coding regulation: Essays on the normative role of information technology. The Hague: T.M.C. Asser Press.
European Commission. 2003. First report on the implementation of the Data Protection Directive 95/46/EC. COM (2003) 265, May 2003.
Goldberg, I. 2003. Privacy enhancing technologies for the Internet, II: Five years later. In *Proceedings of the workshop on privacy enhancing technologies.* Lecture Notes in Computer Science (LNCS), vol. 2482. Heidelberg: Springer.
Grossklags, J., and A. Acquisti. 2009. When 25 cents is too much: An experiment on willingness-to-sell and willingness-to-protect personal information. Working paper.
Gürses, S. 2009. Circumscribing PETs. In *Proceedings of the conference on privacy and data protection, (CPDP 2009).* Heidelberg: Springer.
Hildebrandt, M., and S. Gutwirth. eds. 2008. Profiling the European citizen. Dordrecht: Springer.
ISTPA. 2002. *Privacy framework, version 1.1.* International Security, Trust and Privacy Alliance.
Jacobs, B. 2009. Architecture is politics: Security and privacy issues in transport and beyond. In *Proceedings of the conference on privacy and data protection, (CPDP 2009).* Heidelberg: Springer.
De Jonge, W., and B. Jacobs. 2008. Privacy-friendly electronic traffic pricing via commits. In *Proceedings of the workshop of Formal Aspects of Securiy and Trust (FAST 2008).* Lecture Notes in Computer Science (LNCS), vol. 5491. Heidelberg: Springer.
Kalloniatis, C., E. Kavakli, and S. Gritzalis. 2008. Addressing privacy requirements in system design: The PriS method. *Requirements Engineering* 13 (3): 241–255.
Karat, J., C. Karat, C. Brodie, and J. Feng. 2005. Designing natural language and structured entry methods for privacy policy authoring. In *Proceedings of the 10th IFIP TC13 international conference of human-computer interaction.* Berlin: Springer.
Kosta, E., J. Zibuschka, T. Scherner, and J. Dumortier. 2008. Legal considerations on privacy-enhancing location based services using PRIME technology. *Computer Law and Security Report* 24: 139–146.
Langheinrich, M. 2001. Privacy by design: Principles of privacy aware ubiquitous systems. In *Proceedings of the Ubicomp conference,* 273–291. Lecture Notes in Computer Science (LNCS), vol. 2201. London: Springer.
Le Métayer, D. 2009. A formal privacy management framework. *Proceedings of the workshop of formal aspects of securiy and trust (FAST 2008),* 162–176. Lecture Notes in Computer Science (LNCS), vol. 5491. Berlin: Springer.
Lessig, L. 1999. *Code and other laws in cyberspace.* New York: Basic Books.
OECD. 1980. OECD guidelines on the protection of privacy and transborder flows of personal data. Organization for Economic Co-operation and Development.
Poullet, Y. 2006. The Directive 95/46/EC: Ten years after. *Computer Law and Security Report* 22 (3): 206–217.
Poullet, Y. 2009. About the e-Privacy directive, towards a third generation of data protection legislations. In *Proceedings of the conference on privacy and data protection, (CPDP 2009).* Heidelberg: Springer.
Rezgui, A., A. Bouguettaya, and M.Y. Eltoweissy. 2003. Privacy on the web: Facts, challenges, and solutions. *IEEE Security and Privacy* 1 (6): 40–49.

Rouvroy, A. 2008. Privacy, data protection, and the unprecedented challenges of ambient intelligence. *Studies in Law, Ethics and Technology* 2 (1): 1–51.

Rouvroy, A., and Y. Poullet. 2009. The right to informational self-determination and the value of self-development. Reassessing the importance of privacy for democracy. In *Proceedings of the conference reinventing data protection*. Dordrecht: Springer.

Tynan, D. 2007. The privacy market has many sellers, but few buyers. *Wired.com*. http://www.wired.com/print/techbiz/startups/news/2007/09/privacy.

WP29. 2006. Article 29 Data Protection Working Party, 1611/06/EN, WP 126, Opinion 8/2006 on the review of the regulatory framework for Electronic Communications and Services, with focus on the e-Privacy Directive. Adopted on 26 September.

WP29. 2009. Article 29 Data Protection Working Party, 00350/09/EN, WP 159, Opinion 1/2009 on the proposals amending Directive 2002/58/EC on privacy and electronic communications (e-Privacy Directive). Adopted on 10 February.

Kolibri 360 GmbH
Ferdinand-Jühlke-Straße 7
99095 Erfurt, Deutschland
produktsicherheit@kolibri360.de